ŚRĪ CAITANYA-CARITĀMṚTA

BOOKS by
His Divine Grace A.C. Bhaktivedanta Swami Prabhupāda

Bhagavad-gītā As It Is
Śrīmad-Bhāgavatam, Cantos 1-5 (15 Vols.)
Śrī Caitanya-caritāmṛta (17 Vols.)
Teachings of Lord Caitanya
The Nectar of Devotion
Śrī Īśopaniṣad
Easy Journey to Other Planets
Kṛṣṇa Consciousness: The Topmost Yoga System
Kṛṣṇa, The Supreme Personality of Godhead (3 Vols.)
Transcendental Teachings of Prahlād Mahārāja
Kṛṣṇa, the Reservoir of Pleasure
The Perfection of Yoga
Beyond Birth and Death
On the Way to Kṛṣṇa
Rāja-vidyā: The King of Knowledge
Elevation to Kṛṣṇa Consciousness
Kṛṣṇa Consciousness: The Matchless Gift
Back to Godhead Magazine (Founder)

A complete catalogue is available upon request

International Society for Krishna Consciousness
3764 Watseka Avenue
Los Angeles, California 90034

All Glory to Śrī Guru and Gaurāṅga

Śrī Caitanya-Caritāmṛta

of Kṛṣṇadāsa Kavirāja Gosvāmī

Antya-līlā
Volume Two

"The Glories of the Associates of the Lord"

with the original Bengali text, Roman transliterations, synonyms, translation and elaborate purports

by

HIS DIVINE GRACE

A.C. Bhaktivedanta Swami Prabhupāda

Founder-Ācārya of the International Society for Krishna Consciousness

THE BHAKTIVEDANTA BOOK TRUST
New York · Los Angeles · London · Bombay

Readers interested in the subject matter of this book
are invited by the International Society for Krishna Consciousness
to correspond with its Secretary.

International Society for Krishna Consciousness
3764 Watseka Avenue
Los Angeles, California 90034

Please address all Correspondence To:
Bhaktivedanta Book Trust,
Croome Court, Severn Stoke,
Nr. Worcester, WR8 9DW
Great Britain

Library of Congress Catalogue Card Number: 73-93206
International Standard Book Number: 0-912776-73-0

First printing, 1975: 20,000 copies

Printed in the United States of America

Contents

Introduction

Śrī Caitanya-caritāmṛta is the principal work on the life and teachings of Śrī Kṛṣṇa Caitanya. Śrī Caitanya is the pioneer of a great social and religious movement which began in India a little less than five hundred years ago and which has directly and indirectly influenced the subsequent course of religious and philosophical thinking not only in India but in the recent West as well.

Caitanya Mahāprabhu is regarded as a figure of great historical significance. However, our conventional method of historical analysis—that of seeing a man as a product of his times—fails here. Śrī Caitanya is a personality who transcends the limited scope of historical settings.

At a time when, in the West, man was directing his explorative spirit toward studying the structure of the physical universe and circumnavigating the world in search of new oceans and continents, Śrī Kṛṣṇa Caitanya, in the East, was inaugurating and masterminding a revolution directed inward, toward a scientific understanding of the highest knowledge of man's spiritual nature.

The chief historical sources for the life of Śrī Kṛṣṇa Caitanya are the *kaḍacās* (diaries) kept by Murāri Gupta and Svarūpa Dāmodara Gosvāmī. Murāri Gupta, a physician and close associate of Śrī Caitanya's, recorded extensive notes on the first twenty-four years of Śrī Caitanya's life, culminating in his initiation into the renounced order, *sannyāsa*. The events of the rest of Caitanya Mahāprabhu's forty-eight years are recorded in the diary of Svarūpa Dāmodora Gosvāmī, another of Caitanya Mahāprabhu's intimate associates.

Śrī Caitanya-caritāmṛta is divided into three sections called *līlās,* which literally means "pastimes"—*Ādi-līlā* (the early period), *Madhya-līlā* (the middle period) and *Antya-līlā* (the final period). The notes of Murāri Gupta form the basis of the *Ādi-līlā,* and Svarūpa Dāmodara's diary provides the details for the *Madhya-* and *Antya-līlās.*

The first twelve of the seventeen chapters of *Ādi-līlā* constitute the preface for the entire work. By referring to Vedic scriptural evidence, this preface establishes Śrī Caitanya as the *avatāra* (incarnation) of Kṛṣṇa (God) for the age of Kali—the current epoch, beginning five thousand years ago and characterized by materialism, hypocrisy and dissension. In these descriptions, Caitanya Mahāprabhu, who is identical with Lord Kṛṣṇa, descends to liberally grant pure love of God to the fallen souls of this degraded age by propagating *saṅkīrtana*—literally, "congregational glorification of God"—especially by organizing massive public chanting of the *mahā-mantra* (Great Chant for Deliverance). The esoteric purpose of Lord Caitanya's appearance in the world is revealed, his co-*avatāras* and principal devotees are described and his teachings are summarized. The remaining portion of *Ādi-līlā,* chapters thirteen through seventeen, briefly recounts his divine birth and his life until he accepted the renounced order. This includes his childhood miracles, schooling, marriage and early philosophical confrontations, as well as his organization of a widespread *saṅkīrtana* movement and his civil disobedience against the repression of the Mohammedan government.

The subject of *Madhya-līlā,* the longest of the three divisions, is a detailed narration of Lord Caitanya's extensive and eventful travels throughout India as a renounced mendicant, teacher, philosopher, spiritual preceptor and mystic. During this period of six years, Śrī Caitanya transmits his teachings to his principal disciples. He debates and converts many of the most renowned philosophers and theologians of his time, including Śaṅkarites, Buddhists and Muslims, and incorporates their many thousands of followers and disciples into his own burgeoning numbers. A dramatic account of Caitanya Mahāprabhu's miraculous activities at the giant Jagannātha Cart Festival in Orissa is also included in this section.

Antya-līlā concerns the last eighteen years of Śrī Caitanya's manifest presence, spent in semiseclusion near the famous Jagannātha temple at Jagannātha Purī in Orissa. During these final years, Śrī Caitanya drifted deeper and deeper into trances of spiritual ecstasy unparalleled in all of religious and literary history, Eastern or Western. Śrī Caitanya's perpetual and ever-increasing religious beatitude, graphically described in the eyewitness accounts of Svarūpa Dāmodara Gosvāmī, his constant companion during this period, clearly defy the investigative and descriptive abilities of modern psychologists and phenomenologists of religious experience.

The author of this great classic, Kṛṣṇadāsa Kavirāja Gosvāmī, born in the year 1507, was a disciple of Raghunātha dāsa Gosvāmī, a confidential follower of Caitanya Mahāprabhu. Raghunātha dāsa, a renowned ascetic saint, heard and memorized all the activities of Caitanya Mahāprabhu told to him by Svarūpa Dāmodara. After the passing away of Śrī Caitanya and Svarūpa Dāmodara, Raghunātha dāsa, unable to bear the pain of separation from these objects of his complete devotion, traveled to Vṛndāvana, intending to commit suicide by jumping from Govardhana Hill. In Vṛndāvana, however, he encountered Rūpa Gosvāmī and Sanātana Gosvāmī, the most confidential disciples of Caitanya Mahāprabhu. They convinced him to give up his plan of suicide and impelled him to reveal to them the spiritually inspiring events of Lord Caitanya's later life. Kṛṣṇadāsa Kavirāja Gosvāmī was also residing in Vṛndāvana at this time, and Raghunātha dāsa Gosvāmī endowed him with a full comprehension of the transcendental life of Śrī Caitanya.

By this time, several biographical works had already been written on the life of Śrī Caitanya by contemporary and near-contemporary scholars and devotees. These included *Śrī Caitanya-carita* by Murāri Gupta, *Caitanya-maṅgala* by Locana dāsa Ṭhākura and *Caitanya-bhāgavata.* This latter text, a work by Vṛndāvana dāsa Ṭhākura, who was then considered the principal authority on Śrī Caitanya's life, was highly revered. While composing his important work, Vṛndāvana dāsa, fearing that it would become too voluminous, avoided elaborately describing many of the events of Śrī Caitanya's life, particulary the later ones. Anxious to hear of these later pastimes, the devotees of Vṛndāvana requested Kṛṣṇadāsa Kavirāja Gosvāmī, whom they respected as a great saint, to compose a book to narrate these episodes in detail. Upon this request, and with the permission and blessings of the Madana-mohana Deity of Vṛndāvana, he began compiling *Śrī Caitanya-caritāmṛta,* which, due to its biographical excellence and thorough exposition of Lord Caitanya's profound philosophy and teachings, is regarded as the most significant of biographical works on Śrī Caitanya.

He commenced work on the text while in his late nineties and in failing health, as he vividly describes in the text itself: "I have now become too old and disturbed in invalidity. While writing, my hands tremble. I cannot remember anything, nor can I see or hear properly. Still I write, and this is a great wonder." That he nevertheless completed, under such debilitating conditions, the greatest literary gem of medieval India is surely one of the wonders of literary history.

This English translation and commentary is the work of His Divine Grace A. C. Bhaktivedanta Swami Prabhupāda, the world's most distinguished teacher of Indian religious and philosophical thought. His commentary is based upon two Bengali commentaries, one by his teacher Śrīla Bhaktisiddhānta Sarasvatī Gosvāmī, the eminent Vedic scholar who predicted, "The time will come when the people of the world will learn Bengali to read *Śrī Caitanya-caritāmṛta,*" and the other by Śrīla Bhaktisiddhānta's father, Bhaktivinoda Ṭhākura.

His Divine Grace A. C. Bhaktivedanta Swami Prabhupāda is himself a disciplic descendant of Śrī Caitanya Mahāprabhu, and he is the first scholar to execute systematic English translations of the major works of Śrī Caitanya's followers. His consummate Bengali and Sanskrit scholarship and intimate familiarity with the precepts of Śrī Kṛṣṇa Caitanya are a fitting combination that eminently qualifies him to present this important classic to the English-speaking world. The ease and clarity with which he expounds upon difficult philosophical concepts lures even a reader totally unfamiliar with Indian religious tradition into a genuine understanding and appreciation of this profound and monumental work.

The entire text, with commentary, presented in seventeen lavishly illustrated volumes by the Bhaktivedanta Book Trust, represents a contribution of major importance to the intellectual, cultural and spiritual life of contemporary man.

—The Publishers

His Divine Grace
A. C. Bhaktivedanta Swami Prabhupāda
Founder-Ācārya of the International Society for Krishna Consciousness

The Deity of Śrī Īśvara Purī at the house of Śrīvāsa Ṭhākura in Halisahara. Īśvara Purī pleased Śrīla Mādhavendra Purī by service, and by the blessings of his spiritual master he became such a great personality that Lord Caitanya Mahāprabhu accepted him as His spiritual master.

The temple of Madana-mohana, established by Śrīla Sanātana Gosvāmī, by whose endeavors all the lost places of pilgrimage in the Vṛndāvana area were excavated. By his personal example, he taught people how to stay in Vṛndāvana to execute devotional service. (*p.41*)

Śrīla Raghunātha dāsa Gosvāmī, one of the most dear servants of Śrī Caitanya Mahāprabhu, left all his material possessions to surrender completely unto the Lord and live at His lotus feet.

The site in Pānihāṭi where Raghunātha dāsa Gosvāmī received the mercy of Lord Nityānanda and organized a great feast for the satisfaction of the Lord. (*pp.223-225*)

The *samadhi* tomb and Deities of Uddhārana Datta Ṭhākura, an extremely elevated and liberal devotee of Lord Nityānanda Prabhu, who sat on the raised platform with the Lord at the festival of Raghunātha dāsa Gosvāmī. (*p.232*)

The sacred birthplace of Śrīla Raghunātha dāsa Gosvāmī in the village of Saptagrāma, district of Hugali.

PLATE ONE

Śrīla Rūpa Gosvāmī and Śrīla Sanātana Gosvāmī were ministers directly in charge of the government of Nawab Hussain Shah and they were also householders, but later they became *gosvāmīs*. These two brothers met at Vṛndāvana, where they stayed to execute the will of Śrī Caitanya Mahāprabhu. Śrīla Rūpa Gosvāmī and Sanātana Gosvāmī collected many revealed scriptures, and from the evidence in those scriptures they excavated all the lost sites of pilgrimage. Thus they established temples for the worship of Lord Kṛṣṇa. Being empowered by Lord Caitanya, they both compiled many transcendental literatures to spread the *bhakti* cult.

PLATE TWO

"Sanātana Gosvāmī was very eager to see the lotus feet of Śrī Caitanya Mahāprabhu. Therefore Haridāsa Ṭhākura said, 'The Lord is coming here very soon.' At that very moment, Śrī Caitanya Mahāprabhu, after visiting the temple of Jagannātha to see the offering of *upala-bhoga* [morning refreshments], came with His other devotees to see Haridāsa Ṭhākura. Seeing Śrī Caitanya Mahāprabhu, they both immediately fell flat like rods to offer obeisances. The Lord then lifted Haridāsa and embraced him. Haridāsa Ṭhākura said to Śrī Caitanya Mahāprabhu, 'Here is Sanātana Gosvāmī offering his obeisances.' Seeing Sanātana Gosvāmī, the Lord was greatly surprised. When Śrī Caitanya Mahāprabhu came forward to embrace him, Sanātana backed away and spoke as follows. 'My Lord, please do not touch me. I am the lowest of men, having been born of a low caste. Besides that, I have infections on my body.' Śrī Caitanya Mahāprabhu, however, embraced Sanātana Gosvāmī by force." (*pp.9-11*)

PLATE THREE

"In the village of Pānihāṭi, Raghunātha dāsa obtained an interview with Nityānanda Prabhu, who was accompanied by many *kīrtana* performers, servants and others. Sitting on a rock under a tree on the bank of the Ganges, Lord Nityānanda seemed as effulgent as hundreds and thousands of rising suns. Many devotees sat on the ground surrounding Him. Seeing the influence of Nityānanda Prabhu, Raghunātha dāsa was astonished. Raghunātha dāsa offered his obeisances by falling prostrate at a distant place, and the servant of Nityānanda Prabhu pointed out, 'There is Raghunātha dāsa, offering You obeisances.' Hearing this, Lord Nityānanda Prabhu said, 'You are a thief. Now you have come to see Me. Come here, come here. Today I shall punish you!' The Lord called him, but Raghunātha dāsa did not go near the Lord. Then the Lord forcibly caught him and placed His lotus feet upon Raghunātha dāsa's head." (*pp.223-225*)

PLATE FOUR

"When chipped rice had been served to everyone, Lord Nityānanda Prabhu, in meditation, brought Śrī Caitanya Mahāprabhu. When Śrī Caitanya Mahāprabhu arrived, Lord Nityānanda Prabhu stood up. They then saw how the others were enjoying the chipped rice with yogurt and condensed milk. From each and every pot, Lord Nityānanda Prabhu took one morsel of chipped rice and pushed it into the mouth of Śrī Caitanya Mahāprabhu as a joke. Śrī Caitanya Mahāprabhu, also smiling, took a morsel of food, pushed it into the mouth of Nityānanda and laughed as he made Lord Nityānanda eat it. In this way Lord Nityānanda was walking through all the groups of eaters, and all the Vaiṣṇavas standing there were seeing the fun. No one could understand what Nityānanda Prabhu was doing as He walked about. Some, however, who were very fortunate, could see that Lord Śrī Caitanya Mahāprabhu was also present. Seeing Lord Caitanya Mahāprabhu eating with Him, Lord Nityānanda Prabhu became very happy and exhibited varieties of ecstatic love. Lord Nityānanda Prabhu ordered, 'All of you eat, chanting the holy name of Hari!' Immediately the holy names 'Hari, Hari' resounded, filling the entire universe." (*pp.238-241*)

PLATE FIVE

"When all the Vaiṣṇavas were chanting the holy names 'Hari, Hari' and eating, they remembered how Kṛṣṇa and Balarāma ate with Their companions the cowherd boys on the bank of the Yamunā." (*p.242*)

PLATE SIX

"Nityānanda Prabhu rested for the day, and when the day ended He went to the temple of Rāghava Paṇḍita and began congregational chanting of the holy name of the Lord. Lord Nityānanda Prabhu first influenced all the devotees to dance, and finally He Himself began dancing, thus inundating the entire world in ecstatic love. Lord Śrī Caitanya Mahāprabhu was observing the dancing of Lord Nityānanda Prabhu. Nityānanda Prabhu could see this, but others could not. The dancing of Lord Nityānanda Prabhu, like the dancing of Śrī Caitanya Mahāprabhu, cannot be compared to anything within these three worlds. No one can properly describe the sweetness of Lord Nityānanda's dancing. Śrī Caitanya Mahāprabhu personally comes to see it." (*pp.248-249*)

PLATE SEVEN

"Do not expect honor, but offer all respect to others. Always chant the holy name of Lord Kṛṣṇa, and within your mind render service to Rādhā and Kṛṣṇa in Vṛndāvana." (*p.310*)

PLATE EIGHT

"Lord Jagannātha's *prasāda* is sold by shopkeepers, and that which is not sold decomposes after two or three days. All the decomposed food is thrown before the cows from Tailaṅga at the Siṁha-dvāra gate. Because of its rotten odor, even the cows cannot eat it. At night Raghunātha dāsa would collect that decomposed rice, bring it home and wash it with ample water. Then he ate the hard inner portion of the rice with salt. When Śrī Caitanya Mahāprabhu heard news of this from the mouth of Govinda, He went there the next day and spoke as follows. 'What nice things are you eating? Why don't you give anything to Me?' Saying this, He forcibly took a morsel and began to eat." (*pp.347-350*)

CHAPTER 4

Sanātana Gosvāmī Visits the Lord at Jagannātha Purī

The Fourth Chapter of *Antya-līlā* is summarized by Bhaktivinoda Ṭhākura in his *Amṛta-pravāha-bhāṣya* as follows. Śrīla Sanātana Gosvāmī came alone from Mathurā to Jagannātha Purī to see Lord Caitanya. Because of bathing in bad water and not getting enough food every day while traveling on the path through Jhārikhaṇḍa Forest, he developed a disease that made his body itch. Suffering greatly from this itching, he resolved that in the presence of Śrī Caitanya Mahāprabhu he would throw himself under the wheel of Jagannātha's car and in this way commit suicide.

When Sanātana Gosvāmī came to Jagannātha Purī, he stayed under the care of Haridāsa Ṭhākura for some time, and Śrī Caitanya Mahāprabhu was very happy to see him. The Lord informed Sanātana Gosvāmī about the death of his younger brother, Anupama, who had great faith in the lotus feet of Lord Rāmacandra. One day Śrī Caitanya Mahāprabhu said to Sanātana Gosvāmī, "Your decision to commit suicide is the result of the mode of ignorance. One cannot get love of God simply by committing suicide. You have already dedicated your life and body to My service; therefore your body does not belong to you, nor do you have any right to commit suicide. I have to execute many devotional services through your body. I want you to preach the cult of devotional service and go to Vṛndāvana to excavate the lost holy places." After having thus spoken, Śrī Caitanya Mahāprabhu left, and Haridāsa Ṭhākura and Sanātana Gosvāmī had many talks about this subject.

One day Sanātana Gosvāmī was summoned by Śrī Caitanya Mahāprabhu, who wanted him to come to Yameśvara-ṭoṭā. Sanātana Gosvāmī reached the Lord through the path along the beach by the sea. When Śrī Caitanya Mahāprabhu asked Sanātana Gosvāmī which way he had come, Sanātana replied, "Many servitors of Lord Jagannātha come and go on the path by the Siṁha-dvāra gate of the Jagannātha temple. Therefore, I did not go by that path, but instead went by the beach." Sanātana Gosvāmī did not realize that there were burning blisters on his feet because of the heat of the sand. Śrī Caitanya Mahāprabhu was pleased to hear about Sanātana Gosvāmī's great respect for the temple of Lord Śrī Jagannātha.

Because his disease produced wet sores on his body, Sanātana Gosvāmī used to avoid embracing Śrī Caitanya Mahāprabhu, but nevertheless the Lord would embrace him by force. This made Sanātana Gosvāmī very unhappy, and therefore he consulted Jagadānanda Paṇḍita about what he should do. Jagadānanda advised him to return to Vṛndāvana after the cart festival of Jagannātha, but when Śrī Caitanya Mahāprabhu heard about this instruction, He chastised Jagadānanda Paṇḍita and reminded him that Sanātana Gosvāmī was senior to him and also more learned. Śrī Caitanya Mahāprabhu informed Sanātana Gosvāmī that because Sanātana was a pure devotee, the Lord was never inconvenienced by his bodily condition. Because the Lord was a *sannyāsī,* He did not consider one body better than another. The Lord also informed him that He was maintaining Sanātana and the other devotees just like a father. Therefore the moisture oozing from Sanātana's itching skin did not affect the Lord at all. After speaking with Sanātana Gosvāmī in this way, the Lord again embraced him, and after this embrace, Sanātana Gosvāmī became free from the disease. The Lord ordered Sanātana Gosvāmī to stay with Him for that year, and the next year, after seeing the Ratha-yātrā festival, he left Puruṣottama-kṣetra and returned to Vṛndāvana.

After meeting Śrī Caitanya Mahāprabhu, Śrī Rūpa Gosvāmī also returned to Bengal, where he remained for one year. Whatever money he owned, he distributed among his relatives, the *brāhmaṇas* and the temples. In this way he completely retired and returned to Vṛndāvana to meet Sanātana Gosvāmī.

After narrating these incidents, Kṛṣṇadāsa Kavirāja Gosvāmī has given a list of the main books of Sanātana Gosvāmī, Śrīla Rūpa Gosvāmī and Jīva Gosvāmī.

TEXT 1

বৃন্দাবনাৎ পুনঃ প্রাপ্তং শ্রীগৌরঃ শ্রীসনাতনম্ ।
দেহপাতাদবন্ স্নেহাৎ শুদ্ধং চক্রে পরীক্ষয়া ॥ ১ ॥

vṛndāvanāt punaḥ prāptaṁ
śrī-gauraḥ śrī-sanātanam
deha-pātād avan snehāt
śuddhaṁ cakre parīkṣayā

SYNONYMS

vṛndāvanāt—from Vṛndāvana; *punaḥ*—again; *prāptam*—received; *śrī-gauraḥ*—Lord Śrī Caitanya Mahāprabhu; *śrī-sanātanam*—Śrī Sanātana Gosvāmī; *deha-pātāt*—from giving up his body; *avan*—protecting; *snehāt*—by affection; *śuddham*—pure; *cakre*—made; *parīkṣayā*—by examination.

TRANSLATION

When Sanātana Gosvāmī returned from Vṛndāvana, Śrī Caitanya Mahāprabhu affectionately saved him from his determination to commit suicide. Then, after testing him, Śrī Caitanya Mahāprabhu purified his body.

TEXT 2

জয় জয় শ্রীচৈতন্য জয় নিত্যানন্দ ।
জয়াদ্বৈতচন্দ্র জয় গৌরভক্তবৃন্দ ॥ ২ ॥

jaya jaya śrī-caitanya jaya nityānanda
jayādvaita-candra jaya gaura-bhakta-vṛnda

SYNONYMS

jaya jaya—all glories; *śrī-caitanya*—to Lord Śrī Caitanya Mahāprabhu; *jaya*—all glories; *nityānanda*—to Nityānanda Prabhu; *jaya*—all glories; *advaita-candra*—to Śrī Advaita Ācārya; *jaya*—all glories; *gaura-bhakta-vṛnda*—to the devotees of Lord Śrī Caitanya Mahāprabhu.

TRANSLATION

All glories to Lord Caitanya! All glories to Lord Nityānanda! All glories to Advaitacandra! And all glories to all the devotees of Lord Śrī Caitanya Mahāprabhu!

TEXT 3

নীলাচল হৈতে রূপ গৌড়ে যবে গেলা ।
মথুরা হৈতে সনাতন নীলাচল আইলা ॥ ৩ ॥

nīlācala haite rūpa gauḍe yabe gelā
mathurā haite sanātana nīlācala āilā

SYNONYMS

nīlācala haite—from Nīlācala (Jagannātha Purī); *rūpa*—Śrīla Rūpa Gosvāmī; *gauḍe*—to Bengal; *yabe*—when; *gelā*—went; *mathurā haite*—from Mathurā; *sanātana*—Sanātana Gosvāmī; *nīlācala āilā*—came to Jagannātha Purī.

TRANSLATION

When Śrīla Rūpa Gosvāmī returned from Jagannātha Purī to Bengal, Sanātana Gosvāmī went from Mathurā to Jagannātha Purī to see Śrī Caitanya Mahāprabhu.

TEXT 4

ঝারিখণ্ড-বনপথে আইলা একেলা চলিয়া।
কভু উপবাস, কভু চর্বণ করিয়া ॥ ৪ ॥

jhārikhaṇḍa-vanapathe āilā ekelā caliyā
kabhu upavāsa, kabhu carvaṇa kariyā

SYNONYMS

jhārikhaṇḍa—known as Jhārikhaṇḍa; *vana-pathe*—through the path of the forest of central India; *āilā*—came; *ekelā*—alone; *caliyā*—walking; *kabhu*—sometimes; *upavāsa*—fasting; *kabhu*—sometimes; *carvaṇa kariyā*—chewing.

TRANSLATION

Sanātana Gosvāmī walked alone on the path through Jhārikhaṇḍa Forest in central India. Sometimes he fasted, and sometimes he would eat.

TEXT 5

ঝারিখণ্ডের জলের দোষে, উপবাস হৈতে।
গাত্রে কণ্ডু হৈল, রসা পড়ে খাজুয়াইতে ॥ ৫ ॥

jhārikhaṇḍera jalera doṣe, upavāsa haite
gātre kaṇḍu haila, rasā paḍe khājuyāite

SYNONYMS

jhārikhaṇḍera—at the place known as Jhārikhaṇḍa; *jalera*—of the water; *doṣe*—by the fault; *upavāsa haite*—by fasting; *gātre*—on the body; *kaṇḍu*—itches; *haila*—there were; *rasā*—fluid; *paḍe*—oozes out; *khājuyāite*—by itching.

TRANSLATION

Because of bad water in Jhārikhaṇḍa and because of fasting, Sanātana Gosvāmī contracted a disease that made his body itch. Thus he was afflicted with itching sores from which fluid oozed.

TEXT 6

নির্বেদ হইল পথে, করেন বিচার।
'নীচ-জাতি, দেহ মোর—অত্যন্ত অসার ॥ ৬ ॥

nirveda ha-ila pathe, karena vicāra
'nīca-jāti, deha mora——atyanta asāra

SYNONYMS

nirveda ha-ila—there was disappointment; *pathe*—on the path; *karena vicāra*—he considered; *nīca-jāti*—of a lower caste; *deha mora*—my body; *atyanta*—completely; *asāra*—useless for devotional service.

TRANSLATION

In disappointment, Sanātana Gosvāmī considered, "I am of a low caste, and my body is useless for devotional service.

TEXT 7

জগন্নাথে গেলে তাঁর দর্শন না পাইমু।
প্রভুর দর্শন সদা করিতে নারিমু॥ ৭ ॥

jagannāthe gele tāṅra darśana nā pāimu
prabhura darśana sadā karite nārimu

SYNONYMS

jagannāthe—to Jagannātha Purī; *gele*—when I go; *tāṅra*—His; *darśana*—visit; *nā pāimu*—I shall not get; *prabhura darśana*—seeing Lord Śrī Caitanya Mahāprabhu; *sadā*—always; *karite*—to do; *nārimu*—I shall not be able.

TRANSLATION

"When I go to Jagannātha Purī, I shall not be able to see Lord Jagannātha, nor shall I always be able to see Śrī Caitanya Mahāprabhu.

TEXT 8

মন্দির-নিকটে শুনি তাঁর বাসা-স্থিতি।
মন্দির-নিকটে যাইতে মোর নাহি শক্তি॥ ৮ ॥

mandira-nikaṭe śuni tāṅra vāsā-sthiti
mandira-nikaṭe yāite mora nāhi śakti

SYNONYMS

mandira-nikaṭe—near the temple; *śuni*—I hear; *tāṅra*—His; *vāsā-sthiti*—residential place; *mandira-nikaṭe*—near the temple; *yāite*—to go; *mora*—my; *nāhi śakti*—there is no power.

TRANSLATION

"I have heard that the residential quarters of Śrī Caitanya Mahāprabhu are near the temple of Jagannātha. But I shall not have the power to go near the temple.

TEXT 9

জগন্নাথের সেবক ফেরে কার্য-অনুরোধে ।
তাঁর স্পর্শ হৈলে মোর হবে অপরাধে ॥ ৯ ॥

jagannāthera sevaka phere kārya-anurodhe
tāṅra sparśa haile mora habe aparādhe

SYNONYMS

jagannāthera—of Lord Jagannātha; *sevaka*—different servants; *phere*—move about; *kārya-anurodhe*—because of different duties; *tāṅra*—of them; *sparśa*—touch; *haile*—if there is; *mora*—my; *habe*—there will be; *aparādhe*—offense.

TRANSLATION

"The servants of Lord Jagannātha generally move about tending to their duties, but if they touch me I shall be an offender.

TEXT 10

তাতে যদি এই দেহ ভাল-স্থানে দিয়ে ।
দুঃখ-শান্তি হয় আর সদ্গতি পাইয়ে ॥ ১০ ॥

tāte yadi ei deha bhāla-sthāne diye
duḥkha-śānti haya āra sad-gati pāiye

SYNONYMS

tāte—therefore; *yadi*—if; *ei*—this; *deha*—body; *bhāla-sthāne*—in a good place; *diye*—I sacrifice; *duḥkha-śānti*—appeasement of unhappiness; *haya*—there is; *āra*—and; *sat-gati*—good destination; *pāiye*—I get.

TRANSLATION

"Therefore if I sacrifice this body in a good place, my unhappiness will be mitigated, and I shall attain an exalted destination.

TEXT 11

জগন্নাথ রথযাত্রায় হইবেন বাহির ।
তাঁর রথ-চাকায় ছাড়িমু এই শরীর ॥ ১১ ॥

jagannātha ratha-yātrāya ha-ibena bāhira
tāṅra ratha-cākāya chāḍimu ei śarīra

SYNONYMS

jagannātha ratha-yātrāya—on the occasion of the car festival of Lord Jagannātha; *ha-ibena bāhira*—He will be out; *tāṅra*—of Him; *ratha-cākāya*—under the wheel of the cart; *chāḍimu*—I shall give up; *ei śarīra*—this body.

TRANSLATION

"During the Ratha-yātrā festival, when Lord Jagannātha comes out of the temple, I shall give up this body under the wheel of His cart.

TEXT 12

মহাপ্রভুর আগে, আর দেখি' জগন্নাথ ।
রথে দেহ ছাড়িমু,— এই পরম-পুরুষার্থ'॥ ১২ ॥

mahāprabhura āge, āra dekhi' jagannātha
rathe deha chāḍimu,——ei parama-puruṣārtha'

SYNONYMS

mahāprabhura āge—in front of Śrī Caitanya Mahāprabhu; *āra*—and; *dekhi' jagannātha*—after seeing Lord Jagannātha; *rathe*—under the cart; *deha chāḍimu*—I shall give up this body; *ei*—this; *parama-puruṣa-artha*—the highest benediction of life.

TRANSLATION

"After seeing Lord Jagannātha, I shall give up my body under the wheel of the cart in the presence of Śrī Caitanya Mahāprabhu. This will be the highest benediction of my life."

TEXT 13

এই ত' নিশ্চয় করি' নীলাচলে আইলা ।
লোকে পুছি' হরিদাস-স্থানে উত্তরিলা ॥ ১৩ ॥

ei ta' niścaya kari' nīlācale āilā
loke puchi' haridāsa-sthāne uttarilā

SYNONYMS

ei ta'—in this way; *niścaya kari'*—ascertaining; *nīlācale āilā*—came to Jagannātha Purī; *loke puchi'*—inquiring from people; *haridāsa-sthāne*—the place of Haridāsa Ṭhākura; *uttarilā*—approached.

TRANSLATION

Having made this resolution, Sanātana Gosvāmī went to Nīlācala, where he inquired directions from people and approached the residence of Haridāsa Ṭhākura.

TEXT 14

হরিদাসের কৈলা তেঁহ চরণ বন্দন।
জানি' হরিদাস তাঁরে কৈলা আলিঙ্গন ॥ ১৪ ॥

haridāsera kailā teṅha caraṇa vandana
jāni' haridāsa tāṅre kailā āliṅgana

SYNONYMS

haridāsera—of Haridāsa Ṭhākura; *kailā*—did; *teṅha*—he; *caraṇa vandana*—worshiping the lotus feet; *jāni'*—knowing; *haridāsa*—Haridāsa Ṭhākura; *tāṅre*—him; *kailā āliṅgana*—embraced.

TRANSLATION

He offered his respects to the lotus feet of Haridāsa Ṭhākura, who knew him and thus embraced him.

TEXT 15

মহাপ্রভু দেখিতে তাঁর উৎকণ্ঠিত মন।
হরিদাস কহে,—'প্রভু আসিবেন এখন' ॥ ১৫ ॥

mahāprabhu dekhite tāṅra utkaṇṭhita mana
haridāsa kahe,—'prabhu āsibena ekhana'

SYNONYMS

mahāprabhu—Śrī Caitanya Mahāprabhu; *dekhite*—to see; *tāṅra*—his; *utkaṇṭhita*—anxious; *mana*—mind; *haridāsa kahe*—Haridāsa said; *prabhu*—Śrī Caitanya Mahāprabhu; *āsibena ekhana*—will come here.

TRANSLATION

Sanātana Gosvāmī was very eager to see the lotus feet of Śrī Caitanya Mahāprabhu. Therefore Haridāsa Ṭhākura said, "The Lord is coming here very soon."

TEXT 16

হেনকালে প্রভু 'উপলভোগ' দেখিয়া ।
হরিদাসে মিলিতে আইলা ভক্তগণ লঞা ॥ ১৬ ॥

hena-kāle prabhu 'upala-bhoga' dekhiyā
haridāse milite āilā bhakta-gaṇa lañā

SYNONYMS

hena-kāle—at this time; *prabhu*—Śrī Caitanya Mahāprabhu; *upala-bhoga*—the *upala-bhoga* offering to Lord Jagannātha; *dekhiyā*—after seeing; *haridāse*—Haridāsa; *milite*—to meet; *āilā*—came; *bhakta-gaṇa lañā*—with other devotees.

TRANSLATION

At that very moment, Śrī Caitanya Mahāprabhu, after visiting the temple of Jagannātha to see the offering of upala-bhoga [morning refreshments], came with His other devotees to see Haridāsa Ṭhākura.

TEXT 17

প্রভু দেখি' দুঁহে পড়ে দণ্ডবৎ হঞা ।
প্রভু আলিঙ্গিলা হরিদাসেরে উঠাঞা ॥ ১৭ ॥

prabhu dekhi' duṅhe paḍe daṇḍavat hañā
prabhu āliṅgilā haridāsere uṭhāñā

SYNONYMS

prabhu dekhi'—seeing Lord Śrī Caitanya Mahāprabhu; *duṅhe*—both of them; *paḍe*—fell down; *daṇḍavat hañā*—flat like rods; *prabhu*—Śrī Caitanya Mahāprabhu; *āliṅgilā*—embraced; *haridāsere*—Haridāsa Ṭhākura; *uṭhāñā*—after lifting.

TRANSLATION

Seeing Śrī Caitanya Mahāprabhu, they both immediately fell flat like rods to offer obeisances. The Lord then lifted Haridāsa and embraced him.

TEXT 18

হরিদাস কহে,—'সনাতন করে নমস্কার'।
সনাতনে দেখি' প্রভু হৈলা চমৎকার ॥ ১৮ ॥

haridāsa kahe,——'sanātana kare namaskāra'
sanātane dekhi' prabhu hailā camatkāra

SYNONYMS

haridāsa kahe—Haridāsa said; *sanātana*—Sanātana Gosvāmī; *kare namaskāra*—is offering his obeisances; *sanātane dekhi'*—seeing Sanātana Gosvāmī; *prabhu*—Śrī Caitanya Mahāprabhu; *hailā camatkāra*—became very surprised.

TRANSLATION

Haridāsa Ṭhākura said to Śrī Caitanya Mahāprabhu, "Here is Sanātana Gosvāmī offering his obeisances." Seeing Sanātana Gosvāmī, the Lord was greatly surprised.

TEXT 19

সনাতনে আলিঙ্গিতে প্রভু আগু হৈলা।
পাছে ভাগে সনাতন কহিতে লাগিলা ॥ ১৯ ॥

sanātane āliṅgite prabhu āgu hailā
pāche bhāge sanātana kahite lāgilā

SYNONYMS

sanātane—Sanātana Gosvāmī; *āliṅgite*—to embrace; *prabhu*—Śrī Caitanya Mahāprabhu; *āgu hailā*—came forward; *pāche*—back; *bhāge*—runs; *sanātana*—Sanātana Gosvāmī; *kahite lāgilā*—began to speak.

TRANSLATION

When Śrī Caitanya Mahāprabhu came forward to embrace him, Sanātana backed away and spoke as follows.

TEXT 20

"মোরে না ছুঁইহ, প্রভু, পড়োঁ তোমার পায়।
একে নীচজাতি অধম, আর কণ্ডুরসা গায় ॥" ২০ ॥

"more nā chuṅiha, prabhu, paḍoṅ tomāra pāya
eke nīca-jāti adhama, āra kaṇḍu-rasā gāya

SYNONYMS

more—me; *nā chūṅiha*—please do not touch; *prabhu*—my Lord; *paḍoṅ*—I fall down; *tomāra pāya*—at Your feet; *eke*—on one side; *nīca-jāti*—of a low caste; *adhama*—the lowest of mankind; *āra*—and; *kaṇḍu-rasā*—a disease of wet, itching infections; *gāya*—on the body.

TRANSLATION

"My Lord, please do not touch me. I fall at Your lotus feet. I am the lowest of men, having been born of a low caste. Besides that, I have infections on my body."

TEXT 21

বলাৎকারে প্রভু তাঁরে আলিঙ্গন কৈল।
কণ্ডুক্লেদ মহাপ্রভুর শ্রীঅঙ্গে লাগিল ॥ ২১ ॥

balātkāre prabhu tāṅre āliṅgana kaila
kaṇḍu-kleda mahāprabhura śrī-aṅge lāgila

SYNONYMS

balātkāre—by force; *prabhu*—Śrī Caitanya Mahāprabhu; *tāṅre*—him; *āliṅgana kaila*—embraced; *kaṇḍu-kleda*—the moisture of weeping itches; *mahāprabhura*—of Śrī Caitanya Mahāprabhu; *śrī*—transcendental; *aṅge*—body; *lāgila*—touched.

TRANSLATION

Śrī Caitanya Mahāprabhu, however, embraced Sanātana Gosvāmī by force. Thus the moisture oozing from the itching sores touched the transcendental body of Śrī Caitanya Mahāprabhu.

TEXT 22

সব ভক্তগণে প্রভু মিলাইলা সনাতনে।
সনাতন কৈলা সবার চরণ বন্দনে ॥ ২২ ॥

saba bhakta-gaṇe prabhu milāilā sanātane
sanātana kailā sabāra caraṇa vandane

SYNONYMS

saba—all; *bhakta-gaṇe*—devotees; *prabhu*—Śrī Caitanya Mahāprabhu; *milāilā*—introduced; *sanātane*—to Sanātana Gosvāmī; *sanātana*—Sanātana Gosvāmī; *kailā*—did; *sabāra*—of all of them; *caraṇa vandane*—worshiping the lotus feet.

TRANSLATION

The Lord introduced all the devotees to Sanātana Gosvāmī, who offered his respectful obeisances unto the lotus feet of them all.

TEXT 23

প্রভু লঞা বসিলা পিণ্ডার উপরে ভক্তগণ ।
পিণ্ডার তলে বসিলা হরিদাস সনাতন ॥ ২৩ ॥

prabhu lañā vasilā piṇḍāra upare bhakta-gaṇa
piṇḍāra tale vasilā haridāsa sanātana

SYNONYMS

prabhu lañā—with Śrī Caitanya Mahāprabhu; *vasilā*—sat down; *piṇḍāra upare*—upon the raised platform; *bhakta-gaṇa*—all the devotees; *piṇḍāra tale*—below the platform; *vasilā*—sat down; *haridāsa sanātana*—Haridāsa Ṭhākura and Sanātana Gosvāmī.

TRANSLATION

The Lord and His devotees sat on a raised platform, and below that sat Haridāsa Ṭhākura and Sanātana Gosvāmī.

TEXT 24

কুশলবার্তা মহাপ্রভু পুছেন সনাতনে ।
তেঁহ কহেন,—'পরম মঙ্গল দেখিনু চরণে' ॥ ২৪ ॥

kuśala-vārtā mahāprabhu puchena sanātane
teṅha kahena,——'parama maṅgala dekhinu caraṇe'

SYNONYMS

kuśala—of well-being; *vārtā*—news; *mahāprabhu*—Śrī Caitanya Mahāprabhu; *puchena*—inquires; *sanātane*—from Sanātana Gosvāmī; *teṅha kahena*—he said; *parama maṅgala*—everything is auspicious; *dekhinu caraṇe*—I have seen Your lotus feet.

TRANSLATION

Śrī Caitanya Mahāprabhu inquired from Sanātana about news of his well-being. Sanātana replied, "Everything is auspicious because I have seen Your lotus feet."

TEXT 25

মথুরার বৈষ্ণব-সবের কুশল পুছিলা।
সবার কুশল সনাতন জানাইলা ॥ ২৫ ॥

mathurāra vaiṣṇava-sabera kuśala puchilā
sabāra kuśala sanātana jānāilā

SYNONYMS

mathurāra—of Mathurā; *vaiṣṇava-sabera*—of all the Vaiṣṇavas; *kuśala puchilā*—inquired about the auspiciousness; *sabāra kuśala*—the well-being of all of them; *sanātana*—Sanātana Gosvāmī; *jānāilā*—informed.

TRANSLATION

When the Lord asked about all the Vaiṣṇavas at Mathurā, Sanātana Gosvāmī informed Him of their good health and fortune.

TEXT 26

প্রভু কহে,—"ইহাঁ রূপ ছিল দশমাস।
ইহাঁ হৈতে গৌড়ে গেলা, হৈল দিন দশ ॥ ২৬ ॥

prabhu kahe,——"ihāṅ rūpa chila daśa-māsa
ihāṅ haite gauḍe gelā, haila dina daśa

SYNONYMS

prabhu kahe—Lord Śrī Caitanya Mahāprabhu said; *ihāṅ*—here; *rūpa*—Rūpa Gosvāmī; *chila*—was; *daśa-māsa*—ten months; *ihāṅ haite*—from here; *gauḍe gelā*—has gone to Bengal; *haila*—it was; *dina*—days; *daśa*—ten.

TRANSLATION

Śrī Caitanya Mahāprabhu informed Sanātana Gosvāmī, "Śrīla Rūpa Gosvāmī was here for ten months. He left for Bengal just ten days ago.

TEXT 27

তোমার ভাই অনুপমের হৈল গঙ্গা-প্রাপ্তি।
ভাল ছিল, রঘুনাথে দৃঢ় তার ভক্তি ॥" ২৭ ॥

tomāra bhāi anupamera haila gaṅgā-prāpti
bhāla chila, raghunāthe dṛḍha tāra bhakti"

SYNONYMS

tomāra bhāi—your brother; *anupamera*—of Anupama; *haila*—was; *gaṅgā-prāpti*—death; *bhāla chila*—he was a very good man; *raghu-nāthe*—unto Lord Raghunātha (Lord Rāmacandra); *dṛḍha*—firm; *tāra bhakti*—his devotion.

TRANSLATION

"Your brother Anupama is now dead. He was a very good devotee who had firm conviction in Raghunātha [Lord Rāmacandra]."

TEXT 28

সনাতন কহে,—"নীচ-বংশে মোর জন্ম।
অধর্ম অন্যায় যত,—আমার কুলধর্ম ॥ ২৮ ॥

sanātana kahe,——"nīca-vaṁśe mora janma
adharma anyāya yata,——āmāra kula-dharma

SYNONYMS

sanātana kahe—Sanātana Gosvāmī said; *nīca-vaṁśe*—in a low family; *mora janma*—my birth; *adharma*—irreligion; *anyāya*—sinful activities; *yata*—all; *āmāra*—my; *kula-dharma*—family business.

TRANSLATION

Sanātana Gosvāmī said, "I was born in a low family, for my family commits all kinds of irreligious acts that violate the scriptural injunctions.

TEXT 29

হেন বংশ ঘৃণা ছাড়ি' কৈলা অঙ্গীকার।
তোমার কৃপায় বংশে মঙ্গল আমার ॥ ২৯ ॥

hena vaṁśa ghṛṇā chāḍi' kailā aṅgīkāra
tomāra kṛpāya vaṁśe maṅgala āmāra

SYNONYMS

hena—such; *vaṁśa*—family; *ghṛṇā*—hatred; *chāḍi'*—giving up; *kailā*—You have done; *aṅgīkāra*—acceptance; *tomāra*—Your; *kṛpāya*—by mercy; *vaṁśe*—in the family; *maṅgala*—auspiciousness; *āmāra*—my.

TRANSLATION

"My Lord, without hatred for my family You have accepted me as Your servant. Only by Your mercy is there good fortune in my family.

TEXT 30

সেই অনুপম-ভাই শিশুকাল হৈতে।
রঘুনাথ-উপাসনা করে দৃঢ়চিত্তে ॥ ৩০ ॥

sei anupama-bhāi śiśu-kāla haite
raghunātha-upāsanā kare dṛḍha-citte

SYNONYMS

sei—that; *anupama-bhāi*—brother named Anupama; *śiśu-kāla haite*—from the beginning of childhood; *raghu-nātha*—of Lord Rāmacandra; *upāsanā*—worship; *kare*—performs; *dṛḍha-citte*—with great determination.

TRANSLATION

"From the very beginning of his childhood, my younger brother Anupama was a great devotee of Raghunātha [Lord Rāmacandra], and he worshiped Him with great determination.

TEXT 31

রাত্রি-দিনে রঘুনাথের 'নাম' আর 'ধ্যান'।
রামায়ণ নিরবধি শুনে, করে গান ॥ ৩১ ॥

rātri-dine raghunāthera 'nāma' āra 'dhyāna'
ramayaṇa niravadhl śune, kare gāna

SYNONYMS

rātri-dine—day and night; *raghu-nāthera*—of Lord Rāmacandra; *nāma*—holy name; *āra*—and; *dhyāna*—meditation; *rāmāyaṇa*—the epic about the activities of Lord Rāmacandra known as the *Rāmāyaṇa; niravadhi*—continuously; *śune*—hears; *kare gāna*—chants.

TRANSLATION

"He always chanted the holy name of Raghunātha and meditated upon Him. He continuously heard about the activities of the Lord from the Rāmāyaṇa and chanted about them.

TEXT 32

আমি আর রূপ—তার জ্যেষ্ঠ-সহোদর ।
আমা-দোঁহা-সঙ্গে তেঁহ রহে নিরন্তর ॥ ৩২ ॥

āmi āra rūpa——tāra jyeṣṭha-sahodara
āmā-doṅhā-saṅge teṅha rahe nirantara

SYNONYMS

āmi—I; *āra*—and; *rūpa*—Rūpa Gosvāmī; *tāra*—his; *jyeṣṭha-sahodara*—elder brothers; *āmā-doṅhā*—the two of us; *saṅge*—with; *teṅha*—he; *rahe*—remains; *nirantara*—continuously.

TRANSLATION

"Rūpa and I are his elder brothers. He stayed with us continuously.

TEXT 33

আমা-সবা-সঙ্গে কৃষ্ণকথা, ভাগবত শুনে ।
তাহার পরীক্ষা কৈলুঁ আমি-দুইজনে ॥ ৩৩ ॥

āmā-sabā-saṅge kṛṣṇa-kathā, bhāgavata śune
tāhāra parīkṣā kailuṅ āmi-dui-jane

SYNONYMS

āmā-sabā—all of us; *saṅge*—with; *kṛṣṇa-kathā*—talks about Lord Kṛṣṇa; *bhāgavata śune*—hears *Śrīmad-Bhāgavatam*; *tāhāra*—his; *parīkṣā*—examination; *kailuṅ*—did; *āmi-dui-jane*—both of us.

TRANSLATION

"He heard Śrīmad-Bhāgavatam and talks about Lord Kṛṣṇa with us, and both of us examined him.

TEXT 34

"শুনহ বল্লভ, কৃষ্ণ - পরম-মধুর ।
সৌন্দর্য, মাধুর্য, প্রেম-বিলাস—প্রচুর ॥ ৩৪ ॥

śunaha vallabha, kṛṣṇa——parama-madhura
saundarya, mādhurya, prema-vilāsa——pracura

SYNONYMS

śunaha—please hear; *vallabha*—dear Vallabha; *kṛṣṇa*—Lord Kṛṣṇa; *parama-madhura*—supremely attractive; *saundarya*—beauty; *mādhurya*—sweetness; *prema-vilāsa*—pastimes of love; *pracura*—without limitation.

TRANSLATION

" 'Dear Vallabha,' we said, 'please hear from us. Lord Kṛṣṇa is supremely attractive. His beauty, sweetness and pastimes of love are without limit.

TEXT 35

কৃষ্ণভজন কর তুমি আমা-দুঁহার সঙ্গে ।
তিন ভাই একত্র রহিমু কৃষ্ণকথা-রঙ্গে ॥" ৩৫ ॥

kṛṣṇa-bhajana kara tumi āmā-duṅhāra saṅge
tina bhāi ekatra rahimu kṛṣṇa-kathā-raṅge"

SYNONYMS

kṛṣṇa-bhajana—devotional service to Lord Kṛṣṇa; *kara*—engage in; *tumi*—you; *āmā-duṅhāra*—the two of us; *saṅge*—with; *tina bhāi*—three brothers; *ekatra*—in one place; *rahimu*—we shall stay; *kṛṣṇa-kathā*—of the pastimes of Lord Kṛṣṇa; *raṅge*—in enjoyment.

TRANSLATION

" 'Engage yourself in devotional service to Kṛṣṇa with both of us. We three brothers shall stay together and enjoy discussing the pastimes of Lord Kṛṣṇa.'

TEXT 36

এইমত বারবার কহি দুইজন ।
আমা-দুঁহার গৌরবে কিছু ফিরি' গেল মন ॥ ৩৬ ॥

ei-mata bāra-bāra kahi dui-jana
āmā-duṅhāra gaurave kichu phiri' gela mana

SYNONYMS

ei-mata—in this way; *bāra-bāra*—again and again; *kahi*—we speak; *dui-jana*—two persons; *āmā-duṅhāra*—of us both; *gaurave*—out of respect; *kichu*—somewhat; *phiri' gela*—turned; *mana*—mind.

TRANSLATION

"In this way we both spoke to him again and again, and because of this persuasion and his respect for us, his mind turned somewhat toward our instructions.

TEXT 37

"তোমা-দুহাঁর আজ্ঞা আমি কেমনে লঙ্ঘিমু ?
দীক্ষা-মন্ত্র দেহ' কৃষ্ণ-ভজন করিমু ॥" ৩৭ ॥

"tomā-duṅhāra ājñā āmi kemane laṅghimu?
dīkṣā-mantra deha' kṛṣṇa-bhajana karimu"

SYNONYMS

tomā—of you; *duṅhāra*—of both; *ājñā*—the order; *āmi*—I; *kemane*—how; *laṅghimu*—shall disobey; *dīkṣā*—initiation; *mantra*—mantra; *deha'*—just give; *kṛṣṇa-bhajana*—devotional service to Kṛṣṇa; *karimu*—I shall perform.

TRANSLATION

"Vallabha replied, 'My dear brothers, how can I disobey your orders? Initiate me into the Kṛṣṇa mantra so that I may perform devotional service to Lord Kṛṣṇa.'

TEXT 38

এত কহি' রাত্রিকালে করেন চিন্তন ।
কেমনে ছাড়িমু রঘুনাথের চরণ ॥ ৩৮ ॥

eta kahi' rātri-kāle karena cintana
kemane chāḍimu raghunāthera caraṇa

SYNONYMS

eta kahi'—saying this; *rātri-kāle*—at night; *karena cintana*—began to think; *kemane*—how; *chāḍimu*—shall I give up; *raghu-nāthera caraṇa*—the lotus feet of Lord Raghunātha.

TRANSLATION

"After saying this, at night he began to think, 'How shall I give up the lotus feet of Lord Raghunātha?'

TEXT 39

সব রাত্রি ক্রন্দন করি' কৈল জাগরণ ।
প্রাতঃকালে আমা-দুঁহায় কৈল নিবেদন ॥ ৩৯ ॥

saba rātri krandana kari' kaila jāgaraṇa
prātaḥ-kāle āmā-duṅhāya kaila nivedana

SYNONYMS

saba rātri—throughout the whole night; *krandana*—crying; *kari'*—doing; *kaila jāgaraṇa*—remained awake; *prātaḥ-kāle*—in the morning; *āmā-duṅhāya*—to the two of us; *kaila*—made; *nivedana*—submission.

TRANSLATION

"He stayed up all night and cried. In the morning, he came to us and submitted the following plea.

TEXT 40

'রঘুনাথের পাদপদ্মে বেচিয়াছোঁ মাথা।
কাড়িতে না পারোঁ মাথা, পাঙ বড় ব্যথা ॥ ৪০ ॥

'raghunāthera pāda-padme veciyāchoṅ māthā
kāḍite nā pāroṅ māthā, pāṅa baḍa vyathā

SYNONYMS

raghu-nāthera—of Lord Rāmacandra; *pāda-padme*—at the lotus feet; *veciyāchoṅ māthā*—I have sold my head; *kāḍite*—to take away; *nā pāroṅ*—I am unable; *māthā*—the head; *pāṅa*—I get; *baḍa vyathā*—too much pain.

TRANSLATION

" 'I have sold my head at the lotus feet of Lord Rāmacandra. I cannot take it away. That would be too painful for me.

TEXT 41

কৃপা করি' মোরে আজ্ঞা দেহ' দুইজন।
জন্মে-জন্মে সেবোঁ রঘুনাথের চরণ ॥ ৪১ ॥

kṛpā kari' more ājñā deha' dui-jana
janme-janme sevoṅ raghunāthera caraṇa

SYNONYMS

kṛpā kari'—being merciful; *more*—unto me; *ājñā deha'*—give the order; *dui-jana*—both of you; *janme-janme*—life after life; *sevoṅ*—let me serve; *raghu-nāthera caraṇa*—the lotus feet of Lord Raghunātha.

TRANSLATION

" 'Both of you please be merciful to me and order me in such a way so that life after life I may serve the lotus feet of Lord Raghunātha.

TEXT 42

রঘুনাথের পাদপদ্ম ছাড়ান না যায়।
ছাড়িবার মন হৈলে প্রাণ ফাটি' যায় ॥' ৪২ ॥

raghunāthera pāda-padma chāḍāna nā yāya
chāḍibāra mana haile prāṇa phāṭi' yāya'

SYNONYMS

raghu-nāthera—of Lord Raghunātha; *pāda-padma*—lotus feet; *chāḍāna nā yāya*—it is impossible to give up; *chāḍibāra*—of giving up; *mana haile*—when I think; *prāṇa*—my heart; *phāṭi' yāya*—breaks.

TRANSLATION

" 'It is impossible for me to give up the lotus feet of Lord Raghunātha. When I even think of giving them up, my heart breaks.'

TEXT 43

তবে আমি-দুঁহে তারে আলিঙ্গন কৈলুঁ।
'সাধু, দৃঢ়ভক্তি তোমার'—কহি' প্রশংসিলুঁ ॥ ৪৩ ॥

tabe āmi-duṅhe tāre āliṅgana kailuṅ
'sādhu, dṛḍha-bhakti tomāra'——kahi' praśaṁsiluṅ

SYNONYMS

tabe—at that time; *āmi-duṅhe*—both of us; *tāre*—him; *āliṅgana kailuṅ*—embraced; *sādhu*—very good; *dṛḍha*—very determined; *bhakti*—devotion; *tomāra*—your; *kahi'*—saying; *praśaṁsiluṅ*—we praised.

TRANSLATION

"Upon hearing this, both of us embraced him and encouraged him by saying, 'You are a great saintly devotee, for your determination in devotional service is fixed.' In this way we both praised him.

TEXT 44

যে বংশের উপরে তোমার হয় কৃপা-লেশ ।
সকল মঙ্গল তাহে খণ্ডে সব ক্লেশ ॥' ৪৪ ॥

ye vaṁśera upare tomāra haya kṛpā-leśa
sakala maṅgala tāhe khaṇḍe saba kleśa'

SYNONYMS

ye vaṁśera—which family; *upare*—upon; *tomāra*—Your; *haya*—there is; *kṛpā-leśa*—little mercy; *sakala maṅgala*—all auspiciousness; *tāhe*—on that; *khaṇḍe*—are destroyed; *saba*—all; *kleśa*—miserable conditions.

TRANSLATION

"My dear Lord, the family upon which You bestow even a little mercy is always fortunate, for such mercy makes all miseries disappear."

TEXT 45

গোসাঞি কহেন,—"এইমত মুরারি-গুপ্ত ।
পূর্বে আমি পরীক্ষিলুঁ তার এই রীত ॥ ৪৫ ॥

gosāñi kahena,—"ei-mata murāri-gupta
pūrve āmi parīkṣiluṅ tāra ei rīta

SYNONYMS

gosāñi kahena—Śrī Caitanya Mahāprabhu replied; *ei-mata*—in this way; *murāri-gupta*—Murāri Gupta; *pūrve*—formerly; *āmi*—I; *parīkṣiluṅ*—examined; *tāra*—of him; *ei*—this; *rīta*—manner.

TRANSLATION

Śrī Caitanya Mahāprabhu said, "There was a similar incident concerning Murāri Gupta. Formerly I examined him, and his determination was similar.

TEXT 46

সেই ভক্ত ধন্য, যে না ছাড়ে প্রভুর চরণ ।
সেই প্রভু ধন্য, যে না ছাড়ে নিজ-জন ॥ ৪৬ ॥

sei bhakta dhanya, ye nā chāḍe prabhura caraṇa
sei prabhu dhanya, ye nā chāḍe nija-jana

SYNONYMS

sei bhakta—that devotee; *dhanya*—glorious; *ye*—who; *nā*—not; *chāḍe*—gives up; *prabhura caraṇa*—the lotus feet of the Lord; *sei prabhu*—that Personality of Godhead; *dhanya*—glorious; *ye*—who; *nā*—not; *chāḍe*—gives up; *nija-jana*—His servant.

TRANSLATION

"Glorious is that devotee who does not give up the shelter of his Lord, and glorious is that Lord who does not abandon His servant.

TEXT 47

দুর্দৈবে সেবক যদি যায় অন্য স্থানে ।
সেই ঠাকুর ধন্য তারে চুলে ধরি' আনে ॥ ৪৭ ॥

durdaive sevaka yadi yāya anya sthāne
sei ṭhākura dhanya tāre cule dhari' āne

SYNONYMS

durdaive—by chance; *sevaka*—the servant; *yadi*—if; *yāya*—goes; *anya sthāne*—to another place; *sei ṭhākura*—that master; *dhanya*—glorified; *tāre*—him; *cule*—by the hair; *dhari'*—capturing; *āne*—brings back.

TRANSLATION

"If by chance a servant falls down and goes somewhere else, glorious is that master who captures him and brings him back by the hair.

TEXT 48

ভাল হৈল, তোমার ইহাঁ হৈল আগমনে ।
এই ঘরে রহ ইহাঁ হরিদাস-সনে ॥ ৪৮ ॥

bhāla haila, tomāra ihāṅ haila āgamane
ei ghare raha ihāṅ haridāsa-sane

SYNONYMS

bhāla haila—it was very good; *tomāra*—your; *ihāṅ*—here; *haila*—there was; *āgamane*—arrival; *ei ghare*—in this room; *raha*—remain; *ihāṅ*—here; *haridāsa-sane*—with Haridāsa Ṭhākura.

TRANSLATION

"It is very good that you have arrived here. Now stay in this room with Haridāsa Ṭhākura.

TEXT 49

কৃষ্ণভক্তিরসে দুঁহে পরম প্রধান ।
কৃষ্ণরস আস্বাদন কর, লহ কৃষ্ণনাম ॥" ৪৯ ॥

kṛṣṇa-bhakti-rase duṅhe parama pradhāna
kṛṣṇa-rasa āsvādana kara, laha kṛṣṇa-nāma"

SYNONYMS

kṛṣṇa—of Lord Kṛṣṇa; *bhakti-rase*—in the transcendental mellow of devotional service; *duṅhe*—both of you; *parama pradhāna*—highly expert; *kṛṣṇa-rasa*—the transcendental taste of Kṛṣṇa; *āsvādana*—relishing; *kara*—do; *laha kṛṣṇa-nāma*—chanting the holy name of Kṛṣṇa.

TRANSLATION

"Both of you are expert in understanding the mellows of Lord Kṛṣṇa's devotional service. Therefore you should both continue relishing the taste for such activities and chanting the Hare Kṛṣṇa mahā-mantra."

TEXT 50

এত বলি' মহাপ্রভু উঠিয়া চলিলা ।
গোবিন্দ-দ্বারায় দুঁহে প্রসাদ পাঠাইলা ॥ ৫০ ॥

eta bali' mahāprabhu uṭhiyā calilā
govinda-dvārāya duṅhe prasāda pāṭhāilā

SYNONYMS

eta bali'—saying this; *mahāprabhu*—Śrī Caitanya Mahāprabhu; *uṭhiyā calilā*—got up and left; *govinda-dvārāya*—through Govinda; *duṅhe*—to both of them; *prasāda pāṭhāilā*—sent *prasāda.*

TRANSLATION

Having said this, Śrī Caitanya Mahāprabhu got up and left, and through Govinda He sent prasāda for them to eat.

TEXT 51

এইমত সনাতন রহে প্রভু-স্থানে ।
জগন্নাথের চক্র দেখি' করেন প্রণামে ॥ ৫১ ॥

ei-mata sanātana rahe prabhu-sthāne
jagannāthera cakra dekhi' karena praṇāme

SYNONYMS

ei-mata—in this way; *sanātana*—Sanātana Gosvāmī; *rahe*—remains; *prabhu-sthāne*—under the care of Śrī Caitanya Mahāprabhu; *jagannāthera*—of Lord Jagannātha; *cakra*—the wheel on the top of the temple; *dekhi'*—seeing; *karena praṇāme*—offers respectful obeisances.

TRANSLATION

In this way, Sanātana Gosvāmī stayed under the care of Śrī Caitanya Mahāprabhu. He would see the wheel on the pinnacle of the Jagannātha temple and offer respectful obeisances.

TEXT 52

প্রভু আসি' প্রতিদিন মিলেন দুইজনে ।
ইষ্টগোষ্ঠী, কৃষ্ণকথা কহে কতক্ষণে ॥ ৫২ ॥

prabhu āsi' prati-dina milena dui-jane
iṣṭa-goṣṭhī, kṛṣṇa-kathā kahe kata-kṣaṇe

SYNONYMS

prabhu—Śrī Caitanya Mahāprabhu; *āsi'*—coming; *prati-dina*—every day; *milena dui-jane*—meets both of them; *iṣṭa-goṣṭhī*—discussion; *kṛṣṇa-kathā*—topics of Lord Kṛṣṇa; *kahe*—speaks; *kata-kṣaṇe*—for some time.

TRANSLATION

Every day Śrī Caitanya Mahāprabhu would go there to meet these two stalwart devotees and discuss topics of Kṛṣṇa with them for some time.

TEXT 53

দিব্য প্রসাদ পায় নিত্য জগন্নাথ-মন্দিরে ।
তাহা আনি' নিত্য অবশ্য দেন দোঁহাকারে ॥ ৫৩ ॥

divya prasāda pāya nitya jagannātha-mandire
tāhā āni' nitya avaśya dena doṅhākāre

SYNONYMS

divya—first-class; *prasāda*—*prasāda;* *pāya*—gets; *nitya*—daily; *jagannātha-mandire*—at the temple of Lord Jagannātha; *tāhā āni'*—bringing that; *nitya*—daily; *avaśya*—certainly; *dena*—delivers; *doṅhākāre*—to both of them.

TRANSLATION

The offerings of prasāda in the temple of Lord Jagannātha were of the highest quality. Śrī Caitanya Mahāprabhu would bring this prasāda and deliver it to both devotees.

TEXT 54

একদিন আসি' প্রভু দুঁহারে মিলিলা।
সনাতনে আচম্বিতে কহিতে লাগিলা ॥ ৫৪ ॥

eka-dina āsi' prabhu duṅhāre mililā
sanātane ācambite kahite lāgilā

SYNONYMS

eka-dina—one day; *āsi'*—coming; *prabhu*—Śrī Caitanya Mahāprabhu; *duṅhāre mililā*—met both of them; *sanātane*—unto Sanātana Gosvāmī; *ācambite*—all of a sudden; *kahite lāgilā*—began to speak.

TRANSLATION

One day when the Lord came to meet them, He suddenly began speaking to Sanātana Gosvāmī.

TEXT 55

"সনাতন, দেহত্যাগে কৃষ্ণ যদি পাইয়ে।
কোটি-দেহ ক্ষণেকে তবে ছাড়িতে পারিয়ে ॥ ৫৫ ॥

"sanātana, deha-tyāge kṛṣṇa yadi pāiye
koṭi-deha kṣaṇeke tabe chāḍite pāriye

SYNONYMS

sanātana—My dear Sanātana; *deha-tyāge*—by committing suicide; *kṛṣṇa*—Lord Kṛṣṇa; *yadi*—if; *pāiye*—I can get; *koṭi-deha*—millions of bodies; *kṣaṇeke*—in a moment; *tabe*—then; *chāḍite pāriye*—I can give up.

TRANSLATION

"My dear Sanātana," He said, "if I could attain Kṛṣṇa by committing suicide, I would certainly give up millions of bodies without a moment's hesitation.

TEXT 56

দেহত্যাগে কৃষ্ণ না পাই, পাইয়ে ভজনে।
কৃষ্ণপ্রাপ্ত্যের উপায় কোন নাহি 'ভক্তি' বিনে ॥ ৫৬॥

deha-tyāge kṛṣṇa nā paī, pāiye bhajane
kṛṣṇa-prāptyera upāya kona nāhi 'bhakti' vine

SYNONYMS

deha-tyāge—by giving up the body; *kṛṣṇa*—Lord Kṛṣṇa; *nā pāi*—I do not get; *pāiye*—I get; *bhajane*—by devotional service; *kṛṣṇa-prāptyera*—to get the shelter of Kṛṣṇa; *upāya*—means; *kona*—any; *nāhi*—there is not; *bhakti vine*—without devotional service.

TRANSLATION

"You should know that one cannot attain Kṛṣṇa simply by giving up the body. Kṛṣṇa is attainable by devotional service. There is no other means to attain Him.

TEXT 57

দেহত্যাগাদি যত, সব—তমো-ধর্ম।
তমো-রজো-ধর্মে কৃষ্ণের না পাইয়ে মর্ম ॥ ৫৭ ॥

deha-tyāgādi yata, saba——tamo-dharma
tamo-rajo-dharme kṛṣṇera nā pāiye marma

SYNONYMS

deha-tyāga-ādi—beginning with giving up the material body; *yata*—as many; *saba*—all; *tamaḥ-dharma*—performed under the mode of ignorance; *tamaḥ-rajaḥ-dharme*—by remaining in the modes of ignorance and passion; *kṛṣṇera*—of Lord Kṛṣṇa; *nā pāiye*—I cannot attain; *marma*—the truth.

TRANSLATION

"Acts such as suicide are influenced by the mode of ignorance, and in ignorance and passion one cannot understand who Kṛṣṇa is.

TEXT 58

**'ভক্তি' বিনা কৃষ্ণে কভু নহে 'প্রেমোদয়'।
প্রেম বিনা কৃষ্ণপ্রাপ্তি অন্য হৈতে নয়॥ ৫৮॥**

'bhakti' vinā kṛṣṇe kabhu nahe 'premodaya'
prema vinā kṛṣṇa-prāpti anya haite naya

SYNONYMS

bhakti vinā—without devotional service; *kṛṣṇe*—unto Kṛṣṇa; *kabhu*—at any time; *nahe*—is not; *prema-udaya*—development of dormant love for Kṛṣṇa; *prema vinā*—without love of Kṛṣṇa; *kṛṣṇa-prāpti*—attaining Kṛṣṇa; *anya*—anything else; *haite*—from; *naya*—is not possible.

TRANSLATION

"Unless one discharges devotional service, one cannot awaken one's dormant love for Kṛṣṇa, and there is no means to attain Him other than awakening that dormant love.

TEXT 59

ন সাধয়তি মাং যোগো ন সাংখ্যং ধর্ম উদ্ধব।
ন স্বাধ্যায়স্তপস্ত্যাগো যথা ভক্তির্মমোর্জিতা॥ ৫৯॥

na sādhayati māṁ yogo
na sāṅkhyaṁ dharma uddhava
na svādhyāyas tapas tyāgo
yathā bhaktir mamorjitā

SYNONYMS

na—never; *sādhayati*—causes to remain satisfied; *mām*—Me; *yogaḥ*—the process of control; *na*—nor; *sāṅkhyam*—the process of gaining philosophical knowledge about the Absolute Truth; *dharmaḥ*—such an occupation; *uddhava*—My dear Uddhava; *na*—nor; *svādhyāyaḥ*—study of the *Vedas; tapaḥ*—austerities; *tyāgaḥ*—renunciation, acceptance of *sannyāsa,* or charity; *yathā*—as much as; *bhaktiḥ*—devotional service; *mama*—unto Me; *ūrjitā*—developed.

TRANSLATION

[The Supreme Personality of Godhead, Kṛṣṇa, said:] " 'My dear Uddhava, neither through aṣṭāṅga-yoga [the mystic yoga system to control the senses], nor through impersonal monism or an analytical study of the Absolute Truth,

nor through study of the Vedas, nor through austerities, charity or acceptance of sannyāsa can one satisfy Me as much as by developing unalloyed devotional service unto Me.'

PURPORT

This verse is from *Śrīmad-Bhāgavatam* (11.14.20).

TEXT 60

দেহত্যাগাদি তমো-ধর্ম—পাতক-কারণ।
সাধক না পায় তাতে কৃষ্ণের চরণ ॥ ৬০ ॥

deha-tyāgādi tamo-dharma——pātaka-kāraṇa
sādhaka nā pāya tāte kṛṣṇera caraṇa

SYNONYMS

deha-tyāga—giving up the material body by suicide; *ādi*—beginning with; *tamaḥ-dharma*—on the platform of the mode of ignorance; *pātaka-kāraṇa*—cause of sinful activities; *sādhaka*—the devotee; *nā pāya*—does not get; *tāte*—by that; *kṛṣṇera caraṇa*—the lotus feet of Kṛṣṇa.

TRANSLATION

"Measures like suicide are causes for sin. A devotee never achieves shelter at Kṛṣṇa's lotus feet by such actions.

TEXT 61

প্রেমী ভক্ত বিয়োগে চাহে দেহ ছাড়িতে।
প্রেমে কৃষ্ণ মিলে, সেহ না পারে মরিতে ॥ ৬১ ॥

premī bhakta viyoge cāhe deha chāḍite
preme kṛṣṇa mile, seha nā pāre marite

SYNONYMS

premī bhakta—a devotee attached to Kṛṣṇa by love; *viyoge*—in separation; *cāhe*—wants; *deha chāḍite*—to give up the body; *preme*—by such ecstatic love; *kṛṣṇa mile*—one meets Kṛṣṇa; *seha*—such a devotee; *nā pāre marite*—cannot die.

TRANSLATION

"Because of feelings of separation from Kṛṣṇa, an exalted devotee sometimes wants to give up his life. By such ecstatic love, however, one attains the audience of Kṛṣṇa, and at that time he cannot give up his body.

TEXT 62

গাঢ়ানুরাগের বিয়োগ না যায় সহন।
তাতে অনুরাগী বাঞ্ছে আপন মরণ ॥ ৬২ ॥

gāḍhānurāgera viyoga nā yāya sahana
tāte anurāgī vāñche āpana maraṇa

SYNONYMS

gāḍha-anurāgera—of one who has deep attachment; *viyoga*—separation; *nā*—not; *yāya sahana*—tolerated; *tāte*—therefore; *anurāgī*—a deeply attached devotee; *vāñche*—desires; *āpana maraṇa*—death of himself.

TRANSLATION

"One who is deeply in love with Kṛṣṇa cannot tolerate separation from the Lord. Therefore such a devotee always desires his own death.

TEXT 63

যস্যাঙ্ঘ্রিপঙ্কজরজঃস্নপনং মহান্তো
বাঞ্ছন্ত্যুমাপতিরিবাত্মতমোঽপহত্যৈ।
যর্হ্যম্বুজাক্ষ ন লভেয় ভবৎপ্রসাদং
জহ্যামসূন্ ব্রতকৃশাঞ্ছতজন্মভিঃ স্যাৎ ॥ ৬৩ ॥

yasyāṅghri-paṅkaja-rajaḥ-snapanaṁ mahānto
vāñchanty umā-patir ivātma-tamo 'pahatyai
yarhy ambujākṣa na labheya bhavat-prasādaṁ
jahyām asūn vrata-kṛśāñ chata-janmabhiḥ syāt

SYNONYMS

yasya—whose; *aṅghri*—of feet; *paṅka-ja*—lotus; *rajaḥ*—in the dust; *snapanam*—bathing; *mahāntaḥ*—great personalities; *vāñchanti*—desire; *umā-patiḥ*—Lord Śiva; *iva*—like; *ātma*—personal; *tamaḥ*—ignorance; *apahatyai*—to drive away; *yarhi*—when; *ambuja-akṣa*—O lotus-eyed one; *na labheya*—I do not get; *bhavat-prasādam*—Your mercy; *jahyām*—I shall give up; *asūn*—life; *vrata-kṛśān*—reduced by observing vows; *śata-janmabhiḥ*—by hundreds of births; *syāt*—if it is possible.

TRANSLATION

" 'O lotus-eyed one, great personalities like Lord Śiva desire to bathe in the dust of Your lotus feet to drive away ignorance. If I do not get the mercy of

Your Lordship, I shall observe vows to reduce the duration of my life, and thus I shall give up bodies for hundreds of births if it is possible to get Your mercy in that way.'

PURPORT

This verse was spoken by Rukmiṇīdevī in *Śrīmad-Bhāgavatam* (10.52.43). Rukmiṇīdevī, the daughter of King Bhīṣmaka, had heard about Kṛṣṇa's transcendental attributes, and thus she desired to get Kṛṣṇa as her husband. Unfortunately, her elder brother Rukmī was envious of Kṛṣṇa and therefore wanted her to be offered to Śiśupāla. When Rukmiṇī became aware of this, she was greatly aggrieved. Thus she wrote Kṛṣṇa a confidential letter, which was presented and read to Him by a *brāhmaṇa* messenger. This verse appeared in that letter.

TEXT 64

সিঞ্চাঙ্গ নস্ত্বদধরামৃতপূরকেণ
হাসাবলোক-কলগীতজ-হৃচ্ছয়াগ্নিম্ ।
নো চেদ্বয়ং বিরহজাগ্ন্যুপযুক্তদেহা
ধ্যানেন যাম পদয়োঃ পদবীং সখে তে ॥ ৬৪ ॥

siñcāṅga nas tvad-adharāmṛta-pūrakeṇa
hāsāvaloka-kala-gītaja-hṛc-chayāgnim
no ced vayaṁ virahajāgny-upayukta-dehā
dhyānena yāma padayoḥ padavīṁ sakhe te

SYNONYMS

siñca—just sprinkle water; *aṅga*—O my dear Kṛṣṇa; *naḥ*—our; *tvat*—Your; *adhara*—of the lips; *amṛta*—of nectar; *pūrakeṇa*—by the stream; *hāsa*—smile; *avaloka*—glancing; *kala*—melodious; *gīta*—speaking; *ja*—produced by; *hṛt*—in the heart; *śaya*—resting; *agnim*—upon the fire; *no cet*—if not; *vayam*—we; *viraha*—from separation; *ja*—produced; *agni*—by the fire; *upayukta*—consumed; *dehāḥ*—whose bodies; *dhyānena*—by meditation; *yāma*—shall go; *padayoḥ*—of the lotus feet; *padavīm*—to the site; *sakhe*—O my dear friend; *te*—Your.

TRANSLATION

" 'O dear Kṛṣṇa, by Your smiling glances and melodious talk, You have awakened a fire of lusty desire in our hearts. Now You should extinguish that fire with a stream of nectar from Your lips by kissing us. Kindly do this. Other-

wise, dear friend, the fire within our hearts will burn our bodies to ashes because of separation from You. Thus by meditation we shall claim shelter at Your lotus feet.' "

PURPORT

This verse (*Bhāg.* 10.29.35) was spoken by the *gopīs* when they were attracted by the vibration of Kṛṣṇa's flute in the moonlight of autumn. All of them, being maddened, came to Kṛṣṇa, but to increase their ecstatic love, Kṛṣṇa gave them moral instructions to return home. The *gopīs* did not care for these instructions. They wanted to be kissed by Kṛṣṇa, for they had come there with lusty desires to dance with Him.

TEXT 65

কুবুদ্ধি ছাড়িয়া কর শ্রবণ-কীর্তন ।
অচিরাৎ পাবে তবে কৃষ্ণের চরণ ॥ ৬৫ ॥

kubuddhi chāḍiyā kara śravaṇa-kīrtana
acirāt pābe tabe kṛṣṇera caraṇa

SYNONYMS

ku-buddhi—intelligence not favorable to discharging devotional service; *chāḍiyā*—giving up; *kara*—just do; *śravaṇa-kīrtana*—hearing and chanting; *acirāt*—very soon; *pābe*—you will get; *tabe*—then; *kṛṣṇera caraṇa*—the lotus feet of Kṛṣṇa.

TRANSLATION

Śrī Caitanya Mahāprabhu told Sanātana Gosvāmī, "Give up all your nonsensical desires, for they are unfavorable for getting shelter at the lotus feet of Kṛṣṇa. Engage yourself in chanting and hearing. Then you will soon achieve the shelter of Kṛṣṇa without a doubt.

TEXT 66

নীচ-জাতি নহে কৃষ্ণভজনে অযোগ্য ।
সৎকুল-বিপ্র নহে ভজনের যোগ্য ॥ ৬৬ ॥

nīca-jāti nahe kṛṣṇa-bhajane ayogya
sat-kula-vipra nahe bhajanera yogya

SYNONYMS

nīca-jāti—a lowborn person; *nahe*—is not; *kṛṣṇa-bhajane*—in discharging devotional service; *ayogya*—unfit; *sat-kula-vipra*—a *brāhmaṇa* born in a very respectable aristocratic family; *nahe*—is not; *bhajanera yogya*—fit for discharging devotional service.

TRANSLATION

"A person born in a low family is not unfit for discharging devotional service to Lord Kṛṣṇa, nor is one fit for devotional service simply because he is born in an aristocratic family of brāhmaṇas.

TEXT 67

যেই ভজে সেই বড়, অভক্ত—হীন, ছার।
কৃষ্ণভজনে নাহি জাতি-কুলাদি-বিচার ॥ ৬৭ ॥

yei bhaje sei baḍa, abhakta——hīna, chāra
kṛṣṇa-bhajane nāhi jāti-kulādi-vicāra

SYNONYMS

yei bhaje—anyone who takes to devotional service; *sei*—he; *baḍa*—exalted; *abhakta*—nondevotee; *hīna chāra*—most condemned and abominable; *kṛṣṇa-bhajane*—in discharging devotional service; *nāhi*—there is not; *jāti*—caste; *kula*—family; *ādi*—and so on; *vicāra*—consideration of.

TRANSLATION

"Anyone who takes to devotional service is exalted, whereas a nondevotee is always condemned and abominable. Therefore in the discharge of devotional service to the Lord, there is no consideration of the status of one's family.

TEXT 68

দীনেরে অধিক দয়া করে ভগবান্।
কুলীন, পণ্ডিত, ধনীর বড় অভিমান ॥ ৬৮ ॥

dīnere adhika dayā kare bhagavān
kulīna, paṇḍita, dhanīra baḍa abhimāna

SYNONYMS

dīnere—to the humble; *adhika*—more; *dayā*—mercy; *kare*—shows; *bhagavān*—the Supreme Personality of Godhead; *kulīna*—aristocratic; *paṇḍita*—learned scholar; *dhanīra*—of rich man; *baḍa abhimāna*—great pride.

TRANSLATION

"The Supreme Personality of Godhead, Kṛṣṇa, is always favorable to the humble and meek, but aristocrats, learned scholars and the wealthy are always proud of their positions.

TEXT 69

বিপ্রাদ্দ্বিষড়্‌গুণযুতাদরবিন্দনাভ-
পাদারবিন্দবিমুখাৎ শ্বপচং বরিষ্ঠম্‌।
মন্যে তদর্পিতমনোবচনেহিতার্থ-
প্রাণং পুনাতি স কুলং ন তু ভূরিমানঃ ॥ ৬৯ ॥

viprād dviṣaḍ-guṇa-yutād aravinda-nābha-
pādāravinda-vimukhāt śvapacaṁ variṣṭham
manye tad-arpita-mano-vacane 'hitārtha-
prāṇaṁ punāti sa kulaṁ na tu bhūrimānaḥ

SYNONYMS

viprāt—than a *brāhmaṇa; dvi-ṣaṭ-guṇa-yutāt*—who has twelve brahminical qualifications; *aravinda-nābha*—of Lord Viṣṇu, who has a lotuslike navel; *pāda-aravinda*—unto the lotus feet; *vimukhāt*—than a person bereft of devotion; *śva-pacam*—a *caṇḍāla,* or person accustomed to eating dogs; *variṣṭham*—more glorified; *manye*—I think; *tat-arpita*—dedicated unto Him; *manaḥ*—mind; *vacane*—words; *ahita*—activities; *artha*—wealth; *prāṇam*—life; *punāti*—purifies; *saḥ*—he; *kulam*—his family; *na tu*—but not; *bhūri-mānaḥ*—a *brāhmaṇa* proud of possessing such qualities.

TRANSLATION

" 'One may be born in a brāhmaṇa family and have all twelve brahminical qualities, but if in spite of being thus qualified he is not devoted to the lotus feet of Lord Kṛṣṇa, who has a navel shaped like a lotus, he is not as good as a caṇḍāla who has dedicated his mind, words, activities, wealth and life to the service of the Lord. Simply to take birth in a brāhmaṇa family or to have brahminical qualities is not sufficient. One must be a pure devotee of the Lord. Thus if a śvapaca, or caṇḍāla, is a devotee, he delivers not only himself but his entire family as well, whereas a brāhmaṇa who is not a devotee but simply has brahminical qualifications cannot even purify himself, what to speak of his family.'

PURPORT

This is a verse from *Śrīmad-Bhāgavatam* (7.9.9).

TEXT 70

ভজনের মধ্যে শ্রেষ্ঠ নববিধা ভক্তি ।
'কৃষ্ণপ্রেম', 'কৃষ্ণ' দিতে ধরে মহাশক্তি ॥ ৭০ ॥

bhajanera madhye śreṣṭha nava-vidhā bhakti
'kṛṣṇa-prema', 'kṛṣṇa' dite dhare mahā-śakti

SYNONYMS

bhajanera madhye—in executing devotional service; *śreṣṭha*—the best; *nava-vidhā bhakti*—the nine prescribed methods of devotional service; *kṛṣṇa-prema*—ecstatic love of Kṛṣṇa; *kṛṣṇa*—and Kṛṣṇa; *dite*—to deliver; *dhare*—possess; *mahā-śakti*—great potency.

TRANSLATION

"Among the ways of executing devotional service, the nine prescribed methods are the best, for these processes have great potency to deliver Kṛṣṇa and ecstatic love for Him.

PURPORT

The nine kinds of devotional service are mentioned in *Śrīmad-Bhāgavatam* (7.5.23):

śravaṇaṁ kīrtanaṁ viṣṇoḥ
smaraṇaṁ pāda-sevanam
arcanaṁ vandanaṁ dāsyaṁ
sakhyam ātma-nivedanam

These nine are hearing, chanting, remembering Kṛṣṇa, offering service to Kṛṣṇa's lotus feet, offering worship in the temple, offering prayers, working as a servant, making friendship with Kṛṣṇa and unreservedly surrendering to Kṛṣṇa. These nine processes of devotional service can grant one Kṛṣṇa and ecstatic love for Him. In the beginning one has to discharge devotional service according to regulative principles, but gradually, as devotional service becomes one's life and soul, one achieves the most exalted position of ecstatic love for Kṛṣṇa. Ultimately, Kṛṣṇa is the goal of life. One need not have taken birth in an aristocratic *brāhmaṇa* family to attain the lotus feet of Kṛṣṇa, nor is a person born in a low family unfit to achieve Kṛṣṇa's lotus feet. In *Śrīmad-Bhāgavatam* (3.33.7) Devahūti says to Kapiladeva:

aho bata śva-paco 'to garīyān
yaj-jihvāgre vartate nāma tubhyam

tepus tapas te juhuvuḥ sasnur āryā
brahmānūcur nāma gṛṇanti ye te

"O my Lord, even a person born in a low family of dog-eaters is glorious if he always chants the holy name of the Lord. Such a person has already performed all types of austerities, penances and Vedic sacrifices, has already bathed in the sacred rivers, and has also studied all the Vedic literature. Thus he has become an exalted personality." Similarly, Kuntīdevī says to Lord Kṛṣṇa:

janmaiśvarya-śruta-śrībhir
edhamāna-madaḥ pumān
naivārhaty abhidhātuṁ vai
tvām akiñcana-gocaram

"A person who is proud of his birth, opulence, knowledge and beauty cannot achieve Your lotus feet. You are available only to the humble and meek, not to the proud." (*Bhāg.* 1.8.26.)

TEXT 71

তার মধ্যে সর্বশ্রেষ্ঠ নাম-সঙ্কীর্তন ।
নিরপরাধে নাম লৈলে পায় প্রেমধন ॥ ৭১ ॥

tāra madhye sarva-śreṣṭha nāma-saṅkīrtana
niraparādhe nāma laile pāya prema-dhana

SYNONYMS

tāra madhye—of the nine different types of devotional service; *sarva-śreṣṭha*—the most important of all; *nāma-saṅkīrtana*—chanting of the holy name of the Lord; *niraparādhe*—without offenses; *nāma laile*—if one chants the holy name; *pāya*—he gets; *prema-dhana*—the most valuable ecstatic love of Kṛṣṇa.

TRANSLATION

"Of the nine processes of devotional service, the most important is to always chant the holy name of the Lord. If one does so, avoiding the ten kinds of offenses, one very easily obtains the most valuable love of Godhead."

PURPORT

Śrīla Jīva Gosvāmī Prabhu gives the following directions in his *Bhakti-sandarbha* (270):

iyaṁ ca kīrtanākhyā bhaktir bhagavato dravya-jāti-guṇa-kriyābhir dīna-janaika-viṣayāpāra-karuṇā-mayīti śruti-purāṇādi-viśrutiḥ. ataeva kalau svabhāvata evātidīneṣu lokeṣu āvirbhūya tān anāyāsenaiva tat tad yuga-gata-mahā-sādhanānāṁ sarvam eva phalaṁ dadānā sā kṛtārthayati. yata eva tayaiva kalau bhagavato viśeṣataś ca santoṣo bhavati.

"Chanting the holy name is the chief means of attaining love of Godhead. This chanting or devotional service does not depend on any paraphernalia, nor on one's having taken birth in a good family. By humility and meekness one attracts the attention of Kṛṣṇa. That is the verdict of all the *Vedas.* Therefore if one becomes very humble and meek, he can easily attain the lotus feet of Kṛṣṇa in this age of Kali. That is the fulfillment of all great sacrifices, penances and austerities because when one achieves ecstatic love of Godhead, he attains the complete perfection of life. Therefore whatever one does in executing devotional service must be accompanied with the chanting of the holy name of the Lord." The chanting of the holy name of Kṛṣṇa—Hare Kṛṣṇa, Hare Kṛṣṇa, Kṛṣṇa Kṛṣṇa, Hare Hare/ Hare Rāma, Hare Rāma, Rāma Rāma, Hare Hare—has been praised by Śrīla Rūpa Gosvāmī in his *Nāmāṣṭaka* (verse 1):

nikhila-śruti-mauli-ratna-mālā-
dyuti-nīrājita-pāda-paṅkajānta
ayi mukta-kulair upāsyamānaṁ
paritas tvāṁ hari-nāma saṁśrayāmi

"O Hari-nāma! The tips of the toes of Your lotus feet are constantly being worshiped by the glowing radiance emanating from the string of gems known as the *Upaniṣads,* the crown jewels of all the *Vedas.* You are eternally adored by liberated souls such as Nārada and Śukadeva. O Hari-nāma! I take complete shelter of You."

Similarly, Śrīla Sanātana Gosvāmī has praised the chanting of the holy name as follows in his *Bṛhad-bhāgavatāmṛta* (Chapter One, verse 9):

jayati jayati nāmānanda-rūpaṁ murārer
viramita-nija-dharma-dhyāna-pūjādi-yatnam
kathamapi sakṛd-āttaṁ muktidaṁ prāṇīnāṁ yat
paramam amṛtam ekaṁ jīvanaṁ bhūṣaṇaṁ me

"All glories, all glories to the all-blissful holy name of Śrī Kṛṣṇa, which causes the devotee to give up all conventional religious duties, meditation and worship. When somehow or other uttered even once by a living entity, the holy name awards him liberation. The holy name of Kṛṣṇa is the highest nectar. It is my very life and my only treasure."

In *Śrīmad-Bhāgavatam* (2.1.11) Śukadeva Gosvāmī says:

etan nirvidyamānānām
icchatām akuto-bhayam
yogināṁ nṛpa nirṇītaṁ
harer nāmānukīrtanam

"O King, constant chanting of the holy name of the Lord after the ways of the great authorities is the doubtless and fearless way of success for all, including those who are free from all material desires, those who are desirous of all material enjoyment, and those who are self-satisfied by dint of transcendental knowledge."

Similarly, Śrī Caitanya Mahāprabhu has said in His *Śikṣāṣṭaka* (3):

tṛṇād api sunīcena
taror api sahiṣṇunā
amāninā mānadena
kīrtanīyaḥ sadā hariḥ

"One should chant the holy name of the Lord in a humble state of mind, thinking oneself lower than the straw in the street. One should be more tolerant than a tree, devoid of all sense of false prestige and ready to offer all respect to others. In such a state of mind one can chant the holy name of the Lord constantly." Regarding the ten offenses in chanting the holy name, one may refer to the *Ādi-līlā,* Chapter Eight, verse 24.

TEXT 72

এত শুনি' সনাতনের হৈল চমৎকার ।
প্রভুরে না ভায় মোর মরণ-বিচার ॥ ৭২ ॥

eta śuni' sanātanera haila camatkāra
prabhure nā bhāya mora maraṇa-vicāra

SYNONYMS

eta śuni'—hearing this; *sanātanera*—of Sanātana Gosvāmī; *haila camatkāra*—there was astonishment; *prabhure nā bhāya*—Śrī Caitanya Mahāprabhu does not approve; *mora*—my; *maraṇa-vicāra*—decision to commit suicide.

TRANSLATION

After hearing this, Sanātana Gosvāmī was exceedingly astonished. He could understand, "My decision to commit suicide has not been greatly appreciated by Śrī Caitanya Mahāprabhu."

TEXT 73

সর্বজ্ঞ মহাপ্রভু নিষেধিলা মোরে ।
প্রভুর চরণ ধরি' কহেন তাঁহারে ॥ ৭৩ ॥

sarvajña mahāprabhu niṣedhilā more
prabhura caraṇa dhari' kahena tāṅhāre

SYNONYMS

sarva-jña—who knows everything; *mahāprabhu*—Śrī Caitanya Mahāprabhu; *niṣedhilā*—has forbidden; *more*—me; *prabhura*—of Śrī Caitanya Mahāprabhu; *caraṇa*—the feet; *dhari'*—touching; *kahena tāṅhāre*—began to speak to Him.

TRANSLATION

Sanātana Gosvāmī concluded, "Lord Śrī Caitanya Mahāprabhu, who knows everything—past, present and future—has forbidden me to commit suicide." He then fell down, touching the lotus feet of the Lord, and spoke to Him as follows.

TEXT 74

"সর্বজ্ঞ, কৃপালু তুমি ঈশ্বর স্বতন্ত্র।
যৈছে নাচাও, তৈছে নাচি,—যেন কাষ্ঠযন্ত্র ॥ ৭৪ ॥

"sarvajña, kṛpālu tumi īśvara svatantra
yaiche nācāo, taiche nāci, ——yena kāṣṭha-yantra

SYNONYMS

sarva-jña—all-knowing; *kṛpālu*—merciful; *tumi*—You; *īśvara*—the Supreme Lord; *svatantra*—independent; *yaiche*—as; *nācāo*—You make to dance; *taiche*—so; *nāci*—I dance; *yena*—as if; *kāṣṭha-yantra*—an instrument of wood.

TRANSLATION

"My Lord, You are the omniscient, merciful, independent Supreme Lord. Exactly like an instrument of wood, I dance as You make me do so.

TEXT 75

নীচ, অধম, পামর মুঞি পামর-স্বভাব।
মোরে জিয়াইলে তোমার কিবা হবে লাভ ?" ৭৫ ॥

nīca, adhama, pāmara muñi pāmara-svabhāva
more jiyāile tomāra kibā habe lābha?"

SYNONYMS

nīca—lowborn; *adhama*—lowest; *pāmara*—condemned; *muñi*—I; *pāmara-svabhāva*—naturally sinful; *more jiyāile*—if You save me; *tomāra*—Your; *kibā*—what; *habe*—will be; *lābha*—profit.

TRANSLATION

"I am lowborn. Indeed, I am the lowest. I am condemned, for I have all the characteristics of a sinful man. If You keep me alive, what will be the profit?"

TEXT 76

প্রভু কহে,–"তোমার দেহ মোর নিজ-ধন।
তুমি মোরে করিয়াছ আত্মসমর্পণ ॥ ৭৬ ॥

prabhu kahe, ——"tomāra deha mora nija-dhana
tumi more kariyācha ātma-samarpaṇa

SYNONYMS

prabhu kahe—Śrī Caitanya Mahāprabhu says; *tomāra deha*—your body; *mora*—My; *nija-dhana*—personal property; *tumi*—you; *more*—to Me; *kariyācha*—have done; *ātma-samarpaṇa*—complete surrender.

TRANSLATION

Lord Śrī Caitanya Mahāprabhu said, "Your body is My property. You have already surrendered unto Me. Therefore you no longer have any claim to your body.

TEXT 77

পরের দ্রব্য তুমি কেনে চাহ বিনাশিতে ?
ধর্মাধর্ম বিচার কিবা না পার করিতে ? ৭৭ ॥

parera dravya tumi kene cāha vināśite?
dharmādharma vicāra kibā nā pāra karite?

SYNONYMS

parera dravya—another's property; *tumi*—you; *kene*—why; *cāha*—want; *vināśite*—to destroy; *dharma-adharma*—what is pious and what is impious; *vicāra*—consideration; *kibā*—why; *nā*—not; *pāra*—you can; *karite*—do.

TRANSLATION

"Why should you want to destroy another's property? Can't you consider what is right and wrong?

TEXT 78

তোমার শরীর—মোর প্রধান 'সাধন'।
এ শরীরে সাধিমু আমি বহু প্রয়োজন॥ ৭৮ ॥

tomāra śarīra——mora pradhāna 'sādhana'
e śarīre sādhimu āmi bahu prayojana

SYNONYMS

tomāra śarīra—your body; *mora*—My; *pradhāna*—chief; *sādhana*—instrument; *e śarīre*—by this body; *sādhimu*—shall carry out; *āmi*—I; *bahu*—many; *prayojana*—necessities.

TRANSLATION

"Your body is My principal instrument for executing many necessary functions. By your body I shall carry out many tasks.

TEXT 79

ভক্ত-ভক্তি-কৃষ্ণপ্রেম-তত্ত্বের নিধার।
বৈষ্ণবের কৃত্য, আর বৈষ্ণব-আচার॥ ৭৯ ॥

bhakta-bhakti-kṛṣṇaprema-tattvera nidhāra
vaiṣṇavera kṛtya, āra vaiṣṇava-ācāra

SYNONYMS

bhakta—devotee; *bhakti*—devotional service; *kṛṣṇa-prema*—love of Kṛṣṇa; *tattvera*—of the truth of; *nidhāra*—ascertainment; *vaiṣṇavera kṛtya*—duties of a Vaiṣṇava; *āra*—and; *vaiṣṇava-ācāra*—characteristics of a Vaiṣṇava.

TRANSLATION

"You shall have to ascertain the basic principles of a devotee, devotional service, love of Godhead, Vaiṣṇava duties, and Vaiṣṇava characteristics.

TEXT 80

কৃষ্ণভক্তি, কৃষ্ণপ্রেমসেবা-প্রবর্তন।
লুপ্ততীর্থ-উদ্ধার, আর বৈরাগ্য-শিক্ষণ॥ ৮০ ॥

kṛṣṇa-bhakti, kṛṣṇaprema-sevā-pravartana
lupta-tīrtha-uddhāra, āra vairāgya-śikṣaṇa

SYNONYMS

kṛṣṇa-bhakti—devotional service to Kṛṣṇa; *kṛṣṇa-prema*—love of Kṛṣṇa; *sevā*—service; *pravartana*—establishment of; *lupta-tīrtha*—the lost places of pilgrimage; *uddhāra*—excavating; *āra*—and; *vairāgya-śikṣaṇa*—instruction on the renounced order of life.

TRANSLATION

"You will also have to explain Kṛṣṇa's devotional service, establish centers for cultivation of love of Kṛṣṇa, excavate lost places of pilgrimage and teach people how to adopt the renounced order.

TEXT 81

নিজ-প্রিয়স্থান মোর—মথুরা-বৃন্দাবন।
তাহাঁ এত ধর্ম চাহি করিতে প্রচারণ ॥ ৮১ ॥

nija-priya-sthāna mora——mathurā-vṛndāvana
tāhāṅ eta dharma cāhi karite pracāraṇa

SYNONYMS

nija—own; *priya-sthāna*—very dear place; *mora*—My; *mathurā-vṛndāvana*—Mathurā and Vṛndāvana; *tāhāṅ*—there; *eta*—so many; *dharma*—activities; *cāhi*—I want; *karite*—to do; *pracāraṇa*—preaching.

TRANSLATION

"Mathurā-Vṛndāvana is My own very dear abode. I want to do many things there to preach Kṛṣṇa consciousness.

PURPORT

Śrī Caitanya Mahāprabhu wanted to accomplish many purposes through the exegetical endeavors of Śrīla Sanātana Gosvāmī. First Sanātana Gosvāmī compiled the book called *Bṛhad-bhāgavatāmṛta* to teach people how to become devotees, execute devotional service and attain love of Kṛṣṇa. Second, he compiled the *Hari-bhakti-vilāsa,* wherein he collected authoritative statements from scriptural injunctions regarding how a Vaiṣṇava should behave. Only by the endeavors of Śrī Sanātana Gosvāmī were all the lost places of pilgrimage in the Vṛndāvana area excavated. He established Madana-mohana, the first Deity in the Vṛndāvana area, and by his personal behavior he taught how one should act in the renounced order, completely devoted to the service of the Lord. By his personal example, he taught people how to stay in Vṛndāvana to execute devotional service. The principal mission of Śrī Caitanya Mahāprabhu was to preach Kṛṣṇa consciousness.

Mathurā and Vṛndāvana are the abodes of Lord Kṛṣṇa. Therefore these two places are very dear to Śrī Caitanya Mahāprabhu, and He wanted to develop their glories through Sanātana Gosvāmī.

TEXT 82

মাতার আজ্ঞায় আমি বসি নীলাচলে।
তাহাঁ 'ধর্ম' শিখাইতে নাহি নিজ-বলে ॥ ৮২ ॥

mātāra ājñāya āmi vasi nīlācale
tāhāṅ 'dharma' śikhāite nāhi nija-bale

SYNONYMS

mātāra—of My mother; *ājñāya*—by the order; *āmi*—I; *vasi*—reside; *nīlācale*—at Jagannātha Purī; *tāhāṅ*—in Mathurā and Vṛndāvana; *dharma śikhāite*—to teach religious principles; *nāhi*—not; *nija-bale*—within My ability.

TRANSLATION

"By the order of My mother I am sitting here in Jagannātha Purī; therefore, I cannot go to Mathurā-Vṛndāvana to teach people how to live there according to religious principles.

TEXT 83

এত সব কর্ম আমি যে-দেহে করিমু।
তাহা ছাড়িতে চাহ তুমি, কেমনে সহিমু?" ৮৩ ॥

eta saba karma āmi ye-dehe karimu
tāhā chāḍite cāha tumi, kemane sahimu?"

SYNONYMS

eta saba—all this; *karma*—work; *āmi*—I; *ye-dehe*—by which body; *karimu*—will do; *tāhā*—that; *chāḍite*—to give up; *cāha tumi*—you want; *kemane*—how; *sahimu*—shall I tolerate.

TRANSLATION

"I have to do all this work through your body, but you want to give it up. How can I tolerate this?"

TEXT 84

তবে সনাতন কহে,—"তোমাকে নমস্কারে।
তোমার গম্ভীর হৃদয় কে বুঝিতে পারে? ৮৪ ॥

tabe sanātana kahe,——"tomāke namaskāre
tomāra gambhīra hṛdaya ke bujhite pāre?

SYNONYMS

tabe—at that time; *sanātana kahe*—Sanātana Gosvāmī said; *tomāke namaskāre*—I offer my respectful obeisances unto You; *tomāra*—Your; *gambhīra*—deep; *hṛdaya*—heart; *ke*—who; *bujhite pāre*—can understand.

TRANSLATION

At that time Sanātana Gosvāmī said to Śrī Caitanya Mahāprabhu, "I offer my respectful obeisances unto You. No one can understand the deep ideas You plan within Your heart.

TEXT 85

কাষ্ঠের পুতলী যেন কুহকে নাচায় ।
আপনে না জানে, পুতলী কিবা নাচে গায় ! ৮৫ ॥

kāṣṭhera putalī yena kuhake nācāya
āpane nā jāne, putalī kibā nāce gāya!

SYNONYMS

kāṣṭhera putalī—a doll made of wood; *yena*—as; *kuhake nācāya*—magician causes to dance; *āpane*—personally; *nā jāne*—does not know; *putalī*—the doll; *kibā*—how; *nāce*—dances; *gāya*—sings.

TRANSLATION

"A wooden doll chants and dances according to the direction of a magician but does not know how he is dancing and singing.

TEXT 86

যারে যৈছে নাচাও, সে তৈছে করে নর্তনে ।
কৈছে নাচে, কেবা নাচায়, সেহ নাহি জানে ॥" ৮৬ ॥

yāre yaiche nācāo, se taiche kare nartane
kaiche nāce, kebā nācāya, seha nāhi jāne"

SYNONYMS

yāre—whomever; *yaiche*—as; *nācāo*—You cause to dance; *se*—that person; *taiche*—so; *kare nartane*—dances; *kaiche*—how; *nāce*—he dances; *kebā nācāya*—who causes to dance; *seha*—he; *nāhi jāne*—does not know.

TRANSLATION

"My dear Lord, as You cause one to dance, he dances accordingly, but how he dances and who is causing him to dance he does not know."

TEXT 87

হরিদাসে কহে প্রভু,—"শুন, হরিদাস।
পরের দ্রব্য ইঁহো চাহেন করিতে বিনাশ ॥ ৮৭ ॥

haridāse kahe prabhu, —"śuna, haridāsa
parera dravya iṅho cāhena karite vināśa

SYNONYMS

haridāse—Haridāsa Ṭhākura; *kahe prabhu*—Śrī Caitanya Mahāprabhu addressed; *śuna haridāsa*—My dear Haridāsa, please hear; *parera dravya*—another's property; *iṅho*—this Sanātana Gosvāmī; *cāhena*—wants; *karite vināśa*—to destroy.

TRANSLATION

Śrī Caitanya Mahāprabhu then said to Haridāsa Ṭhākura, "My dear Haridāsa, please hear Me. This gentleman wants to destroy another's property.

TEXT 88

পরের স্থাপ্য দ্রব্য কেহ না খায়, বিলায়।
নিষেধিহ ইঁহারে,—যেন না করে অন্যায় ॥" ৮৮ ॥

parera sthāpya dravya keha nā khāya, vilāya
niṣedhiha iṅhāre, —yena nā kare anyāya"

SYNONYMS

parera—by another; *sthāpya*—to be kept; *dravya*—property; *keha nā khāya*—no one uses; *vilāya*—distributes; *niṣedhiha*—forbid; *iṅhāre*—him; *yena*—so; *nā kare*—he does not do; *anyāya*—something unlawful.

TRANSLATION

"One who is entrusted with another's property does not distribute it or use it for his own purposes. Therefore, tell him not to do such an unlawful thing."

TEXT 89

হরিদাস কহে,—"মিথ্যা অভিমান করি ।
তোমার গম্ভীর হৃদয় বুঝিতে না পারি ॥ ৮৯ ॥

haridāsa kahe, ——"mithyā abhimāna kari
tomāra gambhīra hṛdaya bujhite nā pāri

SYNONYMS

haridāsa kahe—Haridāsa Ṭhākura replied; *mithyā*—falsely; *abhimāna kari*—are proud; *tomāra*—Your; *gambhīra*—deep; *hṛdaya*—intention; *bujhite nā pāri*—we cannot understand.

TRANSLATION

Haridāsa Ṭhākura replied, "We are falsely proud of our capabilities. Actually we cannot understand Your deep intentions.

TEXT 90

কোন্ কোন্ কার্য তুমি কর কোন্ দ্বারে ।
তুমি না জানাইলে কেহ জানিতে না পারে ॥ ৯০ ॥

kon kon kārya tumi kara kon dvāre
tumi nā jānāile keha jānite nā pāre

SYNONYMS

kon kon kārya—what work; *tumi*—You; *kara*—perform; *kon dvāre*—through which; *tumi nā jānāile*—unless You make to understand; *keha jānite nā pāre*—no one can understand.

TRANSLATION

"Unless You inform us, we cannot understand what Your purpose is nor what You want to do through whom.

TEXT 91

এতাদৃশ তুমি ইঁহারে করিয়াছ অঙ্গীকার ।
এত সৌভাগ্য ইহাঁ না হয় কাহার ॥" ৯১ ॥

etādṛśa tumi iṅhāre kariyācha aṅgīkāra
eta saubhāgya ihāṅ nā haya kāhāra"

SYNONYMS

etādṛśa—such; *tumi*—You; *iṅhāre*—him; *kariyācha aṅgīkāra*—have accepted; *eta saubhāgya*—so much fortune; *ihāṅ*—upon him; *nā haya*—is not possible; *kāhāra*—by anyone else.

TRANSLATION

"My dear sir, since You, a great personality, have accepted Sanātana Gosvāmī, he is greatly fortunate; no one can be as fortunate as he."

TEXT 92

তবে মহাপ্রভু করি' দুঁহারে আলিঙ্গন।
'মধ্যাহ্ন' করিতে উঠি' করিলা গমন ॥ ৯২ ॥

tabe mahāprabhu kari' duṅhāre āliṅgana
'madhyāhna' karite uṭhi' karilā gamana

SYNONYMS

tabe—then; *mahāprabhu*—Śrī Caitanya Mahāprabhu; *kari' duṅhāre āliṅgana*—embracing both of them; *madhya-ahna karite*—to perform His noon duties; *uṭhi'*—getting up; *karilā gamana*—left.

TRANSLATION

Thus Śrī Caitanya Mahāprabhu embraced both Haridāsa Ṭhākura and Sanātana Gosvāmī and then got up and left to perform His noon duties.

TEXT 93

সনাতনে কহে হরিদাস করি' আলিঙ্গন।
"তোমার ভাগ্যের সীমা না যায় কথন ॥ ৯৩ ॥

sanātane kahe haridāsa kari' āliṅgana
"tomāra bhāgyera sīmā nā yāya kathana

SYNONYMS

sanātane—unto Sanātana Gosvāmī; *kahe*—said; *haridāsa*—Haridāsa Ṭhākura; *kari' āliṅgana*—embracing; *tomāra*—your; *bhāgyera*—of fortune; *sīmā*—limitation; *nā yāya kathana*—cannot be described.

TRANSLATION

"My dear Sanātana," Haridāsa Ṭhākura said, embracing him, "no one can find the limits of your good fortune.

TEXT 94

তোমার দেহ কহেন প্রভু 'মোর নিজ-ধন'।
তোমা-সম ভাগ্যবান্ নাহি কোন জন ॥ ৯৪ ॥

tomāra deha kahena prabhu 'mora nija-dhana'
tomā-sama bhāgyavān nāhi kona jana

SYNONYMS

tomāra deha—your body; *kahena prabhu*—Śrī Caitanya Mahāprabhu says; *mora*—My; *nija-dhana*—personal property; *tomā-sama*—like you; *bhāgyavān*—fortunate person; *nāhi*—there is not; *kona jana*—anyone.

TRANSLATION

"Śrī Caitanya Mahāprabhu has accepted your body as His own property. Therefore no one can equal you in good fortune.

TEXT 95

নিজ-দেহে যে কার্য না পারেন করিতে।
সে কার্য করাইবে তোমা, সেহ মথুরাতে ॥ ৯৫ ॥

nija-dehe ye kārya nā pārena karite
se kārya karāibe tomā, seha mathurāte

SYNONYMS

nija-dehe—with His personal body; *ye kārya*—whatever business; *nā pārena karite*—He cannot do; *se kārya*—those things; *karāibe*—He will cause to do; *tomā*—you; *seha*—that; *mathurāte*—in Mathurā.

TRANSLATION

"What Śrī Caitanya Mahāprabhu cannot do with His personal body He wants to do through you, and He wants to do it in Mathurā.

TEXT 96

যে করাইতে চাহে ঈশ্বর, সেই সিদ্ধ হয়।
তোমার সৌভাগ্য এই কহিলুঁ নিশ্চয় ॥ ৯৬ ॥

ye karāite cāhe īśvara, sei siddha haya
tomāra saubhāgya ei kahiluṅ niścaya

SYNONYMS

ye—whatever; *karāite*—to cause to do; *cāhe*—wants; *īśvara*—the Supreme Personality of Godhead; *sei*—that; *siddha*—successful; *haya*—is; *tomāra saubhāgya*—your great fortune; *ei*—this; *kahiluṅ*—I have spoken; *niścaya*—my considered opinion.

TRANSLATION

"Whatever the Supreme Personality of Godhead wants us to do will successfully be accomplished. This is your great fortune. That is my mature opinion.

TEXT 97

ভক্তিসিদ্ধান্ত, শাস্ত্র-আচার-নির্ণয়।
তোমা-দ্বারে করাইবেন, বুঝিলুঁ আশয় ॥ ৯৭ ॥

bhakti-siddhānta, śāstra-ācāra-nirṇaya
tomā-dvāre karāibena, bujhiluṅ āśaya

SYNONYMS

bhakti-siddhānta—conclusive decision in devotional service; *śāstra*—according to the scriptural injunctions; *ācāra-nirṇaya*—ascertainment of behavior; *tomā-dvāre*—by you; *karāibena*—will cause to be done; *bujhiluṅ*—I can understand; *āśaya*—His desire.

TRANSLATION

"I can understand from the words of Śrī Caitanya Mahāprabhu that He wants you to write books about the conclusive decision of devotional service and about the regulative principles ascertained from the revealed scriptures.

TEXT 98

আমার এই দেহ প্রভুর কার্যে না লাগিল।
ভারত-ভূমিতে জন্মি' এই দেহ ব্যর্থ হৈল ॥ ৯৮ ॥

āmāra ei deha prabhura kārye nā lāgila
bhārata-bhūmite janmi' ei deha vyartha haila

SYNONYMS

āmāra—my; *ei*—this; *deha*—body; *prabhura*—of Śrī Caitanya Mahāprabhu; *kārye*—in the service; *nā lāgila*—could not be used; *bhārata-bhūmite*—in the land of India; *janmi'*—taking birth; *ei deha*—this body; *vyartha haila*—has become useless.

TRANSLATION

"My body could not be used in the service of Śrī Caitanya Mahāprabhu. Therefore although it took birth in the land of India, this body has been useless."

PURPORT

For a further explanation of the importance of Bhārata-bhūmi, one may refer to the *Ādi-līlā* (9.41) and also *Śrīmad-Bhāgavatam* (5.19.19-27). The special feature of a birth in India is that a person born in India becomes automatically God conscious. In every part of India, and especially in the holy places of pilgrimage, even an ordinary uneducated man is inclined toward Kṛṣṇa consciousness, and as soon as he sees a Kṛṣṇa conscious person, he offers obeisances. India has many sacred rivers like the Ganges, Yamunā, Narmadā, Kāverī and Kṛṣṇā, and simply by bathing in these rivers people are liberated and become Kṛṣṇa conscious. Śrī Caitanya Mahāprabhu therefore says:

bhārata-bhūmite haila manuṣya-janma yāra
janma sārthaka kari' kara para-upakāra

One who has taken birth in the land of Bhārata-bhūmi, India, should take full advantage of his birth. He should become completely well versed in the knowledge of the *Vedas* and spiritual culture and should distribute the experience of Kṛṣṇa consciousness all over the world. People all over the world are madly engaging in sense gratification and in this way spoiling their human lives, with the risk that in the next life they may become animals or less. Human society should be saved from such a risky civilization and the danger of animalism by awakening to God consciousness, Kṛṣṇa consciousness. The Kṛṣṇa consciousness movement has been started for this purpose. Therefore unbiased men of the highest echelon should study the principles of the Kṛṣṇa consciousness movement and fully cooperate with this movement to save human society.

TEXT 99

সনাতন কহে,—"তোমা-সম কেবা আছে আন।
মহাপ্রভুর গণে তুমি—মহাভাগ্যবান্ ! ৯৯ ॥

sanātana kahe, —"tomā-sama kebā āche āna
mahāprabhura gaṇe tumi—mahā-bhāgyavān!

SYNONYMS

sanātana kahe—Sanātana Gosvāmī said; *tomā-sama*—like you; *kebā*—who; *āche*—is there; *āna*—another; *mahāprabhura*—of Śrī Caitanya Mahāprabhu;

gaṇe—among the personal associates; *tumi*—you; *mahā-bhāgyavān*—the most fortunate.

TRANSLATION

Sanātana Gosvāmī replied, "O Haridāsa Ṭhākura, who is equal to you? You are one of the associates of Śrī Caitanya Mahāprabhu. Therefore you are the most fortunate.

TEXT 100

অবতার-কার্য প্রভুর—নাম-প্রচারে ।
সেই নিজ-কার্য প্রভু করেন তোমার দ্বারে ॥ ১০০ ॥

avatāra-kārya prabhura——nāma-pracāre
sei nija-kārya prabhu karena tomāra dvāre

SYNONYMS

avatāra-kārya—mission of the incarnation; *prabhura*—of Śrī Caitanya Mahāprabhu; *nāma-pracāre*—spreading the importance of the holy name of the Lord; *sei*—that; *nija-kārya*—mission of His life; *prabhu*—Śrī Caitanya Mahāprabhu; *karena*—performs; *tomāra dvāre*—through you.

TRANSLATION

"The mission of Śrī Caitanya Mahāprabhu, for which He has descended as an incarnation, is to spread the importance of chanting the holy name of the Lord. Now instead of personally doing so, He is spreading it through you.

TEXT 101

প্রত্যহ কর তিনলক্ষ নাম-সঙ্কীর্তন ।
সবার আগে কর নামের মহিমা কথন ॥ ১০১ ॥

pratyaha kara tina-lakṣa nāma-saṅkīrtana
sabāra āge kara nāmera mahimā kathana

SYNONYMS

prati-aha—daily; *kara*—you do; *tina-lakṣa*—300,000; *nāma-saṅkīrtana*—chanting of the holy name; *sabāra āge*—before everyone; *kara*—you do; *nāmera*—of the holy name; *mahimā kathana*—discussion of the glories.

TRANSLATION

"My dear sir, you are chanting the holy name 300,000 times daily and informing everyone of the importance of such chanting.

TEXT 102

আপনে আচরে কেহ, না করে প্রচার ।
প্রচার করেন কেহ, না করেন আচার ॥ ১০২ ॥

āpane ācare keha, nā kare pracāra
pracāra karena keha, nā karena ācāra

SYNONYMS

āpane—personally; *ācare*—behaves; *keha*—someone; *nā kare pracāra*—does not do preaching work; *pracāra karena*—does preaching work; *keha*—someone; *nā karena ācāra*—does not behave strictly according to the principles.

TRANSLATION

"Some behave very well but do not preach the cult of Kṛṣṇa consciousness, whereas others preach but do not behave properly.

TEXT 103

'আচার', 'প্রচার',—নামের করহ 'দুই' কার্য ।
তুমি—সর্ব-গুরু, তুমি জগতের আর্য ॥" ১০৩ ॥

'ācāra', 'pracāra', ——nāmera karaha 'dui' kārya
tumi——sarva-guru, tumi jagatera ārya

SYNONYMS

ācāra pracāra—behaving well and preaching; *nāmera*—of the holy name; *karaha*—you do; *dui*—two; *kārya*—works; *tumi*—you; *sarva-guru*—everyone's spiritual master; *tumi*—you; *jagatera ārya*—the most advanced devotee within this world.

TRANSLATION

"You simultaneously perform both duties in relation to the holy name by your personal behavior and by your preaching. Therefore you are the spiritual master of the entire world, for you are the most advanced devotee in the world."

PURPORT

Sanātana Gosvāmī clearly defines herein the bona fide spiritual master of the world. The qualifications expressed in this connection are that one must act according to the scriptural injunctions and at the same time preach. One who does so is a bona fide spiritual master. Haridāsa Ṭhākura was the ideal spiritual master because he regularly chanted on his beads a prescribed number of times. Indeed, he was chanting the holy name of the Lord 300,000 times a day. Similarly, the members of the Kṛṣṇa consciousness movement chant a minimum of sixteen rounds a day, which can be done without difficulty, and at the same time they must preach the cult of Caitanya Mahāprabhu according to the gospel of *Bhagavad-gītā As It Is.* One who does so is quite fit to become a spiritual master for the entire world.

TEXT 104

এইমত দুইজন নানা-কথা-রঙ্গে ।
কৃষ্ণকথা আস্বাদয় রহি' একসঙ্গে ॥ ১০৪ ॥

ei-mata dui-jana nānā-kathā-raṅge
kṛṣṇa-kathā āsvādaya rahi' eka-saṅge

SYNONYMS

ei-mata—in this way; *dui-jana*—two persons; *nānā-kathā-raṅge*—in the happiness of discussing various subject matters; *kṛṣṇa-kathā*—the subject matter of Kṛṣṇa; *āsvādaya*—they taste; *rahi' eka-saṅge*—keeping together.

TRANSLATION

In this way the two of them passed their time discussing subjects concerning Kṛṣṇa. Thus they enjoyed life together.

TEXT 105

যাত্রাকালে আইলা সব গৌড়ের ভক্তগণ ।
পূর্ববৎ কৈলা সবে রথযাত্রা দরশন ॥ ১০৫ ॥

yātrā-kāle āilā saba gauḍera bhakta-gaṇa
pūrvavat kailā sabe ratha-yātrā daraśana

SYNONYMS

yātrā-kāle—during the time of the car festival; *āilā*—came; *saba*—all; *gauḍera bhakta-gaṇa*—devotees from Bengal; *pūrvavat*—like previously; *kailā*—did; *sabe*—all; *ratha-yātrā daraśana*—visiting the car festival of Lord Jagannātha.

TRANSLATION

During the time of Ratha-yātrā, all the devotees arrived from Bengal to visit the cart festival as they had done previously.

TEXT 106

রথ-অগ্রে প্রভু তৈছে করিলা নর্তন ।
দেখি চমৎকার হৈল সনাতনের মন ॥ ১০৬ ॥

ratha-agre prabhu taiche karilā nartana
dekhi camatkāra haila sanātanera mana

SYNONYMS

ratha-agre—in front of the car; *prabhu*—Śrī Caitanya Mahāprabhu; *taiche*—similarly; *karilā nartana*—performed dancing; *dekhi*—seeing; *camatkāra haila*—was astonished; *sanātanera mana*—the mind of Sanātana.

TRANSLATION

During the Ratha-yātrā festival, Śrī Caitanya Mahāprabhu again danced before the cart of Jagannātha. When Sanātana Gosvāmī saw this, his mind was astonished.

TEXT 107

বর্ষার চারি-মাস রহিলা সব নিজ ভক্তগণে ।
সবা-সঙ্গে প্রভু মিলাইলা সনাতনে ॥ ১০৭ ॥

varṣāra cāri-māsa rahilā saba nija bhakta-gaṇe
sabā-saṅge prabhu milāilā sanātane

SYNONYMS

varṣāra cāri-māsa—the four months of the rainy season; *rahilā*—remained; *saba*—all; *nija bhakta-gaṇe*—the devotees of Śrī Caitanya Mahāprabhu; *sabā-saṅge*—with all of them; *prabhu*—Śrī Caitanya Mahāprabhu; *milāilā*—introduced; *sanātane*—Sanātana.

TRANSLATION

The Lord's devotees from Bengal stayed at Jagannātha Purī during the four months of the rainy season, and Lord Śrī Caitanya Mahāprabhu introduced Sanātana Gosvāmī to them all.

TEXTS 108-110

অদ্বৈত, নিত্যানন্দ, শ্রীবাস, বক্রেশ্বর ।
বাসুদেব, মুরারি, রাঘব, দামোদর ॥ ১০৮ ॥
পুরী, ভারতী, স্বরূপ, পণ্ডিত-গদাধর ।
সার্বভৌম, রামানন্দ, জগদানন্দ, শঙ্কর ॥ ১০৯ ॥
কাশীশ্বর, গোবিন্দাদি যত ভক্তগণ ।
সবা-সনে সনাতনের করাইলা মিলন ॥ ১১০ ॥

advaita, nityānanda, śrīvāsa, vakreśvara
vāsudeva, murāri, rāghava, dāmodara

purī, bhāratī, svarūpa, paṇḍita-gadādhara
sārvabhauma, rāmānanda, jagadānanda, śaṅkara

kāśīśvara, govindādi yata bhakta-gaṇa
sabā-sane sanātanera karāilā milana

SYNONYMS

advaita—Advaita; *nityānanda*—Nityānanda; *śrīvāsa*—Śrīvāsa; *vakreśvara*—Vakreśvara; *vāsudeva*—Vāsudeva; *murāri*—Murāri; *rāghava*—Rāghava; *dāmodara*—Dāmodara; *purī*—Purī; *bhāratī*—Bhāratī; *svarūpa*—Svarūpa; *paṇḍita-gadādhara*—Gadādhara Paṇḍita; *sārvabhauma*—Sārvabhauma; *rāmānanda*—Rāmānanda; *jagadānanda*—Jagadānanda; *śaṅkara*—Śaṅkara; *kāśīśvara*—Kāśīśvara; *govinda*—Govinda; *ādi*—and others; *yata bhakta-gaṇa*—all the devotees; *sabā-sane*—with all of them; *sanātanera*—of Sanātana Gosvāmī; *karāilā milana*—made introduction.

TRANSLATION

Śrī Caitanya Mahāprabhu introduced Sanātana Gosvāmī to these and other selected devotees: Advaita, Nityānanda, Śrīvāsa, Vakreśvara, Vāsudeva, Murāri, Rāghava, Dāmodara, Paramānanda Purī, Brahmānanda Bhāratī, Svarūpa Dāmodara, Gadādhara Paṇḍita, Sārvabhauma, Rāmānanda, Jagadānanda, Śaṅkara, Kāśīśvara and Govinda.

TEXT 111

যথাযোগ্য করাইল সবার চরণ বন্দন ।
তাঁরে করাইলা সবার কৃপার ভাজন ॥ ১১১ ॥

yathā-yogya karāila sabāra caraṇa vandana
tāṅre karāilā sabāra kṛpāra bhājana

SYNONYMS

yathā-yogya—as it is fit; *karāila*—caused to perform; *sabāra*—of all; *caraṇa vandana*—worshiping the lotus feet; *tāṅre*—him; *karāilā*—made; *sabāra*—of all of them; *kṛpāra bhājana*—object of mercy.

TRANSLATION

The Lord asked Sanātana Gosvāmī to offer obeisances to all the devotees in a way that befitted each one. Thus He introduced Sanātana Gosvāmī to them all, just to make him an object of their mercy.

TEXT 112

সদ্‌গুণে, পাণ্ডিত্যে, সবার প্রিয়—সনাতন ।
যথাযোগ্য কৃপা-মৈত্রী-গৌরব-ভাজন ॥ ১১২ ॥

sad-guṇe, pāṇḍitye, sabāra priya——sanātana
yathā-yogya kṛpā-maitrī-gaurava-bhājana

SYNONYMS

sat-guṇe—in good qualities; *pāṇḍitye*—in learning; *sabāra priya*—dear to everyone; *sanātana*—Sanātana Gosvāmī; *yathā-yogya*—as it is suitable; *kṛpā*—mercy; *maitrī*—friendship; *gaurava*—honor; *bhājana*—worthy of being offered.

TRANSLATION

Sanātana Gosvāmī was dear to everyone because of his exalted qualities in learning. Suitably, therefore, they bestowed upon him mercy, friendship and honor.

TEXT 113

সকল বৈষ্ণব যবে গৌড়দেশে গেলা ।
সনাতন মহাপ্রভুর চরণে রহিলা ॥ ১১৩ ॥

sakala vaiṣṇava yabe gauḍa-deśe gelā
sanātana mahāprabhura caraṇe rahilā

SYNONYMS

sakala—all; *vaiṣṇava*—devotees; *yabe*—when; *gauḍa-deśe*—to Bengal; *gelā*—returned; *sanātana*—Sanātana Gosvāmī; *mahāprabhura*—of Śrī Caitanya Mahāprabhu; *caraṇe rahilā*—stayed at the lotus feet.

TRANSLATION

When all the other devotees returned to Bengal after the Ratha-yātrā festival, Sanātana Gosvāmī stayed under the care of the lotus feet of Śrī Caitanya Mahāprabhu.

TEXT 114

দোলযাত্রা-আদি প্রভুর সঙ্গেতে দেখিল ।
দিনে-দিনে প্রভু-সঙ্গে আনন্দ বাড়িল ॥ ১১৪ ॥

dola-yātrā-ādi prabhura saṅgete dekhila
dine-dine prabhu-saṅge ānanda bāḍila

SYNONYMS

dola-yātrā—the festival of Dola-yātrā; *ādi*—and others; *prabhura saṅgete*—with Śrī Caitanya Mahāprabhu; *dekhila*—he saw; *dine-dine*—day after day; *prabhu-saṅge*—in the association of Śrī Caitanya Mahāprabhu; *ānanda bāḍila*—his pleasure increased.

TRANSLATION

Sanātana Gosvāmī observed the Dola-yātrā ceremony with Lord Śrī Caitanya Mahāprabhu. In this way, his pleasure increased in the company of the Lord.

TEXT 115

পূর্বে বৈশাখ-মাসে সনাতন যবে আইলা ।
জ্যৈষ্ঠমাসে প্রভু তাঁরে পরীক্ষা করিলা ॥ ১১৫ ॥

pūrve vaiśākha-māse sanātana yabe āilā
jyaiṣṭha-māse prabhu tāṅre parīkṣā karilā

SYNONYMS

pūrve—formerly; *vaiśākha-māse*—during the month of April-May; *sanātana*—Sanātana Gosvāmī; *yabe*—when; *āilā*—came; *jyaiṣṭha-māse*—in the month of May-June; *prabhu*—Śrī Caitanya Mahāprabhu; *tāṅre*—him; *parīkṣā karilā*—tested.

TRANSLATION

Sanātana Gosvāmī had come to see Śrī Caitanya Mahāprabhu at Jagannātha Purī during the month of April-May, and during the month of May-June Śrī Caitanya Mahāprabhu tested him.

TEXT 116

জ্যৈষ্ঠমাসে প্রভু যমেশ্বর-টোটা আইলা ।
ভক্ত-অনুরোধে তাহাঁ ভিক্ষা যে করিলা ॥ ১১৬ ॥

jyaiṣṭha-māse prabhu yameśvara-ṭoṭā āilā
bhakta-anurodhe tāhāṅ bhikṣā ye karilā

SYNONYMS

jyaiṣṭha-māse—during the month of May-June; *prabhu*—Śrī Caitanya Mahāprabhu; *yameśvara-ṭoṭā*—to the garden of Lord Śiva, Yameśvara; *āilā*—came; *bhakta-anurodhe*—on the request of the devotees; *tāhāṅ*—there; *bhikṣā ye karilā*—accepted *prasāda.*

TRANSLATION

In that month of May-June, Śrī Caitanya Mahāprabhu came to the garden of Yameśvara [Lord Śiva] and accepted prasāda there at the request of the devotees.

TEXT 117

মধ্যাহ্ন-ভিক্ষাকালে সনাতনে বোলাইল ।
প্রভু বোলাইলা, তাঁর আনন্দ বাড়িল ॥ ১১৭ ॥

madhyāhna-bhikṣā-kāle sanātane bolāila
prabhu bolāilā, tāṅra ānanda bāḍila

SYNONYMS

madhya-ahna—at noon; *bhikṣā-kāle*—at the time for lunch; *sanātane*—for Sanātana Gosvāmī; *bolāila*—He called; *prabhu bolāilā*—Lord Śrī Caitanya Mahāprabhu called; *tāṅra*—his; *ānanda*—happiness; *bāḍila*—increased.

TRANSLATION

At noon, when it was time for lunch, the Lord called for Sanātana Gosvāmī, whose happiness increased because of the call.

TEXT 118

মধ্যাহ্নে সমুদ্র-বালু হঞাছে অগ্নি-সম ।
সেইপথে সনাতন করিলা গমন ॥ ১১৮ ॥

madhyāhne samudra-vālu hañāche agni-sama
sei-pathe sanātana karilā gamana

SYNONYMS

madhya-ahne—at noon; *samudra-vālu*—the sand by the sea; *hañāche*—was; *agni-sama*—as hot as fire; *sei-pathe*—by that path; *sanātana*—Sanātana Gosvāmī; *karilā gamana*—came.

TRANSLATION

At noon the sand on the beach was as hot as fire, but Sanātana Gosvāmī came by that path.

TEXT 119

'প্রভু বোলাঞাছে', —এই আনন্দিত মনে ।
তপ্ত-বালুকাতে পা পোড়ে, তাহা নাহি জানে ॥১১৯॥

'prabhu bolāñāche', ——ei ānandita mane
tapta-vālukāte pā poḍe, tāhā nāhi jāne

SYNONYMS

prabhu bolāñāche—the Lord has called; *ei*—this; *ānandita*—happy; *mane*—within the mind; *tapta-vālukāte*—on the hot sand; *pā*—feet; *poḍe*—were burning; *tāhā*—that; *nāhi jāne*—could not understand.

TRANSLATION

Overwhelmed by joy at being called by the Lord, Sanātana Gosvāmī did not feel that his feet were burning in the hot sand.

TEXT 120

দুই পায়ে ফোস্কা হৈল, তবু গেলা প্রভুস্থানে ।
ভিক্ষা করি' মহাপ্রভু করিয়াছেন বিশ্রামে ॥ ১২০ ॥

dui pāye phoskā haila, tabu gelā prabhu-sthāne
bhikṣā kari' mahāprabhu kariyāchena viśrāme

SYNONYMS

dui pāye—on the two soles; *phoskā haila*—there were blisters; *tabu*—still; *gelā*—came; *prabhu-sthāne*—to Śrī Caitanya Mahāprabhu; *bhikṣā kari'*—after finishing lunch; *mahāprabhu*—Śrī Caitanya Mahāprabhu; *kariyāchena viśrāme*—was taking rest.

TRANSLATION

Although the soles of both his feet were blistered because of the heat, he nevertheless went to Śrī Caitanya Mahāprabhu. There he found that the Lord, having taken His lunch, was resting.

TEXT 121

ভিক্ষা-অবশেষ-পাত্র গোবিন্দ তারে দিলা ।
প্রসাদ পাঞা সনাতন প্রভুপাশে আইলা ॥ ১২১ ॥

bhikṣā-avaśeṣa-pātra govinda tāre dilā
prasāda pāñā sanātana prabhu-pāśe āilā

SYNONYMS

bhikṣā-avaśeṣa—of remnants of the food; *pātra*—plate; *govinda*—Govinda; *tāre dilā*—delivered to him; *prasāda pāñā*—after taking the remnants of food; *sanātana*—Sanātana Gosvāmī; *prabhu-pāśe*—to Lord Śrī Caitanya Mahāprabhu; *āilā*—came.

TRANSLATION

Govinda gave Sanātana Gosvāmī the plate with the remnants of Lord Caitanya's food. After taking the prasāda, Sanātana Gosvāmī approached Lord Śrī Caitanya Mahāprabhu.

TEXT 122

প্রভু কহে,—'কোন্ পথে আইলা, সনাতন ?'
তেঁহ কহে,—'সমুদ্র-পথে, করিলুঁ আগমন ॥' ১২২ ॥

prabhu kahe, —'kon pathe āilā, sanātana?'
teṅha kahe, —'samudra-pathe, kariluṅ āgamana'

SYNONYMS

prabhu kahe—the Lord inquired; *kon pathe*—through which path; *āilā sanātana*—you have come, Sanātana; *teṅha kahe*—he replied; *samudra-pathe*—on the path by the sea; *kariluṅ āgamana*—I have come.

TRANSLATION

When the Lord inquired, "By which path have you come?" Sanātana Gosvāmī replied, "I have come on the path along the beach."

TEXT 123

প্রভু কহে, – "তপ্ত-বালুকাতে কেমনে আইলা ?
সিংহদ্বারের পথ—শীতল, কেনে না আইলা ?১২৩ ॥

prabhu kahe, —"tapta-vālukāte kemane āilā?
siṁha-dvārera patha—śītala, kene nā āilā?

SYNONYMS

prabhu kahe—Śrī Caitanya Mahāprabhu said; *tapta-vālukāte*—on hot sand; *kemane āilā*—how did you come; *siṁha-dvārera patha*—the path of the Siṁha-dvāra gate; *śītala*—very cool; *kene*—why; *nā āilā*—did you not come.

TRANSLATION

Śrī Caitanya Mahāprabhu said, "How did you come through the beach where the sand is so hot? Why didn't you come by the path in front of the Siṁha-dvāra gate? It is very cool.

PURPORT

Siṁha-dvāra refers to the main gate on the eastern side of the Jagannātha temple.

TEXT 124

তপ্ত-বালুকায় তোমার পায় হৈল ব্রণ ।
চলিতে না পার, কেমনে করিলা সহন ?"১২৪ ॥

tapta-vālukāya tomāra pāya haila vraṇa
calite nā pāra, kemane karilā sahana?"

SYNONYMS

tapta-vālukāya—by the hot sand; *tomāra*—your; *pāya*—on the soles; *haila*—there were; *vraṇa*—blisters; *calite nā pāra*—you cannot walk; *kemane*—how; *karilā sahana*—did you tolerate.

TRANSLATION

"The hot sand must have blistered your soles. Now you cannot walk. How did you tolerate it?"

TEXT 125

সনাতন কহে,—"দুখ বহুত না পাইলুঁ ।
পায়ে ব্রণ হঞাছে তাহা না জানিলুঁ ॥ ১২৫ ॥

sanātana kahe, ——"dukha bahuta nā pāiluṅ
pāye vraṇa hañāche tāhā nā jāniluṅ

SYNONYMS

sanātana kahe—Sanātana Gosvāmī replied; *dukha*—pain; *bahuta*—much; *nā pāiluṅ*—I did not feel; *pāye*—on the soles; *vraṇa hañāche*—there were blisters; *tāhā*—that; *nā jāniluṅ*—I did not know.

TRANSLATION

Sanātana Gosvāmī replied, "I did not feel much pain, nor did I know that there are blisters because of the heat.

TEXT 126

সিংহদ্বারে যাইতে মোর নাহি অধিকার ।
বিশেষে—ঠাকুরের তাহাঁ সেবকের প্রচার ॥ ১২৬ ॥

siṁha-dvāre yāite mora nāhi adhikāra
viśeṣe——ṭhākurera tāhāṅ sevakera pracāra

SYNONYMS

siṁha-dvāre—in front of the main gate, known as Siṁha-dvāra; *yāite*—to go; *mora*—my; *nāhi adhikāra*—there is no right; *viśeṣe*—specifically; *ṭhākurera*—of Lord Jagannātha; *tāhāṅ*—there; *sevakera pracāra*—traffic of the servants.

TRANSLATION

"I have no right to pass by the Siṁha-dvāra, for the servants of Jagannātha are always coming and going there.

TEXT 127

সেবক গতাগতি করে, নাহি অবসর ।
তার স্পর্শ হৈলে, সর্বনাশ হবে মোর ॥" ১২৭ ॥

sevaka gatāgati kare, nāhi avasara
tāra sparśa haile, sarva-nāśa habe mora"

SYNONYMS

sevaka—servants; *gatāgati kare*—come and go; *nāhi avasara*—there is no interval; *tāra sparśa haile*—if I touch them; *sarva-nāśa habe mora*—I shall be ruined.

TRANSLATION

"The servants are always coming and going without interval. If I touch them, I shall be ruined."

PURPORT

Herein it is very clearly indicated that priests performing Deity worship should be careful to keep themselves completely pure and not be touched by outsiders. Sanātana Gosvāmī and Haridāsa Ṭhākura, thinking themselves *mlecchas* and *yavanas* because of their past association with Mohammedans, did not enter the temple nor even travel on the path in front of the temple gate. It is customary for the priests of temples in India not even to touch outsiders nor enter the Deity room after having been touched. This is a very important item in temple worship.

TEXT 128

শুনি' মহাপ্রভু মনে সন্তোষ পাইলা ।
তুষ্ট হঞা তাঁরে কিছু কহিতে লাগিলা ॥ ১২৮ ॥

śuni' mahāprabhu mane santoṣa pāilā
tuṣṭa hañā tāṅre kichu kahite lāgilā

SYNONYMS

śuni'—hearing; *mahāprabhu*—Śrī Caitanya Mahāprabhu; *mane*—in the mind; *santoṣa pāilā*—became very happy; *tuṣṭa hañā*—being pleased; *tāṅre*—unto him; *kichu*—something; *kahite lāgilā*—began to speak.

TRANSLATION

Having heard all these details, Śrī Caitanya Mahāprabhu, greatly pleased, spoke as follows.

TEXTS 129-130

"যদ্যপিও তুমি হও জগৎপাবন ।
তোমা-স্পর্শে পবিত্র হয় দেব-মুনিগণ ॥ ১২৯ ॥
তথাপি ভক্ত-স্বভাব—মর্যাদা-রক্ষণ ।
মর্যাদা-পালন হয় সাধুর ভূষণ ॥ ১৩০ ॥

"yadyapio tumi hao jagat-pāvana
tomā-sparśe pavitra haya deva-muni-gaṇa

tathāpi bhakta-svabhāva——maryādā-rakṣaṇa
maryādā-pālana haya sādhura bhūṣaṇa

SYNONYMS

yadyapio—although; *tumi*—you; *hao*—are; *jagat-pāvana*—the deliverer of the entire universe; *tomā*—you; *sparśe*—by touching; *pavitra*—purified; *haya*—becomes; *deva-muni-gaṇa*—the demigods and great saintly persons; *tathāpi*—still; *bhakta-svabhāva*—the nature of a devotee; *maryādā*—etiquette; *rakṣaṇa*—to protect or observe; *maryādā pālana*—to maintain etiquette; *haya*—is; *sādhura bhūṣaṇa*—ornament of devotees.

TRANSLATION

"My dear Sanātana, although you are the deliverer of the entire universe and although even the demigods and great saints are purified by touching you, it is the characteristic of a devotee to observe and protect the Vaiṣṇava etiquette. Maintenance of the Vaiṣṇava etiquette is the ornament of a devotee.

TEXT 131

মর্যাদা-লঙ্ঘনে লোক করে উপহাস ।
ইহলোক, পরলোক—দুই হয় নাশ ॥ ১৩১ ॥

maryādā-laṅghane loka kare upahāsa
iha-loka, para-loka——dui haya nāśa

SYNONYMS

maryādā-laṅghane—by surpassing the customs of etiquette; *loka*—people; *kare upahāsa*—joke; *iha-loka*—this world; *para-loka*—the next world; *dui*—two; *haya nāśa*—become vanquished.

TRANSLATION

"If one transgresses the laws of etiquette, people make fun of him, and thus he is vanquished in both this world and the next.

TEXT 132

মর্যাদা রাখিলে, তুষ্ট কৈলে মোর মন ।
তুমি ঐছে না করিলে করে কোন্ জন ?" ১৩২ ॥

maryādā rākhile, tuṣṭa kaile mora mana
tumi aiche nā karile kare kon jana?"

SYNONYMS

maryādā rākhile—since you have observed the etiquette; *tuṣṭa kaile*—you have satisfied; *mora mana*—My mind; *tumi*—you; *aiche*—like that; *nā karile*—without doing; *kare*—would do; *kon jana*—who.

TRANSLATION

"By observing the etiquette, you have satisfied My mind. Who else but you will show this example?"

TEXT 133

এত বলি' প্রভু তাঁরে আলিঙ্গন কৈল ।
তাঁর কণ্ডুরসা প্রভুর শ্রীঅঙ্গে লাগিল ॥ ১৩৩ ॥

eta bali' prabhu tāṅre āliṅgana kaila
tāṅra kaṇḍu-rasā prabhura śrī-aṅge lāgila

SYNONYMS

eta bali'—saying this; *prabhu*—Śrī Caitanya Mahāprabhu; *tāṅre*—him; *āliṅgana kaila*—embraced; *tāṅra*—his; *kaṇḍu-rasā*—moisture oozing from the itches; *prabhura*—of Śrī Caitanya Mahāprabhu; *śrī-aṅge lāgila*—smeared the body.

TRANSLATION

After saying this, Śrī Caitanya Mahāprabhu embraced Sanātana Gosvāmī, and the moisture oozing from the itching sores on Sanātana's body smeared the body of the Lord.

TEXT 134

বার বার নিষেধেন, তবু করে আলিঙ্গন ।
অঙ্গে রসা লাগে, দুঃখ পায় সনাতন ॥ ১৩৪ ॥

bāra bāra niṣedhena, tabu kare āliṅgana
aṅge rasā lāge, duḥkha pāya sanātana

SYNONYMS

bāra bāra—again and again; *niṣedhena*—forbids; *tabu*—still; *kare āliṅgana*—He embraces; *aṅge*—on the body; *rasā lāge*—oozing moisture touches; *duḥkha*—unhappiness; *pāya*—gets; *sanātana*—Sanātana Gosvāmī.

TRANSLATION

Although Sanātana Gosvāmī forbade Śrī Caitanya Mahāprabhu to embrace him, the Lord did so. Thus His body was smeared with the moisture from Sanātana's body, and Sanātana became greatly distressed.

TEXT 135

এইমতে সেবক-প্রভু দুঁহে ঘর গেলা ।
আর দিন জগদানন্দ সনাতনেরে মিলিলা ॥ ১৩৫ ॥

ei-mate sevaka-prabhu duṅhe ghara gelā
āra dina jagadānanda sanātanere mililā

SYNONYMS

ei-mate—in this way; *sevaka-prabhu*—the servant and the master; *duṅhe*—both of them; *ghara gelā*—returned to their respective places; *āra dina*—the next day; *jagadānanda*—Jagadānanda; *sanātanere mililā*—met Sanātana Gosvāmī.

TRANSLATION

Thus both servant and master departed for their respective homes. The next day, Jagadānanda Paṇḍita went to meet Sanātana Gosvāmī.

TEXT 136

দুইজন বসি' কৃষ্ণকথা-গোষ্ঠী কৈলা ।
পণ্ডিতেরে সনাতন দুঃখ নিবেদিলা ॥ ১৩৬ ॥

dui-jana vasi' kṛṣṇa-kathā-goṣṭhī kailā
paṇḍitere sanātana duḥkha nivedilā

SYNONYMS

dui-jana vasi'—both of them sitting; *kṛṣṇa-kathā*—topics of Lord Kṛṣṇa; *goṣṭhī*—discussion; *kailā*—did; *paṇḍitere*—unto Jagadānanda Paṇḍita; *sanātana*—Sanātana Gosvāmī; *duḥkha nivedilā*—submitted his unhappiness.

TRANSLATION

When Jagadānanda Paṇḍita and Sanātana Gosvāmī sat together and began to discuss topics about Kṛṣṇa, Sanātana Gosvāmī submitted to Jagadānanda Paṇḍita the cause of his distress.

TEXT 137

"ইহাঁ আইলাঙ প্রভুরে দেখি' দুঃখ খণ্ডাইতে ।
যেবা মনে, তাহা প্রভু না দিলা করিতে ॥ ১৩৭ ॥

"ihāṅ āilāṅ prabhure dekhi' duḥkha khaṇḍāite
yebā mane, tāhā prabhu nā dilā karite

SYNONYMS

ihāṅ—here (to Jagannātha Purī); *āilāṅ*—I have come; *prabhure*—Lord Śrī Caitanya Mahāprabhu; *dekhi'*—by seeing; *duḥkha khaṇḍāite*—to diminish my unhappiness; *yebā mane*—what was in my mind; *tāhā*—that; *prabhu*—Lord Śrī Caitanya Mahāprabhu; *nā dilā karite*—did not allow me to do.

TRANSLATION

"I came here to diminish my unhappiness by seeing Lord Śrī Caitanya Mahāprabhu, but the Lord did not allow me to execute what was in my mind.

TEXT 138

নিষেধিতে প্রভু আলিঙ্গন করেন মোরে ।
মোর কণ্ডুরসা লাগে প্রভুর শরীরে ॥ ১৩৮ ॥

niṣedhite prabhu āliṅgana karena more
mora kaṇḍu-rasā lāge prabhura śarīre

SYNONYMS

niṣedhite—although I forbid; *prabhu*—Śrī Caitanya Mahāprabhu; *āliṅgana*—embracing; *karena*—does; *more*—unto me; *mora kaṇḍu-rasā*—my wet sores; *lāge*—touches; *prabhura*—of Śrī Caitanya Mahāprabhu; *śarīre*—on the body.

TRANSLATION

"Although I forbid Him to do so, Śrī Caitanya Mahāprabhu nevertheless embraces me, and therefore His body becomes smeared with the discharges from my itching sores.

TEXT 139

অপরাধ হয় মোর, নাহিক নিস্তার ।
জগন্নাথেহ না দেখিয়ে,—এ দুঃখ অপার ॥ ১৩৯ ॥

aparādha haya mora, nāhika nistāra
jagannātheha nā dekhiye, —e duḥkha apāra

SYNONYMS

aparādha—offense; *haya*—is; *mora*—mine; *nāhika nistāra*—there is no deliverance; *jagannātheha*—also Lord Jagannātha; *nā dekhiye*—I cannot see; *e*—this; *duḥkha apāra*—great unhappiness.

TRANSLATION

"In this way I am committing offenses at His lotus feet, for which I shall certainly not be delivered. At the same time, I cannot see Lord Jagannātha. This is my great unhappiness.

TEXT 140

হিত-নিমিত্ত আইলাঙ আমি, হৈল বিপরীতে ।
কি করিলে হিত হয় নারি নির্ধারিতে ॥" ১৪০ ॥

hita-nimitta āilāṅa āmi, haila viparīte
ki karile hita haya nāri nirdhārite"

SYNONYMS

hita-nimitta—for benefit; *āilāṅa*—came; *āmi*—I; *haila viparīte*—it has become just the opposite; *ki karile*—how; *hita haya*—there will be benefit; *nāri nirdhārite*—I cannot ascertain.

TRANSLATION

"I came here for my benefit, but now I see that I am getting just the opposite. I do not know, nor can I ascertain, how there will be benefit for me."

TEXT 141

পণ্ডিত কহে,—"তোমার বাসযোগ্য 'বৃন্দাবন' ।
রথযাত্রা দেখি' তাহাঁ করহ গমন ॥ ১৪১ ॥

paṇḍita kahe, —"tomāra vāsa-yogya 'vṛndāvana'
ratha-yātrā dekhi' tāhāṅ karaha gamana

SYNONYMS

paṇḍita kahe—Jagadānanda Paṇḍita said; *tomāra*—your; *vāsa-yogya*—a suitable place for residence; *vṛndāvana*—Vṛndāvana; *ratha-yātrā dekhi'*—after seeing the Ratha-yātrā festival; *tāhāṅ*—there; *karaha gamana*—go.

TRANSLATION

Jagadānanda Paṇḍita said, "The most suitable place for you to reside is Vṛndāvana. After seeing the Ratha-yātrā festival, you can return there.

TEXT 142

প্রভুর আজ্ঞা হঞাছে তোমা' দুই ভায়ে ।
বৃন্দাবনে বৈস, তাহাঁ সর্বসুখ পাইয়ে ॥ ১৪২ ॥

prabhura ājñā hañāche tomā' dui bhāye
vṛndāvane vaisa, tāhāṅ sarva-sukha pāiye

SYNONYMS

prabhura—of Śrī Caitanya Mahāprabhu; *ājñā*—order; *hañāche*—has been; *tomā'*—you; *dui bhāye*—to the two brothers; *vṛndāvane vaisa*—sit down at Vṛndāvana; *tāhāṅ*—there; *sarva-sukha*—all happiness; *pāiye*—you will get.

TRANSLATION

"The Lord has already ordered both of you brothers to situate yourselves in Vṛndāvana. There you will achieve all happiness.

TEXT 143

যে-কার্যে আইলা, প্রভুর দেখিলা চরণ ।
রথে জগন্নাথ দেখি' করহ গমন ॥" ১৪৩ ॥

ye-kārye āilā, prabhura dekhilā caraṇa
rathe jagannātha dekhi' karaha gamana"

SYNONYMS

ye-kārye—for which business; *āilā*—you have come; *prabhura*—of Śrī Caitanya Mahāprabhu; *dekhilā*—you have seen; *caraṇa*—the feet; *rathe*—on the car; *jagannātha*—Lord Jagannātha; *dekhi'*—after seeing; *karaha gamana*—go.

TRANSLATION

"Your purpose in coming has been fulfilled, for you have seen the lotus feet of the Lord. Therefore, after seeing Lord Jagannātha on the Ratha-yātrā car, you can leave."

TEXT 144

সনাতন কহে,—"ভাল কৈলা উপদেশ ।
তাহাঁ যাব, সেই মোর 'প্রভুদত্ত দেশ' ॥" ১৪৪ ॥

sanātana kahe, ——"bhāla kailā upadeśa
tāhāṅ yāba, sei mora 'prabhu-datta deśa'"

SYNONYMS

sanātana kahe—Sanātana Gosvāmī replied; *bhāla kailā upadeśa*—you have given good advice; *tāhāṅ yāba*—I shall go there; *sei*—that; *mora*—my; *prabhu-datta*—given by the Lord; *deśa*—residential country.

TRANSLATION

Sanātana Gosvāmī replied, "You have given me very good advice. I shall certainly go there, for that is the place the Lord has given me for my residence."

PURPORT

The words *prabhu-datta deśa* are very significant. Śrī Caitanya Mahāprabhu's devotional cult teaches one not to sit down in one place but to spread the devotional cult all over the world. The Lord dispatched Sanātana Gosvāmī and Rūpa Gosvāmī to Vṛndāvana to excavate and renovate the holy places and from there establish the cult of *bhakti.* Therefore Vṛndāvana was given to Sanātana Gosvāmī and Rūpa Gosvāmī as their place of residence. Similarly, everyone in the line of Śrī Caitanya Mahāprabhu's devotional cult should accept the words of the spiritual master and thus spread the Kṛṣṇa consciousness movement. They should go everywhere, to all parts of the world, accepting those places as *prabhu-datta deśa,* the places of residence given by the spiritual master or Lord Kṛṣṇa. The spiritual master is the representative of Lord Kṛṣṇa; therefore one who has carried out the orders of the spiritual master is understood to have carried out the orders of Kṛṣṇa or Śrī Caitanya Mahāprabhu. Śrī Caitanya Mahāprabhu wanted to spread the *bhakti* cult all over the world (*pṛthivīte āche yata nagarādi grāma*). Therefore devotees in the line of Kṛṣṇa consciousness must go to different parts of the world and preach, as ordered by the spiritual master. That will satisfy Śrī Caitanya Mahāprabhu.

TEXT 145

এত বলি' দুঁহে নিজ-কার্যে উঠি' গেলা ।
আর দিন মহাপ্রভু মিলিবারে আইলা ॥ ১৪৫ ॥

eta bali' duṅhe nija-kārye uṭhi' gelā
āra dina mahāprabhu milibāre āilā

SYNONYMS

eta bali'—talking like this; *duṅhe*—both Jagadānanda Paṇḍita and Sanātana Gosvāmī; *nija-kārye*—to their respective duties; *uṭhi'*—getting up; *gelā*—went; *āra dina*—the next day; *mahāprabhu*—Śrī Caitanya Mahāprabhu; *milibāre āilā*—came to meet.

TRANSLATION

After talking in this way, Sanātana Gosvāmī and Jagadānanda Paṇḍita returned to their respective duties. The next day, Śrī Caitanya Mahāprabhu went to see Haridāsa and Sanātana Gosvāmī.

TEXT 146

হরিদাস কৈলা প্রভুর চরণ বন্দন ।
হরিদাসে কৈলা প্রভু প্রেম-আলিঙ্গন ॥ ১৪৬ ॥

haridāsa kailā prabhura caraṇa vandana
haridāse kailā prabhu prema-āliṅgana

SYNONYMS

haridāsa—Haridāsa Ṭhākura; *kailā*—did; *prabhura*—of Lord Śrī Caitanya Mahāprabhu; *caraṇa vandana*—worshiping the lotus feet; *haridāse*—unto Haridāsa; *kailā*—did; *prabhu*—Śrī Caitanya Mahāprabhu; *prema-āliṅgana*—embracing in ecstatic love.

TRANSLATION

Haridāsa Ṭhākura offered obeisances to the lotus feet of Śrī Caitanya Mahāprabhu, and the Lord embraced him in ecstatic love.

TEXT 147

দূর হৈতে দণ্ড-পরণাম করে সনাতন ।
প্রভু বোলায় বার বার করিতে আলিঙ্গন ॥ ১৪৭ ॥

dūra haite daṇḍa-paraṇāma kare sanātana
prabhu bolāya bāra bāra karite āliṅgana

SYNONYMS

dūra haite—from a distant place; *daṇḍa-paraṇāma*—offering obeisances and *daṇḍavats; kare*—did; *sanātana*—Sanātana Gosvāmī; *prabhu*—Śrī Caitanya Mahāprabhu; *bolāya*—calls; *bāra bāra*—again and again; *karite āliṅgana*—to embrace.

TRANSLATION

Sanātana Gosvāmī offered his obeisances and daṇḍavats from a distant place, but Śrī Caitanya Mahāprabhu called him again and again to embrace him.

TEXT 148

অপরাধ-ভয়ে তেঁহ মিলিতে না আইল।
মহাপ্রভু মিলিবারে সেই ঠাঞি গেল ॥ ১৪৮ ॥

aparādha-bhaye teṅha milite nā āila
mahāprabhu milibāre sei ṭhāñi gela

SYNONYMS

aparādha-bhaye—out of fear of offenses; *teṅha*—Sanātana Gosvāmī; *milite*—to meet; *nā āila*—did not come forward; *mahāprabhu*—Śrī Caitanya Mahāprabhu; *milibāre*—to meet; *sei ṭhāñi*—to Sanātana Gosvāmī; *gela*—went.

TRANSLATION

Out of fear of committing offenses, Sanātana Gosvāmī did not come forward to meet Śrī Caitanya Mahāprabhu. The Lord, however, went forward to meet him.

TEXT 149

সনাতন ভাগি' পাছে করেন গমন।
বলাৎকারে ধরি, প্রভু কৈলা আলিঙ্গন ॥ ১৪৯ ॥

sanātana bhāgi' pāche karena gamana
balātkāre dhari, prabhu kailā āliṅgana

SYNONYMS

sanātana—Sanātana Gosvāmī; *bhāgi'*—running away; *pāche*—back; *karena gamana*—goes; *balātkāre*—by force; *dhari*—capturing; *prabhu*—Śrī Caitanya Mahāprabhu; *kailā āliṅgana*—embraced.

TRANSLATION

Sanātana Gosvāmī backed away, but Śrī Caitanya Mahāprabhu caught him by force and embraced him.

TEXT 150

দুই জন লঞা প্রভু বসিলা পিণ্ডাতে ।
নির্বিণ্ণ সনাতন লাগিলা কহিতে ॥ ১৫০ ॥

dui jana lañā prabhu vasilā piṇḍāte
nirviṇṇa sanātana lāgilā kahite

SYNONYMS

dui jana lañā—taking the two of them; *prabhu*—Śrī Caitanya Mahāprabhu; *vasilā*—sat down; *piṇḍāte*—on the altar; *nirviṇṇa*—advanced in renunciation; *sanātana*—Sanātana Gosvāmī; *lāgilā kahite*—began to speak.

TRANSLATION

The Lord took them both with Him and sat down in a sacred place. Then Sanātana Gosvāmī, who was advanced in renunciation, began to speak.

TEXT 151

"হিত লাগি' আইনু মুঞি, হৈল বিপরীত ।
সেবাযোগ্য নহি, অপরাধ করোঁ নিতি নিতি ॥ ১৫১॥

"hita lāgi' āinu muñi, haila viparīta
sevā-yogya nahi, aparādha karoṅ niti niti

SYNONYMS

hita lāgi'—for benefit; *āinu muñi*—I came; *haila viparīta*—it has become just the opposite; *sevā-yogya nahi*—I am not fit to render service; *aparādha karoṅ*—I commit offenses; *niti niti*—day after day.

TRANSLATION

"I came here for my benefit," he said, "but I see that I am getting just the opposite. I am unfit to render service. I simply commit offenses day after day.

TEXT 152

সহজে নীচ-জাতি মুঞি, দুষ্ট, 'পাপাশয়' ।
মোরে তুমি ছুঁইলে মোর অপরাধ হয় ॥ ১৫২ ॥

sahaje nīca-jāti muñi, duṣṭa, 'pāpāśaya'
more tumi chuṅile mora aparādha haya

SYNONYMS

sahaje—by nature; *nīca-jāti*—lowborn; *muñi*—I; *duṣṭa*—sinful; *pāpa-āśaya*—reservoir of sinful activities; *more*—me; *tumi chuṅile*—if You touch; *mora*—my; *aparādha haya*—there is offense.

TRANSLATION

"By nature I am lowborn. I am a contaminated reservoir of sinful activities. If You touch me, sir, that will be a great offense on my part.

TEXT 153

তাহাতে আমার অঙ্গে কণ্ডু-রসা-রক্ত চলে।
তোমার অঙ্গে লাগে, তবু স্পর্শহ তুমি বলে॥ ১৫৩॥

tāhāte āmāra aṅge kaṇḍu-rasā-rakta cale
tomāra aṅge lāge, tabu sparśaha tumi bale

SYNONYMS

tāhāte—over and above this; *āmāra*—my; *aṅge*—on the body; *kaṇḍu-rasā*—from wet, itching sores; *rakta*—blood; *cale*—runs; *tomāra aṅge lāge*—touches Your body; *tabu*—still; *sparśaha*—touch; *tumi*—You; *bale*—by force.

TRANSLATION

"Moreover, blood is running from infected itching sores on my body, smearing Your body with moisture, but still You touch me by force.

TEXT 154

বীভৎস স্পর্শিতে না কর ঘৃণা-লেশে।
এই অপরাধে মোর হবে সর্বনাশে॥ ১৫৪॥

bībhatsa sparśite nā kara ghṛṇā-leśe
ei aparādhe mora habe sarva-nāśe

SYNONYMS

bībhatsa—horrible; *sparśite*—to touch; *nā kara*—You do not do; *ghṛṇā-leśe*—even a small bit of aversion; *ei aparādhe*—because of this offense; *mora*—my; *habe*—there will be; *sarva-nāśe*—loss of everything auspicious.

TRANSLATION

"My dear sir, You do not have even a pinch of aversion to touching my body, which is in a horrible condition. Because of this offense, everything auspicious will be vanquished for me.

TEXT 155

তাতে ইহাঁ রহিলে মোর না হয় 'কল্যাণ'।
আজ্ঞা দেহ'—রথ দেখি' যাঙ বৃন্দাবন ॥ ১৫৫ ॥

tāte ihāṅ rahile mora nā haya 'kalyāṇa'
ājñā deha'—ratha dekhi' yāṅa vṛndāvana

SYNONYMS

tāte—because of this; *ihāṅ*—here; *rahile*—if I remain; *mora*—my; *nā*—not; *haya*—there is; *kalyāṇa*—auspiciousness; *ājñā deha'*—kindly give the order; *ratha dekhi'*—after witnessing the Ratha-yātrā festival; *yāṅa vṛndāvana*—I may return to Vṛndāvana.

TRANSLATION

"Therefore I see that I will get nothing auspicious by staying here. Kindly give me orders allowing me to return to Vṛndāvana after the Ratha-yātrā festival.

TEXT 156

জগদানন্দ-পণ্ডিতে আমি যুক্তি পুছিল।
বৃন্দাবন যাইতে তেঁহ উপদেশ দিল ॥" ১৫৬ ॥

jagadānanda-paṇḍite āmi yukti puchila
vṛndāvana yāite teṅha upadeśa dila"

SYNONYMS

jagadānanda-paṇḍite—from Jagadānanda Paṇḍita; *āmi*—I; *yukti*—advice; *puchila*—inquired; *vṛndāvana yāite*—to go to Vṛndāvana; *teṅha*—he; *upadeśa dila*—has given instruction.

TRANSLATION

"I have consulted Jagadānanda Paṇḍita for his opinion, and he has also advised me to return to Vṛndāvana."

TEXT 157

এত শুনি' মহাপ্রভু সরোষ-অন্তরে।
জগদানন্দে ক্রুদ্ধ হঞা করে তিরস্কারে ॥ ১৫৭ ॥

eta śuni' mahāprabhu saroṣa-antare
jagadānande kruddha hañā kare tiraṣkāre

SYNONYMS

eta śuni'—hearing this; *mahāprabhu*—Śrī Caitanya Mahāprabhu; *sa-roṣa-antare*—in an angry mood; *jagadānande*—at Jagadānanda Paṇḍita; *kruddha hañā*—becoming very angry; *kare tiraḥ-kāre*—chastises.

TRANSLATION

Hearing this, Śrī Caitanya Mahāprabhu, in an angry mood, began to chastise Jagadānanda Paṇḍita.

TEXT 158

"কালিকার বটুয়া জগা ঐছে গর্বী হৈল।
তোমা-সবারেহ উপদেশ করিতে লাগিল ॥ ১৫৮ ॥

"kālikāra baṭuyā jagā aiche garvī haila
tomā-sabāreha upadeśa karite lāgila

SYNONYMS

kālikāra—new; *baṭuyā*—boy; *jagā*—Jagadānanda Paṇḍita; *aiche*—so; *garvī haila*—has become proud; *tomā-sabāreha*—persons like you; *upadeśa karite*—to advise; *lāgila*—has begun.

TRANSLATION

"Jagā [Jagadānanda Paṇḍita] is only a new boy, but he has become so proud that he thinks himself competent to advise a person like you.

TEXT 159

ব্যবহারে-পরমার্থে তুমি—তার গুরু-তুল্য।
তোমারে উপদেশে, না জানে আপন-মূল্য ॥ ১৫৯ ॥

vyavahāre-paramārthe tumi—tāra guru-tulya
tomāre upadeśe, nā jāne āpana-mūlya

SYNONYMS

vyavahāre—in ordinary dealings; *parama-arthe*—in spiritual matters; *tumi*—you; *tāra*—of him; *guru-tulya*—like a spiritual master; *tomāre*—you; *upadeśe*—he advises; *nā jāne*—does not know; *āpana-mūlya*—his value.

TRANSLATION

"In affairs of spiritual advancement and even in ordinary dealings, you are on the level of his spiritual master. Yet not knowing his own value, he dares to advise you.

TEXT 160

আমার উপদেষ্টা তুমি—প্রামাণিক আর্য ।
তোমারেহ উপদেশে—বালকা করে ঐছে কার্য ॥১৬০॥

āmāra upadeṣṭā tumi——prāmāṇika ārya
tomāreha upadeśe——bālakā kare aiche kārya

SYNONYMS

āmāra—My; *upadeṣṭā*—adviser; *tumi*—you; *prāmāṇika ārya*—authorized person; *tomāreha*—even you; *upadeśe*—he advises; *bālakā*—boy; *kare*—does; *aiche*—such; *kārya*—business.

TRANSLATION

"My dear Sanātana, you are on the level of My adviser, for you are an authorized person. But Jagā wants to advise you. This is but the impudence of a naughty boy."

TEXT 161

শুনি' সনাতন পায়ে ধরি' প্রভুরে কহিল ।
"জগদানন্দের সৌভাগ্য আজি সে জানিল ॥ ১৬১ ॥

śuni' sanātana pāye dhari' prabhure kahila
"jagadānandera saubhāgya āji se jānila

SYNONYMS

śuni'—hearing; *sanātana*—Sanātana Gosvāmī; *pāye dhari'*—capturing the feet; *prabhure kahila*—began to say to Śrī Caitanya Mahāprabhu; *jagadānandera*—of Jagadānanda Paṇḍita; *saubhāgya*—fortune; *āji*—now; *se*—that; *jānila*—I understand.

TRANSLATION

When Śrī Caitanya Mahāprabhu was thus chastising Jagadānanda Paṇḍita, Sanātana Gosvāmī fell at the Lord's feet and said, "I can now understand the fortunate position of Jagadānanda.

TEXT 162

আপনার 'অসৌভাগ্য' আজি হৈল জ্ঞান ।
জগতে নাহি জগদানন্দ-সম ভাগ্যবান্ ॥ ১৬২ ॥

āpanāra 'asaubhāgya' āji haila jñāna
jagate nāhi jagadānanda-sama bhāgyavān

SYNONYMS

āpanāra—my personal; *asaubhāgya*—misfortune; *āji*—today; *haila jñāna*—I can understand; *jagate*—within this world; *nāhi*—there is not; *jagadānanda-sama*—like Jagadānanda Paṇḍita; *bhāgyavān*—fortunate person.

TRANSLATION

"I can also understand my misfortune. No one in this world is as fortunate as Jagadānanda.

TEXT 163

জগদানন্দে পিয়াও আত্মীয়তা-সুধারস ।
মোরে পিয়াও গৌরবস্তুতি-নিম্ব-নিশিন্দা-রস ॥১৬৩॥

jagadānande piyāo ātmīyatā-sudhā-rasa
more piyāo gaurava-stuti-nimba-niśindā-rasa

SYNONYMS

jagadānande—unto Jagadānanda Paṇḍita; *piyāo*—You cause to drink; *ātmīyatā-sudhā-rasa*—the nectar of affectionate relations; *more*—me; *piyāo*—You cause to drink; *gaurava-stuti*—honorable prayers; *nimba-niśindā-rasa*—the juice of *nimba* fruit and *niśindā.*

TRANSLATION

"Sir, You are making Jagadānanda drink the nectar of affectionate relationships, whereas by offering me honorable prayers, You are making me drink the bitter juice of nimba and niśindā.

TEXT 164

আজিহ নহিল মোরে আত্মীয়তা-জ্ঞান !
মোর অভাগ্য, তুমি—স্বতন্ত্র ভগবান্!” ১৬৪ ॥

ājiha nahila more ātmīyatā-jñāna!
mora abhāgya, tumi——svatantra bhagavān!"

SYNONYMS

ājiha—even until now; *nahila*—there has not been; *more*—unto me; *ātmīyatā-jñāna*—feeling as one of Your relations; *mora abhāgya*—my misfortune; *tumi*—You; *svatantra bhagavān*—the independent Personality of Godhead.

TRANSLATION

"It is my misfortune that You have not accepted me as one of Your intimate relations. But You are the completely independent Supreme Personality of Godhead."

TEXT 165

শুনি' মহাপ্রভু কিছু লজ্জিত হৈলা মনে ।
তাঁরে সন্তোষিতে কিছু বলেন বচনে ॥ ১৬৫ ॥

śuni' mahāprabhu kichu lajjita hailā mane
tāṅre santoṣite kichu balena vacane

SYNONYMS

śuni'—hearing; *mahāprabhu*—Śrī Caitanya Mahāprabhu; *kichu*—somewhat; *lajjita*—ashamed; *hailā*—became; *mane*—within the mind; *tāṅre*—him; *santoṣite*—to satisfy; *kichu*—some; *balena*—said; *vacane*—words.

TRANSLATION

Hearing this, Śrī Caitanya Mahāprabhu was somewhat ashamed. Just to satisfy Sanātana Gosvāmī, He spoke the following words.

TEXT 166

“জগদানন্দ প্রিয় আমার নহে তোমা হৈতে ।
মর্যাদা-লঙ্ঘন আমি না পারোঁ সহিতে ॥ ১৬৬ ॥

"jagadānanda priya āmāra nahe tomā haite
maryādā-laṅghana āmi nā pāroṅ sahite

SYNONYMS

jagadānanda—Jagadānanda Paṇḍita; *priya*—more dear; *āmāra*—to Me; *nahe*—is not; *tomā haite*—than you; *maryādā-laṅghana*—transgressing the etiquette; *āmi*—I; *nā*—not; *pāroṅ*—can; *sahite*—tolerate.

TRANSLATION

"My dear Sanātana, please do not think that Jagadānanda is more dear to Me than you. However, I cannot tolerate transgressions of the standard etiquette.

TEXT 167

কাহাঁ তুমি – প্রামাণিক, শাস্ত্রে প্রবীণ !
কাহাঁ জগা—কালিকার বটুয়া নবীন ! ১৬৭ ॥

kāhāṅ tumi——prāmāṇika, śāstre pravīṇa!
kāhāṅ jagā——kālikāra baṭuyā navīna!

SYNONYMS

kāhāṅ—where; *tumi*—you; *prāmāṇika*—authority; *śāstre pravīṇa*—experienced in the learning of the *śāstras*; *kāhāṅ*—where; *jagā*—Jagā; *kālikāra*—recent; *baṭuyā*—youth; *navīna*—new.

TRANSLATION

"You are an experienced authority in the śāstras, whereas Jagā is just a young boy.

TEXT 168

আমাকেহ বুঝাইতে তুমি ধর শক্তি ।
কত ঠাঞি বুঝাঞাছ ব্যবহার-ভক্তি ॥ ১৬৮ ॥

āmākeha bujhāite tumi dhara śakti
kata ṭhāñi bujhāñācha vyavahāra-bhakti

SYNONYMS

āmākeha—even Me; *bujhāite*—to convince; *tumi*—you; *dhara*—have; *śakti*—power; *kata ṭhāñi*—in how many places; *bujhāñācha*—you have convinced; *vyavahāra-bhakti*—ordinary behavior as well as devotional service.

TRANSLATION

"You have the power to convince even Me. In many places you have already convinced Me about ordinary behavior and devotional service.

TEXT 169

তোমারে উপদেশ করে, না যায় সহন ।
অতএব তারে আমি করিয়ে ভৎর্সন ॥ ১৬৯ ॥

tomāre upadeśa kare, nā yāya sahana
ataeva tāre āmi kariye bhartsana

SYNONYMS

tomāre—you; *upadeśa kare*—advises; *nā yāya sahana*—I cannot tolerate; *ataeva*—therefore; *tāre*—unto him; *āmi*—I; *kariye*—do; *bhartsana*—chastisement.

TRANSLATION

"Jagā's advising you is intolerable for Me. Therefore I am chastising him.

TEXT 170

বহিরঙ্গ-জ্ঞানে তোমারে না করি স্তবন ।
তোমার গুণে স্তুতি করায় যৈছে তোমার গুণ ॥১৭০॥

bahiraṅga-jñāne tomāre nā kari stavana
tomāra guṇe stuti karāya yaiche tomāra guṇa

SYNONYMS

bahiraṅga-jñāne—thinking outside My intimate relationship; *tomāre*—unto you; *nā kari*—I do not; *stavana*—offer praise; *tomāra*—your; *guṇe*—by qualifications; *stuti karāya*—one is induced to offer prayers; *yaiche*—as; *tomāra*—your; *guṇa*—attributes.

TRANSLATION

"I offer you praise not because I think of you as being outside an intimate relationship with Me but because you are actually so qualified that one is forced to praise your qualities.

TEXT 171

যদ্যপি কাহার 'মমতা' বহুজনে হয় ।
প্রীতি-স্বভাবে কাহাতে কোন ভাবোদয় ॥ ১৭১ ॥

yadyapi kāhāra 'mamatā' bahu-jane haya
prīti-svabhāve kāhāte kona bhāvodaya

SYNONYMS

yadyapi—although; *kāhāra*—of someone; *mamatā*—affection; *bahu-jane*—unto many persons; *haya*—there is; *prīti-svabhāve*—according to one's affection; *kāhāte*—in someone; *kona*—some; *bhāva-udaya*—awakening of ecstatic love.

TRANSLATION

"Although one has affection for many persons, different types of ecstatic love awaken according to the nature of one's personal relationships.

TEXT 172

তোমার দেহ তুমি কর বীভৎস-জ্ঞান ।
তোমার দেহ আমারে লাগে অমৃত-সমান ॥ ১৭২ ॥

tomāra deha tumi kara bībhatsa-jñāna
tomāra deha āmāre lāge amṛta-samāna

SYNONYMS

tomāra deha—your body; *tumi*—you; *kara bībhatsa-jñāna*—consider horrible; *tomāra deha*—your body; *āmāre*—unto Me; *lāge*—appears; *amṛta-samāna*—as if made of nectar.

TRANSLATION

"You consider your body dangerous and awful, but I think that your body is like nectar.

TEXT 173

অপ্রাকৃত-দেহ তোমার 'প্রাকৃত' কভু নয় ।
তথাপি তোমার তাতে প্রাকৃত-বুদ্ধি হয় ॥ ১৭৩ ॥

aprākṛta-deha tomāra 'prākṛta' kabhu naya
tathāpi tomāra tāte prākṛta-buddhi haya

SYNONYMS

aprākṛta—transcendental; *deha*—body; *tomāra*—your; *prākṛta*—material; *kabhu naya*—is never; *tathāpi*—still; *tomāra*—your; *tāte*—in that; *prākṛta-buddhi*—conception as material; *haya*—is.

TRANSLATION

"Actually your body is transcendental, never material. You are thinking of it, however, in terms of a material conception.

PURPORT

Śrīla Bhaktisiddhānta Sarasvatī Ṭhākura gives his opinion about how a person completely engaged in the service of the Lord transforms his body from material to transcendental. He says: "A pure devotee engaged in the service of Lord Kṛṣṇa has no desire for his personal sense gratification, and thus he never accepts anything for that purpose. He desires only the happiness of the Supreme Personality of Godhead, Kṛṣṇa, and because of his ecstatic love for Kṛṣṇa, he acts in various ways. *Karmīs* think that the material body is an instrument for material enjoyment, and that is why they work extremely hard. A devotee, however, has no such desires. A devotee always engages wholeheartedly in the service of the Lord, forgetting about bodily conceptions and bodily activities. The body of a *karmī* is called material because the *karmī,* being too absorbed in material activities, is always eager to enjoy material facilities, but the body of a devotee who tries his best to work very hard for the satisfaction of Kṛṣṇa by fully engaging in the Lord's service must be accepted as transcendental. Whereas *karmīs* are interested only in the personal satisfaction of their senses, devotees work for the satisfaction of the Supreme Lord. Therefore one who cannot distinguish between devotion and ordinary *karma* may mistakenly consider the body of a pure devotee material. One who knows does not commit such a mistake. Nondevotees who consider devotional activities and ordinary material activities to be on the same level are offenders to the chanting of the transcendental holy name of the Lord. A pure devotee knows that a devotee's body, being always transcendental, is just suitable for rendering service to the Lord.

A devotee on the topmost platform of devotional service always humbly thinks that he is not rendering any devotional service. He thinks that he is poor in devotional service and that his body is material. On the other hand, those known as the *sahajiyās* foolishly think that their material bodies are transcendental. Because of this, they are always bereft of the association of pure devotees, and thus they cannot behave like Vaiṣṇavas. Observing the defects of the *sahajiyās,* Śrīla Bhaktivinoda Ṭhākura has sung as follows in his book *Kalyāṇa-kalpa-taru:*

āmi ta' vaiṣṇava, e-buddhi ha-ile,
amānī nā haba āmi
pratiṣṭhāśā āsi', hṛdaya dūṣibe,
ha-iba niraya-gāmī
nije śreṣṭha jāni', ucchiṣṭādi-dāne,
habe abhimāna bhāra
tāi śiṣya tava, thākiyā sarvadā,
nā la-iba pūjā kāra

"If I think I am a Vaiṣṇava, I shall look forward to receiving respect from others. And if the desire for fame and reputation pollute my heart, certainly I shall go to hell. By giving others the remnants of my food, I shall consider myself superior and shall be burdened with the weight of false pride. Therefore, always remaining your surrendered disciple, I shall not accept worship from anyone else." Śrīla Kṛṣṇadāsa Kavirāja Gosvāmī has written (*Antya-līlā* 20.28):

premera svabhāva——yāhāṅ premera sambandha
sei māne, ——'kṛṣṇe mora nāhi prema-gandha'

"Wherever there is a relationship of love of Godhead, the natural symptoms are that the devotee does not think himself a devotee, but always thinks that he has not even a drop of love for Kṛṣṇa."

TEXT 174

'প্রাকৃত' হৈলেহ তোমার বপু নারি উপেক্ষিতে ।
ভদ্রাভদ্র-বস্তুজ্ঞান নাহিক 'প্রাকৃতে' ॥ ১৭৪ ॥

'prākṛta' haile ha tomāra vapu nāri upekṣite
bhadrābhadra-vastu-jñāna nāhika 'prākṛte'

SYNONYMS

prākṛta—material; *haile ha*—even if it were; *tomāra*—your; *vapu*—body; *nāri*—I cannot; *upekṣite*—neglect; *bhadra-abhadra*—good and bad; *vastu-jñāna*—appreciation of things; *nāhika*—there is not; *prākṛte*—in the material world.

TRANSLATION

"Even if your body were material, I still could not neglect it, for the material body should be considered neither good nor bad.

PURPORT

Śrī Caitanya Mahāprabhu told Sanātana Gosvāmī, "Since you are a Vaiṣṇava, your body is spiritual, not material. Therefore you should not consider this body to be subjected to superior or inferior qualities. Moreover, I am a *sannyāsī*. Therefore even if your body were material, a *sannyāsī* should see no distinction between a good body and a bad body.

TEXT 175

কিং ভদ্রং কিমভদ্রং বা দ্বৈতস্যাবস্তুনঃ কিয়ৎ ।
বাচোদিতং তদনৃতং মনসা ধ্যাতমেব চ ॥ ১৭৫ ॥

kiṁ bhadraṁ kim abhadraṁ vā
dvaitasyāvastunaḥ kiyat

vācoditaṁ tad anṛtaṁ
manasā dhyātam eva ca

SYNONYMS

kim—what; *bhadram*—good; *kim*—what; *abhadram*—bad; *vā*—or; *dvaitasya*—of this material world; *avastunaḥ*—that which has temporary existence; *kiyat*—how much; *vācā*—by words; *uditam*—vibrated; *tat*—that; *anṛtam*—without permanent existence; *manasā*—by the mind; *dhyātam*—conceived; *eva*—certainly; *ca*—and.

TRANSLATION

" 'Anything not conceived in relationship to Kṛṣṇa should be understood to be illusion [māyā]. None of the illusions uttered by words or conceived in the mind are factual. Because illusion is not factual, there is no distinction between what we think is good and what we think is bad. When we speak of the Absolute Truth, such speculations do not apply.'

PURPORT

This is a quotation from *Śrīmad-Bhāgavatam* (11.28.4).

TEXT 176

'দ্বৈতে' ভদ্রাভদ্র-জ্ঞান, সব—'মনোধর্ম' ।
'এই ভাল, এই মন্দ',—এই সব 'ভ্রম' ॥ ১৭৬ ॥

'dvaite' bhadrābhadra-jñāna, saba——'manodharma'
'ei bhāla, ei manda', ——ei saba 'bhrama'

SYNONYMS

dvaite—in the material world; *bhadra-abhadra-jñāna*—understanding of good and bad; *saba*—all; *manaḥ-dharma*—speculative mental creations; *ei bhāla*—this is good; *ei manda*—this is bad; *ei*—this; *saba*—all; *bhrama*—mistake.

TRANSLATION

"In the material world, conceptions of good and bad are all mental speculations. Therefore, saying, 'This is good, and this is bad,' is all a mistake.

PURPORT

Kṛṣṇa, the Supreme Personality of Godhead, is the Absolute Truth, ever existing with different varieties of energies. When one is absorbed in the illusory energy of Kṛṣṇa and cannot understand Kṛṣṇa, one cannot ascertain what is good and bad for him. Conceptions of good and bad are all imaginations or mental speculations. When one forgets that he is an eternal servant of Kṛṣṇa, he wants to enjoy the material world through different plans. At that time he distinguishes between material plans that are good and those that are bad. Actually, however, they are all false.

TEXT 177

বিদ্যাবিনয়সম্পন্নে ব্রাহ্মণে গবি হস্তিনি ।
শুনি চৈব শ্বপাকে চ পণ্ডিতাঃ সমদর্শিনঃ ॥ ১৭৭ ॥

vidyā-vinaya-sampanne
brāhmaṇe gavi hastini
śuni caiva śvapāke ca
paṇḍitāḥ sama-darśinaḥ

SYNONYMS

vidyā—knowledge; *vinaya*—gentleness; *sampanne*—endowed with; *brāhmaṇe*—unto a *brāhmaṇa*; *gavi*—unto a cow; *hastini*—unto an elephant; *śuni*—unto a dog; *ca*—and; *eva*—also; *śva-pāke*—unto a dog-eater; *ca*—also; *paṇḍitāḥ*—those who are actually learned in spiritual understanding; *sama-darśinaḥ*—equipoised.

TRANSLATION

.'' 'The humble sage, by virtue of true knowledge, sees with equal vision a learned and gentle brāhmaṇa, a cow, an elephant, a dog and a dog-eater.'

PURPORT

This is a quotation from *Bhagavad-gītā* (5.18).

TEXT 178

জ্ঞানবিজ্ঞানতৃপ্তাত্মা কূটস্থো বিজিতেন্দ্রিয়ঃ ।
যুক্ত ইত্যুচ্যতে যোগী সমলোষ্ট্রাশ্মকাঞ্চনঃ ॥ ১৭৮ ॥

jñāna-vijñāna-tṛptātmā
kūṭastho vijitendriyaḥ
yukta ity ucyate yogī
sama-loṣṭrāśma-kāñcanaḥ

SYNONYMS

jñāna—by acquired knowledge; *vijñāna*—realized knowledge; *tṛpta*—satisfied; *ātmā*—living entity; *kūṭa-sthaḥ*—fixed in his constitutional position; *vijita*—controlled; *indriyaḥ*—whose senses; *yuktaḥ*—in touch with the Supreme; *iti*—thus; *ucyate*—is said; *yogī*—a *yogī*; *sama*—equal; *loṣṭra*—pebbles; *aśma*—stone; *kāñcanaḥ*—gold.

TRANSLATION

" 'One who is fully satisfied in knowledge obtained and practically applied in life, who is always determined and fixed in his spiritual position, who completely controls his senses, and who sees pebbles, stone and gold on the same level, is understood to be a perfect yogī.'

PURPORT

This is also a quotation from *Bhagavad-gītā* (6.8).

TEXT 179

আমি ত'—সন্ন্যাসী, আমার 'সম-দৃষ্টি' ধর্ম ।
চন্দন-পঙ্কেতে আমার জ্ঞান হয় 'সম' ॥ ১৭৯ ॥

āmi ta'——sannyāsī, āmāra 'sama-dṛṣṭi' dharma
candana-paṅkete āmāra jñāna haya 'sama'

SYNONYMS

āmi—I; *ta'*—certainly; *sannyāsī*—in the renounced order of life; *āmāra*—My; *sama-dṛṣṭi*—seeing everything on the same platform; *dharma*—duty; *candana-paṅkete*—between sandalwood pulp and mud; *āmāra*—My; *jñāna*—knowledge; *haya*—is; *sama*—same.

TRANSLATION

"Since I am in the renounced order, My duty is to make no distinctions but instead be equipoised. My knowledge must be equally disposed toward sandalwood pulp and dirty mud.

PURPORT

It is the duty of a *sannyāsī*, a person in the renounced order, to be always equipoised, and that is also the duty of a learned man and a Vaiṣṇava. A Vaiṣṇava, a *sannyāsī* or a learned person has no conception of the material world; in other words, he has no conception of anything materially important. He has no desire to use sandalwood pulp for sense gratification, nor does sense gratification make him hate mud. Acceptance or rejection of material things is not the concern of a *sannyāsī*, a Vaiṣṇava or a learned person. An advanced devotee has no desire to enjoy or reject anything. His only duty is to accept whatever is favorable for the advancement of Kṛṣṇa consciousness. A Vaiṣṇava should be indifferent to material enjoyment and renunciation and should always hanker for the spiritual life of rendering service to the Lord.

TEXT 180

এই লাগি' তোমা ত্যাগ করিতে না যুয়ায় ।
ঘৃণা-বুদ্ধি করি যদি, নিজ-ধর্ম যায় ॥" ১৮০ ॥

ei lāgi' tomā tyāga karite nā yuyāya
ghṛṇā-buddhi kari yadi, nija-dharma yāya"

SYNONYMS

ei lāgi'—for this reason; *tomā*—you; *tyāga karite*—to reject; *nā yuyāya*—is not befitting; *ghṛṇā-buddhi kari*—I regard with hatred; *yadi*—if; *nija-dharma yāya*—I deviate from My duty.

TRANSLATION

"For this reason, I cannot reject you. If I hated you, I would deviate from My occupational duty."

TEXT 181

হরিদাস কহে,—"প্রভু, যে কহিলা তুমি ।
এই 'বাহ্য প্রতারণা' নাহি মানি আমি ॥ ১৮১ ॥

haridāsa kahe, —"prabhu, ye kahilā tumi
ei 'bāhya pratāraṇā' nāhi māni āmi

SYNONYMS

haridāsa kahe—Haridāsa said; *prabhu*—my Lord; *ye*—what; *kahilā*—have spoken; *tumi*—You; *ei*—this; *bāhya pratāraṇā*—external formality; *nāhi māni āmi*—I do not accept.

TRANSLATION

Haridāsa said, "My dear Lord, what You have spoken deals with external formalities. I do not accept it.

TEXT 182

আমা-সব অধমে যে করিয়াছ অঙ্গীকার ।
দীনদয়ালু-গুণ তোমার তাহাতে প্রচার ॥" ১৮২ ॥

āmā-saba adhame ye kariyācha aṅgīkāra
dīna-dayālu-guṇa tomāra tāhāte pracāra"

SYNONYMS

āmā-saba—all of us; *adhame*—most fallen; *ye*—that; *kariyācha*—You have done; *aṅgīkāra*—acceptance; *dīna-dayālu*—merciful unto the fallen souls; *guṇa*—attribute; *tomāra*—of You; *tāhāte*—in that; *pracāra*—proclaiming.

TRANSLATION

"My Lord, we are all fallen, but You have accepted us due to Your attribute of being merciful to the fallen. This is well known all over the world."

TEXT 183

প্রভু হাসি' কহে,—"শুন, হরিদাস, সনাতন ।
তত্ত্বতঃ কহি তোমা-বিষয়ে যৈছে মোর মন ॥ ১৮৩ ॥

prabhu hāsi' kahe, —"śuna, haridāsa, sanātana
tattvataḥ kahi tomā-viṣaye yaiche mora mana

SYNONYMS

prabhu—Śrī Caitanya Mahāprabhu; *hāsi'*—smiling; *kahe*—says; *śuna*—hear; *haridāsa*—My dear Haridāsa; *sanātana*—My dear Sanātana; *tattvataḥ*—truly; *kahi*—I am speaking; *tomā-viṣaye*—about you; *yaiche*—as; *mora mana*—My mind.

TRANSLATION

Lord Caitanya smiled and said, "Listen, Haridāsa and Sanātana. Now I am speaking the truth about how My mind is attached to you.

TEXT 184

তোমারে 'লাল্য', আপনাকে 'লালক' অভিমান ।
লালকের লাল্যে নহে দোষ-পরিজ্ঞান ॥ ১৮৪ ॥

tomāre 'lālya', āpanāke 'lālaka' abhimāna
lālakera lālye nahe doṣa-parijñāna

SYNONYMS

tomāre—unto you; *lālya*—maintained; *āpanāke*—unto Me; *lālaka*—the maintainer; *abhimāna*—conception; *lālakera*—of the maintainer; *lālye*—unto the maintained; *nahe*—not; *doṣa*—fault; *parijñāna*—understanding.

TRANSLATION

"My dear Haridāsa and Sanātana, I think of you as My little boys, to be maintained by Me. The maintainer never takes seriously any faults of the maintained.

PURPORT

When a father maintains a child and the child is maintained by the father, the father never takes seriously the faults of the child. Even if they actually are faults, the father does not mind them.

TEXT 185

আপনারে হয় মোর অমান্য-সমান ।
তোমা-সবারে করোঁ মুঞি বালক-অভিমান ॥১৮৫ ॥

āpanāre haya mora amānya-samāna
tomā-sabāre karoṅ muñi bālaka-abhimāna

SYNONYMS

āpanāre—unto Myself; *haya*—there is; *mora*—My; *amānya*—not deserving respect; *samāna*—like; *tomā-sabāre*—unto all of you; *karoṅ*—do; *muñi*—I; *bālaka-abhimāna*—considering My sons.

TRANSLATION

"I always think of Myself as deserving no respect, but because of affection I always consider you to be like My little children.

TEXT 186

মাতার যৈছে বালকের 'অমেধ্য' লাগে গায় ।
ঘৃণা নাহি জন্মে, আর মহাসুখ পায় ॥ ১৮৬ ॥

mātāra yaiche bālakera 'amedhya' lāge gāya
ghṛṇā nāhi janme, āra mahā-sukha pāya

SYNONYMS

mātāra—of the mother; *yaiche*—as; *bālakera*—of the child; *amedhya*—stool and urine; *lāge gāya*—touches the body; *ghṛṇā*—hatred; *nāhi janme*—does not arise; *āra*—more; *mahā-sukha*—great pleasure; *pāya*—gets.

TRANSLATION

"When a child passes stool and urine that touch the body of the mother, the mother never hates the child. On the contrary, she takes much pleasure in cleansing him.

TEXT 187

'লাল্যামেধ্য' লালকের চন্দন-সম ভায়।
সনাতনের ক্লেদে আমার ঘৃণা না উপজায়॥" ১৮৭ ॥

'lālyāmedhya' lālakera candana-sama bhāya
sanātanera klede āmāra ghṛṇā nā upajāya"

SYNONYMS

lālya—of the maintained child; *amedhya*—stool and urine; *lālakera*—of the maintainer; *candana-sama*—like sandalwood pulp; *bhāya*—appears; *sanātanera*—of Sanātana Gosvāmī; *klede*—unto the moisture of the sores; *āmāra*—My; *ghṛṇā*—hatred; *nā*—not; *upajāya*—arises.

TRANSLATION

"The stool and urine of the maintained child appear like sandalwood pulp to the mother. Similarly, when the foul moisture oozing from the itches of Sanātana touches My body, I have no hatred for him."

TEXT 188

হরিদাস কহে,—"তুমি ঈশ্বর দয়াময়।
তোমার গম্ভীর হৃদয় বুঝন না যায়॥ ১৮৮ ॥

haridāsa kahe, —"tumi īśvara dayā-maya
tomāra gambhīra hṛdaya bujhana nā yāya

SYNONYMS

haridāsa kahe—Haridāsa Ṭhākura said; *tumi*—You; *īśvara*—the Supreme Personality of Godhead; *dayā-maya*—merciful; *tomāra*—Your; *gambhīra*—deep; *hṛdaya*—heart; *bujhana nā yāya*—cannot be understood.

TRANSLATION

Haridāsa Ṭhākura said, "My dear sir, You are the Supreme Personality of Godhead and are most merciful toward us. No one can understand what is within Your deeply affectionate heart.

TEXT 189

বাসুদেব–গলৎকুষ্ঠী, তাতে অঙ্গ—কীড়াময়।
তারে আলিঙ্গন কৈলা হঞা সদয় ॥ ১৮৯ ॥

vāsudeva——galat-kuṣṭhī, tāte aṅga——kīḍā-maya
tāre āliṅgana kailā hañā sadaya

SYNONYMS

vāsudeva—Vāsudeva; *galat-kuṣṭhī*—suffering from leprosy; *tāte*—over and above that; *aṅga*—the body; *kīḍā-maya*—full of worms; *tāre*—him; *āliṅgana*—embracing; *kailā*—You did; *hañā sa-daya*—being merciful.

TRANSLATION

"You embraced the leper Vāsudeva, whose body was fully infected by worms. You are so kind that in spite of his condition You embraced him.

TEXT 190

আলিঙ্গিয়া কৈলা তার কন্দর্প-সম অঙ্গ।
বুঝিতে না পারি তোমার কৃপার তরঙ্গ ॥" ১৯০ ॥

āliṅgiyā kailā tāra kandarpa-sama aṅga
bujhite nā pāri tomāra kṛpāra taraṅga"

SYNONYMS

āliṅgiyā—by embracing; *kailā*—You made; *tāra*—his; *kandarpa-sama*—as beautiful as Cupid; *aṅga*—body; *bujhite nā pāri*—we cannot understand; *tomāra*—Your; *kṛpāra taraṅga*—waves of mercy.

TRANSLATION

"By embracing him You made his body as beautiful as that of Cupid. We cannot understand the waves of Your mercy."

TEXT 191

প্রভু কহে,—"বৈষ্ণব-দেহ 'প্রাকৃত' কভু নয়।
'অপ্রাকৃত' দেহ ভক্তের 'চিদানন্দময়' ॥ ১৯১ ॥

prabhu kahe, ——"vaiṣṇava-deha 'prākṛta' kabhu naya
'aprākṛta' deha bhaktera 'cid-ānanda-maya'

SYNONYMS

prabhu kahe—Śrī Caitanya Mahāprabhu said; *vaiṣṇava deha*—the body of a Vaiṣṇava; *prākṛta*—material; *kabhu naya*—is never; *aprākṛta*—transcendental; *deha*—body; *bhaktera*—of a devotee; *cit-ānanda-maya*—full of transcendental bliss.

TRANSLATION

Śrī Caitanya Mahāprabhu said, "The body of a devotee is never material. It is considered to be transcendental, full of spiritual bliss.

PURPORT

Śrī Caitanya Mahāprabhu is trying to convince Haridāsa Ṭhākura and Sanātana Gosvāmī that a devotee whose life is dedicated to the service of the Lord is never in the material conception. Because he always engages in the service of the Lord, his body is transcendental and full of spiritual bliss. His body should never be considered material, just as the body of the Deity worshiped in the temple is never considered to be made of stone or wood. Factually, the Deity is directly the Supreme Personality of Godhead, without a doubt. The injunctions of the *Padma Purāṇa* therefore state: *arcye viṣṇau śilādhīr guruṣu nara-matir vaiṣṇave jāti-buddhiḥ. . .yasya vā nārakī saḥ.* The Deity worshiped in the temple is never stone or wood. Similarly, the body of a Vaiṣṇava fully dedicated to the service of the Lord is never considered to belong to the material modes of nature.

TEXT 192

দীক্ষাকালে ভক্ত করে আত্মসমর্পণ।
সেইকালে কৃষ্ণ তারে করে আত্মসম ॥ ১৯২ ॥

dīkṣā-kāle bhakta kare ātma-samarpaṇa
sei-kāle kṛṣṇa tāre kare ātma-sama

SYNONYMS

dīkṣā-kāle—at the time of initiation; *bhakta*—the devotee; *kare*—does; *ātma*—of himself; *samarpaṇa*—full dedication; *sei-kāle*—at that time; *kṛṣṇa*—Lord Kṛṣṇa; *tāre*—him; *kare*—makes; *ātma-sama*—as spiritual as Himself.

TRANSLATION

"At the time of initiation, when a devotee fully surrenders unto the service of the Lord, Kṛṣṇa accepts him to be as good as Himself.

TEXT 193

সেই দেহ করে তার চিদানন্দময় ।
অপ্রাকৃত-দেহে তাঁর চরণ ভজয় ॥ ১৯৩ ॥

sei deha kare tāra cid-ānanda-maya
aprākṛta-dehe tāṅra caraṇa bhajaya

SYNONYMS

sei deha—that body; *kare*—makes; *tāra*—his; *cit-ānanda-maya*—full of transcendental bliss; *aprākṛta-dehe*—in that transcendental body; *tāṅra*—His; *caraṇa*—feet; *bhajaya*—worships.

TRANSLATION

"When the devotee's body is thus transformed into spiritual existence, the devotee, in that transcendental body, renders service to the lotus feet of the Lord.

TEXT 194

মর্ত্যো যদা ত্যক্তসমস্তকর্মা
নিবেদিতাত্মা বিচিকীর্ষিতো মে ।
তদামৃতত্বং প্রতিপদ্যমানো
ময়াত্মভূয়ায় চ কল্পতে বৈ ॥ ১৯৪ ॥

martyo yadā tyakta-samasta-karmā
niveditātmā vicikīrṣito me
tadāmṛtatvaṁ pratipadyamāno
mayātma-bhūyāya ca kalpate vai

SYNONYMS

martyaḥ—the living entity subjected to birth and death; *yadā*—as soon as; *tyakta*—giving up; *samasta*—all; *karmāḥ*—fruitive activities; *nivedita-ātmā*—a fully surrendered soul; *vicikīrṣitaḥ*—desired to act; *me*—by Me; *tadā*—at that time; *amṛtatvam*—immortality; *pratipadyamānaḥ*—attaining; *mayā*—with Me; *ātma-bhūyāya*—for becoming of a similar nature; *ca*—also; *kalpate*—is eligible; *vai*—certainly.

TRANSLATION

" 'The living entity who is subjected to birth and death, when he gives up all material activities dedicating his life to Me for executing My order, and thus acts according to My direction, at that time he reaches the platform of immortality, and becomes fit to enjoy the spiritual bliss of exchange of loving mellows with Me.'

PURPORT

This is a quotation from *Śrīmad-Bhāgavatam* (11.29.34). At the time of initiation, a devotee gives up all his material conceptions. Therefore, being in touch with the Supreme Personality of Godhead, he is situated on the transcendental platform. Thus having attained knowledge and the spiritual platform, he always engages in the service of the spiritual body of Kṛṣṇa. When one is freed from material connections in this way, his body immediately becomes spiritual, and Kṛṣṇa accepts His service. However, Kṛṣṇa does not accept anything from a person with a material conception of life. When a devotee no longer has any desire for material sense gratification, in his spiritual identity he engages in the service of the Lord, for his dormant spiritual consciousness awakens. This awakening of spiritual consciousness makes his body spiritual, and thus he becomes fit to render service to the Lord. *Karmīs* may consider the body of a devotee material, but factually it is not, for a devotee has no conception of material enjoyment. If one thinks that the body of a pure devotee is material, he is an offender, for that is a *vaiṣṇava-aparādha*. In this connection one should consult Śrīla Sanātana Gosvāmī's *Bṛhad-bhāgavatāmṛta* (1.3.45 and 2.3.139).

TEXT 195

সনাতনের দেহে কৃষ্ণ কণ্ডু উপজাঞা ।
আমা পরীক্ষিতে ইহাঁ দিলা পাঠাঞা ॥ ১৯৫ ॥

sanātanera dehe kṛṣṇa kaṇḍu upajāñā
āmā parīkṣite ihāṅ dilā pāṭhāñā

SYNONYMS

sanātanera—of Sanātana Gosvāmī; *dehe*—in the body; *kṛṣṇa*—Lord Kṛṣṇa; *kaṇḍu*—itches; *upajāñā*—manifesting; *āmā*—Me; *parīkṣite*—to test; *ihāṅ*—here; *dilā pāṭhāñā*—has sent.

TRANSLATION

"Kṛṣṇa somehow or other manifested these itching sores on the body of Sanātana Gosvāmī and sent him here to test Me.

TEXT 196

**ঘৃণা করি' আলিঙ্গন না করিতাম যবে ।
কৃষ্ণ-ঠাঞি অপরাধ-দণ্ড পাইতাম তবে ॥ ১৯৬ ॥**

ghṛṇā kari' āliṅgana nā karitāma yabe
kṛṣṇa-ṭhāñi aparādha-daṇḍa pāitāma tabe

SYNONYMS

ghṛṇā kari'—hating; *āliṅgana*—embracing; *nā karitāma*—I would not do; *yabe*—when; *kṛṣṇa-ṭhāñi*—unto Lord Kṛṣṇa; *aparādha-daṇḍa*—punishment for offenses; *pāitāma*—I would have gotten; *tabe*—then.

TRANSLATION

"If I had hated Sanātana Gosvāmī and had not embraced him, I would certainly have been chastised for offenses to Kṛṣṇa.

TEXT 197

**পারিষদ-দেহ এই, না হয় দুর্গন্ধ ।
প্রথম দিবসে পাইলুঁ চতুঃসম-গন্ধ ॥" ১৯৭ ॥**

pāriṣada-deha ei, nā haya durgandha
prathama divase pāiluṅ catuḥsama-gandha"

SYNONYMS

pāriṣada-deha—the body of Kṛṣṇa's associate; *ei*—this; *nā haya*—is not; *durgandha*—having a bad smell; *prathama divase*—on the first day; *pāiluṅ*—I got; *catuḥsama-gandha*—the smell of *catuḥsama,* a mixture of sandalwood pulp, camphor, aguru and musk.

TRANSLATION

"Sanātana Gosvāmī is one of the associates of Kṛṣṇa. There could not be any bad odor from his body. On the first day I embraced him, I smelled the aroma of catuḥsama [a mixture of sandalwood pulp, camphor, aguru and musk]."

PURPORT

An associate of the Lord is one whose body is fully engaged in the service of the Lord. A materialist might see Sanātana Gosvāmī's body as being full of itching sores that exuded foul moisture and a bad smell. Śrī Caitanya Mahāprabhu, however, said that actually the aroma of his body was the excellent scent of a mixture of sandalwood pulp, camphor, musk and aguru. In the *Garuḍa Purāṇa* this mixture, which is called *catuḥsama,* is described as follows:

kastūrikāyā dvau bhāgau
catvāraś candanasya tu
kuṅkumasya trayaś caikaḥ
śaśinaḥ syāt catuḥsamam

"Two parts of musk, four parts of sandalwood, three parts of *aguru* or saffron and one part of camphor, when mixed together, form *catuḥsama.*" The aroma of *catuḥsama* is very pleasing. It is also mentioned in the *Hari-bhakti-vilāsa* (6.115).

TEXT 198

বস্তুতঃ প্রভু যবে কৈলা আলিঙ্গন।
তাঁর স্পর্শে গন্ধ হৈল চন্দনের সম ॥ ১৯৮ ॥

vastutaḥ prabhu yabe kailā āliṅgana
tāṅra sparśe gandha haila candanera sama

SYNONYMS

vastutaḥ—in fact; *prabhu*—Śrī Caitanya Mahāprabhu; *yabe*—when; *kailā*—did; *āliṅgana*—embracing; *tāṅra sparśe*—by His touch; *gandha haila*—there was a fragrance; *candanera sama*—exactly like that of sandalwood pulp.

TRANSLATION

In fact, however, when Śrī Caitanya Mahāprabhu embraced the body of Sanātana Gosvāmī, by the Lord's touch alone there was manifest a fragrance exactly like that of sandalwood pulp.

TEXT 199

প্রভু কহে,——সনাতন, না মানিহ দুঃখ।
তোমার আলিঙ্গনে আমি পাই বড় সুখ ॥ ১৯৯ ॥

prabhu kahe, ——"sanātana, nā māniha duḥkha
tomāra āliṅgane āmi pāi baḍa sukha

SYNONYMS

prabhu kahe—Śrī Caitanya Mahāprabhu continued to speak; *sanātana*—My dear Sanātana; *nā māniha duḥkha*—do not be unhappy; *tomāra āliṅgane*—by embracing you; *āmi*—I; *pāi*—get; *baḍa sukha*—great happiness.

TRANSLATION

Śrī Caitanya Mahāprabhu continued, "My dear Sanātana, do not be aggrieved, for when I embrace you I actually get great pleasure.

TEXT 200

এ-বৎসর তুমি ইহাঁ রহ আমা-সনে ।
বৎসর রহি' তোমারে আমি পাঠাইমু বৃন্দাবনে ॥২০০॥

e-vatsara tumi ihāṅ raha āmā-sane
vatsara rahi' tomāre āmi pāṭhāimu vṛndāvane

SYNONYMS

e-vatsara—this year; *tumi*—you; *ihāṅ*—here; *raha*—remain; *āmā-sane*—with Me; *vatsara*—year; *rahi'*—remaining; *tomāre*—you; *āmi*—I; *pāṭhāimu vṛndāvane*—shall send to Vṛndāvana.

TRANSLATION

"Stay with Me at Jagannātha Purī for one year, and after that I shall send you to Vṛndāvana."

TEXT 201

এত বলি' পুনঃ তাঁরে কৈলা আলিঙ্গন ।
কণ্ডু গেল, অঙ্গ হৈল সুবর্ণের সম ॥ ২০১ ॥

eta bali' punaḥ tāṅre kailā āliṅgana
kaṇḍu gela, aṅga haila suvarṇera sama

SYNONYMS

eta bali'—saying this; *punaḥ*—again; *tāṅre*—him; *kailā*—did; *āliṅgana*—embracing; *kaṇḍu gela*—the itching sores disappeared; *aṅga*—the body; *haila*—became; *suvarṇera sama*—like gold.

TRANSLATION

After saying this, Śrī Caitanya Mahāprabhu again embraced Sanātana Gosvāmī. Thus immediately Sanātana's itches disappeared, and his entire body resembled the color of gold.

TEXT 202

দেখি' হরিদাস মনে হৈলা চমৎকার ।
প্রভুরে কহেন,—"এই ভঙ্গী যে তোমার ॥ ২০২ ॥

dekhi' haridāsa mane hailā camatkāra
prabhure kahena, —"ei bhaṅgī ye tomāra

SYNONYMS

dekhi'—seeing; *haridāsa*—Haridāsa Ṭhākura; *mane*—in the mind; *hailā camatkāra*—became astonished; *prabhure kahena*—spoke to the Lord; *ei*—this; *bhaṅgī*—transcendental activity; *ye*—which; *tomāra*—Your.

TRANSLATION

Seeing the change, Haridāsa Ṭhākura, greatly astonished, told the Lord, "This is Your pastime.

TEXT 203

সেই ঝারিখণ্ডের পানী তুমি খাওয়াইলা ।
সেই পানী-লক্ষ্যে ইঁহার কণ্ডু উপজাইলা ॥ ২০৩ ॥

sei jhārikhaṇḍera pānī tumi khāoyāilā
sei pānī-lakṣye iṅhāra kaṇḍu upajāilā

SYNONYMS

sei—that; *jhārikhaṇḍera*—of Jhārikhaṇḍa; *pānī*—water; *tumi*—You; *khāoyāilā*—made to drink; *sei pānī-lakṣye*—on account of this water; *iṅhāra*—of Sanātana Gosvāmī; *kaṇḍu upajāilā*—You generated the itching.

TRANSLATION

"My dear Lord, You made Sanātana Gosvāmī drink the water of Jhārikhaṇḍa, and You actually generated the consequent itching sores on his body.

TEXT 204

কণ্ডু করি' পরীক্ষা করিলে সনাতনে ।
এই লীলা-ভঙ্গী তোমার কেহ নাহি জানে" ॥২০৪॥

kaṇḍu kari' parīkṣā karile sanātane
ei līlā-bhaṅgī tomāra keha nāhi jāne"

SYNONYMS

kaṇḍu kari'—generating the itching sores; *parīkṣā*—examination; *karile*—You did; *sanātane*—unto Sanātana Gosvāmī; *ei*—this; *līlā*—of pastimes; *bhaṅgī*—trick; *tomāra*—Your; *keha nāhi jāne*—no one knows.

TRANSLATION

"After thus causing these itching sores, You examined Sanātana Gosvāmī. No one can understand Your transcendental pastimes."

TEXT 205

দুঁহে আলিঙ্গিয়া প্রভু গেলা নিজালয় ।
প্রভুর গুণ কহে দুঁহে হঞা প্রেমময় ॥ ২০৫ ॥

duṅhe āliṅgiyā prabhu gelā nijālaya
prabhura guṇa kahe duṅhe hañā prema-maya

SYNONYMS

duṅhe—both of them; *āliṅgiyā*—embracing; *prabhu*—Śrī Caitanya Mahāprabhu; *gelā*—departed; *nija-ālaya*—for His place; *prabhura guṇa*—attributes of Śrī Caitanya Mahāprabhu; *kahe*—discussed; *duṅhe*—both of them; *hañā*—being; *prema-maya*—overwhelmed by ecstasy.

TRANSLATION

After embracing both Haridāsa Ṭhākura and Sanātana Gosvāmī, Śrī Caitanya Mahāprabhu returned to His residence. Then both Haridāsa Ṭhākura and Sanātana Gosvāmī, in great ecstatic love, began to describe the Lord's transcendental attributes.

TEXT 206

এইমত সনাতন রহে প্রভু-স্থানে ।
কৃষ্ণচৈতন্য-গুণ-কথা হরিদাস-সনে ॥ ২০৬ ॥

ei-mata sanātana rahe prabhu-sthāne
kṛṣṇa-caitanya-guṇa-kathā haridāsa-sane

SYNONYMS

ei-mata—in this way; *sanātana*—Sanātana Gosvāmī; *rahe*—remained; *prabhu-sthāne*—at the shelter of Śrī Caitanya Mahāprabhu; *kṛṣṇa-caitanya*—of Lord Śrī Caitanya Mahāprabhu; *guṇa*—of the attributes; *kathā*—discussion; *haridāsa-sane*—with Haridāsa Ṭhākura.

TRANSLATION

In this way Sanātana Gosvāmī stayed under the care of Śrī Caitanya Mahāprabhu and discussed the transcendental qualities of Śrī Caitanya Mahāprabhu with Haridāsa Ṭhākura.

TEXT 207

দোলযাত্রা দেখি' প্রভু তাঁরে বিদায় দিলা ।
বৃন্দাবনে যে করিবেন, সব শিখাইলা ॥ ২০৭ ॥

dola-yātrā dekhi' prabhu tāṅre vidāya dilā
vṛndāvane ye karibena, saba śikhāilā

SYNONYMS

dola-yātrā—the festival of Dola-yātrā; *dekhi'*—seeing; *prabhu*—Śrī Caitanya Mahāprabhu; *tāṅre*—unto him; *vidāya dilā*—bid farewell; *vṛndāvane*—at Vṛndāvana; *ye karibena*—whatever he would do; *saba*—all; *śikhāilā*—instructed.

TRANSLATION

After they saw the Dola-yātrā festival, Śrī Caitanya Mahāprabhu instructed Sanātana Gosvāmī fully about what to do in Vṛndāvana and bade him farewell.

TEXT 208

যে-কালে বিদায় হৈলা প্রভুর চরণে ।
দুইজনার বিচ্ছেদ-দশা না যায় বর্ণনে ॥ ২০৮ ॥

ye-kāle vidāya hailā prabhura caraṇe
dui-janāra viccheda-daśā nā yāya varṇane

SYNONYMS

ye-kāle—when; *vidāya*—farewell; *hailā*—there was; *prabhura caraṇe*—at the lotus feet of Śrī Caitanya Mahāprabhu; *dui-janāra*—both of them; *viccheda-daśā*—condition of separation; *nā yāya varṇane*—cannot be described.

TRANSLATION

The scene of separation that took place when Sanātana Gosvāmī and Śrī Caitanya Mahāprabhu took leave of one another is so piteous that it cannot be described herein.

TEXT 209

যেই বন-পথে প্রভু গেলা বৃন্দাবন ।
সেইপথে যাইতে মন কৈলা সনাতন ॥ ২০৯ ॥

yei vana-pathe prabhu gelā vṛndāvana
sei-pathe yāite mana kailā sanātana

SYNONYMS

yei—which; *vana-pathe*—on the path in the forest; *prabhu*—Śrī Caitanya Mahāprabhu; *gelā vṛndāvana*—went to Vṛndāvana; *sei-pathe*—on the very path; *yāite*—to go; *mana*—mind; *kailā*—made; *sanātana*—Sanātana Gosvāmī.

TRANSLATION

Sanātana Gosvāmī decided to go to Vṛndāvana by the very forest path Śrī Caitanya Mahāprabhu had traversed.

TEXT 210

যে-পথে, যে-গ্রাম-নদী-শৈল, যাহাঁ যেই লীলা।
বলভদ্রভট্ট-স্থানে সব লিখি' নিলা ॥ ২১০ ॥

ye-pathe, ye-grāma-nadī-śaila, yāhāṅ yei līlā
balabhadra-bhaṭṭa-sthāne saba likhi' nilā

SYNONYMS

ye-pathe—on which path; *ye*—which; *grāma*—villages; *nadī*—rivers; *śaila*—hills; *yāhāṅ*—where; *yei*—which; *līlā*—pastimes; *balabhadra-bhaṭṭa-sthāne*—from Balabhadra Bhaṭṭa; *saba*—everything; *likhi'*—writing; *nilā*—he took.

TRANSLATION

Sanātana Gosvāmī noted from Balabhadra Bhaṭṭācārya all the villages, rivers and hills where Śrī Caitanya Mahāprabhu had performed His pastimes.

TEXT 211

মহাপ্রভুর ভক্তগণে সবারে মিলিয়া।
সেইপথে চলি' যায় সে-স্থান দেখিয়া ॥ ২১১ ॥

mahāprabhura bhakta-gaṇe sabāre miliyā
sei-pathe cali' yāya se-sthāna dekhiyā

SYNONYMS

mahāprabhura—of Śrī Caitanya Mahāprabhu; *bhakta-gaṇe*—the devotees; *sabāre*—all; *miliyā*—meeting; *sei-pathe*—on the path; *cali' yāya*—passed through; *se*—those; *sthāna*—places; *dekhiyā*—visiting.

TRANSLATION

Sanātana Gosvāmī met all the devotees of Śrī Caitanya Mahāprabhu and then, traveling by that same path, visited the places through which Śrī Caitanya Mahāprabhu had passed.

PURPORT

Śrīla Bhaktivinoda Ṭhākura writes in a song (*Śaraṇāgati* 31.3):

gaura āmāra, ye saba sthāne,
karala bhramaṇa raṅge
se-saba sthāna, heriba āmi,
praṇayi-bhakata-saṅge.

"May I visit all the holy places associated with the *līlās* of Lord Caitanya and His devotees." A devotee should make a point of visiting all the places where Śrī Caitanya Mahāprabhu performed His pastimes. Indeed, pure devotees of Śrī Caitanya Mahāprabhu even want to see the places He simply visited for only hours or minutes.

TEXT 212

যে-যে-লীলা প্রভু পথে কৈলা যে-যে-স্থানে ।
তাহা দেখি' প্রেমাবেশ হয় সনাতনে ॥ ২১২ ॥

ye-ye-līlā prabhu pathe kailā ye-ye-sthāne
tāhā dekhi' premāveśa haya sanātane

SYNONYMS

ye-ye—whatever; *līlā*—pastimes; *prabhu*—Śrī Caitanya Mahāprabhu; *pathe*—on the way; *kailā*—performed; *ye-ye-sthāne*—in whatever places; *tāhā*—those places; *dekhi'*—by seeing; *prema-āveśa*—ecstatic love; *haya*—there is; *sanātane*—in Sanātana Gosvāmī.

TRANSLATION

As soon as Sanātana Gosvāmī visited a place where Śrī Caitanya Mahāprabhu had performed His pastimes on the way, he was immediately filled with ecstatic love.

TEXT 213

এইমতে সনাতন বৃন্দাবনে আইলা ।
পাছে আসি' রূপ-গোসাঞি তাঁহারে মিলিলা ॥২১৩॥

ei-mate sanātana vṛndāvane āilā
pāche āsi' rūpa-gosāñi tāṅhāre mililā

SYNONYMS

ei-mate—in this way; *sanātana*—Sanātana Gosvāmī; *vṛndāvane āilā*—came to Vṛndāvana; *pāche āsi'*—coming after; *rūpa-gosāñi*—Śrīla Rūpa Gosvāmī; *tāṅhāre*—him; *mililā*—met.

TRANSLATION

In this way Sanātana Gosvāmī reached Vṛndāvana. Later Rūpa Gosvāmī came and met him.

TEXT 214

একবৎসর রূপ-গোসাঞির গৌড়ে বিলম্ব হৈল ।
কুটুম্বের 'স্থিতি'-অর্থ বিভাগ করি' দিল ॥ ২১৪ ॥

eka-vatsara rūpa-gosāñira gauḍe vilamba haila
kuṭumbera 'sthiti'-artha vibhāga kari' dila

SYNONYMS

eka-vatsara—for one year; *rūpa-gosāñira*—of Śrīla Rūpa Gosvāmī; *gauḍe*—in Bengal; *vilamba*—delay; *haila*—there was; *kuṭumbera*—of the relatives; *sthiti-artha*—wealth for maintenance; *vibhāga*—shares; *kari'*—making; *dila*—gave.

TRANSLATION

Śrīla Rūpa Gosvāmī was delayed in Bengal for a year because he was dividing his money among his relatives to situate them in their proper positions.

PURPORT

Although Śrīla Rūpa Gosvāmī renounced his family life, he nevertheless was not unjust to his family members. Even after renunciation, he returned to Bengal, where he properly divided whatever money he had and gave it to his relatives so that they would not be inconvenienced.

TEXT 215

গৌড়ে যে অর্থ ছিল, তাহা আনাইলা ।
কুটুম্ব-ব্রাহ্মণ-দেবালয়ে বাঁটি' দিলা ॥ ২১৫ ॥

gauḍe ye artha chila, tāhā ānāilā
kuṭumba-brāhmaṇa-devālaye bāṅṭi' dilā

SYNONYMS

gauḍe—in Bengal; *ye*—whatever; *artha*—money; *chila*—there was; *tāhā*—that; *ānāilā*—collected; *kuṭumba*—to relatives; *brāhmaṇa*—*brāhmaṇas*; *devālaye*—temples; *bāṅṭi' dilā*—divided and distributed.

TRANSLATION

He collected whatever money he had accumulated in Bengal and divided it among his relatives, the brāhmaṇas and the temples.

TEXT 216

সব মনঃকথা গোসাঞি করি' নির্বাহণ ।
নিশ্চিন্ত হঞা শীঘ্র আইলা বৃন্দাবন ॥ ২১৬ ॥

saba manaḥ-kathā gosāñi kari' nirvāhaṇa
niścinta hañā śīghra āilā vṛndāvana

SYNONYMS

saba—all; *manaḥ-kathā*—decisions; *gosāñi*—Rūpa Gosvāmī; *kari' nirvāhaṇa*—executing properly; *niścinta hañā*—being freed from all anxiety; *śīghra āilā*—very soon returned; *vṛndāvana*—to Vṛndāvana.

TRANSLATION

Thus after finishing all the tasks he had on his mind, he returned to Vṛndāvana fully satisfied.

TEXT 217

দুই ভাই মিলি' বৃন্দাবনে বাস কৈলা ।
প্রভুর যে আজ্ঞা, দুঁহে সব নির্বাহিলা ॥ ২১৭ ॥

dui bhāi mili' vṛndāvane vāsa kailā
prabhura ye ājñā, duṅhe saba nirvāhilā

SYNONYMS

dui bhāi—both brothers; *mili'*—meeting; *vṛndāvane*—in Vṛndāvana; *vāsa kailā*—resided; *prabhura ye ājñā*—whatever was ordered by Śrī Caitanya Mahāprabhu; *duṅhe*—both of them; *saba*—all; *nirvāhilā*—executed.

TRANSLATION

The brothers met at Vṛndāvana, where they stayed to execute the will of Śrī Caitanya Mahāprabhu.

PURPORT

śrī-caitanya-mano-'bhīṣṭaṁ
sthāpitaṁ yena bhū-tale
svayaṁ rūpaḥ kadā mahyaṁ
dadāti sva-padāntikam

"When will Śrīla Rūpa Gosvāmī Prabhupāda, who has established within the material world the mission to fulfill the desire of Lord Caitanya, give me shelter under his lotus feet?" Śrīla Rūpa Gosvāmī and Sanātana Gosvāmī were previously ministers directly in charge of the government of Nawab Hussain Shah, and they were also householders, but later they became *gosvāmīs.* A *gosvāmī,* therefore, is one who executes the will of Śrī Caitanya Mahāprabhu. The title *"gosvāmī"* is not an inherited designation; it is meant for a person who has controlled his sense gratification and dedicated his life to executing the order of Śrī Caitanya Mahāprabhu. Therefore Śrīla Sanātana Gosvāmī and Śrīla Rūpa Gosvāmī became genuine *gosvāmīs* after dedicating their lives to the service of the Lord.

TEXT 218

নানাশাস্ত্র আনি' লুপ্ত-তীর্থ উদ্ধারিলা ।
বৃন্দাবনে কৃষ্ণসেবা প্রকাশ করিলা ॥ ২১৮ ॥

nānā-śāstra āni' lupta-tīrtha uddhārilā
vṛndāvane kṛṣṇa-sevā prakāśa karilā

SYNONYMS

nānā-śāstra—different types of revealed scripture; *āni'*—bringing together; *lupta-tīrtha*—the lost sites of the holy places; *uddhārilā*—excavated; *vṛndāvane*—at Vṛndāvana; *kṛṣṇa-sevā*—Lord Kṛṣṇa's direct service; *prakāśa karilā*—manifested.

TRANSLATION

Śrīla Rūpa Gosvāmī and Sanātana Gosvāmī collected many revealed scriptures, and from the evidence in those scriptures they excavated all the lost sites of pilgrimage. Thus they established temples for the worship of Lord Kṛṣṇa.

TEXT 219

সনাতন গ্রন্থ কৈলা 'ভাগবতামৃতে'।
ভক্ত-ভক্তি-কৃষ্ণ-তত্ত্ব জানি যাহা হৈতে ॥ ২১৯ ॥

sanātana grantha kailā 'bhāgavatāmṛte'
bhakta-bhakti-kṛṣṇa-tattva jāni yāhā haite

SYNONYMS

sanātana—Sanātana Gosvāmī; *grantha*—books; *kailā*—compiled; *bhāgavata-amṛte*—in the *Bhāgavatāmṛta*; *bhakta*—devotee; *bhakti*—devotional service; *kṛṣṇa-tattva*—Kṛṣṇa, the Absolute Truth; *jāni*—we know; *yāhā haite*—from which.

TRANSLATION

Śrīla Sanātana Gosvāmī compiled the Bhāgavatāmṛta. From this book one can understand who is a devotee, what is the process of devotional service, and who is Kṛṣṇa, the Absolute Truth.

TEXT 220

সিদ্ধান্তসার গ্রন্থ কৈলা 'দশম-টিপ্পনী'।
কৃষ্ণলীলারস-প্রেম যাহা হৈতে জানি ॥ ২২০ ॥

siddhānta-sāra grantha kailā 'daśama-ṭippanī'
kṛṣṇa-līlā-rasa-prema yāhā haite jāni

SYNONYMS

siddhānta-sāra—mature understanding; *grantha*—book; *kailā*—compiled; *daśama-ṭippanī*—commentary on the Tenth Canto; *kṛṣṇa-līlā*—of pastimes of Lord Kṛṣṇa; *rasa*—of the transcendental mellow; *prema*—ecstatic love; *yāhā haite*—from which; *jāni*—we can understand.

TRANSLATION

Śrīla Sanātana Gosvāmī wrote a commentary on the Tenth Canto known as Daśama-ṭippanī, from which we can understand the transcendental pastimes and ecstatic love of Lord Kṛṣṇa.

TEXT 221

'হরিভক্তিবিলাস'-গ্রন্থ কৈলা বৈষ্ণব-আচার।
বৈষ্ণবের কর্তব্য যাহাঁ পাইয়ে পার ॥ ২২১ ॥

'hari-bhakti-vilāsa'-grantha kailā vaiṣṇava-ācāra
vaiṣṇavera kartavya yāhāṅ pāiye pāra

SYNONYMS

hari-bhakti-vilāsa—of the name *Hari-bhakti-vilāsa*; *grantha*—book; *kailā*—compiled; *vaiṣṇava-ācāra*—the standard behavior of a Vaiṣṇava; *vaiṣṇavera*—of a devotee; *kartavya*—duty; *yāhāṅ*—in which; *pāiye pāra*—one can understand up to the extreme limit.

TRANSLATION

He also compiled the Hari-bhakti-vilāsa, from which we can understand the standard behavior of a devotee and the full extent of a Vaiṣṇava's duty.

PURPORT

Śrīla Bhaktisiddhānta Sarasvatī Ṭhākura writes: "The *Hari-bhakti-vilāsa* was originally compiled by Śrīla Sanātana Gosvāmī. Later, Gopāla Bhaṭṭa Gosvāmī produced a shortened version of it and added the *Dig-darśinī-ṭīkā.* In the *Hari-bhakti-vilāsa* there are so many quotations from the *sātvata* scriptures that sometimes it is inquired how the atheistic *smārtas* can refuse to accept them and instead imagine some other opinions. What is recorded in the *Hari-bhakti-vilāsa* strictly follows the Vedic scriptures and is certainly pure, but the attitude of the *karmīs* is always one of giving up the conclusion of pure Vaiṣṇava understanding. Because the *karmīs* are very much attached to the world and material activities, they always try to establish atheistic principles that oppose the understanding of the Vaiṣṇavas.

TEXT 222

আর যত গ্রন্থ কৈলা, তাহা কে করে গণন ।
'মদনগোপাল-গোবিন্দের সেবা'-প্রকাশন ॥ ২২২॥

āra yata grantha kailā, tāhā ke kare gaṇana
'madana-gopāla-govindera sevā'-prakāśana

SYNONYMS

āra yata—all other; *grantha*—books; *kailā*—compiled; *tāhā*—that; *ke kare gaṇana*—who can enumerate; *madana-gopāla*—the Deity named Madana-mohana; *govindera*—of the Deity named Śrī Govinda; *sevā*—service; *prakāśana*—exhibition.

TRANSLATION

Śrīla Sanātana Gosvāmī also compiled many other books. Who can enumerate them? The basic principle of all these books is to show us how to love Madana-mohana and Govindajī.

PURPORT

The *Bhakti-ratnākara* refers to the following books by Śrīla Sanātana Gosvāmī: (1) *Bṛhad-bhāgavatāmṛta,* (2) *Hari-bhakti-vilāsa* and his commentary known as *Dig-darśinī,* (3) *Līlā-stava* and (4) the commentary on the Tenth Canto of *Śrīmad-Bhāgavatam* known as *Vaiṣṇava-toṣaṇī.* Sanātana Gosvāmī compiled many, many books, all with the aim of describing how to serve the principal Deities of Vṛndāvana—Govinda and Madana-gopāla. Later, other Deities were gradually established, and the importance of Vṛndāvana increased.

TEXT 223

রূপ-গোসাঞি কৈলা 'রসামৃতসিন্ধু' সার ।
কৃষ্ণভক্তি-রসের যাহাঁ পাইয়ে বিস্তার ॥ ২২৩ ॥

rūpa-gosāñi kailā 'rasāmṛta-sindhu' sāra
kṛṣṇa-bhakti-rasera yāhāṅ pāiye vistāra

SYNONYMS

rūpa-gosāñi—Śrīla Rūpa Gosvāmī; *kailā*—compiled; *rasāmṛta-sindhu*—the book known as *Bhakti-rasāmṛta-sindhu; sāra*—the essence of knowledge in devotional service; *kṛṣṇa-bhakti-rasera*—of the transcendental mellow in devotional service; *yāhāṅ*—wherein; *pāiye*—we can get; *vistāra*—elaboration.

TRANSLATION

Śrīla Rūpa Gosvāmī also wrote many books, the most famous of which is Bhakti-rasāmṛta-sindhu. From that book one can understand the essence of devotional service to Kṛṣṇa and the transcendental mellow one can derive from such service.

TEXT 224

'উজ্জ্বলনীলমণি'-নাম গ্রন্থ কৈল আর ।
রাধাকৃষ্ণ-লীলারস তাহাঁ পাইয়ে পার ॥ ২২৪ ॥

'ujjvala-nīlamaṇi'-nāma grantha kaila āra
rādhā-kṛṣṇa-līlā-rasa tāhāṅ pāiye pāra

SYNONYMS

ujjvala-nīla-maṇi—Ujjvala-nīlamaṇi; nāma—named; *grantha*—scripture; *kaila*—compiled; *āra*—also; *rādhā-kṛṣṇa-līlā-rasa*—the transcendental mellow of the pastimes of Rādhā and Kṛṣṇa; *tāhāṅ*—there; *pāiye*—we get; *pāra*—the extreme limit.

TRANSLATION

Śrīla Rūpa Gosvāmī also compiled the book named Ujjvala-nīlamaṇi, from which one can understand, to the fullest limits, the loving affairs of Śrī Śrī Rādhā and Kṛṣṇa.

TEXT 225

'বিদগ্ধমাধব', 'ললিতমাধব',— নাটকযুগল ।
কৃষ্ণলীলা-রস তাহাঁ পাইয়ে সকল ॥ ২২৫ ॥

'vidagdha-mādhava', 'lalita-mādhava', —nāṭaka-yugala
kṛṣṇa-līlā-rasa tāhāṅ pāiye sakala

SYNONYMS

vidagdha-mādhava—Vidagdha-mādhava; *lalita-mādhava*—Lalita-mādhava; *nāṭaka-yugala*—two dramas; *kṛṣṇa-līlā-rasa*—the mellow derived from the pastimes of Lord Kṛṣṇa; *tāhāṅ*—there; *pāiye sakala*—we can understand all.

TRANSLATION

Śrīla Rūpa Gosvāmī also compiled two important dramas named Vidagdha-mādhava and Lalita-mādhava, from which one can understand all the mellows derived from the pastimes of Lord Kṛṣṇa.

TEXT 226

'দানকেলিকৌমুদী' আদি লক্ষগ্রন্থ কৈল ।
সেই সব গ্রন্থে ব্রজের রস বিচারিল ॥ ২২৬ ॥

'dāna-keli-kaumudī' ādi lakṣa-grantha kaila
sei saba granthe vrajera rasa vicārila

SYNONYMS

dāna-keli-kaumudī—the book named *Dāna-keli-kaumudī; ādi*—beginning with; *lakṣa*—100,000; *grantha*—verses; *kaila*—compiled; *sei*—those; *saba*—all; *granthe*—in scriptures; *vrajera*—of Vṛndāvana; *rasa vicārila*—elaborately explained the transcendental mellows.

TRANSLATION

Śrīla Rūpa Gosvāmī compiled 100,000 verses, beginning with the book Dāna-keli-kaumudī. In all these scriptures he elaborately explained the transcendental mellows of the activities of Vṛndāvana.

PURPORT

Referring to the words *lakṣa-grantha* ("100,000 verses"), Śrīla Bhaktisiddhānta Sarasvatī Ṭhākura says that the total number of verses written by Śrīla Rūpa Gosvāmī is 100,000 (*eka-lakṣa* or *lakṣa-grantha*). The copyists count both the verses and the prose sections of the Sanskrit works. One should not mistakenly think that Śrīla Rūpa Gosvāmī compiled 100,000 books. He actually wrote sixteen books, as mentioned in the First Wave of the *Bhakti-ratnākara* (*śrī-rūpa-gosvāmī grantha ṣoḍaśa karila*).

TEXT 227

তাঁর লঘুভ্রাতা—শ্রীবল্লভ-অনুপম ।
তাঁর পুত্র মহাপণ্ডিত—জীবগোসাঞি নাম ॥ ২২৭ ॥

tāṅra laghu-bhrātā——śrī-vallabha-anupama
tāṅra putra mahā-paṇḍita——jīva-gosāñi nāma

SYNONYMS

tāṅra—his; *laghu-bhrātā*—younger brother; *śrī-vallabha-anupama*—named Śrī Vallabha or Anupama; *tāṅra putra*—his son; *mahā-paṇḍita*--very learned scholar; *jīva gosāñi*—Śrīla Jīva Gosvāmī; *nāma*—named.

TRANSLATION

The son of Śrī Vallabha, or Anupama, Śrīla Rūpa Gosvāmī's younger brother, was the great learned scholar named Śrīla Jīva Gosvāmī.

TEXT 228

সর্ব ত্যজি' তেঁহো পাছে আইলা বৃন্দাবন ।
তেঁহ ভক্তিশাস্ত্র বহু কৈলা প্রচারণ ॥ ২২৮ ॥

sarva tyāji' teṅho pāche āilā vṛndāvana
teṅha bhakti-śāstra bahu kailā pracāraṇa

SYNONYMS

sarva tyāji'—renouncing everything; *teṅho*—he (Śrīla Jīva Gosvāmī); *pāche*—later; *āilā vṛndāvana*—came to Vṛndāvana; *teṅha*—he; *bhakti-śāstra*—books on devotional service; *bahu*—many; *kailā*—did; *pracāraṇa*—spreading.

TRANSLATION

After renouncing everything, Śrīla Jīva Gosvāmī went to Vṛndāvana. Later he also wrote many books on devotional service and expanded the work of preaching.

TEXT 229

'ভাগবত-সন্দর্ভ'-নাম কৈল গ্রন্থ-সার ।
ভাগবত-সিদ্ধান্তের তাহাঁ পাইয়ে পার ॥ ২২৯ ॥

'bhāgavata-sandarbha'-nāma kaila grantha-sāra
bhāgavata-siddhāntera tāhāṅ pāiye pāra

SYNONYMS

bhāgavata-sandarbha—the *Bhāgavata-sandarbha,* which is also known as *Ṣaṭ-sandarbha; nāma*—named; *kaila*—made; *grantha-sāra*—the essence of all scriptures; *bhāgavata-siddhāntera*—of conclusive information about the Supreme Personality of Godhead and His service; *tāhāṅ*—there; *pāiye*—we get; *pāra*—the limit.

TRANSLATION

In particular, Śrīla Jīva Gosvāmī compiled the book named Bhāgavata-sandarbha, or Ṣaṭ-sandarbha, which is the essence of all scriptures. From this book one can obtain a conclusive understanding of devotional service and the Supreme Personality of Godhead.

TEXT 230

'গোপাল-চম্পূ' নাম গ্রন্থ সার কৈল ।
ব্রজ-প্রেম-লীলা-রস-সার দেখাইল ॥ ২৩০ ॥

'gopāla-campū' nāma grantha sāra kaila
vraja-prema-līlā-rasa-sāra dekhāila

SYNONYMS

gopāla-campū—*Gopāla-campū; nāma*—named; *grantha sāra*—the essence of all Vedic literature; *kaila*—made; *vraja*—of Vṛndāvana; *prema*—of love; *līlā*—of pastimes; *rasa*—of mellows; *sāra*—essence; *dekhāila*—exhibited.

TRANSLATION

He also compiled the book named Gopāla-campū, which is the essence of all Vedic literature. In this book he has exhibited the ecstatic loving transactions and pastimes of Rādhā and Kṛṣṇa in Vṛndāvana.

TEXT 231

'ষট্ সন্দর্ভে' কৃষ্ণপ্রেম-তত্ত্ব প্রকাশিল ।
চারিলক্ষ গ্রন্থ তেঁহো বিস্তার করিল ॥ ২৩১ ॥

'ṣaṭ sandarbhe' kṛṣṇa-prema-tattva prakāśila
cāri-lakṣa grantha teṅho vistāra karila

SYNONYMS

ṣaṭ sandarbhe—in the *Ṣaṭ-sandarbha;* *kṛṣṇa-prema-tattva*—the truth about transcendental love of Kṛṣṇa; *prakāśila*—he exhibited; *cāri-lakṣa grantha*—400,000 verses; *teṅho*—he; *vistāra karila*—expanded.

TRANSLATION

In the Ṣaṭ-sandarbha Śrīla Jīva Gosvāmī set forth the truths about the transcendental love of Kṛṣṇa. In this way he expanded 400,000 verses in all his books.

TEXT 232

জীব-গোসাঞি গৌড় হৈতে মথুরা চলিলা ।
নিত্যানন্দপ্রভু-ঠাঞি আজ্ঞা মাগিলা ॥ ২৩২ ॥

jīva-gosāñi gauḍa haite mathurā calilā
nityānanda-prabhu-ṭhāñi ājñā māgilā

SYNONYMS

jīva-gosāñi—Śrīpāda Jīva Gosvāmī; *gauḍa haite*—from Bengal; *mathurā calilā*—started for Mathurā; *nityānanda-prabhu-ṭhāñi*—from Śrīla Nityānanda Prabhu; *ājñā māgilā*—he asked permission.

TRANSLATION

When Jīva Gosvāmī wanted to go to Mathurā from Bengal, he requested permission from Śrīla Nityānanda Prabhu.

TEXT 233

প্রভু প্রীত্যে তাঁর মাথে ধরিলা চরণ ।
রূপ-সনাতন-সম্বন্ধে কৈলা আলিঙ্গন ॥ ২৩৩ ॥

prabhu prītye tāṅra māthe dharilā caraṇa
rūpa-sanātana-sambandhe kailā āliṅgana

SYNONYMS

prabhu prītye—because of the mercy of Śrī Caitanya Mahāprabhu; *tāṅra*—his; *māthe*—on the head; *dharilā caraṇa*—rested His lotus feet; *rūpa-sanātana-sam-*

bandhe—because of his relationship with Rūpa Gosvāmī and Sanātana Gosvāmī; *kailā āliṅgana*—embraced.

TRANSLATION

Because of Jīva Gosvāmī's relationship with Rūpa Gosvāmī and Sanātana Gosvāmī, who were greatly favored by Śrī Caitanya Mahāprabhu, Lord Nityānanda Prabhu placed His feet on the head of Śrīla Jīva Goṣvāmī and embraced him.

TEXT 234

আজ্ঞা দিলা,—"শীঘ্র তুমি যাহ বৃন্দাবনে ।
তোমার বংশে প্রভু দিয়াছেন সেইস্থানে ॥ ২৩৪ ॥

ājñā dilā, ——"śīghra tumi yāha vṛndāvane
tomāra vaṁśe prabhu diyāchena sei-sthāne

SYNONYMS

ājñā dilā—He gave orders; *śīghra*—very soon; *tumi*—you; *yāha*—go; *vṛndāvane*—to Vṛndāvana; *tomāra*—your; *vaṁśe*—to the family; *prabhu*—Lord Śrī Caitanya Mahāprabhu; *diyāchena*—has given; *sei-sthāne*—that place.

TRANSLATION

Lord Nityānanda Prabhu ordered, "Yes, go soon to Vṛndāvana. That place has been awarded to your family, to your father and uncles, by Śrī Caitanya Mahāprabhu, and therefore you must go there immediately."

TEXT 235

তাঁর আজ্ঞায় আইলা, আজ্ঞা-ফল পাইলা ।
শাস্ত্র করি' কতকাল 'ভক্তি' প্রচারিলা ॥ ২৩৫ ॥

tāṅra ājñāya āilā, ājñā-phala pāilā
śāstra kari' kata-kāla 'bhakti' pracārilā

SYNONYMS

tāṅra ājñāya—by His order; *āilā*—came; *ājñā-phala*—the result of His order; *pāilā*—got; *śāstra kari'*—compiling various scriptures; *kata-kāla*—for a long time; *bhakti pracārilā*—preached devotional service.

TRANSLATION

By the order of Nityānanda Prabhu, he went and actually achieved the result of His order, for he compiled many books for a long time and preached the cult of bhakti from Vṛndāvana.

TEXT 236

এই তিনগুরু, আর রঘুনাথদাস ।
ইঁহা-সবার চরণ বন্দোঁ, যাঁর মুঞি 'দাস' ॥২৩৬॥

ei tina-guru, āra raghunātha-dāsa
iṅhā-sabāra caraṇa vandoṅ, yāṅra muñi 'dāsa'

SYNONYMS

ei—these; *tina-guru*—three spiritual masters; *āra*—also; *raghunātha-dāsa*—Raghunātha dāsa Gosvāmī; *iṅhā-sabāra*—of all of them; *caraṇa*—the lotus feet; *vandoṅ*—I worship; *yāṅra*—of whom; *muñi*—I; *dāsa*—the servant.

TRANSLATION

These three—Rūpa Gosvāmī, Sanātana Gosvāmī and Jīva Gosvāmī—are my spiritual masters, and so also is Raghunātha dāsa Gosvāmī. I therefore offer prayers at their lotus feet, for I am their servant.

TEXT 237

এই ত' কহিলুঁ পুনঃ সনাতন-সঙ্গমে ।
প্রভুর আশয় জানি যাহার শ্রবণে ॥ ২৩৭ ॥

ei ta' kahiluṅ punaḥ sanātana-saṅgame
prabhura āśaya jāni yāhāra śravaṇe

SYNONYMS

ei ta' kahiluṅ—thus I have described; *punaḥ*—again; *sanātana-saṅgame*—the meeting with Sanātana Gosvāmī; *prabhura āśaya*—Lord Śrī Caitanya Mahāprabhu's desire; *jāni*—I can understand; *yāhāra śravaṇe*—by hearing of which.

TRANSLATION

Thus I have described the Lord's meeting again with Sanātana Gosvāmī. By hearing this I can understand the Lord's desire.

TEXT 238

চৈতন্যচরিত্র এই—ইক্ষুদণ্ড-সম ।
চর্বণ করিতে হয় রস-আস্বাদন ॥ ২৩৮ ॥

caitanya-caritra ei——ikṣu-daṇḍa-sama
carvaṇa karite haya rasa-āsvādana

SYNONYMS

caitanya-caritra—the characteristics of Lord Śrī Caitanya Mahāprabhu; *ei*—this; *ikṣu-daṇḍa-sama*—exactly like sugar cane; *carvaṇa karite*—chewing; *haya*—there is; *rasa-āsvādana*—a taste of juice.

TRANSLATION

These characteristics of Śrī Caitanya Mahāprabhu are like sugar cane that one can chew to relish transcendental juice.

TEXT 239

শ্রীরূপ-রঘুনাথ-পদে যার আশ ।
চৈতন্যচরিতামৃত কহে কৃষ্ণদাস ॥ ২৩৯ ॥

śrī-rūpa-raghunātha-pade yāra āśa
caitanya-caritāmṛta kahe kṛṣṇadāsa

SYNONYMS

śrī-rūpa—Śrīla Rūpa Gosvāmī; *raghunātha*—Śrīla Raghunātha dāsa Gosvāmī; *pade*—at the lotus feet of; *yāra*—whose; *āśa*—expectation; *caitanya-caritāmṛta*—the book named *Caitanya-caritāmṛta*; *kahe*—describes; *kṛṣṇa-dāsa*—Śrīla Kṛṣṇadāsa Kavirāja Gosvāmī.

TRANSLATION

Praying at the lotus feet of Śrī Rūpa and Śrī Raghunātha, always desiring their mercy, I, Kṛṣṇadāsa, narrate Śrī Caitanya-caritāmṛta, following in their footsteps.

Thus end the Bhaktivedanta purports to the Śrī Caitanya-caritāmṛta, Antya-līlā, *Fourth Chapter, describing Sanātana Gosvāmī's stay with the Lord at Jagannātha Purī.*

CHAPTER 5

How Pradyumna Miśra Received Instructions from Rāmānanda Rāya

The following summary of the Fifth Chapter is given by Śrīla Bhaktivinoda Ṭhākura in his *Amṛta-pravāha-bhāṣya.* Pradyumna Miśra, a resident of Śrīhaṭṭa, came to see Śrī Caitanya Mahāprabhu to hear from Him about Lord Kṛṣṇa and His pastimes. The Lord, however, sent him to Śrīla Rāmānanda Rāya. Śrīla Rāmānanda Rāya was training the *deva-dāsī* dancing girls in the temple, and when Pradyumna Miśra heard about this, he returned to Śrī Caitanya Mahāprabhu. The Lord, however, elaborately described the character of Śrīla Rāmānanda Rāya. Then Pradyumna Miśra went to see Rāmānanda Rāya again to hear about the transcendental truth from him.

A *brāhmaṇa* from Bengal composed a drama about the activities of Śrī Caitanya Mahāprabhu and went to Jagannātha Purī to show it to the associates of the Lord. When Śrī Caitanya Mahāprabhu's secretary, Svarūpa Dāmodara Gosvāmī, heard the drama, he discerned a tinge of Māyāvāda philosophy and pointed it out to the author. Although Svarūpa Dāmodara condemned the entire drama, by reference to secondary meanings of the introductory verse he nevertheless satisfied the *brāhmaṇa.* That *brāhmaṇa* poet thus became greatly obliged to Svarūpa Dāmodara Gosvāmī, renounced his family connections and stayed at Jagannātha Purī with the associates of Śrī Caitanya Mahāprabhu.

TEXT 1

বৈগুণ্যকীটকলিতঃ পৈশুন্য-ব্রণপীড়িতঃ ।
দৈন্যার্ণবে নিমগ্নোঽহং চৈতন্য-বৈদ্যমাশ্রয়ে ॥ ১ ॥

vaiguṇya-kīṭa-kalitaḥ
paiśunya-vraṇa-pīḍitaḥ
dainyārṇave nimagno 'haṁ
caitanya-vaidyam āśraye

SYNONYMS

vaiguṇya—of material activities; *kīṭa*—by the germs; *kalitaḥ*—bitten; *paiśunya*—of envy; *vraṇa*—from boils; *pīḍitaḥ*—suffering; *dainya-arṇave*—in the ocean of humility; *nimagnaḥ*—merged; *aham*—I; *caitanya-vaidyam*—to the physician known as Lord Śrī Caitanya Mahāprabhu; *āśraye*—I surrender.

TRANSLATION

I am infected by germs of material activity and suffering from boils due to envy. Therefore, falling in an ocean of humility, I take shelter of the great physician Lord Śrī Caitanya Mahāprabhu.

TEXT 2

জয় জয় শচীসুত শ্রীকৃষ্ণচৈতন্য ।
জয় জয় কৃপাময় নিত্যানন্দ ধন্য ॥ ২ ॥

jaya jaya śacī-suta śrī-kṛṣṇa-caitanya
jaya jaya kṛpā-maya nityānanda dhanya

SYNONYMS

jaya jaya—all glories; *śacī-suta*—to the son of mother Śacī; *śrī-kṛṣṇa-caitanya*—Śrī Caitanya Mahāprabhu; *jaya jaya*—all glories; *kṛpā-maya*—to the most merciful; *nityānanda dhanya*—the glorious Śrīla Nityānanda Prabhu.

TRANSLATION

All glories to Śrī Caitanya Mahāprabhu, the son of mother Śacī! All glories to Śrī Nityānanda Prabhu! Indeed, He is the most glorious and merciful.

TEXT 3

জয়াদ্বৈত কৃপাসিন্ধু জয় ভক্তগণ ।
জয় স্বরূপ, গদাধর, রূপ, সনাতন ॥ ৩ ॥

jayādvaita kṛpā-sindhu jaya bhakta-gaṇa
jaya svarūpa, gadādhara, rūpa, sanātana

SYNONYMS

jaya advaita—all glories to Advaita Prabhu; *kṛpā-sindhu*—the ocean of mercy; *jaya bhakta-gaṇa*—all glories to the devotees; *jaya svarūpa*—all glories to Svarūpa Dāmodara; *gadādhara*—Gadādhara Paṇḍita; *rūpa*—Śrīla Rūpa; *sanātana*—Sanātana Gosvāmī.

TRANSLATION

I offer my respectful obeisances unto Advaita Prabhu, the ocean of mercy, and to all the devotees, such as Svarūpa Dāmodara Gosvāmī, Gadādhara Paṇḍita, Śrī Rūpa Gosvāmī and Śrī Sanātana Gosvāmī.

TEXT 4

একদিন প্রদ্যুম্ন-মিশ্র প্রভুর চরণে ।
দণ্ডবৎ করি' কিছু করে নিবেদনে ॥ ৪ ॥

eka-dina pradyumna-miśra prabhura caraṇe
daṇḍavat kari' kichu kare nivedane

SYNONYMS

eka-dina—one day; *pradyumna-miśra*—the devotee named Pradyumna Miśra; *prabhura caraṇe*—at the lotus feet of Śrī Caitanya Mahāprabhu; *daṇḍavat kari'*—offering his respects; *kichu*—something; *kare nivedane*—submits as a petition.

TRANSLATION

One day Pradyumna Miśra came to see Śrī Caitanya Mahāprabhu, offering his respects and inquiring from Him with great submission.

TEXT 5

"শুন, প্রভু, মুঞি দীন গৃহস্থ অধম !
কোন ভাগ্যে পাঞাছোঁ তোমার দুর্লভ চরণ ॥ ৫ ॥

"śuna, prabhu, muñi dīna gṛhastha adhama!
kona bhāgye pāñāchoṅ tomāra durlabha caraṇa

SYNONYMS

śuna—please hear; *prabhu*—my Lord; *muñi*—I; *dīna*—very fallen; *gṛhastha*—householder; *adhama*—the lowest of men; *kona bhāgye*—by some good fortune; *pāñāchoṅ*—I have gotten; *tomāra*—Your; *durlabha*—rarely achieved; *caraṇa*—lotus feet.

TRANSLATION

"My Lord," he said, "kindly hear me. I am a cripple-minded householder, the most fallen of men, but somehow, by my good fortune, I have received the shelter of Your lotus feet, which are rarely to be seen.

TEXT 6

কৃষ্ণকথা শুনিবারে মোর ইচ্ছা হয়।
কৃষ্ণকথা কহ মোরে হঞা সদয়॥" ৬॥

kṛṣṇa-kathā śunibāre mora icchā haya
kṛṣṇa-kathā kaha more hañā sadaya"

SYNONYMS

kṛṣṇa-kathā—discussions on the subject of Lord Kṛṣṇa; *śunibāre*—to hear; *mora*—my; *icchā*—desire; *haya*—is; *kṛṣṇa-kathā*—talks about Lord Śrī Kṛṣṇa; *kaha*—kindly speak; *more*—unto me; *hañā*—being; *sa-daya*—kind.

TRANSLATION

"I wish to hear topics concerning Lord Kṛṣṇa constantly. Be merciful unto me and kindly tell me something about Kṛṣṇa."

TEXT 7

প্রভু কহেন,—"কৃষ্ণকথা আমি নাহি জানি।
সবে রামানন্দ জানে, তাঁর মুখে শুনি॥ ৭॥

prabhu kahena,—"kṛṣṇa-kathā āmi nāhi jāni
sabe rāmānanda jāne, tāṅra mukhe śuni

SYNONYMS

prabhu kahena—the Lord replied; *kṛṣṇa-kathā*—talks about Lord Kṛṣṇa; *āmi*—I; *nāhi jāni*—do not know; *sabe*—only; *rāmānanda jāne*—Rāmānanda Rāya knows; *tāṅra mukhe*—from his mouth; *śuni*—I hear.

TRANSLATION

Śrī Caitanya Mahāprabhu replied, "I do not know about topics concerning Lord Kṛṣṇa. I think that only Rāmānanda Rāya knows, for I hear these topics from him.

TEXT 8

ভাগ্যে তোমার কৃষ্ণকথা শুনিতে হয় মন।
রামানন্দ-পাশ যাই' করহ শ্রবণ॥ ৮॥

bhāgye tomāra kṛṣṇa-kathā śunite haya mana
rāmānanda-pāśa yāi' karaha śravaṇa

SYNONYMS

bhāgye—by fortune; *tomāra*—your; *kṛṣṇa-kathā*—topics about Lord Kṛṣṇa; *śunite*—to hear; *haya mana*—there is an inclination; *rāmānanda-pāśa*—to Rāmānanda Rāya; *yāi'*—going; *karaha śravaṇa*—hear.

TRANSLATION

"It is your good fortune that you are inclined to hear topics regarding Kṛṣṇa. The best course for you would be to go to Rāmānanda Rāya and hear these topics from him.

TEXT 9

কৃষ্ণকথায় রুচি তোমার—বড় ভাগ্যবান্।
যার কৃষ্ণকথায় রুচি, সেই ভাগ্যবান্ ॥ ৯ ॥

kṛṣṇa-kathāya ruci tomāra——baḍa bhāgyavān
yāra kṛṣṇa-kathāya ruci, sei bhāgyavān

SYNONYMS

kṛṣṇa-kathāya—in talking of Kṛṣṇa; *ruci*—taste; *tomāra*—your; *baḍa bhāgyavān*—very fortunate; *yāra*—of whom; *kṛṣṇa-kathāya*—in hearing about Kṛṣṇa; *ruci*—taste; *sei bhāgyavān*—he is very fortunate.

TRANSLATION

"I see that you have acquired a taste for hearing talks regarding Kṛṣṇa. Therefore you are extremely fortunate. Not only you but anyone who has awakened such a taste is considered most fortunate.

TEXT 10

ধর্মঃ স্বনুষ্ঠিতঃ পুংসাং বিষ্বক্সেনকথাসু যঃ।
নোৎপাদয়েদ্যদি রতিং শ্রম এব হি কেবলম্ ॥ ১০ ॥

dharmaḥ svanuṣṭhitaḥ puṁsāṁ
viṣvaksena-kathāsu yaḥ
notpādayed yadi ratiṁ
śrama eva hi kevalam

SYNONYMS

dharmaḥ—execution of the system of *varṇa* and *āśrama*; *su-anuṣṭhitaḥ*—properly executed; *puṁsām*—of men; *viṣvaksena-kathāsu*—in talks about Viṣvaksena, or Kṛṣṇa; *yaḥ*—which; *na*—not; *utpādayet*—awakens; *yadi*—if; *ratim*—taste; *śrama*—labor; *eva*—without doubt; *hi*—certainly; *kevalam*—only.

TRANSLATION

" 'A person who properly performs his regulative duties according to varṇa and āśrama but does not develop his dormant attachment for Kṛṣṇa or awaken his taste to hear and chant about Kṛṣṇa is certainly laboring fruitlessly.' "

PURPORT

This is a quotation from *Śrīmad-Bhāgavatam* (1.2.8).

TEXT 11

তবে প্রদ্যুম্ন-মিশ্র গেলা রামানন্দের স্থানে ।
রায়ের সেবক তাঁরে বসাইল আসনে ॥ ১১ ॥

tabe pradyumna-miśra gelā rāmānandera sthāne
rāyera sevaka tāṅre vasāila āsane

SYNONYMS

tabe—thereafter; *pradyumna-miśra*—of the name Pradyumna Miśra; *gelā*—went; *rāmānandera sthāne*—to the place of Rāmānanda Rāya; *rāyera sevaka*—the servant of Rāmānanda Rāya; *tāṅre*—unto him; *vasāila āsane*—gave a sitting place.

TRANSLATION

Pradyumna Miśra, being thus advised by Śrī Caitanya Mahāprabhu, went to the home of Rāmānanda Rāya. There the servant of Rāmānanda Rāya gave him a proper place to sit down.

TEXT 12

দর্শন না পাঞা মিশ্র সেবকে পুছিল ।
রায়ের বৃত্তান্ত সেবক কহিতে লাগিল ॥ ১২ ॥

darśana nā pāñā miśra sevake puchila
rāyera vṛttānta sevaka kahite lāgila

SYNONYMS

darśana—audience; *nā*—not; *pāñā*—getting; *miśra*—Pradyumna Miśra; *sevake*—unto the servant; *puchila*—inquired; *rāyera*—of Rāmānanda Rāya; *vṛttānta*—description; *sevaka*—the servant; *kahite lāgila*—began to speak.

TRANSLATION

Unable to see Rāmānanda Rāya immediately, Pradyumna Miśra inquired from the servant, who then gave a description of Śrī Rāmānanda Rāya.

TEXT 13

"দুই দেব-কন্যা হয় পরম-সুন্দরী ।
নৃত্য-গীতে সুনিপুণা, বয়সে কিশোরী ॥ ১৩ ॥

"dui deva-kanyā haya parama-sundarī
nṛtya-gīte sunipuṇā, vayase kiśorī

SYNONYMS

dui—two; *deva-kanyā*—dancing girls; *haya*—are; *parama-sundarī*—very, very beautiful; *nṛtya-gīte*—in singing and dancing; *su-nipuṇā*—very expert; *vayase*—in age; *kiśorī*—very young.

TRANSLATION

"There are two dancing girls who are extremely beautiful. They are very youthful, and they are expert in dancing and singing.

TEXT 14

সেই দুঁহে লঞা রায় নিভৃত উদ্যানে ।
নিজ-নাটক-গীতের শিখায় নর্তনে ॥ ১৪ ॥

sei duṅhe lañā rāya nibhṛta udyāne
nija-nāṭaka-gītera śikhāya nartane

SYNONYMS

sei duṅhe—those two; *lañā*—taking; *rāya*—Rāmānanda Rāya; *nibhṛta udyāne*—in a solitary place in the garden; *nija-nāṭaka*—of the drama composed by him; *gītera*—of the songs; *śikhāya*—gives direction; *nartane*—in dancing.

TRANSLATION

"Śrīla Rāmānanda Rāya has taken these two girls to a solitary place in his garden, where he is teaching and directing them to dance according to the songs he has composed for his drama.

PURPORT

The drama being rehearsed by Rāmānanda Rāya and the two young girls was the well-known *Jagannātha-vallabha-nāṭaka.* The songs and dances were meant for the pleasure of Lord Jagannātha; therefore Rāmānanda Rāya was personally giving instructions on how to sing and dance for the drama.

TEXT 15

তুমি ইহাঁ বসি' রহ, ক্ষণেকে আসিবেন ।
তবে যেই আজ্ঞা দেহ, সেই করিবেন ॥" ১৫ ॥

tumi ihāṅ vasi' raha, kṣaṇeke āsibena
tabe yei ājñā deha, sei karibena"

SYNONYMS

tumi—you; *ihāṅ*—here; *vasi'*—sitting; *raha*—just wait; *kṣaṇeke āsibena*—he will come within a moment; *tabe*—then; *yei*—whatever; *ājñā*—order; *deha*—you give; *sei*—he; *karibena*—will do.

TRANSLATION

"Please sit here and wait for a few moments. As soon as he comes, he will execute whatever order you give him."

TEXT 16

তবে প্রদ্যুম্ন-মিশ্র তাহাঁ রহিল বসিয়া ।
রামানন্দ নিভৃতে সেই দুই-জন লঞা ॥ ১৬ ॥

tabe pradyumna-miśra tāhāṅ rahila vasiyā
rāmānanda nibhṛte sei dui-jana lañā

SYNONYMS

tabe—then; *pradyumna-miśra*—of the name Pradyumna Miśra; *tāhāṅ*—there; *rahila vasiyā*—remained seated; *rāmānanda*—Rāmānanda Rāya; *nibhṛte*—in a solitary place; *sei*—those; *dui-jana*—two girls; *lañā*—taking.

TRANSLATION

While Pradyumna Miśra remained seated there, Rāmānanda Rāya took the two girls to a solitary place.

TEXT 17

স্বহস্তে করেন তার অভ্যঙ্গ-মর্দন ।
স্বহস্তে করান স্নান, গাত্র সংমার্জন ॥ ১৭ ॥

sva-haste karena tāra abhyaṅga-mardana
sva-haste karāna snāna, gātra sammārjana

SYNONYMS

sva-haste—with his own hand; *karena*—does; *tāra*—of those two girls; *abhyaṅga-mardana*—massaging the body with oil; *sva-haste*—with his own hand; *karāna snāna*—bathes them; *gātra sammārjana*—cleansing the whole body.

TRANSLATION

With his own hand, Śrī Rāmānanda Rāya massaged their bodies with oil and bathed them with water. Indeed, Rāmānanda Rāya cleansed their entire bodies with his own hand.

TEXT 18

স্বহস্তে পরান বস্ত্র, সর্বাঙ্গ মণ্ডন ।
তবু নির্বিকার রায়-রামানন্দের মন ॥ ১৮ ॥

sva-haste parāna vastra, sarvāṅga maṇḍana
tabu nirvikāra rāya-rāmānandera mana

SYNONYMS

sva-haste—with his own hand; *parāna vastra*—dresses them; *sarvāṅga maṇḍana*—decorating the whole body; *tabu*—still; *nirvikāra*—without transformation; *rāya-rāmānandera*—of Rāmānanda Rāya; *mana*—the mind.

TRANSLATION

Although he dressed the two young girls and decorated their bodies with his own hand, he remained unchanged. Such is the mind of Śrīla Rāmānanda Rāya.

TEXT 19

কাষ্ঠ-পাষাণ-স্পর্শে হয় যৈছে ভাব ।
তরুণী-স্পর্শে রামানন্দের তৈছে 'স্বভাব' ॥ ১৯ ॥

kāṣṭha-pāṣāṇa-sparśe haya yaiche bhāva
taruṇī-sparśe rāmānandera taiche 'svabhāva'

SYNONYMS

kāṣṭha—wood; *pāṣāṇa*—stone; *sparśe*—by touching; *haya*—there is; *yaiche*—as; *bhāva*—mental position; *taruṇī-sparśe*—by touching the young girls; *rāmānandera*—of Rāmānanda Rāya; *taiche*—like that; *svabhāva*—nature.

TRANSLATION

While touching the young girls, he was like a person touching wood or stone, for his body and mind were unaffected.

TEXT 20

সেব্য-বুদ্ধি আরোপিয়া করেন সেবন।
স্বাভাবিক দাসীভাব করেন আরোপণ ॥ ২০ ॥

sevya-bujhi āropiyā karena sevana
svābhāvika dāsī-bhāva karena āropaṇa

SYNONYMS

sevya-bujhi āropiyā—considering worshipable; *karena sevana*—engages in service; *svābhāvika*—by his natural position; *dāsī-bhāva*—as a maidservant; *karena āropaṇa*—considers.

TRANSLATION

Śrīla Rāmānanda Rāya used to act in that way because he thought of himself in his original position as a maidservant of the gopīs. Thus although externally he appeared to be a man, internally, in his original spiritual position, he considered himself a maidservant and considered the two girls gopīs.

PURPORT

Śrīla Bhaktivinoda Ṭhākura writes in his *Amṛta-pravāha-bhāṣya:* "Śrīla Rāmānanda Rāya composed a drama named *Jagannātha-vallabha-nāṭaka,* and he engaged two young girls who were professional dancers and singers to demonstrate the ideology of the drama. Such girls, who are called *deva-dāsīs,* are still employed in the temple of Jagannātha, where they are called *māhārīs.* Śrī Rāmānanda Rāya engaged two such girls, and because they were meant to play the parts of *gopīs,* he taught them how to awaken thoughts like those of the *gopīs.* Because the *gopīs* are worshipable personalities, Rāmānanda Rāya, who considered the two girls *gopīs* and himself their maidservant, engaged in their service by massaging their bodies with oil to cleanse them completely. Because Rāmānanda Rāya always placed himself in the position of a maidservant of the *gopīs*, his rehearsal with the girls was actually on the spiritual platform."

Because there was no question of personal sense gratification when Śrī Rāmānanda Rāya was serving the girls, his mind was steady and his body untransformed. This is not to be imitated, nor is such a mentality possible for anyone but Śrī Rāmānanda Rāya, as Śrī Caitanya Mahāprabhu will explain. The example of Śrī Rāmānanda Rāya is certainly unique. The author of *Śrī Caitanya-caritāmṛta* has given this description because in perfect devotional service one can attain such a position. Nevertheless, one must understand this subject very seriously and never attempt to imitate such activities.

TEXT 21

মহাপ্রভুর ভক্তগণের দুর্গম মহিমা ।
তাহে রামানন্দের ভাবভক্তি-প্রেম-সীমা ॥ ২১ ॥

mahāprabhura bhakta-gaṇera durgama mahimā
tāhe rāmānandera bhāva-bhakti-prema-sīmā

SYNONYMS

mahāprabhura—of Lord Śrī Caitanya Mahāprabhu; *bhakta-gaṇera*—of the devotees; *durgama*—difficult to understand; *mahimā*—greatness; *tāhe*—in that connection; *rāmānandera*—of Śrī Rāmānanda Rāya; *bhāva-bhakti*—of ecstatic devotion; *prema-sīmā*—the limit of love of Kṛṣṇa.

TRANSLATION

The greatness of the devotees of Śrī Caitanya Mahāprabhu is exceedingly difficult to understand. Śrī Rāmānanda Rāya is unique among them all, for he showed how one can extend his ecstatic love to the extreme limit.

TEXT 22

তবে সেই দুইজনে নৃত্য শিখাইলা ।
গীতের গূঢ় অর্থ অভিনয় করাইলা ॥ ২২ ॥

tabe sei dui-jane nṛtya śikhāilā
gītera gūḍha artha abhinaya karāilā

SYNONYMS

tabe—thereupon; *sei*—those; *dui-jane*—two young girls; *nṛtya śikhāilā*—directed how to dance; *gītera*—of the songs; *gūḍha artha*—the deep meaning; *abhinaya karāilā*—taught how to express by dramatic performances.

TRANSLATION

Rāmānanda Rāya directed the two girls how to dance and express the deep meaning of his songs through dramatic performances.

TEXT 23

সঞ্চারী, সাত্ত্বিক, স্থায়ি-ভাবের লক্ষণ ।
মুখে নেত্রে অভিনয় করে প্রকটন ॥ ২৩ ॥

sañcārī, sāttvika, sthāyi-bhāvera lakṣaṇa
mukhe netre abhinaya kare prakaṭana

SYNONYMS

sañcārī—passing; *sāttvika*—natural; *sthāyi*—continuously existing; *bhāvera*—of ecstasies; *lakṣaṇa*—symptoms; *mukhe*—in the facial expressions; *netre*—in the movement of the eyes; *abhinaya*—the dramatic performance; *kare prakaṭana*—he demonstrates.

TRANSLATION

He taught them how to express the symptoms of continuous, natural and transitional ecstasies with the movements of their faces, their eyes and the other parts of their bodies.

TEXT 24

ভাবপ্রকটন-লাস্য রায় যে শিখায় ।
জগন্নাথের আগে দুঁহে প্রকট দেখায় ॥ ২৪ ॥

bhāva-prakaṭana-lāsya rāya ye śikhāya
jagannāthera āge duṅhe prakaṭa dekhāya

SYNONYMS

bhāva—ecstasy; *prakaṭana*—manifesting; *lāsya*—feminine poses and dancing; *rāya*—Rāmānanda Rāya; *ye*—which; *śikhāya*—was teaching; *jagannāthera āge*—in front of Lord Jagannātha; *duṅhe*—both of them; *prakaṭa dekhāya*—demonstrated.

TRANSLATION

Through the feminine poses and dances they were taught by Rāmānanda Rāya, the two girls precisely exhibited all these expressions of ecstasy before Lord Jagannātha.

TEXT 25

তবে সেই দুইজনে প্রসাদ খাওয়াইলা ।
নিভৃতে দুঁহারে নিজ-ঘরে পাঠাইলা ॥ ২৫ ॥

tabe sei dui-jane prasāda khāoyāilā
nibhṛte duṅhāre nija-ghare pāṭhāilā

SYNONYMS

tabe—then; *sei*—to those; *dui-jane*—two girls; *prasāda khāoyāilā*—gave *prasāda* to eat; *nibhṛte*—without being exposed; *duṅhāre*—both of them; *nija-ghare*—their homes; *pāṭhāilā*—sent.

TRANSLATION

Then Rāmānanda Rāya fed the two girls sumptuous prasāda and sent them to their homes unexposed.

TEXT 26

প্রতিদিন রায় ঐছে করায় সাধন ।
কোন্ জানে ক্ষুদ্র জীব কাঁহা তাঁর মন ? ২৬ ॥

prati-dina rāya aiche karāya sādhana
kon jāne kṣudra jīva kāṅhā tāṅra mana?

SYNONYMS

prati-dina—daily; *rāya*—Rāmānanda Rāya; *aiche*—in this way; *karāya sādhana*—teaches regularly; *kon jāne*—who can know; *kṣudra jīva*—an insignificant living entity; *kāṅhā*—where; *tāṅra*—his; *mana*—mind.

TRANSLATION

Every day he trained the two deva-dāsīs how to dance. Who among the small living entities, their minds always absorbed in material sense gratification, could understand the mentality of Śrī Rāmānanda Rāya?

PURPORT

Rāmānanda Rāya's service to the *gopīs* for the satisfaction of Kṛṣṇa is purely an affair of the spiritual world. Unless one is fully situated in the spiritual atmosphere, the activities of Rāmānanda Rāya are most difficult to understand.

TEXT 27

মিশ্রের আগমন রায়ে সেবক কহিলা।
শীঘ্র রামানন্দ তবে সভাতে আইলা ॥ ২৭ ॥

miśrera āgamana rāye sevaka kahilā
śīghra rāmānanda tabe sabhāte āilā

SYNONYMS

miśrera—of Pradyumna Miśra; *āgamana*—arrival; *rāye*—to Rāmānanda Rāya; *sevaka kahilā*—the servant informed; *śīghra*—very soon; *rāmānanda*—Rāmānanda Rāya; *tabe*—thereupon; *sabhāte āilā*—came to the assembly room.

TRANSLATION

When the servant informed Rāmānanda Rāya of Pradyumna Miśra's arrival, Rāmānanda Rāya immediately went to the assembly room.

TEXT 28

মিশ্রেরে নমস্কার করে সম্মান করিয়া।
নিবেদন করে কিছু বিনীত হঞা ॥ ২৮ ॥

miśrere namaskāra kare sammāna kariyā
nivedana kare kichu vinīta hañā

SYNONYMS

miśrere—unto Pradyumna Miśra; *namaskāra kare*—offers respectful obeisances; *sammāna kariyā*—with all respect; *nivedana kare*—submitted; *kichu*—something; *vinīta hañā*—with great humility.

TRANSLATION

He offered his obeisances to Pradyumna Miśra with all respect and then, with great humility, spoke as follows.

TEXT 29

"বহুক্ষণ আইলা, মোরে কেহ না কহিল ।
তোমার চরণে মোর অপরাধ হইল ॥ ২৯ ॥

"bahu-kṣaṇa āilā, more keha nā kahila
tomāra caraṇe mora aparādha ha-ila

SYNONYMS

bahu-kṣaṇa—long ago; *āilā*—you came; *more*—me; *keha nā kahila*—no one informed; *tomāra caraṇe*—unto your lotus feet; *mora*—my; *aparādha*—offense; *ha-ila*—there was.

TRANSLATION

"Sir, you came here long ago, but no one informed me. Therefore I have certainly become an offender at your lotus feet.

TEXT 30

তোমার আগমনে মোর পবিত্র হৈল ঘর ।
আজ্ঞা কর, ক্যা করোঁ তোমার কিঙ্কর ॥" ৩০ ॥

tomāra āgamane mora pavitra haila ghara
ājñā kara, kyā karoṅ tomāra kiṅkara"

SYNONYMS

tomāra āgamane—because of your arrival; *mora*—my; *pavitra*—purified; *haila*—became; *ghara*—house; *ājñā kara*—kindly order; *kyā karoṅ*—what can I do; *tomāra kiṅkara*—I am your servant.

TRANSLATION

"My entire home has been purified by your arrival. Kindly order me. What can I do for you? I am your servant."

TEXT 31

মিশ্র কহে,—"তোমা দেখিতে হৈল আগমনে ।
আপনা পবিত্র কৈলুঁ তোমার দরশনে ॥" ৩১ ॥

miśra kahe,—"tomā dekhite haila āgamane
āpanā pavitra kailuṅ tomāra daraśane"

SYNONYMS

miśra kahe—Pradyumna Miśra replied; *tomā*—you; *dekhite*—to see; *haila āgamane*—I came; *āpanā*—myself; *pavitra kailuṅ*—I have purified; *tomāra daraśane*—by seeing you.

TRANSLATION

Pradyumna Miśra replied, "I came simply to see you. Now I have purified myself by seeing Your Honor."

TEXT 32

অতিকাল দেখি' মিশ্র কিছু না কহিল।
বিদায় হইয়া মিশ্র নিজঘর গেল ॥ ৩২ ॥

atikāla dekhi' miśra kichu nā kahila
vidāya ha-iyā miśra nija-ghara gela

SYNONYMS

atikāla dekhi'—seeing that it was too late; *miśra*—Pradyumna Miśra; *kichu*—anything; *nā kahila*—did not say; *vidāya ha-iyā*—taking leave; *miśra*—Pradyumna Miśra; *nija-ghara*—to his own place; *gela*—returned.

TRANSLATION

Because Pradyumna Miśra saw that it was late, he did not say anything else to Rāmānanda Rāya. Instead, he took leave of him and returned to his own home.

TEXT 33

আর দিন মিশ্র আইল প্রভু-বিদ্যমানে।
প্রভু কহে,—'কৃষ্ণকথা শুনিলা রায়স্থানে'? ৩৩ ॥

āra dina miśra āila prabhu-vidyamāne
prabhu kahe,——'kṛṣṇa-kathā śunilā rāya-sthāne'?

SYNONYMS

āra dina—the next day; *miśra*—Pradyumna Miśra; *āila*—came; *prabhu-vidyamāne*—in the presence of Śrī Caitanya Mahāprabhu; *prabhu kahe*—Śrī Caitanya Mahāprabhu inquired; *kṛṣṇa-kathā*—talks about Kṛṣṇa; *śunilā*—have you heard; *rāya-sthāne*—from Śrī Rāmānanda Rāya.

TRANSLATION

The next day, when Pradyumna Miśra arrived in the presence of Śrī Caitanya Mahāprabhu, the Lord inquired, "Have you heard talks about Kṛṣṇa from Śrī Rāmānanda Rāya?"

TEXT 34

তবে মিশ্র রামানন্দের বৃত্তান্ত কহিলা।
শুনি' মহাপ্রভু তবে কহিতে লাগিলা॥ ৩৪॥

tabe miśra rāmānandera vṛttānta kahilā
śuni' mahāprabhu tabe kahite lāgilā

SYNONYMS

tabe—thereupon; *miśra*—Pradyumna Miśra; *rāmānandera*—of Śrī Rāmānanda Rāya; *vṛttānta kahilā*—described the activities; *śuni'*—hearing; *mahāprabhu*—Śrī Caitanya Mahāprabhu; *tabe*—then; *kahite lāgilā*—began to speak.

TRANSLATION

Pradyumna Miśra thereupon described the activities of Śrī Rāmānanda Rāya. After hearing about these activities, Śrī Caitanya Mahāprabhu began to speak.

TEXTS 35-36

"আমি ত' সন্ন্যাসী, আপনারে বিরক্ত করি' মানি।
দর্শন রহু দূরে, 'প্রকৃতির' নাম যদি শুনি॥ ৩৫॥
তবহিঁ বিকার পায় মোর তনু-মন।
প্রকৃতি-দর্শনে স্থির হয় কোন্ জন?" ৩৬॥

"āmi ta' sannyāsī, āpanāre virakta kari' māni
darśana rahu dūre, 'prakṛtira' nāma yadi śuni

tabahiṁ vikāra pāya mora tanu-mana
prakṛti-darśane sthira haya kon jana?"

SYNONYMS

āmi—I; *ta'*—certainly; *sannyāsī*—in the renounced order of life; *āpanāre*—Myself; *virakta kari'*—having renounced everything; *māni*—I consider; *darśana rahu dūre*—what to speak of seeing; *prakṛtira*—of a woman; *nāma*—name; *yadi*—if; *śuni*—I hear; *tabahiṅ*—immediately; *vikāra*—transformation; *pāya*—gets; *mora*—My; *tanu-mana*—mind and body; *prakṛti-darśane*—by seeing a woman; *sthira*—steady; *haya*—is; *kon jana*—what person.

TRANSLATION

"I am a sannyāsī," He said, "and I certainly consider Myself renounced. But not to speak of seeing a woman, if I even hear the name of a woman, I feel changes in My mind and body. Therefore who could remain unmoved by the sight of a woman? It is very difficult.

TEXT 37

রামানন্দ রায়ের কথা শুন, সর্বজন।
কহিবার কথা নহে, যাহা আশ্চর্য-কথন ॥ ৩৭ ॥

rāmānanda rāyera kathā śuna, sarva-jana
kahibāra kathā nahe, yāhā āścarya-kathana

SYNONYMS

rāmānanda rāyera—of Śrī Rāmānanda Rāya; *kathā*—topics; *śuna*—please hear; *sarva-jana*—all people; *kahibāra*—to be spoken; *kathā*—talks; *nahe*—they are not; *yāhā*—which; *āścarya-kathana*—wonderful and uncommon talks.

TRANSLATION

"Everyone please hear these topics about Rāmānanda Rāya, although they are so wonderful and uncommon that they should not be spoken.

TEXT 38

একে দেবদাসী, আর সুন্দরী তরুণী।
তার সব অঙ্গ-সেবা করেন আপনি ॥ ৩৮ ॥

eke deva-dāsī, āra sundarī taruṇī
tāra saba aṅga-sevā karena āpani

SYNONYMS

eke—on one side; *deva-dāsī*—the professional dancing girls; *āra*—and; *sundarī taruṇī*—very beautiful and youthful; *tāra*—their; *saba*—all; *aṅga*—of the body; *sevā*—service; *karena āpani*—performs personally.

TRANSLATION

"The two professional dancing girls are beautiful and youthful, yet Śrī Rāmānanda Rāya personally massages oil upon their bodies.

TEXT 39

স্নানাদি করায়, পরায় বাস-বিভূষণ ।
গুহ্য অঙ্গের হয় তাহা দর্শন-স্পর্শন ॥ ৩৯ ॥

snānādi karāya, parāya vāsa-vibhūṣaṇa
guhya aṅgera haya tāhā darśana-sparśana

SYNONYMS

snāna-ādi karāya—he performs their bathing and so on; *parāya vāsa-vibhūṣaṇa*—dresses and decorates the body with various types of ornaments; *guhya aṅgera*—of the private parts of the body; *haya*—there is; *tāhā*—that; *darśana sparśana*—seeing and touching.

TRANSLATION

"He personally bathes and dresses them and decorates them with ornaments. In this way, he naturally sees and touches the private parts of their bodies.

TEXT 40

তবু নির্বিকার রায়-রামানন্দের মন ।
নানাভাবোদ্গার তারে করায় শিক্ষণ ॥ ৪০ ॥

tabu nirvikāra rāya-rāmānandera mana
nānā-bhāvodgāra tāre karāya śikṣaṇa

SYNONYMS

tabu—still; *nirvikāra*—unchanged; *rāya-rāmānandera mana*—the mind of Śrī Rāmānanda Rāya; *nānā-bhāva-udgāra*—all the symptoms and transformations of ecstasy; *tāre*—unto them; *karāya śikṣaṇa*—he teaches.

TRANSLATION

"Nevertheless, the mind of Śrī Rāmānanda Rāya never changes, although he teaches the girls how to physically express all the transformations of ecstasy.

TEXT 41

নির্বিকার দেহ-মন—কাষ্ঠ-পাষাণ-সম !
আশ্চর্য,—তরুণী-স্পর্শে নির্বিকার মন ॥ ৪১ ॥

nirvikāra deha-mana——kāṣṭha-pāṣāṇa-sama!
āścarya,——taruṇī-sparśe nirvikāra mana

SYNONYMS

nirvikāra—unchanged; *deha-mana*—body and mind; *kāṣṭha-pāṣāṇa-sama*—like wood or stone; *āścarya*—wonderful; *taruṇī-sparśe*—in touching young girls; *nirvikāra*—unchanged; *mana*—mind.

TRANSLATION

"His mind is as steady as wood or stone. Indeed, it is wonderful that even when he touches such young girls, his mind never changes.

TEXT 42

এক রামানন্দের হয় এই অধিকার ।
তাতে জানি অপ্রাকৃত-দেহ তাঁহার ॥ ৪২ ॥

eka rāmānandera haya ei adhikāra
tāte jāni aprākṛta-deha tāṅhāra

SYNONYMS

eka—only one; *rāmānandera*—of Śrī Rāmānanda Rāya; *haya*—there is; *ei*—this; *adhikāra*—special authority; *tāte*—in that way; *jāni*—we can understand; *aprākṛta*—spiritual; *deha*—body; *tāṅhāra*—his.

TRANSLATION

"The authority for such acts is the prerogative of Rāmānanda Rāya alone, for I can understand that his body is not material but has been completely transformed into a spiritual entity.

TEXT 43

তাঁহার মনের ভাব তেঁহ জানে মাত্র ।
তাহা জানিবারে আর দ্বিতীয় নাহি পাত্র ॥ ৪৩ ॥

tāṅhāra manera bhāva teṅha jāne mātra
tāhā jānibāre āra dvitīya nāhi pātra

SYNONYMS

tāṅhāra—his; *manera*—of the mind; *bhāva*—position; *teṅha*—he; *jāne*—knows; *mātra*—only; *tāhā jānibāre*—to understand that; *āra*—other; *dvitīya*—second; *nāhi*—there is not; *pātra*—eligible person.

TRANSLATION

"He alone, and no one else, can understand the position of his mind.

TEXT 44

কিন্তু শাস্ত্রদৃষ্ট্যে এক করি অনুমান।
শ্রীভাগবত-শাস্ত্র—তাহাতে প্রমাণ ॥ ৪৪ ॥

kintu śāstra-dṛṣṭye eka kari anumāna
śrī-bhāgavata-śāstra——tāhāte pramāṇa

SYNONYMS

kintu—but; *śāstra-dṛṣṭye*—according to the direction of the *śāstra*; *eka*—one; *kari anumāna*—I make a guess; *śrī-bhāgavata-śāstra*—*Śrīmad-Bhāgavatam,* the Vedic scripture; *tāhāte*—in that connection; *pramāṇa*—evidence.

TRANSLATION

"But I can make a guess in terms of directions from the śāstra. Śrīmad-Bhāgavatam, the Vedic scripture, gives the direct evidence in this matter.

TEXTS 45-46

ব্রজবধূ-সঙ্গে কৃষ্ণের রাসাদি-বিলাস।
যেই জন কহে, শুনে করিয়া বিশ্বাস ॥ ৪৫ ॥
হৃদ্রোগ-কাম তাঁর তৎকালে হয় ক্ষয়।
তিনগুণ-ক্ষোভ নহে, 'মহাধীর' হয় ॥ ৪৬ ॥

vraja-vadhū-saṅge kṛṣṇera rāsādi-vilāsa
yei jana kahe, śune kariyā viśvāsa

hṛd-roga-kāma tāṅra tat-kāle haya kṣaya
tina-guṇa-kṣobha nahe, 'mahā-dhīra' haya

SYNONYMS

vraja-vadhū-saṅge—in the association of the damsels of Vrajabhūmi; *kṛṣṇera*—of Lord Kṛṣṇa; *rāsa-ādi-vilāsa*—pastimes like the *rāsa* dance; *yei*—which; *jana*—

person; *kahe*—describes; *śune*—hears; *kariyā viśvāsa*—with great faith; *hṛt-roga*—the disease of the heart; *kāma*—lust; *tāṅra*—of him; *tat-kāle*—at that time; *haya kṣaya*—becomes nullified; *tina-guṇa*—of the three modes of material nature; *kṣobha*—agitation; *nahe*—is not; *mahā-dhīra*—very sober; *haya*—becomes.

TRANSLATION

"When one hears or describes with great faith the pastimes of Lord Kṛṣṇa, such as His rāsa dance with the gopīs, the disease of lusty desires in his heart and the agitation caused by the three modes of material nature are immediately nullified, and he becomes sober and silent.

PURPORT

Śrīla Bhaktisiddhānta Sarasvatī Ṭhākura comments in this connection, "Any person seriously inclined to hear about the pastimes of Kṛṣṇa's *rāsa* dance, as mentioned in *Śrīmad-Bhāgavatam,* with great faith and a transcendental, spiritually inspired mind, is immediately freed from the natural lusty desires found within the heart of a materialistic man."

When a pure Vaiṣṇava speaks on *Śrīmad-Bhāgavatam* and another pure Vaiṣṇava hears *Śrīmad-Bhāgavatam* from such a realized soul, both of them live in the transcendental world, where the contamination of the modes of material nature cannot touch them. Freed from the contamination of the modes of nature, the speaker and hearer are fixed in a transcendental mentality, knowing that their position on the transcendental platform is to serve the Supreme Lord. The class known as *prākṛta-sahajiyā,* who consider the transcendental pastimes of Lord Kṛṣṇa something like the behavior between a man and a woman in the material field, artificially think that hearing the *rāsa-līlā* will help them by diminishing the lusty desires of their diseased hearts. But because they do not follow the regulative principles but instead violate even ordinary morals, their contemplation of *rāsa-līlā* is a futile attempt, which sometimes results in their imitating the dealings of the *gopīs* and Lord Kṛṣṇa. To forbid such habits of the *prākṛta-sahajiyās,* Śrī Caitanya Mahāprabhu has excluded their material intelligence by using the word *viśvāsa* ("faith"). In *Śrīmad-Bhāgavatam* (10.33.31), Śrīla Śukadeva Gosvāmī says:

naitat samācarej jātu
manasāpi hy anīśvaraḥ
vinaśyaty ācaran mauḍhyād
yathā rudro 'bdhijaṁ viṣam

"Certainly one who is not the Supreme Personality of Godhead should never, even within his mind, imitate the activities of the transcendental *rāsa-līlā* of Kṛṣṇa. If out of ignorance one does so, he will be destroyed, just as if he were to imitate Lord Śiva, who drank poison produced from the ocean."

TEXT 47

উজ্জ্বল মধুর প্রেমভক্তি সেই পায়।
আনন্দে কৃষ্ণমাধুর্যে বিহরে সদায় ॥ ৪৭ ॥

ujjvala madhura prema-bhakti sei pāya
ānande kṛṣṇa-mādhurye vihare sadāya

SYNONYMS

ujjvala—illuminated; *madhura*—sweet; *prema-bhakti*—ecstatic love of Kṛṣṇa; *sei*—he; *pāya*—gets; *ānande*—in transcendental bliss; *kṛṣṇa-mādhurye*—the sweetness of Kṛṣṇa's pastimes; *vihare*—enjoys; *sadāya*—always.

TRANSLATION

"Tasting the transcendental, effulgent, sweetly ecstatic love of Kṛṣṇa, such a person can enjoy life twenty-four hours a day in the transcendental bliss of the sweetness of Kṛṣṇa's pastimes.

TEXT 48

বিক্রীড়িতং ব্রজবধূভিরিদঞ্চ বিষ্ণোঃ
শ্রদ্ধান্বিতোঽনুশৃণুয়াদথ বর্ণয়েদ্‌যঃ।
ভক্তিং পরাং ভগবতি প্রতিলভ্য কামং
হৃদ্‌রোগমাশ্বপহিনোত্যচিরেণ ধীরঃ ॥ ৪৮ ॥

vikrīḍitaṁ vraja-vadhūbhir idaṁ ca viṣṇoḥ
śraddhānvito 'nuśṛṇuyād atha varṇayed yaḥ
bhaktiṁ parāṁ bhagavati pratilabhya kāmaṁ
hṛd-rogam āśv apahinoty acireṇa dhīraḥ

SYNONYMS

vikrīḍitam—the activity of the *rāsa* dance; *vraja-vadhūbhiḥ*—the damsels of Vraja, the *gopīs*; *idam*—this; *ca*—and; *viṣṇoḥ*—of Lord Kṛṣṇa; *śraddhā-anvitaḥ*—with transcendental faith; *anuśṛṇuyāt*—continuously hears in the *paramparā* system; *atha*—also; *varṇayet*—describes; *yaḥ*—one who; *bhaktim*—devotional service; *parām*—transcendental; *bhagavati*—unto the Supreme Personality of Godhead; *pratilabhya*—attaining; *kāmam*—lusty material desires; *hṛt-rogam*—the disease of the heart; *āśu*—very soon; *apahinoti*—gives up; *acireṇa*—without delay; *dhīraḥ*—one who is sober because of advanced devotional service.

TRANSLATION

" 'A transcendentally sober person who, with faith and love continuously hears from a realized soul about the activities of Lord Kṛṣṇa in His rāsa dance with the gopīs, or one who describes such activities, can attain full transcendental devotional service at the lotus feet of the Supreme Personality of Godhead. Thus lusty material desires, which are the heart disease of all materialistic persons, are for him quickly and completely vanquished.'

PURPORT

All the activities of Lord Kṛṣṇa are transcendental, and the *gopīs* are also transcendentally situated. Therefore the activities of the *gopīs* and Lord Kṛṣṇa, if seriously understood, will certainly free one from material attachment. Then there is no possibility that lusty material desires will awaken.

TEXTS 49-50

যে শুনে, যে পড়ে, তাঁর ফল এতাদৃশী ।
সেই ভাবাবিষ্ট যেই সেবে অহর্নিশি ॥ ৪৯ ॥
তাঁর ফল কি কহিমু, কহনে না যায় ।
নিত্যসিদ্ধ সেই, প্রায়-সিদ্ধ তাঁর কায় ॥ ৫০ ॥

ye śune, ye paḍe, tāṅra phala etādṛśī
sei bhāvāviṣṭa yei seve ahar-niśi

tāṅra phala ki kahimu, kahane nā yāya
nitya-siddha sei, prāya-siddha tāṅra kāya

SYNONYMS

ye śune—anyone who hears; *ye paḍe*—anyone who recites; *tāṅra*—of him; *phala*—the result; *etādṛśī*—this; *sei*—he; *bhāva-āviṣṭa*—always absorbed in thoughts of Kṛṣṇa; *yei seve*—who serves; *ahaḥ-niśi*—day and night; *tāṅra*—his; *phala*—result; *ki kahimu*—what shall I say; *kahane nā yāya*—it is impossible to express; *nitya-siddha*—eternally liberated; *sei*—such a person; *prāya-siddha*—transcendental; *tāṅra*—his; *kāya*—body.

TRANSLATION

"If a transcendentally situated person, following in the footsteps of Śrīla Rūpa Gosvāmī, hears and speaks about the rāsa-līlā dance of Kṛṣṇa and is always absorbed in thoughts of Kṛṣṇa while serving the Lord day and night within his mind, what shall I say about the result? It is so spiritually exalted that it

cannot be expressed in words. Such a person is an eternally liberated associate of the Lord, and his body is completely spiritualized. Although he is visible to material eyes, he is spiritually situated, and all his activities are spiritual. By the will of Kṛṣṇa, such a devotee is understood to possess a spiritual body.

TEXT 51

রাগানুগ-মার্গে জানি রায়ের ভজন।
সিদ্ধদেহ-তুল্য, তাতে 'প্রাকৃত' নহে মন ॥ ৫১ ॥

rāgānuga-mārge jāni rāyera bhajana
siddha-deha-tulya, tāte 'prākṛta' nahe mana

SYNONYMS

rāgānuga-mārge—on the path of spontaneous love of Kṛṣṇa; *jāni*—we can understand; *rāyera bhajana*—the devotional service of Rāmānanda Rāya; *siddha-deha*—spiritual body; *tulya*—equal to; *tāte*—therefore; *prākṛta*—material; *nahe*—is not; *mana*—mind.

TRANSLATION

"Śrīla Rāmānanda Rāya is situated on the path of spontaneous love of Godhead. Therefore he is in his spiritual body, and his mind is not materially affected.

TEXT 52

আমিহ রায়ের স্থানে শুনি কৃষ্ণকথা।
শুনিতে ইচ্ছা হয় যদি, পুনঃ যাহ তথা ॥ ৫২ ॥

āmiha rāyera sthāne śuni kṛṣṇa-kathā
śunite icchā haya yadi, punaḥ yāha tathā

SYNONYMS

āmiha—I also; *rāyera sthāne*—from Rāmānanda Rāya; *śuni*—hear; *kṛṣṇa-kathā*—talks of Kṛṣṇa; *śunite*—to hear; *icchā*—desire; *haya*—there is; *yadi*—if; *punaḥ*—again; *yāha*—go; *tathā*—there.

TRANSLATION

"I also hear topics about Kṛṣṇa from Rāmānanda Rāya. If you want to hear such topics, go to him again.

TEXT 53

মোর নাম লইহ, –'তেহো পাঠাইলা মোরে।
তোমার স্থানে কৃষ্ণকথা শুনিবার তরে॥' ৫৩ ॥

mora nāma la-iha,—'teho pāṭhāilā more
tomāra sthāne kṛṣṇa-kathā śunibāra tare'

SYNONYMS

mora—My; *nāma*—name; *la-iha*—take; *teho*—He; *pāṭhāilā*—sent; *more*—me; *tomāra sthāne*—from you; *kṛṣṇa-kathā*—topics of Kṛṣṇa; *śunibāra tare*—to hear.

TRANSLATION

"You can take My name before him, saying, 'He has sent me to hear about Lord Kṛṣṇa from you.'

TEXT 54

শীঘ্র যাহ, যাবৎ তেঁহো আছেন সভাতে।"
এত শুনি' প্রদ্যুম্ন-মিশ্র চলিলা তুরিতে ॥ ৫৪ ॥

śīghra yāha, yāvat teṅho āchena sabhāte"
eta śuni' pradyumna-miśra calilā turite

SYNONYMS

śīghra yāha—go hastily; *yāvat*—while; *teṅho*—he; *āchena*—is; *sabhāte*—in the assembly room; *eta śuni'*—hearing this; *pradyumna-miśra*—Pradyumna Miśra; *calilā*—went; *turite*—very hastily.

TRANSLATION

"Go hastily while he is in the assembly room." Hearing this, Pradyumna Miśra immediately departed.

TEXT 55

রায়-পাশ গেল, রায় প্রণতি করিল।
'আজ্ঞা কর, যে লাগি' আগমন হৈল' ॥ ৫৫ ॥

rāya-pāśa gela, rāya praṇati karila
'ājñā kara, ye lāgi' āgamana haila'

SYNONYMS

rāya-pāśa—to Rāmānanda Rāya; *gela*—he went; *rāya*—Rāmānanda Rāya; *praṇati karila*—offered his respects; *ājñā kara*—please order me; *ye lāgi'*—for what purpose; *āgamana haila*—have you come.

TRANSLATION

Pradyumna Miśra went to Rāmānanda Rāya, who offered him respectful obeisances and said, "Please order me. For what purpose have you come?"

TEXT 56

মিশ্র কহে,—'মহাপ্রভু পাঠাইলা মোরে ।
তোমার স্থানে কৃষ্ণকথা শুনিবার তরে' ॥ ৫৬ ॥

miśra kahe,—'mahāprabhu pāṭhāilā more
tomāra sthāne kṛṣṇa-kathā śunibāra tare'

SYNONYMS

miśra kahe—Pradyumna Miśra said; *mahāprabhu*—Śrī Caitanya Mahāprabhu; *pāṭhāilā more*—has sent me; *tomāra sthāne*—from you; *kṛṣṇa-kathā*—topics of Lord Kṛṣṇa; *śunibāra tare*—to hear.

TRANSLATION

Pradyumna Miśra answered, "Śrī Caitanya Mahāprabhu has sent me to hear topics about Lord Kṛṣṇa from you."

TEXT 57

শুনি' রামানন্দ রায় হৈলা প্রেমাবেশে ।
কহিতে লাগিলা কিছু মনের হরিষে ॥ ৫৭ ॥

śuni' rāmānanda rāya hailā premāveśe
kahite lāgilā kichu manera hariṣe

SYNONYMS

śuni'—hearing; *rāmānanda rāya*—Rāmānanda Rāya; *hailā*—became; *prema-āveśe*—absorbed in ecstatic love; *kahite lāgilā*—began to speak; *kichu*—something; *manera hariṣe*—in transcendental pleasure.

TRANSLATION

Hearing this, Rāmānanda Rāya became absorbed in ecstatic love and began to speak with great transcendental pleasure.

TEXT 58

"প্রভুর আজ্ঞায় কৃষ্ণকথা শুনিতে আইলা এথা ।
ইহা বই মহাভাগ্য আমি পাব কোথা ?" ৫৮ ॥

"prabhura ājñāya kṛṣṇa-kathā śunite āilā ethā
ihā va-i mahā-bhāgya āmi pāba kothā?"

SYNONYMS

prabhura ājñāya—under the instruction of Śrī Caitanya Mahāprabhu; *kṛṣṇa-kathā*—topics of Lord Kṛṣṇa; *śunite*—to hear; *āilā ethā*—you have come here; *ihā va-i*—without this; *mahā-bhāgya*—great fortune; *āmi*—I; *pāba*—will get; *kothā*—where.

TRANSLATION

"Following the instruction of Śrī Caitanya Mahāprabhu, you have come to hear about Kṛṣṇa. This is my great fortune. How else would I get such an opportunity?"

TEXT 59

এত কহি তারে লঞা নিভৃতে বসিলা ।
'কি কথা শুনিতে চাহ ?' মিশ্রেরে পুছিলা ॥ ৫৯ ॥

eta kahi tāre lañā nibhṛte vasilā
'ki kathā śunite cāha?' miśrere puchilā

SYNONYMS

eta kahi—saying this; *tāre*—him; *lañā*—taking; *nibhṛte vasilā*—sat in a secluded place; *ki kathā*—what kind of topics; *śunite cāha*—do you want to hear; *miśrere puchilā*—he inquired from Pradyumna Miśra.

TRANSLATION

Saying this, Śrī Rāmānanda Rāya took Pradyumna Miśra to a secluded place and inquired from him, "What kind of kṛṣṇa-kathā do you want to hear from me?"

TEXT 60

তেঁহো কহে,—"যে কহিলা বিদ্যানগরে।
সেই কথা ক্রমে তুমি কহিবা আমারে ॥ ৬০ ॥

teṅho kahe,——"ye kahilā vidyānagare
sei kathā krame tumi kahibā āmāre

SYNONYMS

teṅho kahe—he replied; *ye*—what; *kahilā*—you spoke; *vidyā-nagare*—at Vidyānagara; *sei kathā*—those topics; *krame*—according to the order; *tumi*—you; *kahibā*—please speak; *āmāre*—to me.

TRANSLATION

Pradyumna Miśra replied, "Kindly tell me about the same topics you spoke about at Vidyānagara.

TEXT 61

আনের কি কথা, তুমি—প্রভুর উপদেষ্টা!
আমি ত' ভিক্ষুক বিপ্র, তুমি—মোর পোষ্টা ॥ ৬১ ॥

ānera ki kathā, tumi——prabhura upadeṣṭā!
āmi ta' bhikṣuka vipra, tumi——mora poṣṭā

SYNONYMS

ānera ki kathā—what to speak of others; *tumi*—you; *prabhura upadeṣṭā*—an instructor of Śrī Caitanya Mahāprabhu ;*āmi*—I; *ta'*—certainly; *bhikṣuka*—beggar; *vipra*—*brāhmaṇa*; *tumi*—you; *mora*—my; *poṣṭā*—maintainer.

TRANSLATION

"You are an instructor even for Śrī Caitanya Mahāprabhu, not to speak of others. I am but a beggar brāhmaṇa, and you are my maintainer.

TEXT 62

ভাল, মন্দ—কিছু আমি পুছিতে না জানি।
'দীন' দেখি' কৃপা করি' কহিবা আপনি ॥" ৬২ ॥

bhāla, manda——kichu āmi puchite nā jāni
'dīna' dekhi' kṛpā kari' kahibā āpani"

SYNONYMS

bhāla—good; *manda*—bad; *kichu*—something; *āmi*—I; *puchite*—to inquire; *nā jāni*—do not know; *dīna*—very poor in knowledge; *dekhi'*—seeing (me); *kṛpā kari'*—very mercifully; *kahibā*—please; *āpani*—by your own good will.

TRANSLATION

"I do not know how to inquire, for I do not know what is good and what is bad. Seeing me to be poor in knowledge, kindly speak whatever is good for me by your own good will."

TEXT 63

তবে রামানন্দ ক্রমে কহিতে লাগিলা।
কৃষ্ণকথা-রসামৃত-সিন্ধু উথলিলা ॥ ৬৩ ॥

tabe rāmānanda krame kahite lāgilā
kṛṣṇa-kathā-rasāmṛta-sindhu uthalilā

SYNONYMS

tabe—thereupon; *rāmānanda*—Rāmānanda Rāya; *krame*—gradually; *kahite lāgilā*—began to speak; *kṛṣṇa-kathā*—of the topics of Kṛṣṇa; *rasāmṛta-sindhu*—the ocean of transcendental mellow; *uthalilā*—became agitated.

TRANSLATION

Thereupon Rāmānanda Rāya gradually began speaking on topics of Kṛṣṇa. Thus the ocean of the transcendental mellow of those topics became agitated.

TEXT 64

আপনে প্রশ্ন করি' পাছে করেন সিদ্ধান্ত।
তৃতীয় প্রহর হৈল, নহে কথা-অন্ত ॥ ৬৪ ॥

āpane praśna kari' pāche karena siddhānta
tṛtīya prahara haila, nahe kathā-anta

SYNONYMS

āpane—personally; *praśna kari'*—making the question; *pāche*—after that; *karena siddhānta*—gives the conclusion; *tṛtīya prahara haila*—it became afternoon; *nahe kathā-anta*—there was no end to such topics.

TRANSLATION

He began personally posing questions and then answering them with conclusive statements. When afternoon came, the topics still did not end.

TEXT 65

বক্তা শ্রোতা কহে শুনে দুঁহে প্রেমাবেশে ।
আত্মস্মৃতি নাহি, কাহাঁ জানিব দিন-শেষে ॥ ৬৫ ॥

vaktā śrotā kahe śune duṅhe premāveśe
ātma-smṛti nāhi, kāhāṅ jāniba dina-śeṣe

SYNONYMS

vaktā—the speaker; *śrotā*—the listener; *kahe*—speaks; *śune*—hears; *duṅhe*—both of them; *prema-āveśe*—in ecstatic love; *ātma-smṛti nāhi*—there was no bodily consciousness; *kāhāṅ*—where; *jāniba*—can understand; *dina-śeṣe*—the end of day.

TRANSLATION

The speaker and listener spoke and heard in ecstatic love. Thus they forgot their bodily consciousness. How, then, could they perceive the end of the day?

TEXT 66

সেবক কহিল,—'দিন হৈল অবসান' ।
তবে রায় কৃষ্ণকথার করিলা বিশ্রাম ॥ ৬৬ ॥

sevaka kahila,—'dina haila avasāna'
tabe rāya kṛṣṇa-kathāra karilā viśrāma

SYNONYMS

sevaka kahila—the servant informed; *dina*—the day; *haila avasāna*—has ended; *tabe*—at that time; *rāya*—Rāmānanda Rāya; *kṛṣṇa-kathāra*—the talks of Kṛṣṇa; *karilā viśrāma*—ended.

TRANSLATION

The servant informed them, "The day has already ended." Then Rāmānanda Rāya ended his discourses about Kṛṣṇa.

TEXT 67

বহুসম্মান করি' মিশ্রে বিদায় দিলা ।
'কৃতার্থ হইলাঙ' বলি' মিশ্র নাচিতে লাগিলা ॥ ৬৭ ॥

bahu-sammāna kari' miśre vidāya dilā
'kṛtārtha ha-ilāṅa' bali' miśra nācite lāgilā

SYNONYMS

bahu-sammāna—much respectful behavior; *kari'*—doing; *miśre*—unto Pradyumna Miśra; *vidāya dilā*—bade farewell; *kṛtārtha ha-ilāṅa*—I have become very satisfied; *bali'*—saying; *miśra*—Pradyumna Miśra; *nācite lāgilā*—began to dance.

TRANSLATION

Rāmānanda Rāya paid great respect to Pradyumna Miśra and bade him farewell. Pradyumna Miśra said, "I have become very satisfied." He then began to dance.

TEXT 68

ঘরে গিয়া মিশ্র কৈল স্নান, ভোজন ।
সন্ধ্যাকালে দেখিতে আইল প্রভুর চরণ ॥ ৬৮ ॥

ghare giyā miśra kaila snāna, bhojana
sandhyā-kāle dekhite āila prabhura caraṇa

SYNONYMS

ghare giyā—returning home; *miśra*—Pradyumna Miśra; *kaila*—performed; *snāna*—bathing; *bhojana*—eating; *sandhyā-kāle*—in the evening; *dekhite*—to see; *āila*—came; *prabhura caraṇa*—the lotus feet of Śrī Caitanya Mahāprabhu.

TRANSLATION

After returning home, Pradyumna Miśra bathed and ate his meal. In the evening he came to see the lotus feet of Śrī Caitanya Mahāprabhu.

TEXT 69

প্রভুর চরণ বন্দে উল্লসিত-মনে ।
প্রভু কহে,—'কৃষ্ণকথা হইল শ্রবণে' ? ৬৯ ॥

prabhura caraṇa vande ullasita-mane
prabhu kake,——'kṛṣṇa-kathā ha-ila śravaṇe'?

SYNONYMS

prabhura—of Śrī Caitanya Mahāprabhu; *caraṇa*—the lotus feet; *vande*—he worships; *ullasita-mane*—in great happiness; *prabhu kahe*—Śrī Caitanya Mahāprabhu says; *kṛṣṇa-kathā*—talks of Kṛṣṇa; *ha-ila śravaṇe*—did you hear.

TRANSLATION

In great happiness he worshiped the lotus feet of Śrī Caitanya Mahāprabhu. The Lord inquired, "Have you heard topics about Kṛṣṇa?"

TEXT 70

মিশ্র কহে,– "প্রভু, মোরে কৃতার্থ করিলা।
কৃষ্ণকথামৃতার্ণবে মোরে ডুবাইলা ॥ ৭০ ॥

miśra kahe,——"prabhu, more kṛtārtha karilā
kṛṣṇa-kathāmṛtārṇave more ḍubāilā

SYNONYMS

miśra kahe—Pradyumna Miśra said; *prabhu*—my dear Lord; *more*—me; *kṛtārtha*—satisfied; *karilā*—You have made; *kṛṣṇa-kathā*—of talks about Kṛṣṇa; *amṛta-arṇave*—in the ocean of the nectar; *more*—me; *ḍubāilā*—You have drowned.

TRANSLATION

Pradyumna Miśra said, "My dear Lord, You have made me extremely obliged to You because You have drowned me in a nectarean ocean of talks about Kṛṣṇa.

TEXT 71

রামানন্দ রায়-কথা কহিলে না হয়।
'মনুষ্য' নহে রায়, কৃষ্ণভক্তিরসময় ॥ ৭১ ॥

rāmānanda rāya-kathā kahile nā haya
'manuṣya' nahe rāya, kṛṣṇa-bhakti-rasa-maya

SYNONYMS

rāmānanda rāya-kathā—the speeches of Rāmānanda Rāya; *kahile*—describing; *nā haya*—is not possible; *manuṣya*—an ordinary human being; *nahe*—is not; *rāya*—Rāmānanda Rāya; *kṛṣṇa-bhakti-rasa-maya*—absorbed in the devotional service of Lord Kṛṣṇa.

TRANSLATION

"I cannot properly describe the discourses of Rāmānanda Rāya, for he is not an ordinary human being. He is fully absorbed in the devotional service of the Lord.

PURPORT

One is forbidden to accept the *guru,* or spiritual master, as an ordinary human being (*guruṣu nara-matiḥ*). When Rāmānanda Rāya spoke to Pradyumna Miśra, Pradyumna Miśra could understand that Rāmānanda Rāya was not an ordinary human being. A spiritually advanced person who acts with authority, as the spiritual master, speaks as the Supreme Personality of Godhead dictates from within. Thus it is not he that is personally speaking. When a pure devotee or spiritual master speaks, what he says should be accepted as having been directly spoken by the Supreme Personality of Godhead in the *paramparā* system.

TEXT 72

আর এক কথা রায় কহিলা আমারে ।
'কৃষ্ণকথা-বক্তা করি' না জানিহ মোরে ॥ ৭২ ॥

āra eka kathā rāya kahilā āmāre
'kṛṣṇa-kathā-vaktā kari' nā jāniha more

SYNONYMS

āra—another; *eka*—one; *kathā*—topic; *rāya*—Rāmānanda Rāya; *kahilā āmāre*—said to me; *kṛṣṇa-kathā-vaktā*—the speaker on the talks of Kṛṣṇa; *kari'*—as; *nā jāniha more*—do not consider me.

TRANSLATION

"There is one other thing Rāmānanda Rāya said to me. 'Do not consider me the speaker in these talks about Kṛṣṇa.

TEXT 73

মোর মুখে কথা কহেন আপনে গৌরচন্দ্র ।
যৈছে কহায়, তৈছে কহি,—যেন বীণাযন্ত্র ॥ ৭৩ ॥

mora mukhe kathā kahena āpane gauracandra
yaiche kahāya, taiche kahi,——yena vīṇā-yantra

SYNONYMS

mora mukhe—in my mouth; *kathā*—topics; *kahena*—speaks; *āpane*—personally; *gaura-candra*—Lord Śrī Caitanya Mahāprabhu; *yaiche kahāya*—as He causes to speak; *taiche kahi*—so I speak; *yena*—like; *vīṇā-yantra*—the stringed instrument called the *vīṇā.*

TRANSLATION

" 'Whatever I speak is personally spoken by Lord Śrī Caitanya Mahāprabhu. Like a stringed instrument, I vibrate whatever He causes me to speak.

TEXT 74

মোর মুখে কহায় কথা, করে পরচার ।
পৃথিবীতে কে জানিবে এ-লীলা তাঁহার ?' ৭৪ ॥

mora mukhe kahāya kathā, kare paracāra
pṛthivīte ke jānibe e-līlā tāṅhāra?'

SYNONYMS

mora mukhe—in my mouth; *kahāya*—causes to speak; *kathā*—words; *kare paracāra*—preaches; *pṛthivīte*—in this world; *ke jānibe*—who will understand; *e-līlā*—this pastime; *tāṅhāra*—His.

TRANSLATION

" 'In this way the Lord speaks through my mouth to preach the cult of Kṛṣṇa consciousness. Within the world, who will understand this pastime of the Lord?'

TEXT 75

যে-সব শুনিলুঁ, কৃষ্ণ - রসের সাগর ।
ব্রহ্মাদি-দেবের এ সব না হয় গোচর ॥ ৭৫ ॥

ye-saba śuniluṅ, kṛṣṇa-rasera sāgara
brahmādi-devera e saba nā haya gocara

SYNONYMS

ye-saba—all that; *śuniluṅ*—I heard; *kṛṣṇa-rasera*—of the nectar of Lord Kṛṣṇa; *sāgara*—the ocean; *brahmā-ādi-devera*—of the demigods, beginning with Lord Brahmā; *e saba*—all this; *nā haya gocara*—is not possible to be understood.

TRANSLATION

"What I have heard from Rāmānanda Rāya is like a nectarean ocean of discourses about Kṛṣṇa. Even the demigods, beginning with Lord Brahmā, cannot understand all these topics.

TEXT 76

হেন 'রস' পান মোরে করাইলা তুমি।
জন্মে জন্মে তোমার পায় বিকাইলাঙ আমি ॥"৭৬ ॥

hena 'rasa' pāna more karāilā tumi
janme janme tomāra pāya vikāilāṅa āmi

SYNONYMS

hena rasa—such transcendental mellows; *pāna*—to drink; *more*—me; *karāilā tumi*—You have caused; *janme janme*—life after life; *tomāra pāya*—at Your feet; *vikāilāṅa āmi*—I have become sold.

TRANSLATION

"My dear Lord, You have made me drink this transcendental nectar of kṛṣṇa-kathā. Therefore I am sold to Your lotus feet, life after life."

TEXT 77

প্রভু কহে,—"রামানন্দ বিনয়ের খনি।
আপনার কথা পরমুণ্ডে দেন আনি' ॥ ৭৭ ॥

prabhu kahe,—"rāmānanda vinayera khani
āpanāra kathā para-muṇḍe dena āni'

SYNONYMS

prabhu kahe—the Lord replied; *rāmānanda*—Rāmānanda Rāya; *vinayera khani*—the mine of humility; *āpanāra kathā*—his own words; *para-muṇḍe*—on another's head; *dena*—confers; *āni'*—bringing.

TRANSLATION

Śrī Caitanya Mahāprabhu said, "Rāmānanda Rāya is a source of all humility. Therefore he has attributed his own words to another's intelligence.

TEXT 78

মহানুভবের এই সহজ 'স্বভাব' হয় ।
আপনার গুণ নাহি আপনে কহয় ॥" ৭৮ ॥

mahānubhavera ei sahaja 'svabhāva' haya
āpanāra guṇa nāhi āpane kahaya"

SYNONYMS

mahānubhavera—of those who are advanced in realization; *ei*—this; *sahaja*—natural; *svabhāva*—characteristic; *haya*—is; *āpanāra guṇa*—their own personal qualities; *nāhi*—do not; *āpane*—personally; *kahaya*—speak.

TRANSLATION

"This is a natural characteristic of those advanced in devotional service. They do not personally speak of their own good qualities."

TEXT 79

রামানন্দরায়ের এই কহিলু গুণ-লেশ ।
প্রদ্যুম্ন মিশ্রেরে যৈছে কৈলা উপদেশ ॥ ৭৯ ॥

rāmānanda-rāyera ei kahilu guṇa-leśa
pradyumna miśrere yaiche kailā upadeśa

SYNONYMS

rāmānanda-rāyera—of Śrī Rāmānanda Rāya; *ei*—this; *kahilu*—I have spoken; *guṇa-leśa*—a fraction of the transcendental attributes; *pradyumna miśrere*—unto Pradyumna Miśra; *yaiche*—in which way; *kailā upadeśa*—he gave instruction.

TRANSLATION

I have described but a fraction of the transcendental attributes of Rāmānanda Rāya, as revealed when he instructed Pradyumna Miśra.

TEXT 80

'গৃহস্থ' হঞা নহে রায় ষড়্‌বর্গের বশে ।
'বিষয়ী' হঞা সন্ন্যাসীরে উপদেশে ॥ ৮০ ॥

'gṛhastha' hañā nahe rāya ṣaḍ-vargera vaśe
'viṣayī' hañā sannyāsīre upadeśe

SYNONYMS

gṛhastha hañā—being a householder; *nahe*—is not; *rāya*—Rāmānanda Rāya; *ṣaṭ-vargera vaśe*—under the control of the six kinds of bodily change; *viṣayī hañā*—being a pounds-and-shillings man; *sannyāsīre upadeśe*—advises persons in the renounced order of life.

TRANSLATION

Although Rāmānanda Rāya was a householder, he was not under the control of the six kinds of bodily change. Although apparently a pounds-and-shillings man, he advised even persons in the renounced order.

PURPORT

Śrī Rāmānanda Rāya externally appeared to be a *gṛhastha* who was under the influence of the external, material energy, not a self-controlled *brahmacārī, vānaprastha* or *sannyāsī. Gṛhasthas* (householders) who are under the influence of the external energy accept householder life for the purpose of sense enjoyment, but a transcendentally situated Vaiṣṇava is not subjected to the influence of the senses by the Lord's material rule of the six kinds of bodily change (*kāma, krodha, lobha, moha, mada,* and *mātsarya*), even when he plays the part of a *gṛhastha.* Thus although Śrīla Rāmānanda Rāya acted as a *gṛhastha* and was accepted as an ordinary pounds-and-shillings man, he was always absorbed in the transcendental pastimes of Lord Kṛṣṇa. Therefore his mind was spiritually situated, and he was interested only in the subject of Kṛṣṇa. Rāmānanda Rāya was not among the Māyāvādī impersonalists or materialistic logicians who are opposed to the principles of Lord Kṛṣṇa's transcendental pastimes. He was already spiritually situated in the order of renounced life; therefore he was able to turn sand into gold by spiritual potency, or, in other words, to elevate a person from a material to a spiritual position.

TEXT 81

এইসব গুণ তাঁর প্রকাশ করিতে।
মিশ্রেরে পাঠাইলা তাহাঁ শ্রবণ করিতে ॥ ৮১ ॥

ei-saba guṇa tāṅra prakāśa karite
miśrere pāṭhāilā tāhāṅ śravaṇa karite

SYNONYMS

ei-saba—all these; *guṇa*—attributes; *tāṅra*—of Rāmānanda Rāya; *prakāśa karite*—to demonstrate; *miśrere*—Pradyumna Miśra; *pāṭhāilā*—He sent; *tāhāṅ*—there; *śravaṇa karite*—to hear.

TRANSLATION

To demonstrate the transcendental attributes of Rāmānanda Rāya, Śrī Caitanya Mahāprabhu sent Pradyumna Miśra to hear discourses about Kṛṣṇa from him.

TEXT 82

ভক্তগুণ প্রকাশিতে প্রভু ভাল জানে ।
নানা-ভঙ্গীতে গুণ প্রকাশি' নিজ-লাভ মানে ॥ ৮২ ॥

bhakta-guṇa prakāśite prabhu bhāla jāne
nānā-bhaṅgīte guṇa prakāśi' nija-lābha māne

SYNONYMS

bhakta-guṇa—the attributes of a devotee; *prakāśite*—to manifest; *prabhu*—Śrī Caitanya Mahāprabhu; *bhāla jāne*—knows very well how; *nānā-bhaṅgīte*—by various ways; *guṇa*—attributes; *prakāśi'*—manifesting; *nija-lābha*—His profit; *māne*—He considers.

TRANSLATION

The Supreme Personality of Godhead, Śrī Caitanya Mahāprabhu, knows very well how to demonstrate the qualities of His devotees. Therefore, acting like an artistic painter, He does so in various ways and considers this His personal profit.

TEXT 83

আর এক 'স্বভাব' গৌরের শুন, ভক্তগণ ।
ঐশ্বর্য-স্বভাব গূঢ় করে প্রকটন ॥ ৮৩ ॥

āra eka 'svabhāva' gaurera śuna, bhakta-gaṇa
aiśvarya-svabhāva gūḍha kare prakaṭana

SYNONYMS

āra—another; *eka*—one; *svabhāva*—characteristic; *gaurera*—of Lord Śrī Caitanya Mahāprabhu; *śuna*—hear; *bhakta-gaṇa*—O devotees; *aiśvarya-svabhāva*—opulences and characteristics; *gūḍha*—very deep; *kare*—does; *prakaṭana*—manifestation.

TRANSLATION

There is yet another characteristic of Lord Śrī Caitanya Mahāprabhu. O devotees, listen carefully to how He manifests His opulence and characteristics, although they are exceptionally deep.

TEXT 84

সন্ন্যাসী পণ্ডিতগণের করিতে গর্ব্বনাশ ।
নীচ-শূদ্র-দ্বারা করেন ধর্ম্মের প্রকাশ ॥ ৮৪ ॥

sannyāsī paṇḍita-gaṇera karite garva nāśa
nīca-śūdra-dvārā karena dharmera prakāśa

SYNONYMS

sannyāsī—persons in the renounced order; *paṇḍita-gaṇera*—of the learned scholars; *karite*—to do; *garva*—pride; *nāśa*—vanquishing; *nīca*—lowborn; *śūdra*—a fourth-class man; *dvārā*—through; *karena*—does; *dharmera prakāśa*—spreading of real religious principles.

TRANSLATION

To vanquish the false pride of so-called renunciants and learned scholars, He spreads real religious principles, even through a śūdra, or lowborn fourth-class man.

PURPORT

When a man is greatly learned in the *Vedānta-sūtras,* he is known as *paṇḍita,* or a learned scholar. Generally this qualification is attributed to *brāhmaṇas* and *sannyāsīs. Sannyāsa,* the renounced order of life, is the topmost position for a *brāhmaṇa,* a member of the highest of the four *varṇas* (*brāhmaṇa, kṣatriya, vaiśya* and *śūdra*). According to public opinion, a person born in a *brāhmaṇa* family, duly reformed by the purificatory processes and properly initiated by a spiritual master, is an authority on Vedic literature. When such a person is offered the *sannyāsa* order, he comes to occupy the topmost position. The *brāhmaṇa* is supposed to be the spiritual master of the other three *varṇas,* namely *kṣatriya, vaiśya* and *śūdra,* and the *sannyāsī* is supposed to be the spiritual master even of the exalted *brāhmaṇas.*

Generally *brāhmaṇas* and *sannyāsīs* are very proud of their spiritual positions. Therefore, to cut down their false pride, Śrī Caitanya Mahāprabhu preached Kṛṣṇa consciousness through Rāmānanda Rāya, who was neither a member of the renounced order nor a born *brāhmaṇa.* Indeed, Śrī Rāmānanda Rāya was a *gṛhastha* belonging to the *śūdra* class, yet Śrī Caitanya Mahāprabhu arranged for him to be the master who taught Pradyumna Miśra, a highly qualified *brāhmaṇa* born in a *brāhmaṇa* family. Even Śrī Caitanya Mahāprabhu Himself, although belonging to the renounced order, took instruction from Śrī Rāmānanda Rāya. In this way Śrī Caitanya Mahāprabhu exhibited His opulence through Śrī Rāmānanda Rāya. That is the special significance of this incident.

According to Śrī Caitanya Mahāprabhu's philosophy, *yei kṛṣṇa-tattva-vettā, sei 'guru' haya:* anyone who knows the science of Kṛṣṇa can become a spiritual master, without reference to whether or not he is a *brāhmaṇa* or *sannyāsī.* Ordinary people cannot understand the essence of *śāstra,* nor can they understand the pure character, behavior and abilities of strict followers of Śrī Caitanya Mahāprabhu's principles. The Kṛṣṇa consciousness movement is creating pure, exalted Vaiṣṇavas even from those born in families considered lower than those of *śūdras.* This is proof that a Vaiṣṇava may appear in any family, as confirmed in *Śrīmad-Bhāgavatam:*

kirāta-hūṇāndhra-pulinda-pulkaśā
ābhīra-śumbhā yavanāḥ khasādayaḥ
ye 'nye ca pāpā yad-apāśrayāśrayāḥ
śudhyanti tasmai prabhaviṣṇave namaḥ

"Kirāta, Hūṇa, Āndhra, Pulinda, Pulkaśa, Ābhīra, Śumbha, Yavana and the Khasa races, and even others addicted to sinful acts, can be purified by taking shelter of the devotees of the Lord, for He is the supreme power. I beg to offer my respectful obeisances unto Him." (*Bhāg.* 2.4.18) By the grace of the Supreme Lord Viṣṇu, one can be completely purified, become a preacher of Kṛṣṇa consciousness, and become the spiritual master of the entire world. This principle is accepted in all Vedic literature. Evidence can be quoted from authoritative *śāstras* showing how a lowborn person can become the spiritual master of the entire world. Śrī Caitanya Mahāprabhu is to be considered the most munificent personality, for He distributes the real essence of Vedic *śāstras* to anyone who becomes qualified by becoming His sincere servant.

TEXT 85

'ভক্তি', 'প্রেম', 'তত্ত্ব' কহে রায়ে করি' 'বক্তা' ।
আপনি প্রদ্যুম্নমিশ্র-সহ হয় 'শ্রোতা' ॥ ৮৫ ॥

'bhakti', 'prema', 'tattva' kahe rāye kari' 'vaktā'
āpani pradyumna-miśra-saha haya 'śrotā'

SYNONYMS

bhakti—devotional service; *prema*—ecstatic love; *tattva*—truth; *kahe*—He says; *rāye*—Rāmānanda Rāya; *kari'*—by making; *vaktā*—the speaker; *āpani*—Himself; *pradyumna-miśra*—Pradyumna Miśra; *saha*—with; *haya śrotā*—becomes the listener.

TRANSLATION

Śrī Caitanya Mahāprabhu preached about devotional service, ecstatic love and the Absolute Truth by making Rāmānanda Rāya, a gṛhastha born in a low family, the speaker. Then Śrī Caitanya Mahāprabhu Himself, the exalted brāhmaṇa-sannyāsī, and Pradyumna Miśra, the purified brāhmaṇa, both became the hearers of Rāmānanda Rāya.

PURPORT

Śrīla Bhaktivinoda Ṭhākura says in his *Amṛta-pravāha-bhāṣya* that *sannyāsīs* in the line of Śaṅkarācārya always think that they have performed all the duties of *brāhmaṇas* and that, furthermore, having understood the essence of *Vedānta-sūtra* and become *sannyāsīs,* they are the natural spiritual masters of all society. Similarly, persons born in *brāhmaṇa* families think that because they execute the ritualistic ceremonies recommended in the *Vedas* and follow the principles of *smṛti,* they alone can become spiritual masters of society. These highly exalted *brāhmaṇas* think that unless one is born in a *brāhmaṇa* family, one cannot become a spiritual master and teach the Absolute Truth. To cut down the pride of these birthright *brāhmaṇas* and Māyāvādī *sannyāsīs,* Śrī Caitanya Mahāprabhu proved that a person like Rāmānanda Rāya, although born in a *śūdra* family and situated in the *gṛhastha-āśrama,* can become the spiritual master of such exalted personalities as Himself and Pradyumna Miśra. This is the principle of the Vaiṣṇava cult, as evinced in the teachings of Śrī Caitanya Mahāprabhu. A person who knows what is spiritual and what is material and who is firmly fixed in the spiritual position can be *jagad-guru,* the spiritual master of the entire world. One cannot become *jagad-guru* simply by advertising oneself as *jagad-guru* without knowing the essential principles for becoming *jagad-guru.* Even people who never see what a *jagad-guru* is and never talk with other people become puffed-up *sannyāsīs* and declare themselves *jagad-gurus.* Śrī Caitanya Mahāprabhu did not like this. Any person who knows the science of Kṛṣṇa and who is fully qualified in spiritual life can become *jagad-guru.* Thus Śrī Caitanya Mahāprabhu personally took lessons from Śrī Rāmānanda Rāya and also sent Pradyumna Miśra, an exalted *brāhmaṇa,* to take lessons from him.

TEXT 86

হরিদাস-দ্বারা নাম-মাহাত্ম্য-প্রকাশ ।
সনাতন-দ্বারা ভক্তিসিদ্ধান্তবিলাস ॥ ৮৬ ॥

haridāsa-dvārā nāma-māhātmya-prakāśa
sanātana-dvārā bhakti-siddhānta-vilāsa

SYNONYMS

haridāsa-dvārā—by Haridāsa Ṭhākura; *nāma-māhātmya*—of the glories of chanting the Hare Kṛṣṇa *mahā-mantra*; *prakāśa*—manifestation; *sanātana-dvārā*—by Sanātana Gosvāmī; *bhakti-siddhānta-vilāsa*—spreading the essence of devotional life.

TRANSLATION

Śrī Caitanya Mahāprabhu exhibited the glories of the holy name of the Lord through Haridāsa Ṭhākura, who was born in a Mohammedan family. Similarly, He exhibited the essence of devotional service through Sanātana Gosvāmī, who had almost been converted into a Mohammedan.

TEXT 87

শ্রীরূপ-দ্বারা ব্রজের প্রেম-রস-লীলা।
কে বুঝিতে পারে গম্ভীর চৈতন্যের খেলা ? ৮৭ ॥

śrī-rūpa-dvārā vrajera prema-rasa-līlā
ke bujhite pāre gambhīra caitanyera khelā?

SYNONYMS

śrī-rūpa-dvārā—through Śrī Rūpa Gosvāmī; *vrajera*—of Vṛndāvana; *prema-rasa-līlā*—description of ecstatic love and pastimes; *ke*—who; *bujhite pāre*—can understand; *gambhīra*—deep; *caitanyera khelā*—the activities of Śrī Caitanya Mahāprabhu.

TRANSLATION

The Lord also fully exhibited the ecstatic love and transcendental pastimes of Vṛndāvana through Śrīla Rūpa Gosvāmī. Considering all this, who can understand the deep plans of Lord Śrī Caitanya Mahāprabhu?

TEXT 88

শ্রীচৈতন্যলীলা এই—অমৃতের সিন্ধু।
ত্রিজগৎ ভাসাইতে পারে যার এক বিন্দু ॥ ৮৮ ॥

śrī-caitanya-līlā ei——amṛtera sindhu
trijagat bhāsāite pāre yāra eka bindu

SYNONYMS

śrī-caitanya-līlā—transcendental activities of Śrī Caitanya Mahāprabhu; *ei*—these; *amṛtera sindhu*—the ocean of nectar; *tri-jagat*—the three worlds; *bhāsāite*—to inundate; *pāre*—is able; *yāra*—of which; *eka bindu*—one drop.

TRANSLATION

The activities of Śrī Caitanya Mahāprabhu are just like an ocean of nectar. Even a drop of this ocean can inundate all the three worlds.

PURPORT

To inundate the three worlds with nectar is the purpose of the pastimes of Śrī Caitanya Mahāprabhu. How this could be possible was exhibited by Śrīla Raghunātha Gosvāmī and later by Ṭhākura Narottama dāsa and Śyāmānanda Gosvāmī, who all represented the mercy of Śrī Caitanya Mahāprabhu. Now that same mercy is overflooding the entire world through the Kṛṣṇa consciousness movement. The present Kṛṣṇa consciousness movement is nondifferent from the pastimes performed by Śrī Caitanya Mahāprabhu when He was personally present, for the same principles are being followed and the same actions performed without fail.

TEXT 89

চৈতন্যচরিতামৃত নিত্য কর পান ।
যাহা হৈতে 'প্রেমানন্দ', 'ভক্তিতত্ত্ব-জ্ঞান' ॥ ৮৯ ॥

caitanya-caritāmṛta nitya kara pāna
yāhā haite 'premānanda', 'bhakti-tattva-jñāna'

SYNONYMS

caitanya-caritāmṛta—this transcendental literature known as *Caitanya-caritāmṛta*; *nitya*—daily; *kara pāna*—do relish; *yāhā haite*—by which; *prema-ānanda*—transcendental bliss; *bhakti-tattva-jñāna*—transcendental knowledge in devotional service.

TRANSLATION

O devotees, relish daily the nectar of Śrī Caitanya-caritāmṛta and the pastimes of Śrī Caitanya Mahāprabhu, for by doing so one can merge in the transcendental bliss and full knowledge of devotional service.

TEXT 90

এইমত মহাপ্রভু ভক্তগণ লঞা ।
নীলাচলে বিহরয়ে ভক্তি প্রচারিয়া ॥ ৯০ ॥

ei-mata mahāprabhu bhakta-gaṇa lañā
nīlācale viharaye bhakti pracāriyā

SYNONYMS

ei-mata—in this way; *mahāprabhu*—Śrī Caitanya Mahāprabhu; *bhakta-gaṇa lañā*—accompanied by His pure devotees; *nīlācale*—at Jagannātha Purī; *viharaye*—enjoys transcendental bliss; *bhakti pracāriyā*—preaching the cult of devotional service.

TRANSLATION

Thus Lord Śrī Caitanya Mahāprabhu, accompanied by His associates, His pure devotees, enjoyed transcendental bliss in Jagannātha Purī [Nīlācala] preaching the bhakti cult in many ways.

TEXT 91

বঙ্গদেশী এক বিপ্র প্রভুর চরিতে ।
নাটক করি' লঞা আইল প্রভুকে শুনাইতে ॥৯১॥

baṅga-deśī eka vipra prabhura carite
nāṭaka kari' lañā āila prabhuke śunāite

SYNONYMS

baṅga-deśī—from Bengal; *eka vipra*—one *brāhmaṇa*; *prabhura carite*—about Śrī Caitanya Mahāprabhu's characteristics; *nāṭaka kari'*—making a drama; *lañā*—taking; *āila*—came; *prabhuke śunāite*—to induce Lord Śrī Caitanya Mahāprabhu to hear.

TRANSLATION

A brāhmaṇa from Bengal wrote a drama about the characteristics of Śrī Caitanya Mahāprabhu and came with his manuscript to induce the Lord to hear it.

TEXT 92

ভগবান্-আচার্য-সনে তার পরিচয় ।
তাঁরে মিলি' তাঁর ঘরে করিল আলয় ॥ ৯২ ॥

bhagavān-ācārya-sane tāra paricaya
tāṅre mili' tāṅra ghare karila ālaya

SYNONYMS

bhagavān-ācārya—the devotee of Lord Śrī Caitanya Mahāprabhu named Bhagavān Ācārya; *sane*—with; *tāra paricaya*—his acquaintance; *tāṅre mili'*—meeting him; *tāṅra ghare*—at his place; *karila ālaya*—made residence.

TRANSLATION

The brāhmaṇa was acquainted with Bhagavān Ācārya, one of the devotees of Śrī Caitanya Mahāprabhu. Therefore after meeting him at Jagannātha Purī, the brāhmaṇa made his residence at Bhagavān Ācārya's home.

TEXT 93

প্রথমে নাটক তেঁহো তাঁরে শুনাইল ।
তাঁর সঙ্গে অনেক বৈষ্ণব নাটক শুনিল ॥ ৯৩ ॥

prathame nāṭaka teṅho tāṅre śunāila
tāṅra saṅge aneka vaiṣṇava nāṭaka śunila

SYNONYMS

prathame—at first; *nāṭaka*—the drama; *teṅho*—he; *tāṅre*—him; *śunāila*—made to hear; *tāṅra saṅge*—with him; *aneka*—many; *vaiṣṇava*—devotees; *nāṭaka śunila*—listened to the drama.

TRANSLATION

First the brāhmaṇa induced Bhagavān Ācārya to hear the drama, and then many other devotees joined Bhagavān Ācārya in listening to it.

TEXT 94

সবেই প্রশংসে নাটক 'পরম উত্তম' ।
মহাপ্রভুরে শুনাইতে সবার হৈল মন ॥ ৯৪ ॥

sabei praśaṁse nāṭaka 'parama uttama'
mahāprabhure śunāite sabāra haila mana

SYNONYMS

sabei—all; *praśaṁse*—praised; *nāṭaka*—the drama; *parama uttama*—"very good, very good"; *mahāprabhure*—Śrī Caitanya Mahāprabhu; *śunāite*—to cause to hear; *sabāra*—of everyone; *haila*—there was; *mana*—mind.

TRANSLATION

All the Vaiṣṇavas praised the drama, saying, "Very good, very good." They also desired for Śrī Caitanya Mahāprabhu to hear the drama.

TEXT 95

গীত, শ্লোক, গ্রন্থ, কবিত্ব - যেই করি' আনে।
প্রথমে শুনায় সেই স্বরূপের স্থানে ॥ ৯৫ ॥

gīta, śloka, grantha, kavitva——yei kari' āne
prathame śunāya sei svarūpera sthāne

SYNONYMS

gīta—song; *śloka*—verse; *grantha*—literature; *kavitva*—poetry; *yei*—anyone who; *kari'*—making; *āne*—brings; *prathame*—first; *śunāya*—recites; *sei*—that person; *svarūpera sthāne*—before Svarūpa Dāmodara Gosvāmī.

TRANSLATION

Customarily, anyone who composed a song, verse, literary composition or poem about Śrī Caitanya Mahāprabhu first had to bring it to Svarūpa Dāmodara Gosvāmī to be heard.

TEXT 96

স্বরূপ-ঠাঞি উত্তরে যদি, লঞা, তাঁর মন।
তবে মহাপ্রভু-ঠাঞি করায় শ্রবণ ॥ ৯৬ ॥

svarūpa-ṭhāñi uttare yadi, lañā, tāṅra mana
tabe mahāprabhu-ṭhāñi karāya śravaṇa

SYNONYMS

svarūpa-ṭhāñi—before Svarūpa Dāmodara Gosvāmī; *uttare*—passes; *yadi*—if one; *lañā*—taking; *tāṅra mana*—his mind; *tabe*—thereafter; *mahāprabhu-ṭhāñi*—before Śrī Caitanya Mahāprabhu; *karāya śravaṇa*—causes to be heard.

TRANSLATION

If passed by Svarūpa Dāmodara Gosvāmī, it could be presented for Śrī Caitanya Mahāprabhu to hear.

TEXT 97

'রসাভাস' হয় যদি 'সিদ্ধান্তবিরোধ'।
সহিতে না পারে প্রভু, মনে হয় ক্রোধ ॥ ৯৭ ॥

'rasābhāsa' haya yadi 'siddhānta-virodha'
sahite nā pāre prabhu, mane haya krodha

SYNONYMS

rasa-ābhāsa—overlapping of transcendental mellows; *haya*—there is; *yadi*—if; *siddhānta-virodha*—against the principles of the *bhakti* cult; *sahite nā pāre*—cannot tolerate; *prabhu*—Śrī Caitanya Mahāprabhu; *mane*—within the mind; *haya*—is; *krodha*—anger.

TRANSLATION

If there were a hint that transcendental mellows overlapped in a manner contrary to the principles of the bhakti cult, Śrī Caitanya Mahāprabhu would not tolerate it and would become very angry.

PURPORT

Śrīla Bhaktisiddhānta Sarasvatī Ṭhākura quotes the following definition of *rasābhāsa* from the *Bhakti-rasāmṛta-sindhu* (*Uttara-vibhāga,* Ninth Wave, 1-3,20,22,24):

pūrvam evānuśiṣṭena
vikalā rasa-lakṣaṇā
rasā eva rasābhāsā
rasajñair anukīrtitāḥ

syus tridhoparasāś cānu-
rasāś cāparasāś ca te
uttamā madhyamāḥ proktāḥ
kaniṣṭhāś cety amī kramāt

prāptaiḥ sthāyi-vibhāvānu-
bhāvādyais tu virūpatām
śāntādayo rasā eva
dvādaśoparasā matāḥ

bhaktādibhir vibhāvādyaiḥ
kṛṣṇa-sambandha-varjitaiḥ
rasā hāsyādayaḥ sapta
śāntaś cānurasā matāḥ

kṛṣṇa-tat-pratipakṣaś ced
viṣayāśrayatāṁ gatāḥ
hāsādīnāṁ tadā te 'tra
prājñair aparasā matāḥ

bhāvāḥ sarve tadābhāsā
rasābhāsāś ca kecana
amī proktā rasābhijñaiḥ
sarve 'pi rasanād rasāḥ

A mellow temporarily appearing transcendental but contradicting mellows previously stated and lacking some of a mellow's necessities is called *rasābhāsa,* an overlapping mellow, by advanced devotees who know how to taste transcendental mellows. Such mellows are called *uparasa* (submellows), *anurasa* (imitation transcendental mellows) and *aparasa* (opposing transcendental mellows). Thus the overlapping of transcendental mellows is described as being first grade, second grade or third grade. When the twelve mellows—such as neutrality, servitorship and friendship—are characterized by adverse *sthāyi-bhāva, vibhāva* and *anubhāva* ecstasies, they are known as *uparasa,* submellows. When the seven indirect transcendental mellows and the dried up mellow of neutrality are produced by devotees and moods not directly related to Kṛṣṇa and devotional service in ecstatic love, they are described as *anurasa,* imitation mellows. If Kṛṣṇa and the enemies who harbor feelings of opposition toward Him are respectively the object and abodes of the mellow of laughter, the resulting feelings are called *aparasa,* opposing mellows. Experts in distinguishing one mellow from another sometimes accept some overlapping transcendental mellows (*rasābhāsa*) as *rasas* due to their being pleasurable and tasteful. Śrīla Viśvanātha Cakravartī Ṭhākura says, *paraspara-vairayor yadi yogas tadā rasābhāsaḥ:* "When two opposing transcendental mellows overlap, they produce *rasābhāsa,* or an overlapping of transcendental mellows."

TEXT 98

অতএব প্রভু কিছু আগে নাহি শুনে ।
এই মর্যাদা প্রভু করিয়াছে নিয়মে ॥ ৯৮ ॥

ataeva prabhu kichu āge nāhi śune
ei maryādā prabhu kariyāche niyame

SYNONYMS

ataeva—therefore; *prabhu*—Śrī Caitanya Mahāprabhu; *kichu*—anything; *āge*—ahead; *nāhi śune*—does not hear; *ei maryādā*—this etiquette; *prabhu*—Śrī Caitanya Mahāprabhu; *kariyāche niyame*—has made a regulative principle.

TRANSLATION

Therefore Śrī Caitanya Mahāprabhu would not hear anything before Svarūpa Dāmodara heard it first. The Lord made this etiquette a regulative principle.

TEXT 99

স্বরূপের ঠাঞি আচার্য কৈলা নিবেদন।
এক বিপ্র প্রভুর নাটক করিয়াছে উত্তম ॥ ৯৯ ॥

svarūpera ṭhāñi ācārya kailā nivedana
eka vipra prabhura nāṭaka kariyāche uttama

SYNONYMS

svarūpera ṭhāñi—before Svarūpa Dāmodara Gosvāmī; *ācārya*—Bhagavān Ācārya; *kailā*—did; *nivedana*—submission; *eka vipra*—one *brāhmaṇa*; *prabhura*—of Śrī Caitanya Mahāprabhu; *nāṭaka*—drama; *kariyāche*—has composed; *uttama*—very nice.

TRANSLATION

Bhagavān Ācārya submitted to Svarūpa Dāmodara Gosvāmī, "A good brāhmaṇa has prepared a drama about Śrī Caitanya Mahāprabhu that appears exceptionally well composed.

TEXT 100

আদৌ তুমি শুন, যদি তোমার মন মানে।
পাছে মহাপ্রভুরে তবে করাইমু শ্রবণে ॥ ১০০ ॥

ādau tumi śuna, yadi tomāra mana māne
pāche mahāprabhure tabe karāimu śravaṇe

SYNONYMS

ādau—in the beginning; *tumi*—you; *śuna*—hear; *yadi*—if; *tomāra mana māne*—you accept; *pāche*—thereafter; *mahāprabhure*—Śrī Caitanya Mahāprabhu; *tabe*—then; *karāimu śravaṇe*—I shall request to hear.

TRANSLATION

"First you hear it, and if it is acceptable to your mind, I shall request Śrī Caitanya Mahāprabhu to hear it."

TEXT 101

স্বরূপ কহে,—"তুমি 'গোপ' পরম-উদার।
যে-সে শাস্ত্র শুনিতে ইচ্ছা উপজে তোমার ॥ ১০১ ॥

svarūpa kahe,—"tumi 'gopa' parama-udāra
ye-se śāstra śunite icchā upaje tomāra

SYNONYMS

svarūpa kahe—Svarūpa Dāmodara Gosvāmī said; *tumi*—you; *gopa*—cowherd boy; *parama-udāra*—very liberal; *ye-se śāstra*—anything written as scripture; *śunite*—to hear; *icchā*—desire; *upaje*—awakens; *tomāra*—of you.

TRANSLATION

Svarūpa Dāmodara Gosvāmī replied, "Dear Bhagavān Ācārya, you are a very liberal cowherd boy. Sometimes the desire awakens within you to hear any kind of poetry.

TEXT 102

'যদ্বা-তদ্বা' কবির বাক্যে হয় 'রসাভাস'।
সিদ্ধান্তবিরুদ্ধ শুনিতে না হয় উল্লাস ॥ ১০২ ॥

'yadvā-tadvā' kavira vākye haya 'rasābhāsa'
siddhānta-viruddha śunite nā haya ullāsa

SYNONYMS

yadvā-tadvā kavira—of any so-called poet; *vākye*—in the words; *haya*—there is; *rasa-ābhāsa*—overlapping of transcendental mellows; *siddhānta-viruddha*—against the conclusive understanding; *śunite*—to hear; *nā*—not; *haya*—there is; *ullāsa*—joy.

TRANSLATION

"In the writings of so-called poets there is generally a possibility of overlapping transcendental mellows. When the mellows thus go against the conclusive understanding, no one likes to hear such poetry.

PURPORT

Yadvā-tadvā kavi refers to anyone who writes poetry without knowledge of how to do so. Writing poetry, especially poetry concerning the Vaiṣṇava conclusion, is very difficult. If one writes poetry without proper knowledge, there is every possibility that the mellows will overlap. When this occurs, no learned or advanced Vaiṣṇava will like to hear it.

TEXT 103

'রস', 'রসাভাস' যার নাহিক বিচার।
ভক্তিসিদ্ধান্ত-সিন্ধু নাহি পায় পার ॥ ১০৩ ॥

'rasa', 'rasābhāsa' yāra nāhika vicāra
bhakti-siddhānta-sindhu nāhi pāya pāra

SYNONYMS

rasa—transcendental mellows; *rasa-ābhāsa*—overlapping of transcendental mellows; *yāra*—of whom; *nāhika vicāra*—there is no consideration; *bhakti-siddhānta-sindhu*—the ocean of the conclusions of devotional service; *nāhi*—not; *pāya*—attains; *pāra*—the limit.

TRANSLATION

"A so-called poet who has no knowledge of transcendental mellows and the overlapping of transcendental mellows cannot cross the ocean of the conclusions of devotional service.

TEXTS 104-105

'ব্যাকরণ' নাহি জানে, না জানে 'অলঙ্কার' ।
'নাটকালঙ্কার'-জ্ঞান নাহিক যাহার ॥ ১০৪ ॥
কৃষ্ণলীলা বর্ণিতে না জানে সেই ছার !
বিশেষে দুর্গম এই চৈতন্য-বিহার ॥ ১০৫ ॥

'vyākaraṇa' nāhi jāne, nā jāne 'alaṅkāra'
'nāṭakālaṅkāra'-jñāna nāhika yāhāra

kṛṣṇa-līlā varṇite nā jāne sei chāra!
viśeṣe durgama ei caitanya-vihāra

SYNONYMS

vyākaraṇa—grammar; *nāhi jāne*—does not know; *nā jāne*—does not know; *alaṅkāra*—metaphorical ornaments; *nāṭaka-alaṅkāra*—of the metaphorical ornaments of drama; *jñāna*—knowledge; *nāhika*—there is not; *yāhāra*—of whom; *kṛṣṇa-līlā*—the pastimes of Lord Kṛṣṇa; *varṇite*—to describe; *nā jāne*—does not know; *sei*—he; *chāra*—condemned; *viśeṣe*—especially; *durgama*—very, very difficult; *ei*—these; *caitanya-vihāra*—the pastimes of Lord Śrī Caitanya Mahāprabhu.

TRANSLATION

"A poet who does not know the grammatical regulative principles, who is unfamiliar with metaphorical ornaments, especially those employed in drama, and who does not know how to present the pastimes of Lord Kṛṣṇa is condemned. Moreover, the pastimes of Śrī Caitanya Mahāprabhu are especially difficult to understand.

TEXT 106

কৃষ্ণলীলা, গৌরলীলা সে করে বর্ণন ।
গৌর-পাদপদ্ম যাঁর হয় প্রাণ-ধন ॥ ১০৬ ॥

kṛṣṇa-līlā, gaura-līlā se kare varṇana
gaura-pāda-padma yāṅra haya prāṇa-dhana

SYNONYMS

kṛṣṇa-līlā—the pastimes of Lord Kṛṣṇa; *gaura-līlā*—the pastimes of Lord Śrī Caitanya Mahāprabhu; *se*—he; *kare varṇana*—describes; *gaura-pāda-padma*—the lotus feet of Lord Śrī Caitanya Mahāprabhu; *yāṅra*—whose; *haya*—is; *prāṇa-dhana*—the life and soul.

TRANSLATION

"One who has accepted the lotus feet of Śrī Caitanya Mahāprabhu as his life and soul can describe the pastimes of Lord Kṛṣṇa or the pastimes of Lord Śrī Caitanya Mahāprabhu.

TEXT 107

গ্রাম্য-কবির কবিত্ব শুনিতে হয় 'দুঃখ' ।
বিদগ্ধ-আত্মীয়-বাক্য শুনিতে হয় 'সুখ' ॥ ১০৭ ॥

grāmya-kavira kavitva śunite haya 'duḥkha'
vidagdha-ātmīya-vākya śunite haya 'sukha'

SYNONYMS

grāmya-kavira—of a poet who writes poetry concerning man and woman; *kavitva*—poetry; *śunite*—to hear; *haya*—there is; *duḥkha*—unhappiness; *vidagdha-ātmīya*—of a devotee fully absorbed in ecstatic love; *vākya*—the words; *śunite*—to hear; *haya*—there is; *sukha*—happiness.

TRANSLATION

"Hearing the poetry of a person who has no transcendental knowledge and who writes about the relationships between man and woman simply causes unhappiness, whereas hearing the words of a devotee fully absorbed in ecstatic love causes great happiness.

PURPORT

Grāmya-kavi refers to a poet or writer such as the authors of novels and other fiction who write only about the relationships between man and woman.

Vidagdha-ātmīya-vākya, however, refers to words written by a devotee who fully understands pure devotional service. Such devotees, who follow the *paramparā* system, are sometimes described as *sajātīyāśaya-snigdha,* or "pleasing to the same class of people." Only the poetry and other writings of such devotees are accepted with great happiness by devotees.

TEXT 108

রূপ যৈছে দুই নাটক করিয়াছে আরম্ভে।
শুনিতে আনন্দ বাড়ে যার মুখবন্ধে ॥" ১০৮ ॥

rūpa yaiche dui nāṭaka kariyāche ārambhe
śunite ānanda bāḍe yāra mukha-bandhe"

SYNONYMS

rūpa—Rūpa Gosvāmī; *yaiche*—as; *dui*—two; *nāṭaka*—dramas; *kariyāche ārambhe*—has compiled; *śunite*—to hear; *ānanda bāḍe*—transcendental happiness increases; *yāra*—of which; *mukha-bandhe*—even the introductory portion.

TRANSLATION

"The standard for writing dramas has been set by Rūpa Gosvāmī. If a devotee hears the introductory portions of his two dramas, they enhance his transcendental pleasure."

TEXT 109

ভগবান্-আচার্য কহে,—'শুন একবার।
তুমি শুনিলে ভাল-মন্দ জানিবে বিচার ॥'১০৯॥

bhagavān-ācārya kahe,——'śuna eka-bāra
tumi śunile bhāla-manda jānibe vicāra'

SYNONYMS

bhagavān-ācārya—Bhagavān Ācārya; *kahe*—says; *śuna*—please hear; *eka-bāra*—once; *tumi śunile*—if you hear; *bhāla-manda*—good or bad; *jānibe vicāra*—will be able to understand.

TRANSLATION

Despite the explanation of Svarūpa Dāmodara, Bhagavān Ācārya requested, "Please hear the drama once. If you hear it, you can consider whether it is good or bad."

TEXT 110

দুই তিন দিন আচার্য আগ্রহ করিল।
তাঁর আগ্রহে'স্বরূপের শুনিতে ইচ্ছা হইল ॥ ১১০ ॥

dui tina dina ācārya āgraha karila
tāṅra āgrahe svarūpera śunite icchā ha-ila

SYNONYMS

dui tina dina—for two or three days; *ācārya*—Bhagavān Ācārya; *āgraha karila*—expressed his ardent desire; *tāṅra āgrahe*—by his eagerness; *svarūpera*—of Svarūpa Dāmodara; *śunite*—to hear; *icchā*—desire; *ha-ila*—there was.

TRANSLATION

For two or three days Bhagavān Ācārya continually asked Svarūpa Dāmodara Gosvāmī to hear the poetry. Because of his repeated requests, Svarūpa Dāmodara Gosvāmī wanted to hear the poetry written by the brāhmaṇa from Bengal.

TEXT 111

সবা লঞা স্বরূপ গোসাঞি শুনিতে বসিলা।
তবে সেই কবি নান্দী-শ্লোক পড়িলা ॥ ১১১ ॥

sabā lañā svarūpa gosāñi śunite vasilā
tabe sei kavi nāndī-śloka paḍilā

SYNONYMS

sabā lañā—in the company of other devotees; *svarūpa gosāñi*—Svarūpa Dāmodara Gosvāmī; *śunite vasilā*—sat down to hear; *tabe*—thereafter; *sei kavi*—that poet; *nāndī-śloka*—the introductory verse; *paḍilā*—read.

TRANSLATION

Svarūpa Dāmodara Gosvāmī sat down with other devotees to hear the poetry, and then the poet began to read the introductory verse.

TEXT 112

বিকচকমলনেত্রে শ্রীজগন্নাথসংজ্ঞে
কনকরুচিরিহাত্মন্যাত্মতাং যঃ প্রপন্নঃ।

প্রকৃতিজড়মশেষং চেতয়ন্নাবিরাসীৎ
স দিশতু তব ভব্যং কৃষ্ণচৈতন্যদেবঃ ॥ ১১২ ॥

vikaca-kamala-netre śrī-jagannātha-saṁjñe
kanaka-rucir ihātmany ātmatāṁ yaḥ prapannaḥ
prakṛti-jaḍam aśeṣaṁ cetayann āvirāsīt
sa diśatu tava bhavyaṁ kṛṣṇa-caitanya-devaḥ

SYNONYMS

vikaca—expanded; *kamala-netre*—whose lotus eyes; *śrī-jagannātha-saṁjñe*—named Śrī Jagannātha; *kanaka-ruciḥ*—possessing a golden hue; *iha*—here in Jagannātha Purī; *ātmani*—in the body; *ātmatām*—the state of being the self; *yaḥ*—who; *prapannaḥ*—has obtained; *prakṛti*—matter; *jaḍam*—inert; *aśeṣam*—unlimitedly; *cetayan*—enlivening; *āvirāsīt*—has appeared; *saḥ*—He; *diśatu*—may bestow; *tava*—unto you; *bhavyam*—auspiciousness; *kṛṣṇa-caitanya-devaḥ*—Lord Śrī Caitanya Mahāprabhu, known as Kṛṣṇa Caitanya.

TRANSLATION

"The Supreme Personality of Godhead has assumed a golden complexion and has become the soul of the body named Lord Jagannātha, whose blooming lotus eyes are widely expanded. Thus He has appeared in Jagannātha Purī and brought dull matter to life. May that Lord, Śrī Kṛṣṇa Caitanyadeva, bestow upon you all good fortune."

TEXT 113

শ্লোক শুনি' সর্বলোক তাহারে বাখানে ।
স্বরূপ কহে,—'এই শ্লোক করহ ব্যাখ্যানে' ॥ ১১৩ ॥

śloka śuni' sarva-loka tāhāre vākhāne
svarūpa kahe,—'ei śloka karaha vyākhyāne'

SYNONYMS

śloka śuni'—hearing the verse; *sarva-loka*—everyone; *tāhāre*—him; *vākhāne*—praised; *svarūpa kahe*—Svarūpa Dāmodara Gosvāmī said; *ei śloka*—this verse; *karaha vyākhyāne*—kindly explain.

TRANSLATION

When everyone present heard the verse, they all commended the poet, but Svarūpa Dāmodara Gosvāmī requested him, "Kindly explain this verse."

TEXT 114

কবি কহে,—"জগন্নাথ– সুন্দর-শরীর ।
চৈতন্য-গোসাঞি - শরীরী মহাধীর ॥ ১১৪ ॥

kavi kahe,——"jagannātha——sundara-śarīra
caitanya-gosāñi—— śarīrī mahā-dhīra

SYNONYMS

kavi kahe—the poet said; *jagannātha*—Lord Jagannātha; *sundara-śarīra*—very beautiful body; *caitanya-gosāñi*—Śrī Caitanya Mahāprabhu; *śarīrī*—possessor of the body; *mahā-dhīra*—very grave.

TRANSLATION

The poet said, "Lord Jagannātha is a most beautiful body, and Śrī Caitanya Mahāprabhu, who is exceptionally grave, is the owner of that body.

PURPORT

Śarīrī refers to a person who owns the *śarīra,* or body. As stated in *Bhagavad-gītā:*

dehino 'smin yathā dehe
kaumāraṁ yauvanaṁ jarā
tathā dehāntara-prāptir
dhīras tatra na muhyati

"As the embodied soul continually passes, in this body, from boyhood to youth to old age, the soul similarly passes into another body at death. The self-realized soul is not bewildered by such a change." (Bg. 2.13) For the ordinary living being in material existence there is a division or distinction between the body and the owner of the body. In spiritual existence, however, there is no such distinction, for the body is the owner himself and the owner is the body itself. In spiritual existence, everything must be spiritual. Therefore there is no distinction between the body and its owner.

TEXT 115

সহজে জড়জগতের চেতন করাইতে ।
নীলাচলে মহাপ্রভু হৈলা আবির্ভূতে ॥" ১১৫ ॥

sahaje jaḍa-jagatera cetana karāite
nīlācale mahāprabhu hailā āvirbhute

SYNONYMS

sahaje—naturally; *jaḍa-jagatera*—the dull material world; *cetana karāite*—to inspire to spiritual consciousness; *nīlācale*—at Jagannātha Purī; *mahāprabhu*—Śrī Caitanya Mahāprabhu; *hailā āvirbhute*—has appeared.

TRANSLATION

"Śrī Caitanya Mahāprabhu has appeared here in Nīlācala [Jagannātha Purī] to spiritualize the entire dull material world."

TEXT 116

শুনিয়া সবার হৈল আনন্দিত-মন ।
দুঃখ পাঞা স্বরূপ কহে সক্রোধ বচন ॥ ১১৬ ॥

śuniyā sabāra haila ānandita-mana
duḥkha pāñā svarūpa kahe sakrodha vacana

SYNONYMS

śuniyā—hearing; *sabāra*—of all of them; *haila*—there was; *ānandita-mana*—great happiness in the mind; *duḥkha pāñā*—becoming unhappy; *svarūpa kahe*—Svarūpa Dāmodara Gosvāmī began to speak; *sa-krodha vacana*—angry words.

TRANSLATION

Hearing this, everyone present was greatly happy. But Svarūpa Dāmodara, who alone was very unhappy, began to speak in great anger.

TEXT 117

"আরে মূর্খ, আপনার কৈলি সর্বনাশ !
দুই ত' ঈশ্বরে তোর নাহিক বিশ্বাস ॥ ১১৭ ॥

"āre mūrkha, āpanāra kaili sarva-nāśa!
dui ta' īśvare tora nāhika viśvāsa

SYNONYMS

āre mūrkha—O fool; *āpanāra*—of yourself; *kaili*—you have done; *sarva-nāśa*—loss of all auspiciousness; *dui ta' īśvare*—in the two controllers; *tora*—your; *nāhika viśvāsa*—there is no faith.

TRANSLATION

"You are a fool," he said. "You have brought ill fortune upon yourself, for you have no knowledge of the existence of the two Lords, Jagannāthadeva and Śrī Caitanya Mahāprabhu, nor have you faith in Them.

TEXT 118

পূর্ণানন্দ-চিৎস্বরূপ জগন্নাথ-রায়।
তাঁরে কৈলি জড়-নশ্বর-প্রাকৃত-কায়!! ১১৮ ॥

pūrṇānanda-cit-svarūpa jagannātha-rāya
tāṅre kaili jaḍa-naśvara-prākṛta-kāya!!

SYNONYMS

pūrṇa-ānanda—complete transcendental bliss; *cit-svarūpa*—the spiritual identity; *jagannātha-rāya*—Lord Jagannātha; *tāṅre*—Him; *kaili*—you have made; *jaḍa*—inert; *naśvara*—perishable; *prākṛta*—material; *kāya*—possessing a body.

TRANSLATION

"Lord Jagannātha is completely spiritual and full of transcendental bliss, but you have compared Him to a dull, destructible body composed of the inert, external energy of the Lord.

PURPORT

If one thinks that the form of Lord Jagannātha is an idol made of wood, he immediately brings ill fortune into his life. According to the direction of the *Padma Purāṇa: arcye viṣṇau śilā-dhīḥ. . .yasya vā nārakī saḥ.* Thus one who thinks that the body of Lord Jagannātha is made of matter and who distinguishes between Lord Jagannātha's body and soul is condemned, for he is an offender. A pure devotee who knows the science of Kṛṣṇa consciousness makes no distinction between Lord Jagannātha and His body. He knows that they are identical, just as Lord Kṛṣṇa and His soul are one and the same. When one's eyes are purified by devotional service performed on the spiritual platform, one can actually envision Lord Jagannātha and His body as being completely spiritual. The advanced devotee, therefore, does not see the worshipable Deity to have a soul within a body like an ordinary human being. There is no distinction between the body and soul of Lord Jagannātha, for Lord Jagannātha is *sac-cid-ānanda-vigraha,* just as the body of Kṛṣṇa is *sac-cid-ānanda-vigraha.* There is actually no difference between Lord Jagannātha and Śrī Caitanya Mahāprabhu, but the ignorant poet from Bengal applied a material distinction to the body of Lord Śrī Jagannātha.

TEXT 119

পূর্ণ-ষড়ৈশ্বর্য চৈতন্য—স্বয়ং ভগবান্।
তাঁরে কৈলি ক্ষুদ্র জীব স্ফুলিঙ্গ-সমান!! ১১৯ ॥

pūrṇa-ṣaḍ-aiśvarya caitanya——svayaṁ bhagavān
tāṅre kaili kṣudra jīva sphuliṅga-samāna!!

SYNONYMS

pūrṇa—complete; *ṣaṭ-aiśvarya*—possessing six opulences; *caitanya*—Lord Śrī Caitanya Mahāprabhu; *svayam*—Himself; *bhagavān*—the Supreme Personality of Godhead; *tāṅre*—Him; *kaili*—you have made; *kṣudra jīva*—an ordinary living entity; *sphuliṅga-samāna*—exactly equal to the spark.

TRANSLATION

"You have calculated Śrī Caitanya Mahāprabhu, who is the Supreme Personality of Godhead, full in six opulences, to be on the level of an ordinary living being. Instead of knowing Him as the supreme fire, you have accepted Him as a spark."

PURPORT

In the *Upaniṣads* it is said, *yathāgner visphuliṅgā vyuccaranti:* the living entities are like sparks of fire, and His Lordship the Supreme Personality of Godhead is considered the original great fire. When we hear this *śruti-vākya,* or message from the *Vedas,* we should understand the distinction between the Supreme Lord Kṛṣṇa and the living entities. A person under the control of the external energy, however, cannot understand that distinction. Such a person cannot understand that the Supreme Person is the original great fire, whereas the living entities are simply small fragmental parts of that Supreme Personality of Godhead. As Kṛṣṇa says in *Bhagavad-gītā* (15.7):

mamaivāṁśo jīva-loke
jīva-bhūtaḥ sanātanaḥ
manaḥ ṣaṣṭhānīndriyāṇi
prakṛti-sthāni karṣati

"The living entities in this conditioned world are My eternal, fragmental parts. Due to conditioned life, they are struggling very hard with the six senses, which include the mind."

There is a distinction between the body and soul of the materially existing living being, but because Śrī Caitanya Mahāprabhu and Lord Jagannātha do not possess material bodies, there is no distinction between Their bodies and souls. On the spiritual platform, body and soul are identical; there is no distinction between them. As stated in *Śrīmad-Bhāgavatam:*

etad īśanam īśasya
prakṛti-stho 'pi tad-guṇaiḥ
na yujyate sadātma-sthair
yathā buddhis tad-āśrayā

"This is the divinity of the Personality of Godhead. He is not affected by the qualities of material nature, even though He is in contact with them. Similarly, the devotees who have taken shelter of the Lord cannot be influenced by the material qualities." (*Bhāg.* 1.11.38) His Lordship the Supreme Personality of Godhead, Kṛṣṇa, is unaffected by the influence of the three modes of material nature. Indeed, His devotees are also unpolluted by the influence of the external energy because they engage in the service of His Lordship. Even the very body of a devotee becomes spiritualized, just as an iron rod put into fire becomes as qualified as fire because it becomes red hot and will immediately burn anything it touches. Therefore the poet from Bengal committed a great offense by treating Lord Jagannātha's body and Lord Jagannātha, the Supreme Personality of Godhead, as two different entities, material and spiritual, as if the Lord were an ordinary living being. The Lord is always the master of the material energy; therefore He is not doomed to be covered by the material energy like an ordinary living entity.

TEXT 120

দুই-ঠাঞি অপরাধে পাইবি দুর্গতি !
অতত্ত্বজ্ঞ 'তত্ত্ব' বর্ণে, তার এই রীতি ! ১২০ ॥

dui-ṭhāñi aparādhe pāibi durgati!
atattva-jña 'tattva' varṇe, tāra ei rīti!

SYNONYMS

dui-ṭhāñi—unto both; *aparādhe*—by offense; *pāibi*—you will get; *durgati*—hellish destination; *a-tattva-jña*—one who has no knowledge of the Absolute Truth; *tattva varṇe*—describes the Absolute Truth; *tāra*—his; *ei*—this; *rīti*—course.

TRANSLATION

Svarūpa Dāmodara continued, "Because you have committed an offense to Lord Jagannātha and Śrī Caitanya Mahāprabhu, you will attain a hellish destination. You do not know how to describe the Absolute Truth, but nevertheless you have tried to do so. Therefore you must be condemned.

PURPORT

The *brāhmaṇa* poet from Bengal was an offender in the estimation of Svarūpa Dāmodara Gosvāmī, for although the poet had no knowledge of the Absolute Truth, he had nevertheless tried to describe it. The Bengali poet was an offender to both Śrī Caitanya Mahāprabhu and Lord Jagannātha. Because he had made a distinction between Lord Jagannātha's body and soul and because he had indicated that Lord Śrī Caitanya Mahāprabhu was different from Lord Jagannātha, he had committed offenses to Them both. *A-tattva-jña* refers to one who has no knowledge of the Absolute Truth or who worships his own body as the Supreme Personality of Godhead. If an *ahaṅgrahopāsaka-māyāvādī,* a person engaged in fruitive activities or a person interested only in sense gratification, describes the Absolute Truth, he immediately becomes an offender.

TEXT 121

আর এক করিয়াছ পরম 'প্রমাদ' !
দেহ-দেহি-ভেদ ঈশ্বরে কৈলে 'অপরাধ' ! ১২১ ॥

āra eka kariyācha parama 'pramāda'!
deha-dehi-bheda īśvare kaile 'aparādha'!

SYNONYMS

āra eka—another one; *kariyācha*—you have done; *parama*—the supreme; *pramāda*—illusion; *deha-dehi-bheda*—the distinction between the body and soul; *īśvare*—in His Lordship; *kaile*—you have done; *aparādha*—an offense.

TRANSLATION

"You are in complete illusion, for you have distinguished between the body and soul of His Lordship [Lord Jagannātha or Śrī Caitanya Mahāprabhu]. That is a great offense.

PURPORT

When one differentiates between the body and soul of the Supreme Personality of Godhead, he immediately becomes an offender. Because the living entities in the material world are generally covered by material bodies, the body and soul of an ordinary human being cannot be identical. The Supreme Lord bestows the fruits of one's activities, for He is the Lord of the results of fruitive action. He is also the cause of all causes, and He is the master of the material energy. Therefore He is supreme. An ordinary living being, however, in his material condition, enjoys the results of his own fruitive activities and therefore falls under their influence. Even in the liberated stage of *brahma-bhūta* identification, he engages in rendering service to His Lordship. Thus there are distinctions between an ordinary human being and the Supreme Lord. *Karmīs* and *jñānīs* who ignore these distinctions are offenders against the lotus feet of the Supreme Personality of Godhead.

An ordinary human being is prone to be subjugated by the material energy, whereas His Lordship the Supreme Personality of Godhead—Śrī Caitanya Mahāprabhu, Lord Kṛṣṇa or Lord Jagannātha—is always the master of the material energy and is therefore never subject to its influence. His Lordship the Supreme

Personality of Godhead has an unlimited spiritual identity, never to be broken, whereas the consciousness of the living entity is limited and fragmented. The living entities are fragmental portions of the Supreme Personality of Godhead eternally (*mamaivāṁśo jīva-loke jīva-bhūtaḥ sanātanaḥ*). It is not that they are covered by the material energy in conditioned life but become one with the Supreme Personality of Godhead when freed from the influence of material energy. Such an idea is offensive.

According to the considerations of Māyāvādī fools, the Supreme Personality of Godhead accepts a material body when He appears in the material world. A Vaiṣṇava, however, knows perfectly well that for Kṛṣṇa, Lord Jagannātha or Śrī Caitanya Mahāprabhu—unlike ordinary human beings—there is no distinction between the body and the soul. Even in the material world His Lordship retains His spiritual identity; therefore Lord Kṛṣṇa exhibited all opulences even in His childhood body. There is no distinction between the body and soul of Kṛṣṇa; whether He is in His childhood body or His youthful body, He is always identical with His body. Even though Kṛṣṇa appears like an ordinary human being, He is never subjected to the rules and regulations of the material world. He is *svarāṭ*, or fully independent. He can appear in the material world, but contrary to the offensive conclusion of the Māyāvda school, He has no material body. In this connection one may again refer to the above-mentioned verse from *Śrīmad-Bhāgavatam* (1.11.38):

etad īśanam īśasya
prakṛti-stho 'pi tad-guṇaiḥ
na yujyate sadātma-sthair
yathā buddhis tad-āśrayā

The Supreme Person has an eternal spiritual body. If one tries to distinguish between the body and soul of the Supreme Personality of Godhead, he commits a great offense.

TEXT 122

ঈশ্বরের নাহি কভু দেহ-দেহি-ভেদ ।
স্বরূপ, দেহ,—চিদানন্দ, নাহিক বিভেদ ॥ ১২২ ॥

īśvarera nāhi kabhu deha-dehi-bheda
svarūpa, deha,——cid-ānanda, nāhika vibheda

SYNONYMS

īśvarera—of the Supreme Personality of Godhead; *nāhi*—there is not; *kabhu*—at any time; *deha-dehi-bheda*—distinction between the body and soul;

svarūpa—personal identity; *deha*—body; *cit-ānanda*—all made of blissful spiritual energy; *nāhika vibheda*—there is no distinction.

TRANSLATION

"At no time is there a distinction between the body and soul of the Supreme Personality of Godhead. His personal identity and His body are made of blissful spiritual energy. There is no distinction between them.

PURPORT

Lord Kṛṣṇa, the son of Nanda Mahārāja, is *advaya-jñāna;* in other words, there is no distinction between His body and soul, for His existence is completely spiritual. According to the verse from *Śrīmad-Bhāgavatam* beginning with the words *vadanti tat tattva-vidas tattvam* (1.2.11), the Absolute Truth is always to be understood from three angles of vision as Brahman, Paramātmā and Bhagavān. Unlike the objects of the material world, however, the Absolute Truth is always one and always the same. Thus there is no distinction between His body and soul. His form, name, attributes and pastimes, therefore, are completely distinct from those of the material world. One should know perfectly well that there is no difference between the body and soul of the Supreme Personality of Godhead. When one conceives of a distinction between His body and soul, one is immediately conditioned by material nature. Because a person in the material world makes such distinctions, he is called *baddha-jīva,* a conditioned soul.

TEXT 123

"দেহ-দেহি-বিভাগোঽয়ং নেশ্বরে বিদ্যতে ক্বচিৎ ॥" ১২৩ ॥

"deha-dehi-vibhāgo 'yaṁ
neśvare vidyate kvacit"

SYNONYMS

deha—of the body; *dehi*—of the embodied; *vibhāgaḥ*—distinction; *ayam*—this; *na*—not; *īśvare*—in the Supreme Personality of Godhead; *vidyate*—exists; *kvacit*—at any time.

TRANSLATION

" 'There is no distinction between the body and soul of the Supreme Personality of Godhead at any time.'

PURPORT

This quotation, which is included in the *Laghu-bhāgavatāmṛta* (1.5.342), is from the *Kūrma Purāṇa*.

TEXTS 124-125

নাতঃ পরং পরম যদ্ভবতঃ স্বরূপ-
মানন্দমাত্রমবিকল্পমবিদ্ধবর্চঃ ।
পশ্যামি বিশ্বসৃজমেকমবিশ্বমাত্মন্
ভূতেন্দ্রিয়াত্মকমদস্ত উপাশ্রিতোঽস্মি ॥ ১২৪ ॥
তদ্বা ইদং ভুবনমঙ্গল মঙ্গলায়
ধ্যানে স্ম নো দরশিতং ত উপাসকানাম্ ।
তস্মৈ নমো ভগবতেঽনুবিধেম তুভ্যং
যোঽনাদৃতো নরকভাগ্ভিরসংপ্রসঙ্গৈঃ ॥ ১২৫ ॥

nātaḥ paraṁ parama yad bhavataḥ svarūpam
ānanda-mātram avikalpam aviddha-varcaḥ
paśyāmi viśva-sṛjam ekam aviśvam ātman
bhūtendriyātmaka-madas ta upāśrito 'smi

tad vā idaṁ bhuvana-maṅgala maṅgalāya
dhyāne sma no daraśitaṁ ta upāsakānām
tasmai namo bhagavate 'nuvidhema tubhyaṁ
yo 'nādṛto naraka-bhāgbhir asat-prasaṅgaiḥ

SYNONYMS

na—do not; *ataḥ param*—here after; *parama*—O Supreme; *yat*—that which; *bhavataḥ*—of Your Lordship; *svarūpam*—eternal form; *ānanda-mātram*—impersonal Brahman effulgence; *avikalpam*—without changes; *aviddha-varcaḥ*—without deterioration of potency; *paśyāmi*—do I see; *viśva-sṛjam*—creator of the cosmic manifestation; *ekam*—one without a second; *aviśvam*—and yet not of matter; *ātman*—O supreme cause; *bhūta*—body; *indriya*—senses; *ātmaka*—on such identification; *madaḥ*—pride; *te*—unto You; *upāśritaḥ*—surrendered; *asmi*—I am; *tat*—the Supreme Personality of Godhead; *vā*—or; *idam*—this present form; *bhuvana-maṅgala*—they are all-auspicious for all the universes; *maṅgalāya*—for the sake of all prosperity; *dhyāne*—in meditation; *sma*—as it were; *naḥ*—unto us; *daraśitam*—manifested; *te*—Your; *upāsakānām*—of the devotees; *tasmai*—

unto Him; *namaḥ*—my respectful obeisances; *bhagavate*—unto the Personality of Godhead; *anuvidhema*—I perform; *tubhyam*—unto You; *yaḥ*—which; *anādṛtaḥ*—is neglected; *naraka-bhāgbhiḥ*—by persons destined for hell; *asat-prasaṅgaiḥ*—by material topics.

TRANSLATION

" 'O my Lord, I do not see a form superior to Your present form of eternal bliss and knowledge. In Your impersonal Brahman effulgence in the spiritual sky, there is no occasional change and no deterioration of internal potency. I surrender unto You because, whereas I am proud of my material body and senses, Your Lordship is the cause of the cosmic manifestation. Yet You are untouched by matter.

" 'This present form, or any transcendental form expanded by the Supreme Personality of Godhead, Śrī Kṛṣṇa, is equally auspicious for all the universes. Since You have manifested this eternal personal form upon whom Your devotees meditate, I therefore offer my respectful obeisances unto You. Those who are destined to be dispatched to the path of hell neglect Your personal form because of speculating on material topics.'

PURPORT

These verses from *Śrīmad-Bhāgavatam* (3.9.3,4) were spoken by Lord Brahmā.

TEXT 126

কাহাঁ 'পূর্ণানন্দৈশ্বর্য' কৃষ্ণ 'মায়েশ্বর' !
কাহাঁ 'ক্ষুদ্র' জীব 'দুঃখী', 'মায়ার কিঙ্কর' ! ১২৬ ॥

kāhāṅ 'pūrṇānandaiśvarya' kṛṣṇa 'māyeśvara'!
kāhāṅ 'kṣudra' jīva 'duḥkhī', 'māyāra kiṅkara'!

SYNONYMS

kāhāṅ—whereas; *pūrṇa*—full; *ānanda*—bliss; *aiśvarya*—opulences; *kṛṣṇa*—Lord Kṛṣṇa; *māyā-īśvara*—the master of the material energy; *kāhāṅ*—whereas; *kṣudra jīva*—the little conditioned soul; *duḥkhī*—unhappy; *māyāra kiṅkara*—the servant of the material energy.

TRANSLATION

"Whereas Kṛṣṇa, the Absolute Truth, the Supreme Personality of Godhead, is full of transcendental bliss, possesses all six spiritual opulences in full, and is the master of the material energy, the small conditioned soul, who is always unhappy, is the servant of the material energy.

PURPORT

The living entity is an ever-conditioned servant of the material energy, whereas Kṛṣṇa, the Supreme Personality of Godhead, is master of the material energy. How, then, could they be on an equal level? There can be no comparison between them. His Lordship is always in a happy condition of transcendental bliss, whereas the conditioned soul is always unhappy because of his contact with the material energy. The Supreme Lord controls the material energy, and the material energy controls the conditioned souls. There is therefore no comparison between the Supreme Personality of Godhead and the ordinary living entities.

TEXT 127

"হ্লাদিন্যা সম্বিদাশ্লিষ্টঃ সচ্চিদানন্দ ঈশ্বরঃ ।
স্বাবিদ্যা-সংবৃতো জীবঃ সংক্লেশনিকরাকরঃ ॥" ১২৭ ॥

"hlādinyā samvidāśliṣṭaḥ
sac-cid-ānanda-īśvaraḥ
svāvidyā saṁvṛto jīvaḥ
saṅkleśa-nikārākara"

SYNONYMS

hlādinyā—by the *hlādinī* potency; *samvidā*—by the *samvit* potency; *āśliṣṭaḥ*—surrounded; *sat-cit-ānanda*—always transcendentally blissful; *īśvaraḥ*—the Supreme Controller; *sva*—own; *avidyā*—by ignorance; *saṁvṛtaḥ*—surrounded; *jīvaḥ*—the living entity; *saṅkleśa*—of the three fold miseries; *nikāra*—of the multitude; *ākara*—the mine.

TRANSLATION

" 'The Supreme Personality of Godhead, the Supreme Controller, is always full of transcendental bliss and is accompanied by the potencies known as hlādinī and samvit. The conditioned soul, however, is always covered by ignorance and embarassed by the threefold miseries of life. Thus he is a treasure house of all kinds of tribulations.' "

PURPORT

This verse is found in Śrīdhara Svāmī's *Bhāvārtha-dīpikā* (1.7.6), wherein he quotes Śrī Viṣṇusvāmī.

TEXT 128

শুনি' সভাসদের চিত্তে হৈল চমৎকার ।
'সত্য কহে গোসাঞি, দুঁহার করিয়াছে তিরস্কার' ॥

śuni' sabhā-sadera citte haila camatkāra
'satya kahe gosāñi, duṅhāra kariyāche tiraskāra'

SYNONYMS

śuni'—hearing; *sabhā-sadera*—of all the members of the assembly; *citte*—in the minds; *haila*—there was; *camatkāra*—wonder; *satya*—the truth; *kahe*—said; *gosāñi*—Svarūpa Dāmodara Gosvāmī; *duṅhāra*—of both; *kariyāche*—has done; *tiraskāra*—offense.

TRANSLATION

Hearing this explanation, all the members of the assembly were struck with wonder. "Svarūpa Dāmodara Gosvāmī has spoken the real truth," they admitted. "The brāhmaṇa from Bengal has committed an offense by wrongly describing Lord Jagannātha and Lord Śrī Caitanya Mahāprabhu."

TEXT 129

শুনিয়া কবির হৈল লজ্জা, ভয়, বিস্ময় ।
হংস-মধ্যে বক যৈছে কিছু নাহি কয় ॥ ১২৯ ॥

śuniyā kavira haila lajjā, bhaya, vismaya
haṁsa-madhye baka yaiche kichu nāhi kaya

SYNONYMS

śuniyā—hearing; *kavira*—of the poet; *haila*—there was; *lajjā*—shame; *bhaya*—fear; *vismaya*—astonishment; *haṁsa-madhye*—in a society of white swans; *baka*—a duck; *yaiche*—just as; *kichu*—anything; *nāhi*—not; *kaya*—utters.

TRANSLATION

When the Bengali poet heard this chastisement from Svarūpa Dāmodara Gosvāmī, he was ashamed, fearful and astonished. Indeed, being like a duck in a society of white swans, he could not say anything.

TEXT 130

তার দুঃখ দেখি, স্বরূপ সদয়-হৃদয় ।
উপদেশ কৈলা তারে যৈছে 'হিত' হয় ॥ ১৩০ ॥

tāra duḥkha dekhi, svarūpa sadaya-hṛdaya
upadeśa kailā tāre yaiche 'hita' haya

SYNONYMS

tāra—his; *duḥkha dekhi*—observing the unhappiness; *svarūpa*—Svarūpa Dāmodara Gosvāmī; *sadaya-hṛdaya*—very kindhearted; *upadeśa kailā*—gave instruction; *tāre*—unto him; *yaiche*—so that; *hita*—benefit; *haya*—there can be.

TRANSLATION

Seeing the poet's unhappiness, Svarūpa Dāmodara Gosvāmī, who was naturally very kindhearted, advised him so that he could derive some benefit.

TEXT 131

"যাহ, ভাগবত পড় বৈষ্ণবের স্থানে ।
একান্ত আশ্রয় কর চৈতন্য-চরণে ॥ ১৩১ ॥

"yāha, bhāgavata paḍa vaiṣṇavera sthāne
ekānta āśraya kara caitanya-caraṇe

SYNONYMS

yāha—just go; *bhāgavata paḍa*—read *Śrīmad-Bhāgavatam; vaiṣṇavera sthāne*—from a self-realized Vaiṣṇava; *ekānta āśraya kara*—fully surrender; *caitanya-caraṇe*—at the lotus feet of Śrī Caitanya Mahāprabhu.

TRANSLATION

"If you want to understand Śrīmad-Bhāgavatam," he said, "you must approach a self-realized Vaiṣṇava and hear from him. You can do this when you have completely taken shelter of the lotus feet of Śrī Caitanya Mahāprabhu."

PURPORT

Herein Svarūpa Dāmodara Gosvāmī instructs the poet from Bengal to hear *Śrīmad-Bhāgavatam* from a pure Vaiṣṇava and learn from him. In India especially, there is now a class of professional *Bhāgavatam* readers whose means of livelihood is to go from village to village, town to town, reading *Bhāgavatam* and collecting *dakṣiṇa,* or rewards, in the form of money or goods, like umbrellas, cloth and fruit. Thus there is now a system of *Bhāgavata* business, with recitations called *Bhāgavata-saptāha* that continue for one week, although this is not mentioned in *Śrīmad-Bhāgavatam.* Nowhere does *Śrīmad-Bhāgavatam* say that the *Bhāgavatam* should be heard for one week from professionals. Rather, *Śrīmad-Bhāgavatam* (1.2.17) says: *śṛṇvatāṁ sva-kathāḥ kṛṣṇaḥ puṇya-śravaṇa-kīrtanaḥ.* One should regularly hear *Śrīmad-Bhāgavatam* from a self-realized Vaiṣṇava. By such hearing, one becomes pious. *Hṛdy antaḥstho hy abhadrāṇi vidhunoti suhṛt-satām.* As one thus hears the *Bhāgavatam* regularly and sincerely, his heart is purified of all material contamination.

naṣṭa-prāyeṣv abhadreṣu
nityaṁ bhāgavata-sevayā
bhagavaty uttama-śloke
bhaktir bhavati naiṣṭhikī

"As one regularly hears the *Bhāgavatam* or renders service unto the pure devotee, all that is troublesome to the heart is practically destroyed, and loving service unto the glorious Lord, who is praised with transcendental songs, is established as an irrevocable fact." (*Bhāg.* 1.2.18)

This is the proper process, but people are accustomed to being misled by professional *Bhāgavatam* reciters. Therefore Svarūpa Dāmodara Gosvāmī herein advises that one should not hear *Śrīmad-Bhāgavatam* from professional reciters. Instead, one must hear and learn the *Bhāgavatam* from a self-realized Vaiṣṇava. Sometimes it is seen that when a Māyāvādī *sannyāsī* reads the *Bhāgavatam,* flocks of men go to hear jugglery of words that cannot awaken their dormant love for Kṛṣṇa. Sometimes people go to see professional dramas and offer food and money to the players, who are expert at collecting these offerings very nicely. The result is that the members of the audience remain in the same position of *gṛham andha-kūpam,* family affection, and do not awaken their love for Kṛṣṇa.

In the *Bhāgavatam* (7.5.30), it is said, *matir na kṛṣṇe parataḥ svato vā mitho 'bhipadyeta gṛha-vratānām:* the *gṛhavratas,* those who are determined to continue following the materialistic way of life, will never awaken their dormant love of Kṛṣṇa, for they hear the *Bhāgavatam* only to solidify their position in household life and to be happy in family affairs and sex. Condemning this process of hearing the *Bhāgavatam* from professionals, Svarūpa Dāmodara Gosvāmī says, *yāha, bhāgavata paḍa vaiṣṇavera sthāne:* "To understand the *Śrīmad-Bhāgavatam,* you must approach a self-realized Vaiṣṇava." One should rigidly avoid hearing the *Bhāgavatam* from a Māyāvādī or other nondevotee who simply performs a grammatical jugglery of words to twist some meaning from the text, collect money from the innocent public, and thus keep people in darkness.

Svarūpa Dāmodara Gosvāmī strictly prohibits the behavior of the materialistic so-called hearers of *Śrīmad-Bhāgavatam.* Instead of awakening real love for Kṛṣṇa, such hearers of the *Bhāgavatam* become more and more attached to household affairs and sex life (*yan maithunādi-gṛhamedhi-sukhaṁ hi tuccham*). One should hear *Śrīmad-Bhāgavatam* from a person who has no connection with material activities, or, in other words, from a *paramahaṁsa* Vaiṣṇava, one who has achieved the highest stage of *sannyāsa.* This, of course, is not possible unless one takes shelter of the lotus feet of Śrī Caitanya Mahāprabhu. The *Śrīmad-Bhāgavatam* is understandable only for one who can follow in the footsteps of Śrī Caitanya Mahāprabhu.

TEXT 132

চৈতন্যের ভক্তগণের নিত্য কর 'সঙ্গ'।
তবেত জানিবা সিদ্ধান্তসমুদ্র-তরঙ্গ ॥ ১৩২ ॥

caitanyera bhakta-gaṇera nitya kara 'saṅga'
tabeta jānibā siddhānta-samudra-taraṅga

SYNONYMS

caitanyera—of Lord Śrī Caitanya Mahāprabhu; *bhakta-gaṇera*—of the devotees; *nitya*—regularly; *kara*—do; *saṅga*—association; *tabeta*—then only; *jānibā*—you will understand; *siddhānta-samudra-taraṅga*—the waves of the ocean of devotional service.

TRANSLATION

Svarūpa Dāmodara continued, "Associate regularly with the devotees of Śrī Caitanya Mahāprabhu, for then only will you understand the waves of the ocean of devotional service.

PURPORT

It is clearly to be understood in this connection that the followers of Śrī Caitanya Mahāprabhu's way of devotional service are eternally associates of the Supreme Personality of Godhead and perfect knowers of the Absolute Truth. If one immediately follows the principles of Śrī Caitanya Mahāprabhu by associating with His devotees, lusty desires for material enjoyment will vanish from one's heart. Then one will be able to understand the meaning of *Śrīmad-Bhāgavatam* and the purpose of listening to it. Otherwise such understanding is impossible.

TEXT 133

তবেত পাণ্ডিত্য তোমার হইবে সফল।
কৃষ্ণের স্বরূপ-লীলা বর্ণিবা নির্মল ॥ ১৩৩ ॥

tabeta pāṇḍitya tomāra ha-ibe saphala
kṛṣṇera svarūpa-līlā varṇibā nirmala

SYNONYMS

tabeta—then only; *pāṇḍitya*—learning; *tomāra*—your; *ha-ibe*—will become; *sa-phala*—successful; *kṛṣṇera*—of Lord Kṛṣṇa; *svarūpa-līlā*—the transcendental pastimes; *varṇibā*—you will describe; *nirmala*—without material contamination.

TRANSLATION

"Only if you follow the principles of Śrī Caitanya Mahāprabhu and His devotees will your learning be successful. Then you will be able to write about the transcendental pastimes of Kṛṣṇa without material contamination.

TEXT 134

এই শ্লোক করিয়াছ পাঞা সন্তোষ।
তোমার হৃদয়ের অর্থে দুঁহায় লাগে 'দোষ' ॥১৩৪॥

ei śloka kariyācha pāñā santoṣa
tomāra hṛdayera arthe duṅhāya lāge 'doṣa'

SYNONYMS

ei śloka—this verse; *kariyācha*—you have composed; *pāñā santoṣa*—getting satisfaction; *tomāra hṛdayera*—of your heart; *arthe*—by the meaning; *duṅhāya*—to both; *lāge doṣa*—there is an offense.

TRANSLATION

"You have composed this introductory verse to your great satisfaction, but the meaning you have expressed is contaminated by offenses to both Lord Jagannātha and Śrī Caitanya Mahāprabhu.

TEXT 135

তুমি যৈছে-তৈছে কহ, না জানিয়া রীতি।
সরস্বতী সেই-শব্দে করিয়াছে স্তুতি ॥ ১৩৫ ॥

tumi yaiche-taiche kaha, nā jāniyā rīti
sarasvatī sei-śabde kariyāche stuti

SYNONYMS

tumi—you; *yaiche-taiche*—somehow or other; *kaha*—speak; *nā jāniyā rīti*—not knowing the regulative principles; *sarasvatī*—the goddess of learning; *sei-śabde*—in those words; *kariyāche stuti*—has made prayers.

TRANSLATION

"You have written something irregular, not knowing the regulative principles, but the goddess of learning, Sarasvatī, has used your words to offer her prayers to the Supreme Lord.

PURPORT

Svarūpa Dāmodara Gosvāmī informed the Bengali poet, "Because of your ignorance and your leaning toward Māyāvāda philosophy, you cannot distinguish the difference between the Māyāvāda and Vaiṣṇava philosophies. Therefore the process you have adopted to praise Lord Śrī Caitanya Mahāprabhu and Lord Jagannātha does not follow the proper system; indeed, it is irregular and offensive. Fortunately, however, through your words, the goddess of learning, mother Sarasvatī, has tactfully offered her prayers to her master, Lord Śrī Caitanya Mahāprabhu."

TEXT 136

যৈছে ইন্দ্র, দৈত্যাদি করে কৃষ্ণের ভৎর্সন ।
সেইশব্দে সরস্বতী করেন স্তবন ॥ ১৩৬ ॥

yaiche indra, daityādi kare kṛṣṇera bhartsana
sei-śabde sarasvatī karena stavana

SYNONYMS

yaiche—just like; *indra*—Lord Indra, the King of heaven; *daitya*—demons; *ādi*—and others; *kare*—do; *kṛṣṇera bhartsana*—chastisement to Kṛṣṇa; *sei-śabde*—by those words; *sarasvatī*—the goddess of learning; *karena stavana*—offers prayers.

TRANSLATION

"Sometimes demons, and even Lord Indra, the King of heaven, chastised Kṛṣṇa, but mother Sarasvatī, taking advantage of their words, offered prayers to the Lord.

TEXT 137

বাচালং বালিশং স্তব্ধমজ্ঞং পণ্ডিতমানিনম্ ।
কৃষ্ণং মর্ত্যমুপাশ্রিত্য গোপা মে চক্রুরপ্রিয়ম্ ॥ ১৩৭ ॥

vācālaṁ bāliśaṁ stabdhaṁ
ajñaṁ paṇḍita-māninam
kṛṣṇaṁ martyam upāśritya
gopā me cakrur apriyam

SYNONYMS

vācālam—talkative; *bāliśam*—childish; *stabdham*—impudent; *ajñam*—foolish; *paṇḍita-māninam*—thinking Himself a very learned scholar; *kṛṣṇam*—Kṛṣṇa; *mar-*

tyam—an ordinary mortal human being; *upāśritya*—taking shelter of; *gopāḥ*—the cowherd men; *me*—unto me; *cakruḥ*—committed; *apriyam*—that which is not very much appreciated.

TRANSLATION

"[Lord Indra said:] 'This Kṛṣṇa, who is an ordinary human being, is talkative, childish, impudent and ignorant, although He thinks Himself very learned. The cowherd men in Vṛndāvana have offended me by accepting Him. This has not been greatly appreciated by me.'

PURPORT

This verse is from *Śrīmad-Bhāgavatam* (10.25.5).

TEXT 138

ঐশ্বর্য-মদে মত্ত ইন্দ্র,—যেন মাতোয়াল ।
বুদ্ধিনাশ হৈল, কেবল নাহিক সাম্ভাল ॥ ১৩৮ ॥

aiśvarya-made matta indra,——yena mātoyāla
buddhi-nāśa haila, kevala nāhika sāmbhāla

SYNONYMS

aiśvarya-made—being proud of his opulence; *matta*—maddened; *indra*—the King of heaven; *yena*—as if; *mātoyāla*—a mad person; *buddhi-nāśa*—bereft of intelligence; *haila*—became; *kevala*—only; *nāhika*—there is not; *sāmbhāla*—caution.

TRANSLATION

"Indra, the King of heaven, being too proud of his heavenly opulences, became like a madman. Thus bereft of his intelligence, he could not restrain himself from speaking nonsensically about Kṛṣṇa.

TEXT 139

ইন্দ্র বলে,—"মুঞি কৃষ্ণের করিয়াছি নিন্দন" ।
তারই মুখে সরস্বতী করেন স্তবন ॥ ১৩৯ ॥

indra bale,——"muñi kṛṣṇera kariyāchi nindana"
tāra-i mukhe sarasvatī karena stavana

SYNONYMS

indra bale—Indra says; *muñi*—I; *kṛṣṇera*—of Lord Kṛṣṇa; *kariyāchi*—have done; *nindana*—chastisement and defamation; *tāra-i mukhe*—from his mouth; *sarasvatī*—mother Sarasvatī, the goddess of learning; *karena stavana*—offers prayers.

TRANSLATION

"Thus Indra thought, 'I have properly chastised Kṛṣṇa and defamed Him.' But Sarasvatī, the goddess of learning, took this opportunity to offer prayers to Kṛṣṇa.

TEXT 140

'বাচাল' কহিয়ে—'বেদপ্রবর্তক' ধন্য ।
'বালিশ'—তথাপি 'শিশু-প্রায়' গর্বশূন্য ॥ ১৪০ ॥

'vācāla kahiye—'veda-pravartaka' dhanya
'bāliśa'—tathāpi 'śiśu-prāya' garva-śūnya

SYNONYMS

vācāla—talkative; *kahiye*—I say; *veda-pravartaka*—one who can speak with the authority of the *Vedas;* *dhanya*—glorious; *bāliśa*—childish; *tathāpi*—still; *śiśu-prāya*—like a child; *garva-śūnya*—without pride.

TRANSLATION

"The word 'vācāla' is used to refer to a person who can speak according to Vedic authority, and the word 'bāliśa' means 'innocent.' Kṛṣṇa spoke the Vedic knowledge, yet He always presents Himself as a prideless, innocent boy.

TEXT 141

বন্দ্যাভাবে 'অনম্র'—'স্তব্ধ'-শব্দে কয় ।
যাহা হৈতে অন্য 'বিজ্ঞ' নাহি—সে 'অজ্ঞ' হয় ॥১৪১॥

vandyābhāve 'anamra'—'stabdha'-śabde kaya
yāhā haite anya 'vijña' nāhi—se 'ajña' haya

SYNONYMS

vandya-abhāve—because there is no one else to be offered obeisances; *anamra*—the one who does not offer obeisances; *stabdha-śadbe*—by the word *stabdha* ("impudent"); *kaya*—says; *yāhā haite*—than whom; *anya*—other; *vijña*—learned scholar; *nāhi*—is not; *se*—He; *ajña*—one by whom nothing is unknown; *haya*—is.

TRANSLATION

"When there is no one else to receive obeisances, one may be called 'anamra,' or one who offers obeisances to no one. This is the meaning of the word 'stabdha.' And because no one is found to be more learned than Kṛṣṇa, He may be called 'ajña,' indicating that nothing is unknown to Him.

TEXT 142

'পণ্ডিতের মান্য-পাত্র – হয় 'পণ্ডিতমানী' ।
তথাপি ভক্তবাৎসল্যে 'মনুষ্য' অভিমানী ॥ ১৪২ ॥

'paṇḍitera mānya-pātra——haya 'paṇḍita-mānī'
tathāpi bhakta-vātsalye 'manuṣya' abhimānī

SYNONYMS

paṇḍitera—of learned scholars; *mānya-pātra*—worshipable object; *haya*—is; *paṇḍita-mānī*—a person honored by the learned scholars; *tathāpi*—still; *bhakta-vātsalye*—because of being very affectionate to the devotees; *manuṣya abhimānī*—presents Himself as an ordinary human being.

TRANSLATION

"The word 'paṇḍita-mānī' can be used to indicate that Kṛṣṇa is honored even by learned scholars. Nevertheless, because of affection for His devotees, Kṛṣṇa appears like an ordinary human being and may therefore be called 'martya.'

TEXT 143

জরাসন্ধ কহে,—"কৃষ্ণ—পুরুষ-অধম ।
তোর সঙ্গে না যুঝিমু, "যাহি বন্ধুহন্" ॥ ১৪৩ ॥

jarāsandha kahe,——"kṛṣṇa——puruṣa-adhama
tora saṅge nā yujhimu, "yāhi bandhu-han"

SYNONYMS

jarāsandha kahe—Jarāsandha says; *kṛṣṇa*—Kṛṣṇa; *puruṣa-adhama*—the lowest of human beings; *tora saṅge*—with You; *nā yujhimu*—I shall not fight; *yāhi*—because; *bandhu-han*—killer of Your own relatives.

TRANSLATION

"The demon Jarāsandha chastised Kṛṣṇa, saying, 'You are the lowest of human beings. I shall not fight with You, for You killed Your own relatives.'

PURPORT

In this verse also, mother Sarasvatī offers prayers to Kṛṣṇa. The word *puruṣa-adhama* refers to the Personality of Godhead, under whom all other persons remain, or, in other words, *puruṣa-uttama,* the best of all living beings. Similarly, the word *bandhu-han* means "the killer of *māyā.*" In the conditioned state of life, one is closely related with *māyā* as a friend, but when one comes in contact with Kṛṣṇa one is freed from that relationship.

TEXT 144

যাহা হৈতে অন্য পুরুষসকল—'অধম'।
সেই হয় 'পুরুষাধম'—সরস্বতীর মন ॥ ১৪৪ ॥

yāhā haite anya puruṣa-sakala——'adhama'
sei haya 'puruṣādhama'——sarasvatīra mana

SYNONYMS

yāhā haite—from whom; *anya*—other; *puruṣa*—persons; *sakala*—all; *adhama*—subordinate; *sei*—he; *haya*—is; *puruṣa-adhama*—the person under whom all others remain; *sarasvatīra mana*—the explanation of mother Sarasvatī.

TRANSLATION

"Mother Sarasvatī takes 'puruṣādhama' to mean 'puruṣottama,' He to whom all men are subordinate.

TEXT 145

'বান্ধে সবারে'—তাতে অবিদ্যা 'বন্ধু' হয়।
'অবিদ্যা-নাশক'—'বন্ধুহন্'-শব্দে কয় ॥ ১৪৫ ॥

'bāndhe sabāre'——tāte avidyā 'bandhu' haya
'avidyā-nāśaka'——'bandhu-han'-śabde kaya

SYNONYMS

bāndhe—binds; *sabāre*—everyone; *tāte*—therefore; *avidyā*—nescience, or *māyā; bandhu*—binder or relative; *haya*—is; *avidyā-nāśaka*—vanquisher of *māyā; bandhu-han-śabde*—by the word *"bandhu-han"*; *kaya*—mother Sarasvatī says.

TRANSLATION

"Nescience, or māyā, may be called 'bandhu' because she entangles everone in the material world. Therefore by using the word 'bandhu-han,' mother Sarasvatī says that Lord Kṛṣṇa is the vanquisher of māyā.

PURPORT

Everyone is entangled in the illusory energy, but as stated in *Bhagavad-gītā, mām eva ye prapadyante māyām etāṁ taranti te:* as soon as one surrenders to Kṛṣṇa, he is freed from *māyā.* Therefore Kṛṣṇa may be called *bandhu-han,* the killer of *māyā.*

TEXT 146

এইমত শিশুপাল করিল নিন্দন।
সেইবাক্যে সরস্বতী করেন স্তবন ॥ ১৪৬ ॥

ei-mata śiśupāla karila nindana
sei-vākye sarasvatī karena stavana

SYNONYMS

ei-mata—in this way; *śiśu-pāla*—of the name Śiśupāla; *karila nindana*—blasphemed; *sei-vākye*—by those words; *sarasvatī*—the goddess of learning; *karena stavana*—offers prayers.

TRANSLATION

"Śiśupāla also blasphemed Kṛṣṇa in this way, but the goddess of learning, Sarasvatī, offered her prayers to Kṛṣṇa even by his words.

TEXT 147

তৈছে এই শ্লোকে তোমার অর্থে 'নিন্দা' আইসে।
সরস্বতীর অর্থ শুন, যাতে 'স্তুতি' ভাসে ॥ ১৪৭ ॥

taiche ei śloke tomāra arthe 'nindā' āise
sarasvatīra artha śuna, yāte 'stuti' bhāse

SYNONYMS

taiche—in that way; *ei śloke*—in this verse; *tomāra*—your; *arthe*—by the meaning; *nindā*—blasphemy; *āise*—comes; *sarasvatīra artha*—the meaning of mother Sarasvatī; *śuna*—hear; *yāte*—by which; *stuti*—prayers; *bhāse*—appear.

TRANSLATION

"In that way, although your verse is blasphemous according to your meaning, mother Sarasvatī has taken advantage of it to offer prayers to the Lord.

TEXT 148

**জগন্নাথ হন কৃষ্ণের 'আত্মস্বরূপ' ।
কিন্তু ইহাঁ দারুব্রহ্ম –স্থাবর-স্বরূপ ॥ ১৪৮ ॥**

jagannātha hana kṛṣṇera 'ātma-svarūpa'
kintu ihāṅ dāru-brahma——sthāvara-svarūpa

SYNONYMS

jagannātha—Lord Jagannātha; *hana*—is; *kṛṣṇera ātma-svarūpa*—identical with Kṛṣṇa; *kintu*—but; *ihāṅ*—here, at Jagannātha Purī; *dāru-brahma*—the Absolute appearing as wood; *sthāvara-svarūpa*—nonmoving identity.

TRANSLATION

"There is no difference between Lord Jagannātha and Kṛṣṇa, but here Lord Jagannātha is fixed as the Absolute Person appearing in wood. Therefore He does not move.

TEXT 149

**তাঁহা-সহ আত্মতা একরূপ হঞা ।
কৃষ্ণ একতত্ত্বরূপ—দুই রূপ হঞা ॥ ১৪৯ ॥**

tāṅhā-saha ātmatā eka-rūpa hañā
kṛṣṇa eka-tattva-rūpa——dui rūpa hañā

SYNONYMS

tāṅhā-saha—with Him; *ātmatā*—the quality of being the self; *eka-rūpa hañā*—being one form; *kṛṣṇa*—Lord Kṛṣṇa; *eka-tattva-rūpa*—one principle; *dui*—two; *rūpa*—forms; *hañā*—becoming.

TRANSLATION

"Thus Lord Jagannātha and Śrī Caitanya Mahāprabhu, although appearing as two, are one because They are both Kṛṣṇa, who is one alone.

TEXT 150

**সংসারতারণ-হেতু যেই ইচ্ছা-শক্তি ।
তাহার মিলন করি' একতা যৈছে প্রাপ্তি ॥ ১৫০ ॥**

saṁsāra-tāraṇa-hetu yei icchā-śakti
tāhāra milana kari' ekatā yaiche prāpti

SYNONYMS

saṁsāra-tāraṇa-hetu—for delivering the entire world; *yei*—that; *icchā-śakti*—the potency of will; *tāhāra*—of that will; *milana kari'*—by the meeting; *ekatā*—oneness; *yaiche*—so that; *prāpti*—obtainment.

TRANSLATION

"The supreme desire to deliver the entire world meets in both of Them, and for that reason also They are one and the same.

TEXT 151

সকল সংসারী লোকের করিতে উদ্ধার ।
গৌর-জঙ্গম-রূপে কৈলা অবতার ॥ ১৫১ ॥

sakala saṁsārī lokera karite uddhāra
gaura-jaṅgama-rūpe kailā avatāra

SYNONYMS

sakala—all; *saṁsārī*—materially contaminated; *lokera*—persons; *karite uddhāra*—to deliver; *gaura*—Śrī Caitanya Mahāprabhu; *jaṅgama*—moving; *rūpe*—in the form; *kailā avatāra*—has descended.

TRANSLATION

"To deliver all the materially contaminated people of the world, that same Kṛṣṇa has descended, moving as Lord Śrī Caitanya Mahāprabhu.

TEXT 152

জগন্নাথের দর্শনে খণ্ডায় সংসার ।
সব-দেশের সব-লোক নারে আসিবার ॥ ১৫২ ॥

jagannāthera darśane khaṇḍāya saṁsāra
saba-deśera saba-loka nāre āsibāra

SYNONYMS

jagannāthera—of Lord Jagannātha; *darśane*—by visiting; *khaṇḍāya saṁsāra*—one is freed from material existence; *saba-deśera*—of all countries; *saba-loka*—all men; *nāre āsibāra*—cannot come.

TRANSLATION

"By visiting Lord Jagannātha one is freed from material existence, but not all men of all countries can come or be admitted here in Jagannātha Purī.

TEXT 153

শ্রীকৃষ্ণচৈতন্যপ্রভু দেশে দেশে যাঞা ।
সব-লোকে নিস্তারিলা জঙ্গম-ব্রহ্ম হঞা ॥ ১৫৩ ॥

śrī-kṛṣṇa-caitanya-prabhu deśe deśe yāñā
saba-loke nistārilā jaṅgama-brahma hañā

SYNONYMS

śrī-kṛṣṇa-caitanya-prabhu—Lord Śrī Caitanya Mahāprabhu; *deśe deśe yāñā*—moving from one country to another; *saba-loke nistārilā*—delivered all conditioned souls; *jaṅgama-brahma*—moving Brahman; *hañā*—being.

TRANSLATION

"Śrī Caitanya Mahāprabhu, however, moves from one country to another, personally or by His representative. Thus He, as the moving Brahman, delivers all the people of the world.

TEXT 154

সরস্বতীর অর্থ এই কহিলুঁ বিবরণ ।
এহো ভাগ্য তোমার ঐছে করিলে বর্ণন ॥ ১৫৪ ॥

sarasvatīra artha ei kahiluṅ vivaraṇa
eho bhāgya tomāra aiche karile varṇana

SYNONYMS

sarasvatīra—of Sarasvatī; *artha*—meaning; *ei*—this; *kahiluṅ vivaraṇa*—I have explained; *eho*—this; *bhāgya*—great fortune; *tomāra aiche*—in such a way; *karile varṇana*—you have described.

TRANSLATION

"Thus I have explained the meaning intended by mother Sarasvatī, the goddess of learning. It is your great fortune that you have described Lord Jagannātha and Lord Śrī Caitanya Mahāprabhu in that way.

TEXT 155

কৃষ্ণে গালি দিতে করে নাম উচ্চারণ ।
সেই নাম হয় তার 'মুক্তির' কারণ ॥" ১৫৫ ॥

kṛṣṇe gāli dite kare nāma uccāraṇa
sei nāma haya tāra 'muktira' kāraṇa"

SYNONYMS

kṛṣṇe—Lord Kṛṣṇa; *gāli dite*—to blaspheme or chastise; *kare nāma uccāraṇa*—chants the name of Kṛṣṇa; *sei nāma*—that holy name; *haya*—becomes; *tāra*—his; *muktira kāraṇa*—the cause of liberation.

TRANSLATION

"Sometimes it so happens that one who wants to chastise Kṛṣṇa utters the holy name, and thus the holy name becomes the cause of his liberation."

TEXT 156

তবে সেই কবি সবার চরণে পড়িয়া ।
সবার শরণ লৈল দন্তে তৃণ লঞা ॥ ১৫৬ ॥

tabe sei kavi sabāra caraṇe paḍiyā
sabāra śaraṇa laila dante tṛṇa lañā

SYNONYMS

tabe—thereupon; *sei*—that; *kavi*—poet; *sabāra*—of all; *caraṇe*—at the feet; *paḍiyā*—falling down; *sabāra*—of all the devotees; *śaraṇa laila*—took shelter; *dante*—in the mouth; *tṛṇa lañā*—taking a straw.

TRANSLATION

Upon hearing this proper explanation by Svarūpa Dāmodara Gosvāmī, the Bengali poet fell down at the feet of all the devotees and took shelter of them with a straw in his mouth.

TEXT 157

তবে সব ভক্ত তারে অঙ্গীকার কৈলা ।
তার গুণ কহি' মহাপ্রভুরে মিলাইলা ॥ ১৫৭ ॥

tabe saba bhakta tāre aṅgīkāra kailā
tāra guṇa kahi' mahāprabhure milāilā

SYNONYMS

tabe—thereupon; *saba bhakta*—all the devotees; *tāre*—him; *aṅgīkāra kailā*—accepted as one of the associates; *tāra guṇa kahi'*—explaining his humble behavior; *mahāprabhure milāilā*—introduced him to Śrī Caitanya Mahāprabhu.

TRANSLATION

Thereupon all the devotees accepted his association. Explaining his humble behavior, they introduced him to Śrī Caitanya Mahāprabhu.

TEXT 158

সেই কবি সর্ব ত্যজি' রহিলা নীলাচলে ।
গৌরভক্তগণের কৃপা কে কহিতে পারে ? ১৫৮ ॥

sei kavi sarva tyaji' rahilā nīlācale
gaura-bhakta-gaṇera kṛpā ke kahite pāre?

SYNONYMS

sei kavi—that poet; *sarva tyaji'*—giving up all nonsensical activities; *rahilā*—remained; *nīlācale*—at Jagannātha Purī; *gaura-bhakta-gaṇera*—of the devotees of Lord Śrī Caitanya Mahāprabhu; *kṛpā*—the mercy; *ke*—who; *kahite pāre*—can explain.

TRANSLATION

By the mercy of the devotees of Lord Śrī Caitanya Mahāprabhu, that poet from Bengal gave up all other activities and stayed with them at Jagannātha Purī. Who can explain the mercy of the devotees of Śrī Caitanya Mahāprabhu?

TEXT 159

এই ত' কহিলুঁ প্রদ্যুম্নমিশ্র-বিবরণ ।
প্রভুর আজ্ঞায় কৈল কৃষ্ণকথার শ্রবণ ॥ ১৫৯ ॥

ei ta' kahiluṅ pradyumna-miśra-vivaraṇa
prabhura ājñāya kaila kṛṣṇa-kathāra śravaṇa

SYNONYMS

ei ta' kahiluṅ—thus I have described; *pradyumna-miśra-vivaraṇa*—the descriptive narration of Pradyumna Miśra; *prabhura ājñāya*—on the order of Śrī Caitanya Mahāprabhu; *kaila*—did; *kṛṣṇa-kathāra śravaṇa*—listening to discourses on topics concerning Kṛṣṇa.

TRANSLATION

I have thus described the narration concerning Pradyumna Miśra and how, following the order of Śrī Caitanya Mahāprabhu, he listened to discourses about Kṛṣṇa spoken by Rāmānanda Rāya.

TEXT 160

তার মধ্যে কহিলুঁ রামানন্দের মহিমা।
আপনে শ্রীমুখে প্রভু বর্ণে যাঁর সীমা ॥ ১৬০ ॥

tāra madhye kahiluṅ rāmānandera mahimā
āpane śrī-mukhe prabhu varṇe yāṅra sīmā

SYNONYMS

tāra madhye—within these statements; *kahiluṅ*—I have explained; *rāmānandera mahimā*—the glories of Rāmānanda Rāya; *āpane*—personally; *śrī-mukhe*—from his mouth; *prabhu*—the Lord; *varṇe*—explains; *yāṅra*—of whom; *sīmā*—the limit of ecstatic love.

TRANSLATION

Within the narration I have explained the glorious characteristics of Śrī Rāmānanda Rāya, through whom Śrī Caitanya Mahāprabhu personally described the limits of ecstatic love for Kṛṣṇa.

TEXT 161

প্রস্তাবে কহিলুঁ কবির নাটক-বিবরণ।
অজ্ঞ হঞা শ্রদ্ধায় পাইল প্রভুর চরণ ॥ ১৬১ ॥

prastāve kahiluṅ kavira nāṭaka-vivaraṇa
ajña hañā śraddhāya pāila prabhura caraṇa

SYNONYMS

prastāve—by the way; *kahiluṅ*—I have explained; *kavira*—of the poet; *nāṭaka-vivaraṇa*—description of the drama; *ajña hañā*—although being ignorant; *śraddhāya*—with faith and love; *pāila*—got; *prabhura caraṇa*—the shelter of Lord Śrī Caitanya Mahāprabhu.

TRANSLATION

In the course of the narration, I have also told about the drama by the poet from Bengal. Although he was ignorant, because of his faith and humility he nevertheless obtained the shelter of Śrī Caitanya Mahāprabhu.

TEXT 162

শ্রীকৃষ্ণচৈতন্য-লীলা—অমৃতের সার ।
একলীলা-প্রবাহে বহে শত-শত ধার ॥ ১৬২ ॥

śrī-kṛṣṇa-caitanya-līlā——amṛtera sāra
eka-līlā-pravāhe vahe śata-śata dhāra

SYNONYMS

śrī-kṛṣṇa-caitanya-līlā—the pastimes of Lord Śrī Caitanya Mahāprabhu; *amṛtera sāra*—the essence of nectar; *eka-līlā*—of one pastime; *pravāhe*—by the stream; *vahe*—flow; *śata-śata dhāra*—hundreds and hundreds of branches.

TRANSLATION

The pastimes of Lord Śrī Kṛṣṇa Caitanya Mahāprabhu are the essence of nectar. From the stream of one of His pastimes flow hundreds and thousands of branches.

TEXT 163

শ্রদ্ধা করি' এই লীলা যেই পড়ে, শুনে ।
গৌরলীলা, ভক্তি-ভক্ত-রস-তত্ত্ব জানে ॥ ১৬৩ ॥

śraddhā kari' ei līlā yei paḍe, śune
gaura-līlā, bhakti-bhakta-rasa-tattva jāne

SYNONYMS

śraddhā kari'—with faith and love; *ei līlā*—these pastimes; *yei*—anyone who; *paḍe, śune*—reads and hears; *gaura-līlā*—the pastimes of Lord Śrī Caitanya Mahāprabhu; *bhakti-bhakta-rasa-tattva*—the truth about devotional service, devotees and their transcendental mellows; *jāne*—understands.

TRANSLATION

Anyone who reads and hears these pastimes with faith and love can understand the truth about devotional service, devotees and the transcendental mellows of the pastimes of Lord Śrī Caitanya Mahāprabhu.

TEXT 164

শ্রীরূপ-রঘুনাথ-পদে যার আশ ।
চৈতন্যচরিতামৃত কহে কৃষ্ণদাস ॥ ১৬৪ ॥

śrī-rūpa-raghunātha-pade yāra āśa
caitanya-caritāmṛta kahe kṛṣṇadāsa

SYNONYMS

śrī-rūpa—Śrīla Rūpa Gosvāmī; *raghunātha*—Śrīla Raghunātha dāsa Gosvāmī; *pade*—at the lotus feet; *yāra*—whose; *āśa*—expectation; *caitanya-caritāmṛta*—the book named *Caitanya-caritāmṛta; kahe*—describes; *kṛṣṇadāsa*—Śrīla Kṛṣṇadāsa Kavirāja Gosvāmī.

TRANSLATION

Praying at the lotus feet of Śrī Rūpa and Śrī Raghunātha, always desiring their mercy, I, Kṛṣṇadāsa, narrate Śrī Caitanya-caritāmṛta, following in their footsteps.

Thus end the Bhaktivedanta purports to the Śrī Caitanya-caritāmṛta, Antya-līlā, *Fifth Chapter, describing how Pradyumna Miśra received instructions from Rāmānanda Rāya.*

CHAPTER 6

The Meeting of Śrī Caitanya Mahāprabhu and Raghunātha dāsa Gosvāmī

A summary of this chapter is given by Bhaktivinoda Ṭhākura in his *Amṛta-pravāha-bhāṣya* as follows. When Śrī Caitanya Mahāprabhu went into transcendental fits of ecstatic love, Rāmānanda Rāya and Svarūpa Dāmodara Gosvāmī attended to Him and satisfied Him as He desired. Raghunātha dāsa Gosvāmī had been attempting to come to the lotus feet of Śrī Caitanya Mahāprabhu for a long time, and finally he left his home and met the Lord. When Śrī Caitanya Mahāprabhu had gone to Śāntipura on His way to Vṛndāvana, Raghunātha dāsa Gosvāmī had offered to dedicate his life at the Lord's lotus feet. In the meantime, however, a Mohammedan official became envious of Hiraṇya dāsa, Raghunātha dāsa Gosvāmī's uncle, and induced some big official court minister to have him arrested. Thus Hiraṇya dāsa left his home, but by the intelligence of Raghunātha dāsa the misunderstanding was mitigated. Then Raghunātha dāsa went to Pānihāṭi, and, following the order of Nityānanda Prabhu, he observed a festival (*ciḍā-dadhi-mahotsava*) by distributing chipped rice mixed with yogurt. The day after the festival, Nityānanda Prabhu gave Raghunātha dāsa the blessing that he would very soon attain the shelter of Śrī Caitanya Mahāprabhu. After this incident, Raghunātha dāsa, with the help of his priest, whose name was Yadunandana Ācārya, got out of his house by trickery and thus ran away. Not touching the general path, Raghunātha dāsa Gosvāmī secretly went to Jagannātha Purī. After twelve days, he arrived in Jagannātha Purī at the lotus feet of Śrī Caitanya Mahāprabhu.

Śrī Caitanya Mahāprabhu entrusted Raghunātha dāsa Gosvāmī to Svarūpa Dāmodara Gosvāmī. Therefore another name for Raghunātha dāsa Gosvāmī is Svarūpera Raghu, or the Raghunātha of Svarūpa Dāmodara. For five days Raghunātha dāsa Gosvāmī took *prasāda* at the temple, but later he would stand at the Siṁha-dvāra gate and eat only whatever he could gather by alms. Later he lived by taking alms from various *chatras,* or food distributing centers. When Raghunātha's father received news of this, he sent some men and money, but Raghunātha dāsa Gosvāmī refused to accept the money. Understanding that Raghunātha dāsa Gosvāmī was living by begging from the *chatras,* Śrī Caitanya Mahāprabhu presented him with His own *guñjā-mālā* and a stone from Govardhana Hill. Thereafter, Raghunātha dāsa Gosvāmī used to eat rejected food that he had collected and washed. This renounced life greatly pleased both

Svarūpa Dāmodara Gosvāmī and Śrī Caitanya Mahāprabhu. One day Śrī Caitanya Mahāprabhu took by force some of the same food, thus blessing Raghunātha dāsa Gosvāmī for his renunciation.

TEXT 1

কৃপাগুণৈর্যঃ কুগৃহান্ধকূপা-
দুদ্ধৃত্য ভঙ্গ্যা রঘুনাথদাসম্ ।
ন্যস্য স্বরূপে বিদধেঽন্তরঙ্গং
শ্রীকৃষ্ণচৈতন্যমমুং প্রপদ্যে ॥ ১ ॥

kṛpā-guṇair yaḥ kugṛhāndha-kūpād
uddhṛtya bhaṅgyā raghunātha-dāsam
nyasya svarūpe vidadhe 'ntaraṅgaṁ
śrī-kṛṣṇa-caitanyam amuṁ prapadye

SYNONYMS

kṛpā-guṇaiḥ—by the ropes of causeless mercy; *yaḥ*—who; *ku-gṛha*—of contemptible family life; *andha-kūpāt*—from the blind well; *uddhṛtya*—having raised; *bhaṅgyā*—by a trick; *raghunātha-dāsam*—Raghunātha dāsa Gosvāmī; *nyasya*—giving over; *svarūpe*—to Svarūpa Dāmodara Gosvāmī; *vidadhe*—made; *antaraṅgam*—one of His personal associates; *śrī-kṛṣṇa-caitanyam*—unto Lord Śrī Kṛṣṇa Caitanya Mahāprabhu; *amum*—unto Him; *prapadye*—I offer my obeisances.

TRANSLATION

With the ropes of His causeless mercy, Śrī Kṛṣṇa Caitanya Mahāprabhu employed a trick to deliver Raghunātha dāsa Gosvāmī from the blind well of contemptible family life. He made Raghunātha dāsa Gosvāmī one of His personal associates, placing him under the charge of Svarūpa Dāmodara Gosvāmī. I offer my obeisances unto Him.

TEXT 2

জয় জয় শ্রীচৈতন্য জয় নিত্যানন্দ ।
জয়াদ্বৈতচন্দ্র জয় গৌরভক্তবৃন্দ ॥ ২ ॥

jaya jaya śrī-caitanya, jaya nityānanda
jayādvaita-candra, jaya gaura-bhakta-vṛnda

SYNONYMS

jaya jaya—all glories; *śrī-caitanya*—to Lord Caitanya; *jaya*—all glories; *nityānanda*—to Lord Nityānanda; *jaya*—all glories; *advaita-candra*—to Advaita Ācārya; *jaya*—all glories; *gaura-bhakta-vṛnda*—to the devotees of Lord Caitanya Mahāprabhu.

TRANSLATION

All glory to Lord Caitanya Mahāprabhu! All glory to Lord Nityānanda! All glory to Śrī Advaita Ācārya! And all glory to all the devotees of Lord Śrī Caitanya Mahāprabhu!

TEXT 3

এইমত গৌরচন্দ্র ভক্তগণ-সঙ্গে ।
নীলাচলে নানা লীলা করে নানা-রঙ্গে ॥ ৩ ॥

ei-mata gauracandra bhakta-gaṇa-saṅge
nīlācale nānā līlā kare nānā-raṅge

SYNONYMS

ei-mata—in this way; *gauracandra*—Lord Śrī Caitanya Mahāprabhu; *bhakta-gaṇa-saṅge*—with His associates; *nīlācale*—at Nīlācala (Jagannātha Purī); *nānā*—various; *līlā*—pastimes; *kare*—performs; *nānā-raṅge*—in varieties of transcendental pleasure.

TRANSLATION

Thus Lord Gauracandra performed various pastimes with His associates at Jagannātha Purī in varieties of transcendental pleasure.

TEXT 4

যদ্যপি অন্তরে কৃষ্ণ-বিয়োগ বাধয়ে ।
বাহিরে না প্রকাশয় ভক্ত-দুঃখ-ভয়ে ॥ ৪ ॥

yadyapi antare kṛṣṇa-viyoga bādhaye
bāhire nā prakāśaya bhakta-duḥkha-bhaye

SYNONYMS

yadyapi—although; *antare*—within the heart; *kṛṣṇa-viyoga*—separation from Kṛṣṇa; *bādhye*—obstructs; *bāhire*—externally; *nā prakāśaya*—does not exhibit; *bhakta-duḥkha-bhaye*—fearing the unhappiness of the devotees.

TRANSLATION

Although Śrī Caitanya Mahāprabhu felt pangs of separation from Kṛṣṇa, He did not manifest His feelings externally, for He feared the unhappiness of His devotees.

TEXT 5

উৎকট বিরহ-দুঃখ যবে বাহিরায় ।
তবে যে বৈকল্য প্রভুর বর্ণন না যায় ॥ ৫ ॥

utkaṭa viraha-duḥkha yabe bāhirāya
tabe ye vaikalya prabhura varṇana nā yāya

SYNONYMS

utkaṭa—severe; *viraha-duḥkha*—unhappiness of separation; *yabe*—when; *bāhirāya*—is manifested; *tabe*—at that time; *ye*—what; *vaikalya*—transformations; *prabhura*—of the Lord; *varṇana nā yāya*—cannot be described.

TRANSLATION

The transformations undergone by the Lord when He manifested severe unhappiness due to separation from Kṛṣṇa cannot be described.

TEXT 6

রামানন্দের কৃষ্ণকথা, স্বরূপের গান ।
বিরহ-বেদনায় প্রভুর রাখয়ে পরাণ ॥ ৬ ॥

rāmānandera kṛṣṇa-kathā, svarūpera gāna
viraha-vedanāya prabhura rākhaye parāṇa

SYNONYMS

rāmānandera—of Rāmānanda Rāya; *kṛṣṇa-kathā*—talks of Lord Kṛṣṇa; *svarūpera gāna*—the songs of Svarūpa Dāmodara; *viraha-vedanāya*—at the time of pangs of separation; *prabhura*—of Lord Śrī Caitanya Mahāprabhu; *rākhaye*—keep; *parāṇa*—the life.

TRANSLATION

When the Lord acutely felt pangs of separation from Kṛṣṇa, only Śrī Rāmānanda Rāya's talk about Kṛṣṇa and the sweet songs of Svarūpa Dāmodara kept Him alive.

TEXT 7

দিনে প্রভু নানা-সঙ্গে হয় অন্য মন ।
রাত্রিকালে বাড়ে প্রভুর বিরহ-বেদন ॥ ৭ ॥

dine prabhu nānā-saṅge haya anya mana
rātri-kāle bāḍe prabhura viraha-vedana

SYNONYMS

dine—during the daytime; *prabhu*—Lord Śrī Caitanya Mahāprabhu; *nānā-saṅge*—by different association; *haya*—becomes; *anya*—diverted; *mana*—His mind; *rātri-kāle*—at night; *bāḍe*—increase; *prabhura*—of Lord Śrī Caitanya Mahāprabhu; *viraha-vedana*—pangs of separation.

TRANSLATION

Because the Lord associated with various devotees during the day, His mind was somewhat diverted, but at night the pangs of separation from Kṛṣṇa increased very rapidly.

TEXT 8

তাঁর সুখ-হেতু সঙ্গে রহে দুই জনা ।
কৃষ্ণরস-শ্লোক-গীতে করেন সান্ত্বনা ॥ ৮ ॥

tāṅra sukha-hetu saṅge rahe dui janā
kṛṣṇa-rasa-śloka-gīte karena sāntvanā

SYNONYMS

tāṅra sukha-hetu—for His happiness; *saṅge*—in His association; *rahe*—remain; *dui janā*—two personalities; *kṛṣṇa-rasa*—of the transcendental mellows of Kṛṣṇa; *śloka*—verses; *gīte*—by songs; *karena sāntvanā*—they pacified.

TRANSLATION

Two people—Rāmānanda Rāya and Svarūpa Dāmodara Gosvāmī—stayed with the Lord to pacify Him by reciting various verses about Kṛṣṇa's pastimes and by singing appropriate songs for His satisfaction.

TEXT 9

সুবল যৈছে পূর্বে কৃষ্ণসুখের সহায় ।
গৌরসুখদান-হেতু তৈছে রাম-রায় ॥ ৯ ॥

subala yaiche pūrve kṛṣṇa-sukhera sahāya
gaura-sukha-dāna-hetu taiche rāma-rāya

SYNONYMS

subala—Subala, one of the cowherd boy friends of Kṛṣṇa; *yaiche*—just as; *pūrve*—previously; *kṛṣṇa-sukhera*—to give happiness to Kṛṣṇa; *sahāya*—helper; *gaura-sukha-dāna-hetu*—for giving happiness to Lord Śrī Caitanya Mahāprabhu; *taiche*—similarly; *rāma-rāya*—Rāmānanda Rāya.

TRANSLATION

Previously, when Lord Kṛṣṇa was personally present, Subala, one of His cowherd boy friends, gave Him happiness when He felt separation from Rādhārāṇī. Similarly, Rāmānanda Rāya helped give happiness to Lord Śrī Caitanya Mahāprabhu.

TEXT 10

পূর্বে যৈছে রাধার ললিতা সহায়-প্রধান ।
তৈছে স্বরূপ-গোসাঞি রাখে মহাপ্রভুর প্রাণ ॥১০॥

pūrve yaiche rādhāra lalitā sahāya-pradhāna
taiche svarūpa-gosāñi rākhe mahāprabhura prāṇa

SYNONYMS

pūrve—previously; *yaiche*—just as; *rādhāra*—of Śrīmatī Rādhārāṇī; *lalitā*—Her companion named Lalitā; *sahāya-pradhāna*—the best helper; *taiche*—similarly; *svarūpa-gosāñi*—Svarūpa Dāmodara Gosvāmī; *rākhe*—keeps; *mahāprabhura prāṇa*—the life of Śrī Caitanya Mahāprabhu.

TRANSLATION

Previously, when Śrīmatī Rādhārāṇī felt the pangs of separation from Kṛṣṇa, Her constant companion Lalitā kept Her alive by helping Her in many ways. Similarly, when Śrī Caitanya Mahāprabhu felt Rādhārāṇī's emotions, Svarūpa Dāmodara Gosvāmī helped Him maintain His life.

TEXT 11

এই দুই জনার সৌভাগ্য কহন না যায় ।
প্রভুর 'অন্তরঙ্গ' বলি' যাঁরে লোকে গায় ॥ ১১ ॥

ei dui janāra saubhāgya kahana nā yāya
prabhura 'antaraṅga' bali' yāṅre loke gāya

SYNONYMS

ei dui janāra—of these two personalities; *saubhāgya*—fortune; *kahana nā yāya*—cannot be described; *prabhura*—of Lord Śrī Caitanya Mahāprabhu; *antaraṅga*—very intimate and confidential associates; *bali'*—as; *yāṅre*—whom; *loke*—people; *gāya*—say.

TRANSLATION

To describe the fortunate position of Rāmānanda Rāya and Svarūpa Dāmodara Gosvāmī is extremely difficult. They were renowned as intimately confidential friends of Śrī Caitanya Mahāprabhu.

TEXT 12

এইমত বিহরে গৌর লঞা ভক্তগণ ।
রঘুনাথ-মিলন এবে শুন, ভক্তগণ ॥ ১২ ॥

ei-mata vihare gaura lañā bhakta-gaṇa
raghunātha-milana ebe śuna, bhakta-gaṇa

SYNONYMS

ei-mata—in this way; *vihare*—enjoys; *gaura*—Lord Śrī Caitanya Mahāprabhu; *lañā bhakta-gaṇa*—keeping company with His devotees; *raghunātha-milana*—meeting with Raghunātha dāsa Gosvāmī; *ebe*—now; *śuna*—hear; *bhakta-gaṇa*—O devotees.

TRANSLATION

The Lord thus enjoyed His life with His devotees. O devotees of Lord Śrī Caitanya Mahāprabhu, now hear how Raghunātha dāsa Gosvāmī met the Lord.

TEXT 13

পূর্বে শান্তিপুরে রঘুনাথ যবে আইলা ।
মহাপ্রভু কৃপা করি' তাঁরে শিখাইলা ॥ ১৩ ॥

pūrve śāntipure raghunātha yabe āilā
mahāprabhu kṛpā kari' tāṅre śikhāilā

SYNONYMS

pūrve—previously; *śāntipure*—to Śāntipura; *raghunātha*—Raghunātha dāsa; *yabe āilā*—when he came; *mahāprabhu*—Śrī Caitanya Mahāprabhu; *kṛpā kari'*—showing causeless mercy; *tāṅre śikhāilā*—gave him lessons.

TRANSLATION

When Raghunātha dāsa, during his family life, went to meet Śrī Caitanya Mahāprabhu at Śāntipura, the Lord gave him worthy instructions by His causeless mercy.

TEXT 14

প্রভুর শিক্ষাতে তেঁহো নিজ-ঘরে যায় ।
মর্কট-বৈরাগ্য ছাড়ি' হৈলা 'বিষয়ি-প্রায়' ॥ ১৪ ॥

prabhura śikṣāte teṅho nija-ghare yāya
markaṭa-vairāgya chāḍi' hailā 'viṣayi-prāya'

SYNONYMS

prabhura śikṣāte—by the instruction of Śrī Caitanya Mahāprabhu; *teṅho*—he; *nija-ghare yāya*—returned to his home; *markaṭa-vairāgya*—monkey renunciation; *chāḍi'*—giving up; *hailā*—became; *viṣayi-prāya*—like a pounds-and-shillings man.

TRANSLATION

Instead of becoming a so-called renunciate, Raghunātha dāsa, following the instructions of the Lord, returned home and played exactly like a pounds-and-shillings man.

TEXT 15

ভিতরে বৈরাগ্য, বাহিরে করে সর্ব-কর্ম ।
দেখিয়া ত' মাতা-পিতার আনন্দিত মন ॥ ১৫ ॥

bhitare vairāgya, bāhire kare sarva-karma
dekhiyā ta' mātā-pitāra ānandita mana

SYNONYMS

bhitare—within his heart; *vairāgya*—complete renunciation; *bāhire*—externally; *kare*—does; *sarva*—all; *karma*—activities; *dekhiyā*—seeing; *ta'*—certainly; *mātā-pitāra*—of the father and mother; *ānandita*—satisfied; *mana*—the mind.

TRANSLATION

Raghunātha dāsa was inwardly completely renounced, even in family life, but he did not express his renunciation externally. Instead, he acted just like an ordinary businessman. Seeing this, his father and mother were satisfied.

TEXT 16

‘মথুরা হৈতে প্রভু আইলা’,—বার্তা যবে পাইলা ।
প্রভু-পাশ চলিবারে উদ্‌যোগ করিলা ॥ ১৬ ॥

‘mathurā haite prabhu āilā’,——vārtā yabe pāilā
prabhu-pāśa calibāre udyoga karilā

SYNONYMS

mathurā haite—from Mathurā; *prabhu āilā*—Lord Śrī Caitanya Mahāprabhu has come back; *vārtā*—message; *yabe pāilā*—when he received; *prabhu-pāśa*—to Śrī Caitanya Mahāprabhu; *calibāre*—to go; *udyoga karilā*—made an endeavor.

TRANSLATION

When he received a message that Lord Śrī Caitanya Mahāprabhu had returned from Mathurā City, Raghunātha dāsa endeavored to go to the lotus feet of the Lord.

TEXT 17

হেন-কালে মুলুকের এক ম্লেচ্ছ অধিকারী ।
সপ্তগ্রাম-মুলুকের সে হয় ‘চৌধুরী’ ॥ ১৭ ॥

hena-kāle mulukera eka mleccha adhikārī
saptagrāma-mulukera se haya ‘caudhurī’

SYNONYMS

hena-kāle—at this time; *mulukera*—of the country; *eka*—one; *mleccha*—Mohammedan; *adhikārī*—official; *saptagrāma-mulukera*—of the place known as Saptagrāma; *se*—that person; *haya*—is; *caudhurī*—tax collector.

TRANSLATION

At that time there was a Mohammedan official collecting the taxes of Saptagrāma.

PURPORT

Formerly, when the Mohammedan government was in power, the person appointed tax collector would collect the taxes of the local Zamindars, or landholders. He would keep one-fourth of the collection for himself as a profit, and the balance he would deliver to the treasury of the government.

TEXT 18

হিরণ্যদাস মুলুক নিল 'মক্‌ররি' করিয়া ।
তার অধিকার গেল, মরে সে দেখিয়া ॥ ১৮ ॥

hiraṇya-dāsa muluka nila 'makrari' kariyā
tāra adhikāra gela, mare se dekhiyā

SYNONYMS

hiraṇya-dāsa—the uncle of Raghunātha dāsa Gosvāmī; *muluka nila*—took charge of the country; *makrari kariyā*—by some agreement; *tāra adhikāra gela*—the Mohammedan *caudhurī* lost his position; *mare se dekhiyā*—became extremely envious of Hiraṇya dāsa.

TRANSLATION

When Hiraṇya dāsa, Raghunātha dāsa's uncle, made an agreement with the government to collect taxes, the Mohammedan caudhurī, or tax collector, having lost his position, became extremely envious of him.

TEXT 19

বার লক্ষ দেয় রাজায়, সাধে বিশ লক্ষ ।
সে 'তুরুক্‌' কিছু না পাঞা হৈল প্রতিপক্ষ ॥ ১৯ ॥

bāra lakṣa deya rājāya, sādhe biśa lakṣa
se 'turuk' kichu nā pāñā haila pratipakṣa

SYNONYMS

bāra lakṣa—1,200,000 coins; *deya*—delivers; *rājāya*—unto the Mohammedan government; *sādhe*—collects; *biśa lakṣa*—2,000,000 coins; *se turuk*—that Turk; *kichu*—anything; *nā pāñā*—not getting; *haila pratipakṣa*—became his rival.

TRANSLATION

Hiraṇya dāsa was collecting 2,000,000 coins and therefore should have delivered 1,500,000 to the government. Instead, he was giving only 1,200,-

000, thus making an extra profit of 300,000 coins. Seeing this, the Mohammedan caudhurī, who was a Turk, became his rival.

TEXT 20

রাজ-ঘরে কৈফিয়ৎ দিয়া উজীরে আনিল ।
হিরণ্যদাস পলাইল, রঘুনাথেরে বান্ধিল ॥ ২০ ॥

rāja-ghare kaiphiyat diyā ujīre ānila
hiraṇya-dāsa palāila, raghunāthere bāndhila

SYNONYMS

rāja-ghare—to the government treasury; *kaiphiyat diyā*—sending a confidential account; *ujīre ānila*—brought the minister in charge; *hiraṇya-dāsa palāila*—Hiraṇya dāsa fled; *raghunāthere bāndhila*—he arrested Raghunātha dāsa.

TRANSLATION

After sending a confidential account to the government treasury, the caudhurī brought the minister in charge. The caudhurī came, wanting to arrest Hiraṇya dāsa, but Hiraṇya dāsa had left home. Therefore the caudhurī arrested Raghunātha dāsa.

TEXT 21

প্রতিদিন রঘুনাথে করয়ে ভৎর্সনা ।
'বাপ-জ্যেঠারে আন', নহে পাইবা যাতনা ॥ ২১ ॥

prati-dina raghunāthe karaye bhartsanā
'bāpa-jyeṭhāre āna', nahe pāibā yātanā

SYNONYMS

prati-dina—daily; *raghunāthe*—Raghunātha dāsa; *karaye bhartsanā*—he chastised; *bāpa-jyeṭhāre āna*—bring your father and his elder brother; *nahe*—otherwise; *pāibā yātanā*—you will be punished.

TRANSLATION

Every day, the Mohammedan would chastise Raghunātha dāsa and tell him, "Bring your father and his elder brother. Otherwise you will be punished."

TEXT 22

মারিতে আনয়ে যদি দেখে রঘুনাথে ।
মন ফিরি' যায়, তবে না পারে মারিতে ॥ ২২ ॥

mārite ānaye yadi dekhe raghunāthe
mana phiri' yāya, tabe nā pāre mārite

SYNONYMS

mārite—to beat; *ānaye*—brings; *yadi*—when; *dekhe*—sees; *raghunāthe*—Raghunātha dāsa; *mana*—his mind; *phiri' yāya*—becomes changed; *tabe*—at that time; *nā pāre mārite*—he could not beat.

TRANSLATION

The caudhurī wanted to beat him, but as soon as he saw Raghunātha's face, his mind changed, and he could not beat him.

TEXT 23

বিশেষে কায়স্থ-বুদ্ধ্যে অন্তরে করে ডর ।
মুখে তর্জে গর্জে, মারিতে সভয় অন্তর ॥ ২৩ ॥

viśeṣe kāyastha-buddhye antare kare ḍara
mukhe tarje garje, mārite sabhaya antara

SYNONYMS

viśeṣe—specifically; *kāyastha-buddhye*—considering a *kāyastha; antare*—within his heart; *kare ḍara*—is afraid; *mukhe*—with his mouth; *tarje garje*—threatens; *mārite*—to beat; *sa-bhaya*—afraid; *antara*—at heart.

TRANSLATION

Indeed, the caudhurī was afraid of Raghunātha dāsa because Raghunātha dāsa belong to the kāyastha community. Although the caudhurī would chastise him with oral vibrations, he was afraid to beat him.

PURPORT

Raghunātha dāsa belonged to a very aristocratic family of the *kāyastha* community. He had substantial influence with the local people, and therefore the *caudhurī,* or minister, was afraid to beat him. Superficially he would chastise Raghunātha dāsa with threatening vibrations, but he did not beat him. The members of the *kāyastha* community in India are generally very intelligent and expert in business management. Formerly they were mostly government officers. They were mentioned even by Yājñavalkya, as quoted by Śrīla Bhaktivinoda Ṭhākura in his *Amṛta-pravāha-bhāṣya:*

cāṭa-taṣkara-durvṛttair
mahā-sāhasikādibhiḥ
pīḍyamānā prajā rakṣet
kāyasthaiś ca viśeṣtaḥ

From this verse it appears that the governmental officials of the *kāyastha* community would sometimes chastise the citizens, and thus it was the duty of the king to protect the people in general from the atrocities of the *kāyasthas*. In Bengal the *kāyastha* community is honored almost as much as the *brāhmaṇa* community, but in the up-country of India the *kāyasthas* are considered *śūdras* because they generally eat meat and drink wine. In any case, from history the *kāyasthas* appear very intelligent. Thus the Mohammedan *caudhurī* was afraid of Raghunātha dāsa because he belonged to the *kāyastha* community.

TEXT 24

তবে রঘুনাথ কিছু চিন্তিলা উপায়।
বিনতি করিয়া কহে সেই ম্লেচ্ছ-পায় ॥ ২৪ ॥

tabe raghunātha kichu cintilā upāya
vinati kariyā kahe sei mleccha-pāya

SYNONYMS

tabe—then; *raghunātha*—Raghunātha dāsa Gosvāmī; *kichu*—some; *cintilā*—thought of; *upāya*—means; *vinati kariyā*—in great humility; *kahe*—he says; *sei mleccha*—of that Mohammedan *caudhurī; pāya*—at the feet.

TRANSLATION

While this was going on, Raghunātha dāsa thought of a tricky method of escape. Thus he humbly submitted this plea at the feet of the Mohammedan caudhurī.

TEXT 25

"আমার পিতা, জ্যেঠা হয় তোমার দুই ভাই।
ভাই-ভাইয়ে তোমরা কলহ কর সর্বদাই ॥ ২৫ ॥

"āmāra pitā, jyeṭhā haya tomāra dui bhāi
bhāi-bhāiye tomarā kalaha kara sarvadāi

SYNONYMS

āmāra pitā—my father; *jyeṭhā*—and his elder brother; *haya*—are; *tomāra*—your; *dui bhāi*—two brothers; *bhāi-bhāiye*—between brother and brother; *tomarā*—all of you; *kalaha kara*—fight; *sarvadāi*—always.

TRANSLATION

"My dear sir, my father and his elder brother are both your brothers. All brothers always fight about something.

TEXT 26

কভু কলহ, কভু প্রীতি—ইহার নিশ্চয় নাই।
কালি পুনঃ তিন ভাই হইবা এক-ঠাঞি ॥ ২৬ ॥

kabhu kalaha, kabhu prīti——ihāra niścaya nāi
kāli punaḥ tina bhāi ha-ibā eka-ṭhāñi

SYNONYMS

kabhu—sometimes; *kalaha*—fight; *kabhu*—sometimes; *prīti*—very intimate friendly behavior; *ihāra*—of these things; *niścaya nāi*—there is no certainty; *kāli*—the next day; *punaḥ*—again; *tina bhāi*—three brothers; *ha-ibā*—will be; *eka-ṭhāñi*—at one place.

TRANSLATION

"Sometimes brothers fight among themselves, and sometimes they have very friendly dealings. There is no certainty when such changes will take place. Thus I am sure that although today you are fighting, tomorrow you three brothers will be sitting together in peace.

TEXT 27

আমি যৈছে পিতার, তৈছে তোমার বালক।
আমি তোমার পাল্য, তুমি আমার পালক ॥ ২৭ ॥

āmi yaiche pitāra, taiche tomāra bālaka
āmi tomāra pālya, tumi āmāra pālaka

SYNONYMS

āmi—I; *yaiche*—just like; *pitāra*—of my father; *taiche*—similarly; *tomāra*—your; *bālaka*—son; *āmi*—I; *tomāra*—your; *pālya*—person to be maintained; *tumi*—you; *āmāra*—my; *pālaka*—maintainer.

TRANSLATION

"Just as I am my father's son, so I am also yours. I am your dependent, and you are my maintainer.

TEXT 28

পালক হঞা পাল্যেরে তাড়িতে না যুয়ায় ।
তুমি সর্বশাস্ত্র জান 'জিন্দাপীর'-প্রায় ॥" ২৮ ॥

pālaka hañā pālyere tāḍite nā yuyāya
tumi sarva-śāstra jāna 'jindā-pīra'-prāya"

SYNONYMS

pālaka hañā—being a maintainer; *pālyere*—the person who is maintained; *tāḍite*—to punish; *nā yuyāya*—is not good; *tumi*—you; *sarva-śāstra*—all scriptures; *jāna*—know; *jindā-pīra*—a living saintly person; *prāya*—just like.

TRANSLATION

"For a maintainer to punish the person he maintains is not good. You are expert in all the scriptures. Indeed, you are like a living saint."

TEXT 29

এত শুনি' সেই ম্লেচ্ছের মন আর্দ্র হৈল ।
দাড়ি বাহি' অশ্রু পড়ে, কাঁদিতে লাগিল ॥ ২৯ ॥

eta śuni' sei mlecchera mana ārdra haila
dāḍi vāhi' aśru paḍe, kāṅdite lāgila

SYNONYMS

eta śuni'—hearing this; *sei mlecchera*—of that Mohammedan; *mana*—mind; *ārdra haila*—became softened; *dāḍi vāhi'*—flowing over his beard; *aśru paḍe*—tears fell; *kāṅdite lāgila*—began to cry.

TRANSLATION

Hearing Raghunātha dāsa's appealing voice, the Mohammedan's heart softened. He began to cry, and tears glided down his beard.

TEXT 30

ম্লেচ্ছ বলে,—"আজি হৈতে তুমি—মোর 'পুত্র' ।
আজি ছাড়াইমু তোমা' করি' এক সূত্র ॥" ৩০ ॥

mleccha bale,——"āji haite tumi——mora 'putra'
āji chāḍāimu tomā' kari' eka sūtra"

SYNONYMS

mleccha bale—the Mohammedan said; *āji haite*—from this day; *tumi*—you; *mora putra*—my son; *āji*—today; *chāḍāimu tomā'*—I shall get you released; *kari' eka sūtra*—by some means.

TRANSLATION

The Mohammedan caudhurī told Raghunātha dāsa, "You are my son from this day on. Today, by some means, I shall have you released."

TEXT 31

উজিরে কহিয়া রঘুনাথে ছাড়াইল ।
প্রীতি করি' রঘুনাথে কহিতে লাগিল ॥ ৩১ ॥

ujire kahiyā raghunāthe chāḍāila
prīti kari' raghunāthe kahite lāgila

SYNONYMS

ujire—unto the minister; *kahiyā*—speaking; *raghunāthe chāḍāila*—released Raghunātha dāsa; *prīti kari'*—with great affection; *raghunāthe*—unto Raghunātha dāsa; *kahite lāgila*—began to say.

TRANSLATION

After informing the minister, the caudhurī released Raghunātha dāsa and then began to speak to him with great affection.

TEXT 32

"তোমার জ্যেঠা নির্বুদ্ধি অষ্টলক্ষ খায় ।
আমি—ভাগী, আমারে কিছু দিবারে যুয়ায় ॥ ৩২ ॥

"tomāra jyeṭhā nirbuddhi aṣṭa-lakṣa khāya
āmi——bhāgī, āmāre kichu dibāre yuyāya

SYNONYMS

tomāra jyeṭhā—the elder brother of your father; *nirbuddhi*—bereft of intelligence; *aṣṭa-lakṣa khāya*—enjoys 800,000 coins; *āmi*—I; *bhāgī*—shareholder; *āmāre*—unto me; *kichu*—something; *dibāre*—to give; *yuyāya*—is proper.

TRANSLATION

"The elder brother of your father is less intelligent," he said. "He enjoys 800,000 coins, but since I am also a shareholder, he should give some portion of it to me.

TEXT 33

যাহ তুমি, তোমার জ্যেঠারে মিলাহ আমারে ।
যে-মতে ভাল হয় করুন, ভার দিলুঁ তাঁরে ॥ ৩৩ ॥

yāha tumi, tomāra jyeṭhāre milāha āmāre
ye-mate bhāla haya karuna, bhāra diluṅ tāṅre

SYNONYMS

yāha—go; *tumi*—you; *tomāra*—your; *jyeṭhāre*—the elder brother of your father; *milāha āmāre*—arrange to meet with me; *ye-mate*—in whatever way; *bhāla*—good; *haya*—is; *karuna*—let him do; *bhāra diluṅ tāṅre*—I shall completely depend upon him.

TRANSLATION

"Now you go arrange a meeting between me and your uncle. Let him do whatever he thinks best. I shall completely depend on his decision."

TEXT 34

রঘুনাথ আসি' তবে জ্যেঠারে মিলাইল ।
ম্লেচ্ছ-সহিত বশ কৈল—সব শান্ত হৈল ॥ ৩৪ ॥

raghunātha āsi' tabe jyeṭhāre milāila
mleccha-sahita vaśa kaila——saba śānta haila

SYNONYMS

raghunātha—Raghunātha dāsa; *āsi'*—coming; *tabe*—then; *jyeṭhāre milāila*—arranged a meeting between the *caudhurī* and the elder brother of his father; *mleccha-sahita*—with the Mohammedan; *vaśa kaila*—he settled; *saba*—everything; *śānta haila*—became peaceful.

TRANSLATION

Raghunātha dāsa arranged a meeting between his uncle and the caudhurī. He settled the matter, and everything was peaceful.

TEXT 35

এইমত রঘুনাথের বৎসরেক গেল ।
দ্বিতীয় বৎসরে পলাইতে মন কৈল ॥ ৩৫ ॥

ei-mata raghunāthera vatsareka gela
dvitīya vatsare palāite mana kaila

SYNONYMS

ei-mata—in this way; *raghunāthera*—of Raghunātha dāsa; *vatsareka*—one year; *gela*—passed; *dvitīya vatsare*—the next year; *palāite*—to go away from home; *mana kaila*—he decided.

TRANSLATION

In this way Raghunātha dāsa passed one year exactly like a first-class business manager, but the next year he again decided to leave home.

TEXT 36

রাত্রে উঠি' একেলা চলিলা পলাঞা ।
দূর হৈতে পিতা তাঁরে আনিল ধরিয়া ॥ ৩৬ ॥

rātre uṭhi' ekelā calilā palāñā
dūra haite pitā tāṅre ānila dhariyā

SYNONYMS

rātre—at night; *uṭhi'*—getting up; *ekelā*—alone; *calilā*—left; *palāñā*—running away; *dūra haite*—from a distant place; *pitā*—his father; *tāṅre*—him; *ānila*—brought back; *dhariyā*—catching.

TRANSLATION

He got up alone one night and left, but his father caught him in a distant place and brought him back.

TEXT 37

এইমতে বারে বারে পলায়, ধরি' আনে ।
তবে তাঁর মাতা কহে তাঁর পিতা সনে ॥ ৩৭ ॥

ei-mate bāre bāre palāya, dhari' āne
tabe tāṅra mātā kahe tāṅra pitā sane

SYNONYMS

ei-mate—in this way; *bāre bāre*—again and again; *palāya*—he goes away; *dhari' āne*—brings him back; *tabe*—then; *tāṅra mātā*—his mother; *kahe*—speaks; *tāṅra pitā sane*—with his father.

TRANSLATION

This became almost a daily affair. Raghunātha would run away from home, and his father would again bring him back. Then Raghunātha dāsa's mother began speaking to his father.

TEXT 38

"পুত্র 'বাতুল' হইল, ইহায় রাখহ বান্ধিয়া"।
তাঁর পিতা কহে তারে নির্বিণ্ণ হঞা ॥ ৩৮ ॥

"putra 'bātula' ha-ila, ihāya rākhaha bāndhiyā"
tāṅra pitā kahe tāre nirviṇṇa hañā

SYNONYMS

putra—son; *bātula ha-ila*—has become mad; *ihāya*—him; *rākhaha bāndhiyā*—just keep by binding; *tāṅra pitā*—his father; *kahe*—says; *tāre*—to her; *nirviṇṇa hañā*—being very unhappy.

TRANSLATION

"Our son has become mad," she said. "Just keep him by binding him with ropes." His father, being very unhappy, replied to her as follows.

TEXT 39

"ইন্দ্রসম ঐশ্বর্য, স্ত্রী অপ্সরা-সম।
এ সব বান্ধিতে নারিলেক যাঁর মন ॥ ৩৯ ॥

"indra-sama aiśvarya, strī apsarā-sama
e saba bāndhite nārileka yāṅra mana

SYNONYMS

indra-sama—like the heavenly King, Indra; *aiśvarya*—material opulence; *strī*—wife; *apsarā-sama*—like an angel of heaven; *e saba*—all this; *bāndhite*—to bind; *nārileka*—was not able; *yāṅra mana*—whose mind.

TRANSLATION

"Raghunātha dāsa, our son, has opulences like Indra, the heavenly King, and his wife is as beautiful as an angel. Yet all this could not tie down his mind.

TEXT 40

দড়ির বন্ধনে তাঁরে রাখিবা কেমতে ?
জন্মদাতা পিতা নারে 'প্রারব্ধ' খণ্ডাইতে ॥ ৪০ ॥

daḍira bandhane tāṅre rākhibā ke-mate?
janma-dātā pitā nāre 'prārabdha' khaṇḍāite

SYNONYMS

daḍira bandhane—by bonds of ropes; *tāṅre*—him; *rākhibā*—will you keep; *ke-mate*—how; *janma-dātā pitā*—the father who begets the child; *nāre*—is not able; *prārabdha*—the reaction of previous activities; *khaṇḍāite*—to nullify.

TRANSLATION

"How then could we keep this boy home by binding him with ropes? It is not possible even for one's father to nullify the reactions of one's past activities.

TEXT 41

চৈতন্যচন্দ্রের কৃপা হঞাছে ইঁহারে ।
চৈতন্যচন্দ্রের 'বাতুল' কে রাখিতে পারে ?" ॥ ৪১ ॥

caitanya-candrera kṛpā hañāche iṅhāre
caitanya-candrera 'bātula' ke rākhite pāre?"

SYNONYMS

caitanya-candrera—of Lord Śrī Caitanya Mahāprabhu; *kṛpā*—mercy; *hañāche iṅhāre*—has been bestowed upon him; *caitanya-candrera*—of Lord Śrī Caitanya Mahāprabhu; *bātula*—madman; *ke*—who; *rākhite pāre*—can keep.

TRANSLATION

"Lord Śrī Caitanya Mahāprabhu has fully bestowed His mercy on him. Who can keep home such a madman of Caitanyacandra?"

TEXT 42

তবে রঘুনাথ কিছু বিচারিলা মনে।
নিত্যানন্দ-গোসাঞির পাশ চলিলা আর দিনে ॥ ৪২ ॥

tabe raghunātha kichu vicārilā mane
nityānanda-gosāñira pāśa calilā āra dine

SYNONYMS

tabe—thereupon; *raghunātha*—Raghunātha dāsa; *kichu*—something; *vicārilā mane*—considered within his mind; *nityānanda-gosāñira pāśa*—unto Nityānanda Gosāñi; *calilā*—went; *āra dine*—the next day.

TRANSLATION

Then Raghunātha dāsa considered something in his mind, and the next day he went to Nityānanda Gosāñi.

TEXT 43

পানিহাটি-গ্রামে পাইলা প্রভুর দরশন।
কীর্তনীয়া সেবক সঙ্গে আর বহুজন ॥ ৪৩ ॥

pānihāṭi-grāme pāilā prabhura daraśana
kīrtanīyā sevaka saṅge āra bahu-jana

SYNONYMS

pānihāṭi-grāme—in the village known as Pānihāṭi; *pāilā*—got; *prabhura daraśana*—the audience of Nityānanda Prabhu; *kīrtanīyā sevaka*—performers of *saṅkīrtana* and servants; *saṅge*—with; *āra*—and; *bahu-jana*—many other persons.

TRANSLATION

In the village of Pānihāṭi, Raghunātha dāsa obtained an interview with Nityānanda Prabhu, who was accompanied by many kīrtana performers, servants and others.

TEXT 44

গঙ্গাতীরে বৃক্ষ-মূলে পিণ্ডার উপরে।
বসিয়াছেন—যেন কোটী সূর্যোদয় করে ॥ ৪৪ ॥

gaṅgā-tīre vṛkṣa-mūle piṇḍāra upare
vasiyāchena——yena koṭī sūryodaya kare

SYNONYMS

gaṅgā-tīre—on the bank of the Ganges; *vṛkṣa-mūle*—underneath a tree; *piṇḍāra upare*—on a rock; *vasiyāchena*—was sitting; *yena*—as if; *koṭī sūrya*—hundreds of thousands of suns; *udaya kare*—rise.

TRANSLATION

Sitting on a rock under a tree on the bank of the Ganges, Lord Nityānanda seemed as effulgent as hundreds and thousands of rising suns.

TEXT 45

তলে উপরে বহুভক্ত হঞাছে বেষ্টিত।
দেখি' প্রভুর প্রভাব রঘুনাথ—বিস্মিত ॥ ৪৫ ॥

tale upare bahu-bhakta hañāche veṣṭita
dekhi' prabhura prabhāva raghunātha——vismita

SYNONYMS

tale—the surface; *upare*—upon; *bahu-bhakta*—many devotees; *hañāche veṣṭita*—He was surrounded; *dekhi'*—seeing; *prabhura prabhāva*—the influence of Nityānanda Prabhu; *raghunātha*—Raghunātha dāsa; *vismita*—astonished.

TRANSLATION

Many devotees sat on the ground surrounding Him. Seeing the influence of Nityānanda Prabhu, Raghunātha dāsa was astonished.

TEXT 46

দণ্ডবৎ হঞা সেই পড়িলা কতদূরে।
সেবক কহে,—'রঘুনাথ দণ্ডবৎ করে' ॥ ৪৬ ॥

daṇḍavat hañā sei paḍilā kata-dūre
sevaka kahe,——'raghunātha daṇḍavat kare'

SYNONYMS

daṇḍavat hañā—falling flat like a rod; *sei*—he; *paḍilā kata-dūre*—fell down at a distant place; *sevaka kahe*—the servant of Nityānanda Prabhu said; *raghunātha*—Raghunātha dāsa; *daṇḍavat kare*—is offering obeisances.

TRANSLATION

Raghunātha dāsa offered his obeisances by falling prostrate at a distant place, and the servant of Nityānanda Prabhu pointed out, "There is Raghunātha dāsa, offering You obeisances."

TEXT 47

শুনি' প্রভু কহে,—"চোরা দিলি দরশন ।
আয়, আয়, আজি তোর করিমু দণ্ডন" ॥ ৪৭ ॥

śuni' prabhu kahe,——"corā dili daraśana
āya, āya, āji tora karimu daṇḍana"

SYNONYMS

śuni'—hearing; *prabhu kahe*—Lord Nityānanda Prabhu said; *corā*—thief; *dili daraśana*—you have come to see Me; *āya āya*—come here, come here; *āji*—today; *tora*—your; *karimu*—I shall do; *daṇḍana*—punishment.

TRANSLATION

Hearing this, Lord Nityānanda Prabhu said, "You are a thief. Now you have come to see Me. Come here, come here. Today I shall punish you!"

TEXT 48

প্রভু বোলায়, তেঁহো নিকটে না করে গমন ।
আকর্ষিয়া তাঁর মাথে প্রভু ধরিলা চরণ ॥ ৪৮ ॥

prabhu bolāya, teṅho nikaṭe nā kare gamana
ākarṣiyā tāṅra māthe prabhu dharilā caraṇa

SYNONYMS

prabhu bolāya—the Lord calls; *teṅho*—he; *nikaṭe*—nearby; *nā kare gamana*—does not come; *ākarṣiyā*—bringing him near; *tāṅra māthe*—on his head; *prabhu*—Nityānanda Prabhu; *dharilā caraṇa*—placed His feet.

TRANSLATION

The Lord called him, but Raghunātha dāsa did not go near the Lord. Then the Lord forcibly caught him and placed His lotus feet upon Raghunātha dāsa's head.

TEXT 49

কৌতুকী নিত্যানন্দ সহজে দয়াময়।
রঘুনাথে কহে কিছু হঞা সদয় ॥ ৪৯ ॥

kautukī nityānanda sahaje dayāmaya
raghunāthe kahe kichu hañā sadaya

SYNONYMS

kautukī—very funny; *nityānanda*—Lord Nityānanda; *sahaje*—by nature; *dayāmaya*—very merciful; *raghunāthe*—unto Raghunātha dāsa; *kahe*—says; *kichu*—something; *hañā sa-daya*—being merciful.

TRANSLATION

Lord Nityānanda was by nature very merciful and funny. Being merciful, He spoke to Raghunātha dāsa as follows.

TEXT 50

"নিকটে না আইস, চোরা, ভাগ' দূরে দূরে।
আজি লাগ্ পাঞাছি, দণ্ডিমু তোমারে ॥ ৫০ ॥

"nikaṭe nā āisa, corā, bhāga' dūre dūre
āji lāg pāñāchi, daṇḍimu tomāre

SYNONYMS

nikaṭe—nearby; *nā āisa*—you do not come; *corā*—thief; *bhāga'*—you go away; *dūre dūre*—a long distance; *āji*—today; *lāg pāñāchi*—I have caught; *daṇḍimu tomāre*—I shall punish you.

TRANSLATION

"You are just like a thief, for instead of coming near, you stay away at a distant place. Now that I have captured you, I shall punish you.

TEXT 51

দধি, চিড়া ভক্ষণ করাহ মোর গণে।"
শুনি' আনন্দিত হৈল রঘুনাথ মনে ॥ ৫১ ॥

dadhi, ciḍā bhakṣaṇa karāha mora gaṇe"
śuni' ānandita haila raghunātha mane

SYNONYMS

dadhi—yogurt; *ciḍā*—chipped rice; *bhakṣaṇa karāha*—feed; *mora gaṇe*—My associates; *śuni'*—hearing; *ānandita haila*—became very happy; *raghunātha*—Raghunātha dāsa; *mane*—in the mind.

TRANSLATION

"Make a festival and feed all My associates yogurt and chipped rice." Hearing this, Raghunātha dāsa was greatly pleased.

TEXT 52

সেইক্ষণে নিজ-লোক পাঠাইলা গ্রামে।
ভক্ষ্য-দ্রব্য লোক সব গ্রাম হৈতে আনে॥ ৫২ ॥

sei-kṣaṇe nija-loka pāṭhāilā grāme
bhakṣya-dravya loka saba grāma haite āne

SYNONYMS

sei-kṣaṇe—immediately; *nija-loka*—his servants; *pāṭhāilā grāme*—he sent to the nearby village; *bhakṣya-dravya*—eatables; *loka saba*—all the persons; *grāma haite*—from the village; *āne*—bring.

TRANSLATION

Raghunātha dāsa immediately sent his own men to the village to purchase all kinds of eatables and bring them back.

TEXT 53

চিড়া, দধি, দুগ্ধ, সন্দেশ, আর চিনি, কলা।
সব দ্রব্য আনাঞা চৌদিকে ধরিলা॥ ৫৩ ॥

ciḍā, dadhi, dugdha, sandeśa, āra cini, kalā
saba dravya ānāñā caudike dharilā

SYNONYMS

ciḍā—chipped rice; *dadhi*—yogurt; *dugdha*—milk; *sandeśa*—sweetmeats; *āra*—and; *cini*—sugar; *kalā*—banana; *saba*—all; *dravya*—materials; *ānāñā*—causing to be brought; *cau-dike*—all around; *dharilā*—kept.

TRANSLATION

Raghunātha dāsa brought chipped rice, yogurt, milk, sweetmeats, sugar, bananas and other eatables and placed them all around.

TEXT 54

'মহোৎসব'-নাম শুনি' ব্রাহ্মণ-সজ্জন।
আসিতে লাগিল লোক অসঙ্খ্য-গণন ॥ ৫৪ ॥

'mahotsava'-nāma śuni' brāhmaṇa-sajjana
āsite lāgila loka asaṅkhya-gaṇana

SYNONYMS

mahotsava—festival; *nāma*—name; *śuni*—hearing; *brāhmaṇa-sat-jana*—*brāhmaṇas* and other gentlemen; *āsite lāgila*—began to pour in; *loka*—people; *asaṅkhya-gaṇana*—innumerable.

TRANSLATION

As soon as they heard that a festival was going to be held, all kinds of brāhmaṇas and other gentlemen began to arrive. Thus there were innumerable people.

TEXT 55

আর গ্রামান্তর হৈতে সামগ্রী আনিল।
শত দুই-চারি হোল্না তাঁহা আনাইল ॥ ৫৫ ॥

āra grāmāntara haite sāmagrī ānila
śata dui-cāri holnā tāṅhā ānāila

SYNONYMS

āra—also; *grāma-antara haite*—from other villages; *sāmagrī*—articles; *ānila*—brought; *śata*—hundred; *dui-cāri*—two to four; *holnā*—round earthen pots; *tāṅhā*—there; *ānāila*—caused to be brought.

TRANSLATION

Seeing the crowd increasing, Raghunātha dāsa arranged to get more eatables from other villages. He also brought two to four hundred large, round earthen pots.

TEXT 56

বড় বড় মৃৎকুণ্ডিকা আনাইল পাঁচ সাতে।
এক বিপ্র প্রভু লাগি' চিড়া ভিজায় তাতে ॥ ৫৬ ॥

baḍa baḍa mṛt-kuṇḍikā ānāila pāṅca sāte
eka vipra prabhu lāgi' ciḍā bhijāya tāte

SYNONYMS

baḍa baḍa—big, big; *mṛt-kuṇḍikā*—earthen basins; *ānāila*—arranged to be brought; *pāṅca sāte*—five or seven; *eka vipra*—one *brāhmaṇa; prabhu lāgi'*—for Nityānanda Prabhu; *ciḍā*—the chipped rice; *bhijāya*—soaked; *tāte*—in those.

TRANSLATION

He also obtained five or seven especially large earthen pots, and in these pots a brāhmaṇa began soaking chipped rice for the satisfaction of Lord Nityānanda.

TEXT 57

এক-ঠাঞি তপ্ত-দুগ্ধে চিড়া ভিজাঞা ।
অর্ধেক ছানিল দধি, চিনি, কলা দিয়া ॥ ৫৭ ॥

eka-ṭhāñi tapta-dugdhe ciḍā bhijāñā
ardheka chānila dadhi, cini, kalā diyā

SYNONYMS

eka-ṭhāñi—in one place; *tapta-dugdhe*—in hot milk; *ciḍa*—the chipped rice; *bhijāñā*—soaking; *ardheka*—half of it; *chānila*—mixed; *dadhi*—yogurt; *cini*—sugar; *kalā*—bananas; *diyā*—putting in.

TRANSLATION

In one place, chipped rice was soaked in hot milk in each of the large pots. Then half the rice was mixed with yogurt, sugar and bananas.

TEXT 58

আর অর্ধেক ঘনাবৃত-দুগ্ধেতে ছানিল ।
চাঁপাকলা, চিনি, ঘৃত, কর্পূর তাতে দিল ॥ ৫৮ ॥

āra ardheka ghanāvṛta-dugdhete chānila
cāṅpā-kalā, cini, ghṛta, karpūra tāte dila

SYNONYMS

āra ardheka—the other half; *ghana-āvṛta*—condensed; *dugdhete*—in milk; *chānila*—mixed; *cāṅpā-kalā*—a special type of banana; *cini*—sugar; *ghṛta*—clarified butter, ghee; *karpūra*—camphor; *tāte dila*—put into that.

TRANSLATION

The other half was mixed with condensed milk and a special type of banana known as cāṅpā-kalā. Then sugar, clarified butter and camphor were added.

TEXT 59

ধুতি পরি' প্রভু যদি পিণ্ডাতে বসিলা ।
সাতকুণ্ডী বিপ্র তাঁর আগেতে ধরিলা ॥ ৫৯ ॥

dhuti pari' prabhu yadi piṇḍāte vasilā
sāta-kuṇḍī vipra tāṅra āgete dharilā

SYNONYMS

dhuti pari'—putting on a new cloth; *prabhu*—Lord Nityānanda; *yadi*—when; *piṇḍāte vasilā*—sat on a high platform; *sāta-kuṇḍī*—the seven big, big earthen pots; *vipra*—the *brāhmaṇa; tāṅra āgete*—in front of Him; *dharilā*—placed.

TRANSLATION

After Nityānanda Prabhu had changed His cloth for a new one and sat on a raised platform, the brāhmaṇa brought before Him the seven huge pots.

TEXT 60

চবুতরা-উপরে যত প্রভুর নিজগণে ।
বড় বড় লোক বসিলা মণ্ডলী-রচনে ॥ ৬০ ॥

cabutarā-upare yata prabhura nija-gaṇe
baḍa baḍa loka vasilā maṇḍalī-racane

SYNONYMS

cabutarā-upare—on the raised platform; *yata*—all; *prabhura nija-gaṇe*—very intimate associates of the Lord; *baḍa baḍa loka*—big, big people; *vasilā*—sat down; *maṇḍalī-racane*—in a circle.

TRANSLATION

On that platform, all the most important associates of Śrī Nityānanda Prabhu, as well as other important men, sat down in a circle around the Lord.

TEXT 61

রামদাস, সুন্দরানন্দ, দাস-গদাধর ।
মুরারি, কমলাকর, সদাশিব, পুরন্দর ॥ ৬১ ॥

rāmadāsa, sundarānanda, dāsa-gadādhara
murāri, kamalākara, sadāśiva, purandara

SYNONYMS

rāmadāsa—Rāmadāsa; *sundarānanda*—Sundarānanda; *dāsa-gadādhara*—Gadādhara dāsa; *murāri*—Murāri; *kamalākara*—Kamalākara; *sadāśiva*—Sadāśiva; *purandara*—Purandara.

TRANSLATION

Among them were Rāmadāsa, Sundarānanda, Gadādhara dāsa, Murāri, Kamalākara, Sadāśiva and Purandara.

TEXT 62

ধনঞ্জয়, জগদীশ, পরমেশ্বর-দাস ।
মহেশ, গৌরীদাস, হোড়-কৃষ্ণদাস ॥ ৬২ ॥

dhanañjaya, jagadīśa, parameśvara-dāsa
maheśa, gaurīdāsa, hoḍa-kṛṣṇadāsa

SYNONYMS

dhanañjaya—Dhanañjaya; *jagadīśa*—Jagadīśa; *parameśvara-dāsa*—Parameśvara dāsa; *maheśa*—Maheśa; *gaurīdāsa*—Gaurīdāsa; *hoḍa-kṛṣṇadāsa*—Hoḍa Kṛṣṇadāsa.

TRANSLATION

Dhanañjaya, Jagadīśa, Parameśvara dāsa, Maheśa, Gaurīdāsa and Hoḍa Kṛṣṇadāsa were also there.

TEXT 63

উদ্ধারণ দত্ত আদি যত নিজগণ ।
উপরে বসিলা সব, কে করে গণন ? ৬৩ ॥

uddhāraṇa datta ādi yata nija-gaṇa
upare vasilā saba, ke kare gaṇana?

SYNONYMS

uddhāraṇa datta—Uddhāraṇa Datta; *ādi*—and similar other persons; *yata nija-gaṇa*—all personal associates; *upare*—above; *vasilā*—sat down; *saba*—all; *ke*—who; *kare gaṇana*—can count.

TRANSLATION

Similarly, Uddhāraṇa Datta Ṭhākura and many other personal associates of the Lord sat on the raised platform with Nityānanda Prabhu. No one could count them all.

PURPORT

The devotees mentioned herein are described by Śrīla Bhaktisiddhānta Sarasvatī Ṭhākura in his *Anubhāṣya.* For further information one may consult the following references in the *Ādi-līlā.* Rāmadāsa—Chapter Ten, texts 116 and 118, and Chapter Eleven, texts 13 and 16. Sundarānanda—11.23. Gadādhara dāsa—10.53, 11.13-14 and 11.17. The Murāri mentioned herein is different from Murāri Gupta. His full name is Murāri Caitanya dāsa, and he is a personal associate of Nityānanda Prabhu. Thus one should consult Chapter Eleven, text 20. Kamalākara—11.24. Sadāśiva—11.38. Purandara—11.28. Dhanañjaya—11.31. Jagadīśa—11.30. Parameśvara—11.29. Maheśa—11.32. Gaurīdāsa—11.26. Hoḍa Kṛṣṇadāsa—11.47. Uddhāraṇa Datta Ṭhākura—11.41.

TEXT 64

শুনি' পণ্ডিত ভট্টাচার্য যত বিপ্র আইলা ।
মান্য করি' প্রভু সবারে উপরে বসাইলা ॥ ৬৪ ॥

śuni' paṇḍita bhaṭṭācārya yata vipra āilā
mānya kari' prabhu sabāre upare vasāilā

SYNONYMS

śuni'—hearing; *paṇḍita bhaṭṭācārya*—learned scholars and priests; *yata*—all; *vipra*—*brāhmaṇas; āilā*—came; *mānya kari'*—giving honor; *prabhu*—Lord Nityānanda Prabhu; *sabāre*—all of them; *upare vasāilā*—seated on the top.

TRANSLATION

Hearing about the festival, all kinds of learned scholars, brāhmaṇas and priests went there. Lord Nityānanda Prabhu honored them and made them sit on the raised platform with Him.

TEXT 65

দুই দুই মৃৎকুণ্ডিকা সবার আগে দিল ।
একে দুগ্ধ-চিড়া, আরে দধি-চিড়া কৈল ॥ ৬৫ ॥

dui dui mṛt-kuṇḍikā sabāra āge dila
eke dugdha-ciḍā, āre dadhi-ciḍā kaila

SYNONYMS

dui dui—two and two; *mṛt-kuṇḍikā*—earthen pots; *sabāra āge*—before everyone; *dila*—offered; *eke*—in one; *dugdha-ciḍā*—chipped rice with condensed milk; *āre*—in the other; *dadhi-ciḍā*—chipped rice with yogurt; *kaila*—put.

TRANSLATION

Everyone was offered two earthen pots. In one was put chipped rice with condensed milk and in the other chipped rice with yogurt.

TEXT 66

আর যত লোক সব চোতরা-তলানে।
মণ্ডলী-বন্ধে বসিলা, তার না হয় গণনে ॥ ৬৬ ॥

āra yata loka saba cotarā-talāne
maṇḍalī-bandhe vasilā, tāra nā haya gaṇane

SYNONYMS

āra—other; *yata*—as many as; *loka*—people; *saba*—all; *cotarā-talāne*—at the base of the platform; *maṇḍalī-bandhe*—in groups; *vasilā*—sat down; *tāra*—of them; *nā haya gaṇane*—there was no counting.

TRANSLATION

All the other people sat in groups around the platform. No one could count how many people there were.

TEXT 67

একেক জনারে দুই দুই হোল্‌না দিল।
দধি-চিড়া দুগ্ধ-চিড়া, দুইতে ভিজাইল ॥ ৬৭ ॥

ekeka janāre dui dui holnā dila
dadhi-ciḍā dugdha-ciḍā, duite bhijāila

SYNONYMS

ekeka janāre—to each and every one of them; *dui dui*—two and two; *holnā dila*—earthen pots were supplied; *dadhi-ciḍā*—chipped rice with yogurt; *dugdha-ciḍā*—chipped rice with condensed milk; *duite*—in the two pots; *bhijāila*—were soaked.

TRANSLATION

Each and every one of them was supplied two earthen pots—one of chipped rice soaked in yogurt and the other of chipped rice soaked in condensed milk.

TEXT 68

কোন কোন বিপ্র উপরে স্থান না পাঞা ।
দুই হোল্‌নায় চিড়া ভিজায় গঙ্গাতীরে গিয়া ॥ ৬৮ ॥

kona kona vipra upare sthāna nā pāñā
dui holnāya ciḍā bhijāya gaṅgā-tīre giyā

SYNONYMS

kona kona—some; *vipra*—*brāhmaṇas; upare*—on the platform; *sthāna nā pāñā*—not having gotten a place; *dui holnāya*—in two earthen pots; *ciḍā bhijāya*—soak chipped rice; *gaṅgā-tīre*—on the bank of the Ganges; *giyā*—going.

TRANSLATION

Some of the brāhmaṇas, not having gotten a place on the platform, went to the bank of the Ganges with their two earthen pots and soaked their chipped rice there.

TEXT 69

তীরে স্থান না পাঞা আর কত জন ।
জলে নামি' দধি-চিড়া করয়ে ভক্ষণ ॥ ৬৯ ॥

tīre sthāna nā pāñā āra kata jana
jale nāmi' dadhi-ciḍā karaye bhakṣaṇa

SYNONYMS

tīre—on the bank; *sthāna*—place; *nā pāñā*—not having gotten; *āra*—other; *kata*—some; *jana*—persons; *jale nāmi'*—getting down into the water; *dadhi-ciḍā*—yogurt and chipped rice; *karaye bhakṣaṇa*—began to eat.

TRANSLATION

Others, who could not get a place even on the bank of the Ganges, got down into the water and began eating their two kinds of chipped rice.

TEXT 70

কেহ উপরে, কেহ তলে, কেহ গঙ্গাতীরে ।
বিশজন তিন-ঠাঞি পরিবেশন করে ॥ ৭০ ॥

keha upare, keha tale, keha gaṅgā-tīre
biśa-jana tina-ṭhāñi pariveśana kare

SYNONYMS

keha upare—some on the platform; *keha tale*—some at the base of the platform; *keha gaṅgā-tīre*—some on the bank of the Ganges; *biśa-jana*—twenty men; *tina-ṭhāñi*—in three places; *pariveśana kare*—distributed.

TRANSLATION

Thus some sat on the platform, some at the base of the platform, and some on the bank of the Ganges, and they were all supplied two pots each by the twenty men who distributed the food.

TEXT 71

হেনকালে আইলা তথা রাঘব পণ্ডিত ।
হাসিতে লাগিলা দেখি' হঞা বিস্মিত ॥ ৭১ ॥

hena-kāle āilā tathā rāghava paṇḍita
hāsite lāgilā dekhi' hañā vismita

SYNONYMS

hena-kāle—at this time; *āilā*—arrived; *tathā*—there; *rāghava paṇḍita*—the great scholar named Rāghava Paṇḍita; *hāsite lāgilā*—began to laugh; *dekhi'*—seeing; *hañā vismita*—being astonished.

TRANSLATION

At that time, Rāghava Paṇḍita arrived there. Seeing the situation, he began to laugh in great surprise.

TEXT 72

নি-সক্‌ড়ি নানামত প্রসাদ আনিল ।
প্রভুরে আগে দিয়া ভক্তগণে বাঁটি দিল ॥ ৭২ ॥

ni-sakḍi nānā-mata prasāda ānila
prabhure āge diyā bhakta-gaṇe bāṅṭi dila

SYNONYMS

ni-sakḍi—food cooked in ghee; *nānā-mata*—various types; *prasāda*—remnants of the Lord's food; *ānila*—he brought; *prabhure āge*—in front of Lord Nityānanda; *diyā*—placing; *bhakta-gaṇe*—to all the devotees; *bāṅṭi dila*—distributed.

TRANSLATION

He brought many other kinds of food cooked in ghee and offered to the Lord. This prasāda he first placed before Lord Nityānanda and then distributed among the devotees.

TEXT 73

**প্রভুরে কহে,—"তোমা লাগি' ভোগ লাগাইল।
তুমি ইহাঁ উৎসব কর, ঘরে প্রসাদ রহিল॥" ৭৩॥**

prabhure kahe, ——"tomā lāgi' bhoga lāgāila
tumi ihāṅ utsava kara, ghare prasāda rahila"

SYNONYMS

prabhure kahe—he said to Lord Nityānanda Prabhu; *tomā lāgi'*—for You; *bhoga lāgāila*—I have offered food to the Deity; *tumi*—You; *ihāṅ*—here; *utsava kara*—are engaged in a festival; *ghare*—at home; *prasāda*—the *prasāda; rahila*—remained.

TRANSLATION

Rāghava Paṇḍita said to Lord Nityānanda, "For You, sir, I have already offered food to the Deity, but You are engaged in a festival here, and so the food is lying there untouched."

TEXT 74

**প্রভু কহে,—"এ-দ্রব্য দিনে করিয়ে ভোজন।
রাত্র্যে তোমার ঘরে প্রসাদ করিমু ভক্ষণ॥ ৭৪॥**

prabhu kahe, ——"e-dravya dine kariye bhojana
rātrye tomāra ghare prasāda karimu bhakṣaṇa

SYNONYMS

prabhu kahe—Lord Nityānanda Prabhu said; *e-dravya*—this food; *dine*—during the daytime; *kariye bhojana*—let Me eat; *rātrye*—at night; *tomāra ghare*—in your house; *prasāda*—the *prasāda; karimu bhakṣaṇa*—I shall eat.

TRANSLATION

Lord Nityānanda replied, "Let Me eat all this food here during the day, and I shall eat at your home at night.

TEXT 75

গোপ-জাতি আমি বহু গোপগণ সঙ্গে ।
আমি সুখ পাই এই পুলিনভোজন-রঙ্গে ॥" ৭৫ ॥

gopa-jāti āmi bahu gopa-gaṇa saṅge
āmi sukha pāi ei pulina-bhojana-raṅge"

SYNONYMS

gopa-jāti—belonging to the community of cowherd boys; *āmi*—I; *bahu*—many; *gopa-gaṇa*—cowherd boys; *saṅge*—with; *āmi*—I; *sukha pāi*—become very happy; *ei*—this; *pulina*—by the riverside; *bhojana-raṅge*—in the enjoyment of eating.

TRANSLATION

"I belong to a community of cowherd boys, and therefore I generally have many cowherd associates with Me. I am happy when we eat together in a picnic like this by the sandy bank of the river."

TEXT 76

রাঘবে বসাঞা দুই কুণ্ডী দেওয়াইলা ।
রাঘব দ্বিবিধ চিড়া তাতে ভিজাইলা ॥ ৭৬ ॥

rāghave vasāñā dui kuṇḍī deoyāilā
rāghava dvividha ciḍā tāte bhijāilā

SYNONYMS

rāghave—Rāghava Paṇḍita; *vasāñā*—making sit down; *dui*—two; *kuṇḍī*—earthen pots; *deoyāilā*—arranged to be delivered to him; *rāghava*—Rāghava Paṇḍita; *dvi-vidha*—two kinds; *ciḍā*—chipped rice; *tāte*—in them; *bhijāilā*—soaked.

TRANSLATION

Lord Nityānanda made Rāghava Paṇḍita sit down and had two pots delivered to him also. There were two kinds of chipped rice soaked in them.

TEXT 77

সকল-লোকের চিড়া পূর্ণ যবে হইল ।
ধ্যানে তবে প্রভু মহাপ্রভুরে আনিল ॥ ৭৭ ॥

sakala-lokera ciḍā pūrṇa yabe ha-ila
dhyāne tabe prabhu mahāprabhure ānila

SYNONYMS

sakala-lokera—of everyone; *ciḍā*—chipped rice; *pūrṇa*—full; *yabe*—when; *ha-ila*—was; *dhyāne*—in meditation; *tabe*—at that time; *prabhu*—Lord Nityānanda Prabhu; *mahāprabhure ānila*—brought Śrī Caitanya Mahāprabhu.

TRANSLATION

When chipped rice had been served to everyone, Lord Nityānanda Prabhu, in meditation, brought Śrī Caitanya Mahāprabhu.

TEXT 78

মহাপ্রভু আইলা দেখি' নিতাই উঠিলা ।
তাঁরে লঞা সবার চিড়া দেখিতে লাগিলা ॥ ৭৮ ॥

mahāprabhu āilā dekhi' nitāi uṭhilā
tāṅre lañā sabāra ciḍā dekhite lāgilā

SYNONYMS

mahāprabhu—Śrī Caitanya Mahāprabhu; *āilā*—came; *dehki'*—seeing; *nitāi*—Lord Nityānanda; *uṭhilā*—stood up; *tāṅre lañā*—with Him; *sabāra*—of everyone; *ciḍā*—chipped rice; *dekhite lāgilā*—began to see.

TRANSLATION

When Śrī Caitanya Mahāprabhu arrived, Lord Nityānanda Prabhu stood up. They then saw how the others were enjoying the chipped rice with yogurt and condensed milk.

TEXT 79

সকল কুণ্ডীর, হোল্‌নার চিড়ার এক এক গ্রাস ।
মহাপ্রভুর মুখে দেন করি' পরিহাস ॥ ৭৯ ॥

sakala kuṇḍīra, holnāra ciḍāra eka eka grāsa
mahāprabhura mukhe dena kari' parihāsa

SYNONYMS

sakala kuṇḍīra—from all the pots; *holnāra*—from the big pots; *ciḍāra*—of chipped rice; *eka eka grāsa*—one morsel; *mahāprabhura mukhe*—into the mouth of Śrī Caitanya Mahāprabhu; *dena*—puts; *kari' parihāsa*—making a joke.

TRANSLATION

From each and every pot, Lord Nityānanda Prabhu took one morsel of chipped rice and pushed it into the mouth of Śrī Caitanya Mahāprabhu as a joke.

TEXT 80

হাসি' মহাপ্রভু আর এক গ্রাস লঞা।
তাঁর মুখে দিয়া খাওয়ায় হাসিয়া হাসিয়া ॥ ৮০ ॥

hāsi' mahāprabhu āra eka grāsa lañā
tāṅra mukhe diyā khāoyāya hāsiyā hāsiyā

SYNONYMS

hāsi'—smiling; *mahāprabhu*—Śrī Caitanya Mahāprabhu; *āra*—another; *eka grāsa*—one morsel; *lañā*—taking; *tāṅra mukhe*—in the mouth of Lord Nityānanda Prabhu; *diyā*—putting; *khāoyāya*—makes eat; *hāsiyā hāsiyā*—laughing.

TRANSLATION

Śrī Caitanya Mahāprabhu, also smiling, took a morsel of food, pushed it into the mouth of Nityānanda and laughed as He made Lord Nityānanda eat it.

TEXT 81

এইমত নিতাই বুলে সকল মণ্ডলে।
দাণ্ডাঞা রঙ্গ দেখে বৈষ্ণব সকলে ॥ ৮১ ॥

ei-mata nitāi bule sakala maṇḍale
dāṇḍāñā raṅga dekhe vaiṣṇava sakale

SYNONYMS

ei-mata—in this way; *nitāi bule*—Lord Nityānanda was walking; *sakala maṇḍale*—through all the groups; *dāṇḍāñā*—standing; *raṅga dekhe*—see the fun; *vaiṣṇava sakale*—all the Vaiṣṇavas.

TRANSLATION

In this way Lord Nityānanda was walking through all the groups of eaters, and all the Vaiṣṇavas standing there were seeing the fun.

TEXT 82

কি করিয়া বেড়ায়,—ইহা কেহ নাহি জানে।
মহাপ্রভুর দর্শন পায় কোন ভাগ্যবানে ॥ ৮২ ॥

ki kariyā beḍāya, —ihā keha nāhi jāne
mahāprabhura darśana pāya kona bhāgyavāne

SYNONYMS

ki kariyā—doing what; *beḍāya*—walks through; *ihā*—this; *keha nāhi jāne*—no one could understand; *mahāprabhura darśana pāya*—see Śrī Caitanya Mahāprabhu; *kona bhāgyavāne*—some fortunate men.

TRANSLATION

No one could understand what Nityānanda Prabhu was doing as He walked about. Some, however, who were very fortunate, could see that Lord Śrī Caitanya Mahāprabhu was also present.

TEXT 83

তবে হাসি' নিত্যানন্দ বসিলা আসনে।
চারি কুণ্ডী আরোয়া চিড়া রাখিলা ডাহিনে ॥ ৮৩ ॥

tabe hāsi' nityānanda vasilā āsane
cāri kuṇḍī āroyā ciḍā rākhilā ḍāhine

SYNONYMS

tabe hāsi'—thereupon smiling; *nityānanda*—Lord Nityānanda Prabhu; *vasilā āsane*—sat down on His seat; *cāri kuṇḍī*—four earthen pots; *āroyā ciḍā*—chipped rice not made from boiled paddy; *rākhilā ḍāhine*—He kept on His right side.

TRANSLATION

Then Nityānanda Prabhu smiled and sat down. On His right side He kept four pots of chipped rice that had not been made from boiled paddy.

TEXT 84

আসন দিয়া মহাপ্রভুরে তাহাঁ বসাইলা।
দুই ভাই তবে চিড়া খাইতে লাগিলা ॥ ৮৪ ॥

āsana diyā mahāprabhure tāhāṅ vasāilā
dui bhāi tabe ciḍā khāite lāgilā

SYNONYMS

āsana diyā—offering a sitting place; *mahāprabhure*—unto Śrī Caitanya Mahāprabhu; *tāhāṅ*—there; *vasāilā*—made sit; *dui bhāi*—the two brothers; *tabe*—at that time; *ciḍā*—chipped rice; *khāite lāgilā*—began to eat.

TRANSLATION

Lord Nityānanda offered Śrī Caitanya Mahāprabhu a place and had Him sit down. Then together the two brothers began eating chipped rice.

TEXT 85

দেখি' নিত্যানন্দপ্রভু আনন্দিত হৈলা ।
কত কত ভাবাবেশ প্রকাশ করিলা ॥ ৮৫ ॥

dekhi' nityānanda-prabhu ānandita hailā
kata kata bhāvāveśa prakāśa karilā

SYNONYMS

dekhi'—seeing; *nityānanda-prabhu*—Lord Nityānanda Prabhu; *ānandita hailā*—became very happy; *kata kata*—so much; *bhāva-āveśa*—ecstatic love; *prakāśa karilā*—He manifested.

TRANSLATION

Seeing Lord Caitanya Mahāprabhu eating with Him, Lord Nityānanda Prabhu became very happy and exhibited varieties of ecstatic love.

TEXT 86

আজ্ঞা দিলা,—'হরি বলি' করহ ভোজন' ।
'হরি' 'হরি'-ধ্বনি উঠি' ভরিল ভুবন ॥ ৮৬ ॥

ājñā dilā, —'hari bali' karaha bhojana'
'hari' 'hari'-dhvani uṭhi' bharila bhuvana

SYNONYMS

ājñā dilā—He ordered; *hari bali'*—saying "Hari"; *karaha bhojana*—all of you eat; *hari hari-dhvani*—the resounding of "Hari, Hari"; *uṭhi'*—rising; *bharila bhuvana*—filled the universe.

TRANSLATION

Lord Nityānanda Prabhu ordered, "All of you eat, chanting the holy name of Hari." Immediately the holy names "Hari, Hari" resounded, filling the entire universe.

TEXT 87

'হরি' 'হরি' বলি' বৈষ্ণব করয়ে ভোজন ।
পুলিন-ভোজন সবার হইল স্মরণ ॥ ৮৭ ॥

'hari' 'hari' bali' vaiṣṇava karaye bhojana
pulina-bhojana sabāra ha-ila smaraṇa

SYNONYMS

hari hari bali'—chanting Hari, Hari; *vaiṣṇava*—all the Vaiṣṇavas; *karaye bhojana*—eat; *pulina-bhojana*—eating on the bank of the Yamunā; *sabāra ha-ila smaraṇa*—everyone could remember.

TRANSLATION

When all the Vaiṣṇavas were chanting the holy names "Hari, Hari" and eating, they remembered how Kṛṣṇa and Balarāma ate with Their companions the cowherd boys on the bank of the Yamunā.

TEXT 88

নিত্যানন্দ মহাপ্রভু—কৃপালু, উদার ।
রঘুনাথের ভাগ্যে এত কৈলা অঙ্গীকার ॥ ৮৮ ॥

nityānanda mahāprabhu——kṛpālu, udāra
raghunāthera bhāgye eta kailā aṅgīkāra

SYNONYMS

nityānanda mahāprabhu—Lord Nityānanda Prabhu and Lord Śrī Caitanya Mahāprabhu; *kṛpālu*—merciful; *udāra*—liberal; *raghunāthera bhāgye*—by the great fortune of Raghunātha dāsa; *eta*—all this; *kailā aṅgīkāra*—They accepted.

TRANSLATION

Śrī Caitanya Mahāprabhu and Lord Nityānanda Prabhu are extremely merciful and liberal. It was Raghunātha dāsa's good fortune that They accepted all these dealings.

TEXT 89

নিত্যানন্দ-প্রভাব-কৃপা জানিবে কোন্ জন ?
মহাপ্রভু আনি' করায় পুলিন-ভোজন ॥ ৮৯ ॥

nityānanda-prabhāva-kṛpā jānibe kon jana?
mahāprabhu āni' karāya pulina-bhojana

SYNONYMS

nityānanda—of Nityānanda Prabhu; *prabhāva-kṛpā*—influence and mercy; *jānibe*—can know; *kon jana*—who; *mahāprabhu āni'*—bringing Śrī Caitanya Mahāprabhu; *karāya pulina-bhojana*—induces Him to eat on the river bank.

TRANSLATION

Who can understand the influence and mercy of Lord Nityānanda Prabhu? He is so powerful that He induced Lord Śrī Caitanya Mahāprabhu to come eat chipped rice on the bank of the Ganges.

TEXT 90

শ্রীরামদাসাদি গোপ প্রেমাবিষ্ট হৈলা ।
গঙ্গাতীরে 'যমুনা-পুলিন' জ্ঞান কৈলা ॥ ৯০ ॥

śrī-rāmadāsādi gopa premāviṣṭa hailā
gaṅgā-tīre 'yamunā-pulina' jñāna kailā

SYNONYMS

śrī-rāmadāsa-ādi—headed by Śrī Rāmadāsa; *gopa*—the cowherd boys; *prema-āviṣṭa hailā*—became absorbed in ecstatic love; *gaṅgā-tīre*—the bank of the Ganges River; *yamunā-pulina*—the bank of the Yamunā River; *jñāna kailā*—they thought.

TRANSLATION

All the confidential devotees who were cowherd boys, headed by Śrī Rāmadāsa, were absorbed in ecstatic love. They thought the bank of the Ganges to be the bank of the Yamunā.

TEXT 91

মহোৎসব শুনি' পসারি নানা-গ্রাম হৈতে ।
চিড়া, দধি, সন্দেশ, কলা আনিল বেচিতে ॥ ৯১ ॥

mahotsava śuni' pasāri nānā-grāma haite
ciḍā, dadhi, sandeśa, kalā ānila vecite

SYNONYMS

mahotsava śuni'—hearing about this festival; *pasāri*—the shopkeepers; *nānā-grāma*—various villages; *haite*—from; *ciḍā*—chipped rice; *dadhi*—yogurt; *sandeśa*—sweetmeats; *kalā*—bananas; *ānila*—brought; *vecite*—to sell.

TRANSLATION

When the shopkeepers of many other villages heard about the festival, they arrived there to sell chipped rice, yogurt, sweetmeats and bananas.

TEXT 92

যত দ্রব্য লঞা আইসে, সব মূল্য করি' লয়।
তার দ্রব্য মূল্য দিয়া তাহারে খাওয়ায় ॥ ৯২ ॥

yata dravya lañā āise, saba mūlya kari' laya
tāra dravya mūlya diyā tāhāre khāoyāya

SYNONYMS

yata dravya—all materials; *lañā*—bringing; *āise*—come; *saba*—all; *mūlya kari' laya*—Raghunātha purchased; *tāra dravya*—of their goods; *mūlya diyā*—giving the price; *tāhāre khāoyāya*—fed them.

TRANSLATION

As they came, bringing all kinds of food, Raghunātha dāsa purchased it all. He gave them the price for their goods and later fed them the very same food.

TEXT 93

কৌতুক দেখিতে আইল যত যত জন।
সেই চিড়া, দধি, কলা করিল ভক্ষণ ॥ ৯৩ ॥

kautuka dekhite āila yata yata jana
sei ciḍā, dadhi, kalā karila bhakṣaṇa

SYNONYMS

kautuka—these funny things; *dekhite*—to see; *āila*—arrived; *yata yata jana*—all kinds of men; *sei*—they; *ciḍā*—chipped rice; *dadhi*—yogurt; *kalā*—bananas; *karila bhakṣaṇa*—ate.

TRANSLATION

Anyone who came to see how these funny things were going on was also fed chipped rice, yogurt and bananas.

TEXT 94

ভোজন করি' নিত্যানন্দ আচমন কৈলা।
চারি কুণ্ডীর অবশেষ রঘুনাথে দিলা ॥ ৯৪ ॥

bhojana kari' nityānanda ācamana kailā
cāri kuṇḍīra avaśeṣa raghunāthe dilā

SYNONYMS

bhojana kari'—after finishing eating; *nityānanda*—Nityānanda Prabhu; *ācamana kailā*—washing His hands and mouth; *cāri kuṇḍīra*—of the four pots; *avaśeṣa*—what was remaining; *raghunāthe dilā*—delivered to Raghunātha dāsa.

TRANSLATION

After Lord Nityānanda Prabhu finished eating, He washed His hands and mouth and gave Raghunātha dāsa the food remaining in the four pots.

TEXT 95

আর তিন কুণ্ডিকায় অবশেষ ছিল ।
গ্রাসে-গ্রাসে করি' বিপ্র সব ভক্তে দিল ॥ ৯৫ ॥

āra tina kuṇḍikāya avaśeṣa chila
grāse-grāse kari' vipra saba bhakte dila

SYNONYMS

āra—other; *tina kuṇḍikāya*—in three pots; *avaśeṣa chila*—there was food remaining; *grāse-grāse*—by morsel; *kari'*—delivering; *vipra*—a *brāhmaṇa; saba bhakte*—to all the devotees; *dila*—delivered.

TRANSLATION

There was food remaining in the three other big pots of Lord Nityānanda, and a brāhmaṇa distributed it to all the devotees, giving a morsel to each.

TEXT 96

পুষ্পমালা বিপ্র আনি' প্রভু-গলে দিল ।
চন্দন আনিয়া প্রভুর সর্বাঙ্গে লেপিল ॥ ৯৬ ॥

puṣpa-mālā vipra āni' prabhu-gale dila
candana āniyā prabhura sarvāṅge lepila

SYNONYMS

puṣpa-mālā—a flower garland; *vipra*—one *brāhmaṇa; āni'*—bringing; *prabhu-gale*—on the neck of Lord Nityānanda Prabhu; *dila*—placed; *candana āniyā*—bringing sandalwood pulp; *prabhura*—of Lord Nityānanda Prabhu; *sarvāṅge lepila*—smeared all over the body.

TRANSLATION

Then a brāhmaṇa brought a flower garland, placed the garland on Nityānanda Prabhu's neck and smeared sandalwood pulp all over His body.

TEXT 97

সেবক তাম্বূল লঞা করে সমর্পণ ।
হাসিয়া হাসিয়া প্রভু করয়ে চর্বণ ॥ ৯৭ ॥

sevaka tāmbūla lañā kare samarpaṇa
hāsiyā hāsiyā prabhu karaye carvaṇa

SYNONYMS

sevaka—servant; *tāmbūla*—betel nuts; *lañā*—bringing; *kare samarpaṇa*—offers; *hāsiyā hāsiyā*—smiling; *prabhu*—Lord Nityānanda Prabhu; *karaye carvaṇa*—chews.

TRANSLATION

When a servant brought betel nuts and offered them to Lord Nityānanda, the Lord smiled and chewed them.

TEXT 98

মালা-চন্দন-তাম্বূল শেষ যে আছিল ।
শ্রীহস্তে প্রভু তাহা সবাকারে বাঁটি' দিল ॥ ৯৮ ॥

mālā-candana-tāmbūla śeṣa ye āchila
śrī-haste prabhu tāhā sabākāre bāṅṭi' dila

SYNONYMS

mālā-candana-tāmbūla—the flower garlands, sandalwood pulp and betel; *śeṣa ye āchila*—whatever remained; *śrī-haste*—in His own hand; *prabhu*—Nityānanda Prabhu; *tāhā*—that; *sabākāre*—to all; *bāṅṭi' dila*—distributed.

TRANSLATION

With His own hands Lord Nityānanda Prabhu distributed to all the devotees whatever flower garlands, sandalwood pulp and betel nuts remained.

TEXT 99

আনন্দিত রঘুনাথ প্রভুর 'শেষ' পাঞা ।
আপনার গণ-সহ খাইলা বাঁটিয়া ॥ ৯৯ ॥

ānandita raghunātha prabhura 'śeṣa' pāñā
āpanāra gaṇa-saha khāilā bāṅṭiyā

SYNONYMS

ānandita—being very happy; *raghunātha*—Raghunātha dāsa; *prabhura śeṣa pāñā*—after getting the remnants left by Lord Nityānanda Prabhu; *āpanāra gaṇa*—his own associates; *saha*—with; *khāilā*—ate; *bāṅṭiyā*—distributing.

TRANSLATION

After receiving the remnants of food left by Lord Nityānanda Prabhu, Raghunātha dāsa, who was greatly happy, ate some and distributed the rest among his own associates.

TEXT 100

এই ত' কহিলুঁ নিত্যানন্দের বিহার ।
'চিড়া-দধি-মহোৎসব'-নামে খ্যাতি যার ॥ ১০০ ॥

ei ta' kahiluṅ nityānandera vihāra
'ciḍā-dadhi-mahotsava'-nāme khyāti yāra

SYNONYMS

ei ta'—in this way; *kahiluṅ*—I have described; *nityānandera vihāra*—the pastimes of Lord Nityānanda Prabhu; *ciḍā-dadhi-mahotsava*—the festival of eating chipped rice and yogurt; *nāme*—of the name; *khyāti*—the fame; *yāra*—of which.

TRANSLATION

Thus I have described the pastimes of Lord Nityānanda Prabhu in relation to the celebrated festival of chipped rice and yogurt.

TEXT 101

প্রভু বিশ্রাম কৈলা, যদি দিন-শেষ হৈল ।
রাঘব-মন্দিরে তবে কীর্তন আরম্ভিল ॥ ১০১ ॥

prabhu viśrāma kailā, yadi dina-śeṣa haila
rāghava-mandire tabe kīrtana ārambhila

SYNONYMS

prabhu—Nityānanda Prabhu; *viśrāma kailā*—took rest; *yadi*—when; *dina-śeṣa haila*—the day was ended; *rāghava-mandire*—at the temple of Rāghava Paṇḍita;

tabe—at that time; *kīrtana ārambhila*—began congregational chanting of the holy name.

TRANSLATION

Nityānanda Prabhu rested for the day, and when the day ended He went to the temple of Rāghava Paṇḍita and began congregational chanting of the holy name of the Lord.

TEXT 102

ভক্ত সব নাচাঞা নিত্যানন্দ-রায় ।
শেষে নৃত্য করে প্রেমে জগৎ ভাসায় ॥ ১০২ ॥

bhakta saba nācāñā nityānanda-rāya
śeṣe nṛtya kare preme jagat bhāsāya

SYNONYMS

bhakta saba—all the devotees; *nācāñā*—making to dance; *nityānanda-rāya*—Lord Nityānanda Prabhu; *śeṣe*—at the end; *nṛtya kare*—began to dance; *preme*—in ecstatic love; *jagat bhāsāya*—inundated the entire world.

TRANSLATION

Lord Nityānanda Prabhu first influenced all the devotees to dance, and finally He Himself began dancing, thus inundating the entire world in ecstatic love.

TEXT 103

মহাপ্রভু তাঁর নৃত্য করেন দরশন ।
সবে নিত্যানন্দ দেখে, না দেখে অন্যজন ॥ ১০৩ ॥

mahāprabhu tāṅra nṛtya karena daraśana
sabe nityānanda dekhe, nā dekhe anya-jana

SYNONYMS

mahāprabhu—Śrī Caitanya Mahāprabhu; *tāṅra*—His; *nṛtya*—dancing; *karena daraśana*—sees; *sabe*—all; *nityānanda dekhe*—Nityānanda Prabhu sees; *nā dekhe*—do not see; *anya-jana*—others.

TRANSLATION

Lord Śrī Caitanya Mahāprabhu was observing the dancing of Lord Nityānanda Prabhu. Nityānanda Prabhu could see this, but the others could not.

TEXT 104

নিত্যানন্দের নৃত্য,—যেন তাঁহার নর্তনে ।
উপমা দিবার নাহি এ-তিন ভুবনে ॥ ১০৪ ॥

nityānandera nṛtya, —yena tāṅhāra nartane
upamā dibāra nāhi e-tina bhuvane

SYNONYMS

nityānandera nṛtya—the dancing of Lord Nityānanda Prabhu; *yena*—as; *tāṅhāra nartane*—with the dancing of Śrī Caitanya Mahāprabhu; *upamā dibāra nāhi*—there cannot be any comparison; *e-tina bhuvane*—within these three worlds.

TRANSLATION

The dancing of Lord Nityānanda Prabhu, like the dancing of Śrī Caitanya Mahāprabhu, cannot be compared to anything within these three worlds.

TEXT 105

নৃত্যের মাধুরী কেবা বর্ণিবারে পারে ।
মহাপ্রভু আইসে যেই নৃত্য দেখিবারে ॥ ১০৫ ॥

nṛtyera mādhurī kebā varṇibāre pāre
mahāprabhu āise yei nṛtya dekhibāre

SYNONYMS

nṛtyera mādhurī—the sweetness of the dancing; *kebā*—who; *varṇibāre pāre*—can describe; *mahāprabhu āise*—Śrī Caitanya Mahāprabhu comes; *yei*—that; *nṛtya*—dancing; *dekhibāre*—to see.

TRANSLATION

No one can properly describe the sweetness of Lord Nityānanda's dancing. Śrī Caitanya Mahāprabhu personally comes to see it.

TEXT 106

নৃত্য করি' প্রভু যবে বিশ্রাম করিলা ।
ভোজনের লাগি' পণ্ডিত নিবেদন কৈলা ॥ ১০৬ ॥

nṛtya kari' prabhu yabe viśrāma karilā
bhojanera lāgi' paṇḍita nivedana kailā

SYNONYMS

nṛtya kari'—after dancing; *prabhu*—Lord Nityānanda; *yabe*—when; *viśrāma karilā*—took rest; *bhojanera lāgi'*—for His eating; *paṇḍita*—Rāghava Paṇḍita; *nivedana kailā*—submitted a request.

TRANSLATION

After the dancing and after Lord Nityānanda had rested, Rāghava Paṇḍita submitted his request that the Lord take supper.

TEXT 107

ভোজনে বসিলা প্রভু নিজগণ লঞা ।
মহাপ্রভুর আসন ডাহিনে পাতিয়া ॥ ১০৭ ॥

bhojane vasilā prabhu nija-gaṇa lañā
mahāprabhura āsana ḍāhine pātiyā

SYNONYMS

bhojane—to eat; *vasilā*—sat down; *prabhu*—Lord Nityānanda Prabhu; *nija-gaṇa lañā*—with His own personal associates; *mahāprabhura*—of Śrī Caitanya Mahāprabhu; *āsana*—sitting place; *ḍāhine pātiyā*—setting on the right side.

TRANSLATION

Lord Nityānanda Prabhu sat down for supper with His personal associates and made a sitting place on His right side for Śrī Caitanya Mahāprabhu.

TEXT 108

মহাপ্রভু আসি' সেই আসনে বসিল ।
দেখি' রাঘবের মনে আনন্দ বাড়িল ॥ ১০৮ ॥

mahāprabhu āsi' sei āsane vasila
dekhi' rāghavera mane ānanda bāḍila

SYNONYMS

mahāprabhu—Śrī Caitanya Mahāprabhu; *āsi'*—coming; *sei āsane*—on that seat; *vasila*—sat down; *dekhi'*—seeing; *rāghavera mane*—in the mind of Rāghava Paṇḍita; *ānanda*—great happiness; *bāḍila*—increased.

TRANSLATION

Śrī Caitanya Mahāprabhu came there and sat down at His place. Seeing this, Rāghava Paṇḍita felt increasing happiness.

TEXT 109

দুইভাই-আগে প্রসাদ আনিয়া ধরিলা।
সকল বৈষ্ণবে পিছে পরিবেশন কৈলা ॥ ১০৯ ॥

dui-bhāi-āge prasāda āniyā dharilā
sakala vaiṣṇave piche pariveśana kailā

SYNONYMS

dui-bhāi-āge—in front of the two brothers; *prasāda*—the remnants of food offered to Lord Kṛṣṇa; *āniyā*—bringing; *dharilā*—put; *sakala vaiṣṇave*—to all the Vaiṣṇavas; *piche*—thereafter; *pariveśana kailā*—distributed.

TRANSLATION

Rāghava Paṇḍita brought the prasāda before the two brothers and thereafter distributed prasāda to all the other Vaiṣṇavas.

TEXT 110

নানাপ্রকার পিঠা, পায়স, দিব্য শাল্যন্ন।
অমৃত নিন্দয়ে ঐছে বিবিধ ব্যঞ্জন ॥ ১১০ ॥

nānā-prakāra piṭhā, pāyasa, divya śālyanna
amṛta nindaye aiche vividha vyañjana

SYNONYMS

nānā-prakāra piṭhā—various types of cake; *pāyasa*—sweet rice; *divya śālyanna*—fine cooked rice; *amṛta*—nectar; *nindaye*—surpassed; *aiche*—such; *vividha vyañjana*—varieties of vegetables.

TRANSLATION

There were varieties of cakes, sweet rice and fine cooked rice that surpassed the taste of nectar. There were also varieties of vegetables.

TEXT 111

রাঘব-ঠাকুরের প্রসাদ অমৃতের সার।
মহাপ্রভু যাহা খাইতে আইসে বার বার ॥ ১১১ ॥

rāghava-ṭhākurera prasāda amṛtera sāra
mahāprabhu yāhā khāite āise bāra bāra

SYNONYMS

rāghava-ṭhākurera—of Rāghava Paṇḍita; *prasāda*—food offered to the Deity; *amṛtera sāra*—the essence of nectar; *mahāprabhu*—Śrī Caitanya Mahāprabhu; *yāhā*—which; *khāite*—to eat; *āise*—came; *bāra bāra*—again and again.

TRANSLATION

The food prepared and offered to the Deity by Rāghava Paṇḍita was like the essence of nectar. Śrī Caitanya Mahāprabhu came there again and again to eat such prasāda.

TEXT 112

পাক করি' রাঘব যবে ভোগ লাগায়।
মহাপ্রভুর লাগি' ভোগ পৃথক্ বাড়য় ॥ ১১২ ॥

pāka kari' rāghava yabe bhoga lāgāya
mahāprabhura lāgi' bhoga pṛthak bāḍaya

SYNONYMS

pāka kari'—after cooking; *rāghava*—Rāghava Paṇḍita; *yabe*—when; *bhoga lāgāya*—offers food to the Deity; *mahāprabhura lāgi'*—for Lord Śrī Caitanya Mahāprabhu; *bhoga*—offering; *pṛthak*—separate; *bāḍaya*—arranges.

TRANSLATION

When Rāghava Paṇḍita offered the food to the Deity after cooking, he would make a separate offering for Śrī Caitanya Mahāprabhu.

TEXT 113

প্রতিদিন মহাপ্রভু করেন ভোজন।
মধ্যে মধ্যে প্রভু তাঁরে দেন দরশন ॥ ১১৩ ॥

prati-dina mahāprabhu karena bhojana
madhye madhye prabhu tāṅre dena daraśana

SYNONYMS

prati-dina—daily; *mahāprabhu*—Śrī Caitanya Mahāprabhu; *karena bhojana*—eats; *madhye madhye*—sometimes; *prabhu*—Śrī Caitanya Mahāprabhu; *tāṅre*—unto him; *dena daraśana*—gives His audience.

TRANSLATION

Every day, Śrī Caitanya Mahāprabhu would eat at the house of Rāghava Paṇḍita. Sometimes He would give Rāghava Paṇḍita the opportunity to see Him.

TEXT 114

দুই ভাইরে রাঘব আনি' পরিবেশে ।
যত্ন করি' খাওয়ায়, না রহে অবশেষে ॥ ১১৪ ॥

dui bhāire rāghava āni' pariveśe
yatna kari' khāoyāya, nā rahe avaśeṣe

SYNONYMS

dui bhāire—to the two brothers; *rāghava*—Rāghava Paṇḍita; *āni'*—bringing; *pariveśe*—distributed; *yatna kari'*—with great attention; *khāoyāya*—fed Them; *nā rahe avaśeṣe*—there were no remnants.

TRANSLATION

Rāghava Paṇḍita would bring and distribute prasāda to the two brothers, feeding Them with great attention. They ate everything, and therefore there were no remnants left.

TEXT 115

কত উপহার আনে, হেন নাহি জানি ।
রাঘবের ঘরে রান্ধে রাধা-ঠাকুরাণী ॥ ১১৫ ॥

kata upahāra āne, hena nāhi jāni
rāghavera ghare rāndhe rādhā-ṭhākurāṇī

SYNONYMS

kata upahāra—many presentations; *āne*—brings; *hena*—such; *nāhi jāni*—I cannot understand; *rāghavera ghare*—at the house of Rāghava Paṇḍita; *rāndhe*—cooks; *rādhā-ṭhākurāṇī*—the supreme mother, Śrīmatī Rādhārāṇī.

TRANSLATION

He brought so many presentations that no one could know them perfectly. Indeed, it was a fact that the supreme mother, Rādhārāṇī, personally cooked in the house of Rāghava Paṇḍita.

TEXT 116

দুর্বাসার ঠাঞি তেঁহো পাঞাছেন বর ।
অমৃত হইতে পাক তাঁর অধিক মধুর ॥ ১১৬ ॥

durvāsāra ṭhāñi teṅho pāñāchena vara
amṛta ha-ite pāka tāṅra adhika madhura

SYNONYMS

durvāsāra ṭhāñi—from Durvāsā Muni; *teṅho*—She; *pāñāchena vara*—got the benediction; *amṛta ha-ite*—than nectar; *pāka*—cooking; *tāṅra*—Her; *adhika madhura*—more sweet.

TRANSLATION

Śrīmatī Rādhārāṇī received from Durvāsā Muni the benediction that whatever She cooked would be sweeter than nectar. That is the special feature of Her cooking.

TEXT 117

সুগন্ধি সুন্দর প্রসাদ—মাধুর্যের সার ।
দুই ভাই তাহা খাঞা সন্তোষ অপার ॥ ১১৭ ॥

sugandhi sundara prasāda——mādhuryera sāra
dui bhāi tāhā khāñā santoṣa apāra

SYNONYMS

su-gandhi—fragrant; *sundara*—beautiful; *prasāda*—food; *mādhuryera sāra*—the essence of all sweetness; *dui bhāi*—the two brothers; *tāhā*—that; *khāñā*—eating; *santoṣa apāra*—very, very happy.

TRANSLATION

Aromatic and pleasing to see, the food was the essence of all sweetness. Thus the two brothers, Lord Caitanya Mahāprabhu and Lord Nityānanda Prabhu, ate it with great satisfaction.

TEXT 118

ভোজনে বসিতে রঘুনাথে কহে সর্বজন ।
পণ্ডিত কহে,—'ইঁহ পাছে করিবে ভোজন ॥' ১১৮ ॥

bhojane vasite raghunāthe kahe sarva-jana
paṇḍita kahe, —— iṅha pāche karibe bhojana'

SYNONYMS

bhojane—to eat; *vasite*—to sit down; *raghunāthe*—unto Raghunātha dāsa; *kahe*—requested; *sarva-jana*—everyone; *paṇḍita kahe*—Rāghava Paṇḍita said; *iṅha*—this; *pāche*—later; *karibe bhojana*—will take food.

TRANSLATION

All the devotees present requested Raghunātha dāsa to sit down and take prasāda, but Rāghava Paṇḍita told them, "He will take prasāda later."

TEXT 119

ভক্তগণ আকণ্ঠ ভরিয়া করিল ভোজন।
'হরি' ধ্বনি করি' উঠি' কৈলা আচমন ॥ ১১৯ ॥

bhakta-gaṇa ākaṇṭha bhariyā karila bhojana
'hari' dhvani kari' uṭhi' kailā ācamana

SYNONYMS

bhakta-gaṇa—all the devotees; *ākaṇṭha*—up to the neck; *bhariyā*—filling; *karila bhojana*—took *prasāda; hari dhvani*—chanting of the holy name of Hari; *kari'*—doing; *uṭhi'*—getting up; *kailā ācamana*—washed their mouths and hands.

TRANSLATION

All the devotees took prasāda, filling themselves to the brim. Thereafter, chanting the holy name of Hari, they stood up and washed their hands and mouths.

TEXT 120

ভোজন করি' দুই ভাই কৈলা আচমন।
রাঘব আনি' পরাইলা মাল্য-চন্দন ॥ ১২০ ॥

bhojana kari' dui bhāi kailā ācamana
rāghava āni' parāilā mālya-candana

SYNONYMS

bhojana kari'—after eating; *dui bhāi*—the two brothers; *kailā ācamana*—washed Their hands and mouths; *rāghava*—Rāghava Paṇḍita; *āni'*—bringing;

parāilā—decorated Them with; *mālya-candana*—flower garlands and sandalwood pulp.

TRANSLATION

After eating, the two brothers washed Their hands and mouths. Then Rāghava Paṇḍita brought flower garlands and sandalwood pulp and decorated Them.

TEXT 121

বিড়া খাওয়াইলা, কৈলা চরণ বন্দন।
ভক্তগণে দিলা বিড়া, মাল্য-চন্দন ॥ ১২১ ॥

biḍā khāoyāilā, kailā caraṇa vandana
bhakta-gaṇe dilā biḍā, mālya-candana

SYNONYMS

biḍā khāoyāilā—he offered betel nuts; *kailā caraṇa vandana*—prayed to the lotus feet; *bhakta-gaṇe*—unto the devotees; *dilā*—gave; *biḍā*—betel nuts; *mālya-candana*—garlands and sandalwood pulp.

TRANSLATION

Rāghava Paṇḍita offered Them betel nuts and worshiped Their lotus feet. He also distributed betel nuts, flower garlands and sandalwood pulp to the devotees.

TEXT 122

রাঘবের কৃপা রঘুনাথের উপরে।
দুই ভাইএর অবশিষ্ট পাত্র দিলা তাঁরে ॥ ১২২ ॥

rāghavera kṛpā raghunāthera upare
dui bhāiera avaśiṣṭa pātra dilā tāṅre

SYNONYMS

rāghavera—of Rāghava Paṇḍita; *kṛpā*—mercy; *raghunāthera upare*—unto Raghunātha dāsa; *dui bhāiera*—of the two brothers; *avaśiṣṭa*—of remnants of food; *pātra*—the dishes; *dilā tāṅre*—offered to him.

TRANSLATION

Rāghava Paṇḍita, being very merciful toward Raghunātha dāsa, offered him the dishes with the remnants of food left by the two brothers.

TEXT 123

**কহিলা,—"চৈতন্য গোসাঞি করিয়াছেন ভোজন।
তাঁর শেষ পাইলে, তোমার খণ্ডিল বন্ধন॥" ১২৩॥**

kahilā, —"caitanya gosāñi kariyāchena bhojana
tāṅra śeṣa pāile, tomāra khaṇḍila bandhana"

SYNONYMS

kahilā—he said; *caitanya gosāñi*—Lord Śrī Caitanya Mahāprabhu; *kariyāchena bhojana*—has eaten; *tāṅra śeṣa*—His remnants; *pāile*—if you take; *tomāra*—your; *khaṇḍila*—will cease; *bandhana*—bondage.

TRANSLATION

He said, "Lord Śrī Caitanya Mahāprabhu has eaten this food. If you take His remnants, you will be released from the bondage of your family."

TEXT 124

**ভক্ত-চিত্তে ভক্ত-গৃহে সদা অবস্থান।
কভু গুপ্ত, কভু ব্যক্ত, স্বতন্ত্র ভগবান্॥ ১২৪॥**

bhakta-citte bhakta-gṛhe sadā avasthāna
kabhu gupta, kabhu vyakta, svatantra bhagavān

SYNONYMS

bhakta-citte—in the heart of a devotee; *bhakta-gṛhe*—at the house of a devotee; *sadā avasthāna*—always resides; *kabhu gupta*—sometimes hidden; *kabhu vyakta*—sometimes manifest; *svatantra*—fully independent; *bhagavān*—the Supreme Personality of Godhead.

TRANSLATION

The Supreme Personality of Godhead always resides either in the heart or in the home of a devotee. This fact is sometimes hidden and sometimes manifest, for the Supreme Personality of Godhead is fully independent.

TEXT 125

**সর্বত্র 'ব্যাপক' প্রভুর সদা সর্বত্র বাস।
ইহাতে সংশয় যার, সেই যায় নাশ॥ ১২৫॥**

sarvatra 'vyāpaka' prabhura sadā sarvatra vāsa
ihāte saṁśaya yāra, sei yāya nāśa

SYNONYMS

sarvatra—everywhere; *vyāpaka*—pervading; *prabhura*—of the Supreme Personality of Godhead; *sadā*—always; *sarvatra*—everywhere; *vāsa*—residence; *ihāte*—about this; *saṁśaya*—doubt; *yāra*—of whom; *sei*—he; *yāya nāśa*—becomes annihilated.

TRANSLATION

The Supreme Personality of Godhead is all-pervasive, and therefore He resides everywhere. Anyone who doubts this will be annihilated.

TEXT 126

প্রাতে নিত্যানন্দ প্রভু গঙ্গাস্নান করিয়া ।
সেই বৃক্ষমূলে বসিলা নিজগণ লঞা ॥ ১২৬ ॥

prāte nityānanda prabhu gaṅgā-snāna kariyā
sei vṛkṣa-mūle vasilā nija-gaṇa lañā

SYNONYMS

prāte—in the morning; *nityānanda prabhu*—Lord Nityānanda Prabhu; *gaṅgā-snāna*—bathing in the Ganges; *kariyā*—after doing; *sei vṛkṣa-mūle*—under that tree; *vasilā*—sat down; *nija-gaṇa lañā*—with His associates.

TRANSLATION

In the morning, after taking His bath in the Ganges, Nityānanda Prabhu sat down with His associates beneath the same tree under which He had previously sat.

TEXT 127

রঘুনাথ আসি' কৈলা চরণ বন্দন ।
রাঘবপণ্ডিত-দ্বারা কৈলা নিবেদন ॥ ১২৭ ॥

raghunātha āsi' kailā caraṇa vandana
rāghava-paṇḍita-dvārā kailā nivedana

SYNONYMS

raghunātha—Raghunātha dāsa; *āsi'*—coming; *kailā caraṇa vandana*—worshiped His lotus feet; *rāghava-paṇḍita-dvārā*—through Rāghava Paṇḍita; *kailā nivedana*—submitted his desire.

TRANSLATION

Raghunātha dāsa went there and worshiped Lord Nityānanda's lotus feet. Through Rāghava Paṇḍita, he submitted his desire.

TEXT 128

“অধম, পামর মুই হীন জীবাধম !
মোর ইচ্ছা হয়—পাঙ চৈতন্য-চরণ ॥ ১২৮ ॥

"adhama, pāmara mui hīna jīvādhama!
mora icchā haya——pāṅa caitanya-caraṇa

SYNONYMS

adhama—the most fallen; *pāmara*—the most sinful; *mui*—I; *hīna*—condemned; *jīva-adhama*—the lowest of all living beings; *mora*—my; *icchā*—desire; *haya*—is; *pāṅa*—I can get; *caitanya-caraṇa*—the shelter of the lotus feet of Śrī Caitanya Mahāprabhu.

TRANSLATION

"I am the lowest of men, the most sinful, fallen and condemned. Nevertheless, I desire to attain the shelter of Śrī Caitanya Mahāprabhu.

TEXT 129

বামন হঞা যেন চান্দ ধরিবারে চায়।
অনেক যত্ন কৈনু, তাতে কভু সিদ্ধ নয় ॥ ১২৯ ॥

vāmana hañā yena cānda dharibāre cāya
aneka yatna kainu, tāte kabhu siddha naya

SYNONYMS

vāmana hañā—being a dwarf; *yena*—as if; *cānda*—the moon; *dharibāre*—to catch; *cāya*—wants; *aneka yatna*—many attempts; *kainu*—I have made; *tāte*—in that; *kabhu siddha naya*—I have not been successful.

TRANSLATION

"Like a dwarf who wants to catch the moon, I have tried my best many times, but I have never been successful.

TEXT 130

যতবার পলাই আমি গৃহাদি ছাড়িয়া।
পিতা, মাতা—দুই মোরে রাখয়ে বান্ধিয়া॥ ১৩০॥

yata-bāra palāi āmi gṛhādi chāḍiyā
pitā, mātā——dui more rākhaye bāndhiyā

SYNONYMS

yata-bāra—as many times; *palāi*—go away; *āmi*—I; *gṛha-ādi chāḍiyā*—giving up my relationship with home; *pitā mātā*—father and mother; *dui*—both of them; *more*—me; *rākhaye bāndhiyā*—keep bound.

TRANSLATION

"Every time I tried to go away and give up my home relationships, my father and mother unfortunately kept me bound.

TEXT 131

তোমার কৃপা বিনা কেহ 'চৈতন্য' না পায়।
তুমি কৃপা কৈলে তাঁরে অধমেহ পায়॥ ১৩১॥

tomāra kṛpā vinā keha 'caitanya' nā pāya
tumi kṛpā kaile tāṅre adhameha pāya

SYNONYMS

tomāra kṛpā—Your mercy; *vinā*—without; *keha*—anyone; *caitanya*—Lord Śrī Caitanya Mahāprabhu; *nā pāya*—cannot get; *tumi kṛpā kaile*—if You are merciful; *tāṅre*—Him; *adhameha*—even the fallen soul; *pāya*—can get.

TRANSLATION

"No one can attain the shelter of Śrī Caitanya Mahāprabhu without Your mercy, but if You are merciful, even the lowest of men can attain shelter at His lotus feet.

TEXT 132

অযোগ্য মুই নিবেদন করিতে করি ভয়।
মোরে 'চৈতন্য' দেহ' গোসাঞি হঞা সদয় ॥ ১৩২ ॥

ayogya mui nivedana karite kari bhaya
more 'caitanya' deha' gosāñi hañā sadaya

SYNONYMS

ayogya—unfit; *mui*—I; *nivedana karite*—to submit my desires; *kari bhaya*—I am afraid; *more*—unto me; *caitanya deha'*—kindly give the shelter of Lord Śrī Caitanya Mahāprabhu; *gosāñi*—O my Lord; *hañā sa-daya*—being merciful.

TRANSLATION

"Although I am unfit and greatly afraid to submit this plea, I nevertheless request You, sir, to be especially merciful toward me by granting me shelter at the lotus feet of Śrī Caitanya Mahāprabhu.

TEXT 133

মোর মাথে পদ ধরি' করহ প্রসাদ।
'নির্বিঘ্নে চৈতন্য পাঙ—কর আশীর্বাদ ॥" ১৩৩ ॥

mora māthe pada dhari' karaha prasāda
nirvighne caitanya pāṅa——kara āśīrvāda"

SYNONYMS

mora māthe—upon my head; *pada dhari'*—keeping Your feet; *karaha prasāda*—bless me; *nirvighne*—without difficulty; *caitanya pāṅa*—I may get the shelter of Śrī Caitanya Mahāprabhu; *kara āśīrvāda*—give this benediction.

TRANSLATION

"Placing Your feet on my head, give me the benediction that I may achieve the shelter of Śrī Caitanya Mahāprabhu without difficulty. I pray for this benediction."

TEXT 134

শুনি' হাসি' কহে প্রভু সব ভক্তগণে।
"ইহার বিষয়সুখ—ইন্দ্রসুখ-সমে ॥ ১৩৪ ॥

śuni' hāsi' kahe prabhu saba bhakta-gaṇe
"ihāra viṣaya-sukha——indra-sukha-sama

SYNONYMS

śuni'—hearing; *hāsi'*—smiling; *kahe*—says; *prabhu*—Lord Nityānanda Prabhu; *saba bhakta-gaṇe*—unto all the devotees; *ihāra*—of Raghunātha dāsa; *viṣaya-sukha*—material happiness; *indra-sukha*—the material happiness of the King of heaven, Indra; *sama*—equal to.

TRANSLATION

After hearing this appeal by Raghunātha dāsa, Lord Nityānanda Prabhu smiled and told all the devotees, "Raghunātha dāsa's standard of material happiness is equal to that of Indra, the King of heaven.

TEXT 135

চৈতন্য-কৃপাতে সেহ নাহি ভায় মনে।
সবে আশীর্বাদ কর—পাউক চৈতন্য-চরণে ॥ ১৩৫ ॥

caitanya-kṛpāte seha nāhi bhāya mane
sabe āśīrvāda kara——pāuka caitanya-caraṇe

SYNONYMS

caitanya-kṛpāte—by the mercy of Lord Śrī Caitanya Mahāprabhu; *seha*—such a standard of material happiness; *nāhi bhāya*—he does not take as valuable; *mane*—at mind; *sabe*—all of you; *āśīrvāda kara*—give the benediction; *pāuka*—let him get; *caitanya-caraṇe*—the shelter of the lotus feet of Śrī Caitanya Mahāprabhu.

TRANSLATION

"Because of the mercy bestowed upon him by Śrī Caitanya Mahāprabhu, Raghunātha dāsa, although situated in such material happiness, does not like it at all. Therefore let every one of you be merciful toward him and give him the benediction that he may very soon attain shelter at the lotus feet of Śrī Caitanya Mahāprabhu.

TEXT 136

কৃষ্ণপাদপদ্ম-গন্ধ যেই জন পায়।
ব্রহ্মলোক-আদি-সুখ তাঁরে নাহি ভায় ॥"১৩৬ ॥

kṛṣṇa-pāda-padma-gandha yei jana pāya
brahmaloka-ādi-sukha tāṅre nāhi bhāya"

SYNONYMS

kṛṣṇa—of Lord Kṛṣṇa; *pāda-padma*—of the lotus feet; *gandha*—the fragrance; *yei jana*—anyone who; *pāya*—gets; *brahma-loka*—of Brahmaloka; *ādi*—and so on; *sukha*—happiness; *tāṅre*—to him; *nāhi bhāya*—does not appear valuable.

TRANSLATION

"One who experiences the fragrance of the lotus feet of Lord Kṛṣṇa does not even value the standard of happiness available in Brahmaloka, the topmost planet. And what to speak of heavenly happiness?

TEXT 137

যো দুস্ত্যজান্ দারসুতান্ সুহৃদ্রাজ্যং হৃদিস্পৃশঃ ।
জহৌ যুবৈব মলবদুত্তম-শ্লোকলালসঃ ॥ ১৩৭ ॥

yo dustyajān dāra-sutān
suhṛd-rājyaṁ hṛdi-spṛśaḥ
jahau yuvaiva malavad
uttama-śloka-lālasaḥ

SYNONYMS

yaḥ—who (Bharata Mahārāja); *dustyajān*—difficult to give up; *dāra-sutān*—wife and children; *suhṛt*—friends; *rājyam*—kingdom; *hṛdi-spṛśaḥ*—dear to the core of the heart; *jahau*—gave up; *yuvā*—youth; *eva*—at that time; *malavat*—like stool; *uttama-śloka-lālasaḥ*—being captivated by the transcendental qualities, pastimes and association of the Supreme Personality of Godhead.

TRANSLATION

" 'Lord Kṛṣṇa, the Supreme Personality of Godhead, is offered sublime, poetic prayers by those trying to attain His favor. Thus He is known as Uttamaśloka. Being very eager to gain the association of Lord Kṛṣṇa, King Bharata, although in the prime of youth, gave up his very attractive wife, affectionate children, most beloved friends and opulent kingdom, exactly as one gives up stool after excreting it.' "

PURPORT

This verse is from *Śrīmad-Bhāgavatam* (5.14.43).

TEXT 138

তবে রঘুনাথে প্রভু নিকটে বোলাইলা ।
তাঁর মাথে পদ ধরি' কহিতে লাগিলা ॥ ১৩৮ ॥

tabe raghunāthe prabhu nikaṭe bolāilā
tāṅra māthe pada dhari' kahite lāgilā

SYNONYMS

tabe—then; *raghunāthe*—Raghunātha dāsa; *prabhu*—Lord Nityānanda Prabhu; *nikaṭe bolāilā*—called nearby; *tāṅra māthe*—on his head; *pada dhari'*—keeping His feet; *kahite lāgilā*—began to speak.

TRANSLATION

Then Lord Nityānanda Prabhu called Raghunātha dāsa near Him, placed His lotus feet upon Raghunātha dāsa's head and began to speak.

TEXT 139

"তুমি যে করাইলা এই পুলিন-ভোজন ।
তোমায় কৃপা করি' গৌর কৈলা আগমন ॥ ১৩৯ ॥

"tumi ye karāilā ei pulina-bhojana
tomāya kṛpā kari' gaura kailā āgamana

SYNONYMS

tumi—you; *ye*—that; *karāilā*—caused to do; *ei*—this; *pulina-bhojana*—picnic on the bank of the Ganges; *tomāya*—unto you; *kṛpā kari'*—being merciful; *gaura*—Lord Śrī Caitanya Mahāprabhu; *kailā āgamana*—came.

TRANSLATION

"My dear Raghunātha dāsa," He said, "since you arranged the feast on the bank of the Ganges, Śrī Caitanya Mahāprabhu came here just to show you His mercy.

TEXT 140

কৃপা করি' কৈলা চিড়া-দুগ্ধ ভোজন ।
নৃত্য দেখি' রাত্র্যে কৈলা প্রসাদ ভক্ষণ ॥ ১৪০ ॥

kṛpā kari' kailā ciḍā-dugdha bhojana
nṛtya dekhi' rātrye kailā prasāda bhakṣaṇa

SYNONYMS

kṛpā kari'—by His causeless mercy; *kailā*—did; *ciḍā-dugdha bhojana*—eating of the chipped rice and milk; *nṛtya dekhi'*—after seeing the dancing; *rātrye*—at night; *kailā prasāda bhakṣaṇa*—ate the *prasāda.*

TRANSLATION

"By His causeless mercy He ate the chipped rice and milk. Then, after seeing the dancing of the devotees at night, He took His supper.

TEXT 141

তোমা উদ্ধারিতে গৌর আইলা আপনে ।
ছুটিল তোমার যত বিঘ্নাদি-বন্ধনে ॥ ১৪১ ॥

tomā uddhārite gaura āilā āpane
chuṭila tomāra yata vighnādi-bandhane

SYNONYMS

tomā—you; *uddhārite*—to deliver; *gaura*—Lord Śrī Caitanya Mahāprabhu, Gaurahari; *āilā āpane*—came personally; *chuṭila*—have gone; *tomāra*—your; *yata*—all kinds of; *vighna-ādi-bandhane*—impediments for bondage.

TRANSLATION

"Lord Śrī Caitanya Mahāprabhu, Gaurahari, came here personally to deliver you. Now rest assured that all the impediments meant for your bondage are gone.

TEXT 142

স্বরূপের স্থানে তোমা করিবে সমর্পণে ।
'অন্তরঙ্গ' ভৃত্য বলি' রাখিবে চরণে ॥ ১৪২ ॥

svarūpera sthāne tomā karibe samarpaṇe
'antaraṅga' bhṛtya bali' rākhibe caraṇe

SYNONYMS

svarūpera sthāne—unto Svarūpa Dāmodara; *tomā*—you; *karibe samarpaṇe*—He will give; *antaraṅga*—very confidential; *bhṛtya*—servant; *bali'*—as; *rākhibe caraṇe*—will keep under His lotus feet.

TRANSLATION

"Śrī Caitanya Mahāprabhu will accept you and place you under the charge of His secretary, Svarūpa Dāmodara. You will thus become one of the most confidential internal servants and will attain the shelter of Śrī Caitanya Mahāprabhu.

TEXT 143

নিশ্চিন্ত হঞা যাহ আপন-ভবন ।
অচিরে নির্বিঘ্নে পাবে চৈতন্য-চরণ ॥" ১৪৩ ॥

niścinta hañā yāha āpana-bhavana
acire nirvighne pābe caitanya-caraṇa"

SYNONYMS

niścinta—without anxiety; *hañā*—being; *yāha*—go; *āpana-bhavana*—to your own place; *acire*—very soon; *nirvighne*—without impediments; *pābe*—you will get; *caitanya-caraṇa*—the shelter of Lord Śrī Caitanya Mahāprabhu.

TRANSLATION

"Being assured of all this, return to your own home. Very soon, without impediments, you will attain the shelter of Lord Śrī Caitanya Mahāprabhu."

TEXT 144

সব ভক্তদ্বারে তাঁরে আশীর্বাদ করাইলা ।
তাঁ-সবার চরণ রঘুনাথ বন্দিলা ॥ ১৪৪ ॥

saba bhakta-dvāre tāṅre āśīrvāda karāilā
tāṅ-sabāra caraṇa raghunātha vandilā

SYNONYMS

saba—all; *bhakta-dvāre*—by the devotees; *tāṅre āśīrvāda karāilā*—had him blessed; *tāṅ-sabāra*—of all of them; *caraṇa*—the lotus feet; *raghunātha*—Raghunātha dāsa; *vandilā*—worshiped.

TRANSLATION

Lord Nityānanda had Raghunātha dāsa blessed by all the devotees, and Raghunātha dāsa offered his respects to their lotus feet.

TEXT 145

প্রভু-আজ্ঞা লঞা বৈষ্ণবের আজ্ঞা লইলা।
রাঘব-সহিতে নিভৃতে যুক্তি করিলা॥ ১৪৫॥

prabhu-ājñā lañā vaiṣṇavera ājñā la-ilā
rāghava-sahite nibhṛte yukti karilā

SYNONYMS

prabhu-ājñā—the order of Lord Nityānanda Prabhu; *lañā*—taking; *vaiṣṇavera ājñā*—the permission of all the Vaiṣṇavas; *la-ilā*—he took; *rāghava-sahite*—with Rāghava Paṇḍita; *nibhṛte*—in a solitary place; *yukti karilā*—he consulted.

TRANSLATION

After taking leave of Lord Nityānanda Prabhu and then all the other Vaiṣṇavas, Śrī Raghunātha dāsa consulted secretly with Rāghava Paṇḍita.

TEXT 146

যুক্তি করি' শত মুদ্রা, সোণা তোলা-সাতে।
নিভৃতে দিলা প্রভুর ভাণ্ডারীর হাতে॥ ১৪৬॥

yukti kari' śata mudrā, soṇā tolā-sāte
nibhṛte dilā prabhura bhāṇḍārīra hāte

SYNONYMS

yukti kari'—after consultation; *śata mudrā*—one hundred coins; *soṇā*—in gold pieces; *tolā-sāte*—about seven *tolās* (about two and a half ounces); *nibhṛte*—secretly; *dilā*—delivered; *prabhura*—of Lord Nityānanda Prabhu; *bhāṇḍārīra*—of the treasurer; *hāte*—into the hand.

TRANSLATION

After consulting with Rāghava Paṇḍita, he secretly delivered one hundred gold coins and about seven tolās of gold to the hand of Nityānanda Prabhu's treasurer.

TEXT 147

তাঁরে নিষেধিলা,—"প্রভুরে এবে না কহিবা।
নিজ-ঘরে যাবেন যবে তবে নিবেদিবা॥" ১৪৭॥

tāṅre niṣedhilā, —"prabhure ebe nā kahibā
nija-ghare yābena yabe tabe nivedibā"

SYNONYMS

tāṅre—him; *niṣedhilā*—he forbade; *prabhure*—unto Lord Nityānanda Prabhu; *ebe*—now; *nā kahibā*—do not speak; *nija-ghare*—to His home; *yābena*—will return; *yabe*—when; *tabe*—then; *nivedibā*—kindly inform Him.

TRANSLATION

Raghunātha dāsa admonished the treasurer, "Do not speak about this to Lord Nityānanda Prabhu now, but when He returns home, kindly inform Him about this presentation."

TEXT 148

তবে রাঘব-পণ্ডিত তাঁরে ঘরে লঞা গেলা ।
ঠাকুর দর্শন করাঞা মালা-চন্দন দিলা ॥ ১৪৮ ॥

tabe rāghava-paṇḍita tāṅre ghare lañā gelā
ṭhākura darśana karāñā mālā-candana dilā

SYNONYMS

tabe—thereupon; *rāghava-paṇḍita*—Rāghava Paṇḍita; *tāṅre*—him; *ghare lañā gelā*—took to his home; *ṭhākura darśana karāñā*—after inducing him to see the Deity; *mālā-candana*—a garland and sandalwood pulp; *dilā*—delivered.

TRANSLATION

Thereupon, Rāghava Paṇḍita took Raghunātha dāsa to his home. After inducing him to see the Deity, he gave Raghunātha dāsa a garland and sandalwood pulp.

TEXT 149

অনেক 'প্রসাদ' দিলা পথে খাইবারে ।
তবে পুনঃ রঘুনাথ কহে পণ্ডিতেরে ॥ ১৪৯ ॥

aneka 'prasāda' dilā pathe khāibāre
tabe punaḥ raghunātha kahe paṇḍitere

SYNONYMS

aneka prasāda—much *prasāda; dilā*—delivered; *pathe khāibāre*—to eat on his way; *tabe*—then; *punaḥ*—again; *raghunātha kahe*—Raghunātha dāsa said; *paṇḍitere*—to Rāghava Paṇḍita.

TRANSLATION

He gave Raghunātha dāsa a large quantity of prasāda to eat on his way home. Then Raghunātha dāsa again spoke to Rāghava Paṇḍita.

TEXT 150

"প্রভুর সঙ্গে যত মহান্ত, ভৃত্য, আশ্রিত জন ।
পূজিতে চাহিয়ে আমি সবার চরণ ॥ ১৫০ ॥

"prabhura saṅge yata mahānta, bhṛtya, āśrita jana
pūjite cāhiye āmi sabāra caraṇa

SYNONYMS

prabhura saṅge—with Lord Nityānanda Prabhu; *yata*—all; *mahānta*—great devotees; *bhṛtya*—servants; *āśrita jana*—subservient people; *pūjite*—to worship; *cāhiye*—want; *āmi*—I; *sabāra caraṇa*—the lotus feet of all of them.

TRANSLATION

"I want to give money," he said, "just to worship the lotus feet of all the great devotees, servants and subservants of Lord Nityānanda Prabhu.

TEXT 151

বিশ, পঞ্চদশ, বার, দশ, পঞ্চ হয় ।
মুদ্রা দেহ' বিচারি' যার যত যোগ্য হয় ॥ ১৫১ ॥

biśa, pañca-daśa, bāra, daśa, pañca haya
mudrā deha' vicāri' yāra yata yogya haya

SYNONYMS

biśa—twenty; *pañca-daśa*—fifteen; *bāra*—twelve; *daśa*—ten; *pañca*—five; *haya*—are; *mudrā*—coins; *deha'*—give; *vicāri'*—considering; *yāra*—of whom; *yata*—as much; *yogya haya*—is fit.

TRANSLATION

"As you think fit, give twenty, fifteen, twelve, ten or five coins to each of them."

TEXT 152

সব লেখা করিয়া রাঘব-পাশ দিলা ।
যাঁর নামে যত রাঘব চিঠি লেখাইলা ॥ ১৫২ ॥

saba lekhā kariyā rāghava-pāśa dilā
yāṅra nāme yata rāghava ciṭhi lekhāilā

SYNONYMS

saba—all; *lekhā kariyā*—writing; *rāghava-pāśa dilā*—delivered to Rāghava Paṇḍita; *yāṅra nāme*—in whose name; *yata*—as much; *rāghava*—Rāghava Paṇḍita; *ciṭhi*—a list; *lekhāilā*—had written.

TRANSLATION

Raghunātha dāsa drew up an account of the amount to be given and submitted it to Rāghava Paṇḍita, who then made up a list showing how much money was to be paid to each and every devotee.

TEXT 153

একশত মুদ্রা আর সোণা তোলা-দ্বয় ।
পণ্ডিতের আগে দিল করিয়া বিনয় ॥ ১৫৩ ॥

eka-śata mudrā āra soṇā tolā-dvaya
paṇḍitera āge dila kariyā vinaya

SYNONYMS

eka-śata mudrā—one hundred coins; *āra*—and; *soṇā*—gold; *tolā-dvaya*—two *tolās; paṇḍitera āge*—before Rāghava Paṇḍita; *dila*—presented; *kariyā vinaya*—with great humility.

TRANSLATION

With great humility, Raghunātha dāsa placed one hundred gold coins and about two tolās of gold before Rāghava Paṇḍita for all the other devotees.

TEXT 154

তাঁর পদধূলি লঞা স্বগৃহে আইলা ।
নিত্যানন্দ-কৃপা পাঞা কৃতার্থ মানিলা ॥ ১৫৪ ॥

tāṅra pada-dhūli lañā svagṛhe āilā
nityānanda-kṛpā pāñā kṛtārtha mānilā

SYNONYMS

tāṅra—his; *pada-dhūli*—the dust of the feet; *lañā*—taking; *sva-gṛhe āilā*—returned to his home; *nityānanda-kṛpā*—the mercy of Lord Nityānanda Prabhu; *pāñā*—getting; *kṛtārtha mānilā*—he felt greatly obligated.

TRANSLATION

After taking dust from the feet of Rāghava Paṇḍita, Raghunātha dāsa returned to his home, feeling greatly obligated to Lord Nityānanda Prabhu because of having received His merciful benediction.

TEXT 155

সেই হৈতে অভ্যন্তরে না করেন গমন ।
বাহিরে দুর্গামণ্ডপে যাঞা করেন শয়ন ॥ ১৫৫ ॥

sei haite abhyantare nā karena gamana
bāhire durgā-maṇḍape yāñā karena śayana

SYNONYMS

sei haite—from that day; *abhyantare*—in the interior rooms; *nā karena gamana*—did not go; *bāhire*—outside; *durgā-maṇḍape*—to the place where Durgā worship was performed; *yāñā*—going; *karena śayana*—he sleeps.

TRANSLATION

From that day on, he did not go into the interior section of the house. Instead, he would sleep on the Durgā-maṇḍapa [the place where mother Durgā was worshiped].

TEXT 156

তাঁহা জাগি' রহে সব রক্ষকগণ ।
পলাইতে করেন নানা উপায় চিন্তন ॥ ১৫৬ ॥

tāṅhā jāgi' rahe saba rakṣaka-gaṇa
palāite karena nānā upāya cintana

SYNONYMS

tāṅhā—there; *jāgi'*—keeping awake; *rahe*—stay; *saba*—all; *rakṣaka-gaṇa*—the watchmen; *palāite*—to go away; *karena*—does; *nānā*—various; *upāya*—means; *cintana*—thinking of.

TRANSLATION

There, however, the watchmen alertly kept guard. Raghunātha dāsa was thinking of various means by which to escape their vigilance.

TEXT 157

হেনকালে গৌড়দেশের সব ভক্তগণ ।
প্রভুরে দেখিতে নীলাচলে করিলা গমন ॥ ১৫৭ ॥

hena-kāle gauḍa-deśera saba bhakta-gaṇa
prabhure dekhite nīlācale karilā gamana

SYNONYMS

hena-kāle—at this time; *gauḍa-deśera*—of Bengal; *saba*—all; *bhakta-gaṇa*—devotees; *prabhure*—Lord Śrī Caitanya Mahāprabhu; *dekhite*—to see; *nīlācale*—to Jagannātha Purī; *karilā gamana*—went.

TRANSLATION

At that time, all the devotees of Bengal were going to Jagannātha Purī to see Lord Caitanya Mahāprabhu.

TEXT 158

তাঁ-সবার সঙ্গে রঘুনাথ যাইতে না পারে ।
প্রসিদ্ধ প্রকট সঙ্গ, তবহিঁ ধরা পড়ে ॥ ১৫৮ ॥

tāṅ-sabāra saṅge raghunātha yāite nā pāre
prasiddha prakaṭa saṅga, tabahiṅ dharā paḍe

SYNONYMS

tāṅ-sabāra—all of them; *saṅge*—with; *raghunātha*—Raghunātha dāsa; *yāite nā pāre*—could not go; *prasiddha*—famous; *prakaṭa*—known; *saṅga*—group; *tabahiṅ*—immediately; *dharā paḍe*—he would be caught.

TRANSLATION

Raghunātha dāsa could not accompany them, for they were so famous that he would immediately have been caught.

TEXTS 159-160

এইমত চিন্তিতে দৈবে একদিনে ।
বাহিরে দেবীমণ্ডপে করিয়াছেন শয়নে ॥ ১৫৯ ॥
দণ্ড-চারি রাত্রি যবে আছে অবশেষ ।
যদুনন্দন-আচার্য তবে করিলা প্রবেশ ॥ ১৬০ ॥

ei-mata cintite daive eka-dine
bāhire devī-maṇḍape kariyāchena śayane

daṇḍa-cāri rātri yabe āche avaśeṣa
yadunandana-ācārya tabe karilā praveśa

SYNONYMS

ei-mata—in this way; *cintite*—while he was thinking; *daive*—by chance; *eka-dine*—one day; *bāhire*—outside the house; *devī-maṇḍape*—on the Durgā platform; *kariyāchena śayane*—was sleeping; *daṇḍa-cāri*—four *daṇḍas* (ninety-six minutes); *rātri*—night; *yabe*—when; *āche avaśeṣa*—there remained; *yadunandana-ācārya*—the priest of the name Yadunandana Ācārya; *tabe*—then; *karilā praveśa*—entered.

TRANSLATION

Thus Raghunātha dāsa thought deeply about how to escape, and one night while he was sleeping on the Durgā-maṇḍapa, the priest Yadunandana Ācārya entered the house when only four daṇḍas remained until the end of the night.

TEXT 161

বাসুদেব-দত্তের তেঁহ হয় 'অনুগৃহীত' ।
রঘুনাথের 'গুরু' তেঁহো হয় 'পুরোহিত' ॥ ১৬১ ॥

vāsudeva-dattera teṅha haya 'anugṛhīta'
raghunāthera 'guru' teṅho haya 'purohita'

SYNONYMS

vāsudeva-dattera—of Vāsudeva Datta; *teṅha*—he; *haya anugṛhīta*—was given the mercy; *raghunāthera*—of Raghunātha dāsa; *guru*—the spiritual master; *teṅho*—he; *haya*—was; *purohita*—the priest.

TRANSLATION

Yadunandana Ācārya was the priest and spiritual master of Raghunātha dāsa. Although born in a brāhmaṇa family, he had accepted the mercy of Vāsudeva Datta.

PURPORT

Śrīla Bhaktisiddhānta Sarasvatī Ṭhākura comments that although the atheists who have deviated from the order of Śrī Advaita Ācārya introduce themselves as followers of Advaita Ācārya, they do not accept Śrī Caitanya Mahāprabhu as the Supreme Personality of Godhead, Kṛṣṇa. Yadunandana Ācārya, one of the most confidential followers of Śrī Caitanya Mahāprabhu, was the initiated disciple of Advaita Ācārya. He was not polluted by sentimental distinctions classifying Vaiṣṇavas according to birth. Therefore although Vāsudeva Datta had not been born in a *brāhmaṇa* family, Yadunandana Ācārya accepted Vāsudeva Datta as his spiritual master.

TEXT 162

অদ্বৈত-আচার্যের তেঁহ 'শিষ্য অন্তরঙ্গ'।
আচার্য-আজ্ঞাতে মানে—চৈতন্য 'প্রাণধন' ॥ ১৬২ ॥

advaita-ācāryera teṅha 'śiṣya antaraṅga'
ācārya-ājñāte māne——caitanya 'prāṇa-dhana'

SYNONYMS

advaita-ācāryera—of Advaita Ācārya; *teṅha*—Yadunandana Ācārya; *śiṣya*—disciple; *antaraṅga*—very confidential; *ācārya-ājñāte*—by the order of Advaita Ācārya; *māne*—he accepted; *caitanya prāṇa-dhana*—Lord Śrī Caitanya Mahāprabhu as his life and soul.

TRANSLATION

Yadunandana Ācārya had been officially initiated by Advaita Ācārya. Thus he considered Lord Caitanya his life and soul.

TEXT 163

অঙ্গনে আসিয়া তেঁহো যবে দাণ্ডাইলা।
রঘুনাথ আসি' তবে দণ্ডবৎ কৈলা ॥ ১৬৩ ॥

aṅgane āsiyā teṅho yabe dāṇḍāilā
raghunātha āsi' tabe daṇḍavat kailā

SYNONYMS

aṅgane—in the courtyard; *āsiyā*—entering; *teṅho*—Yadunandana Ācārya; *yabe*—when; *dāṇḍāilā*—stood up; *raghunātha*—Raghunātha dāsa; *āsi'*—coming; *tabe*—at that time; *daṇḍavat kailā*—offered his respects, falling down.

TRANSLATION

When Yadunandana Ācārya entered the house of Raghunātha dāsa and stood in the courtyard, Raghunātha dāsa went there and fell down to offer his obeisances.

TEXT 164

তাঁর এক শিষ্য তাঁর ঠাকুরের সেবা করে।
সেবা ছাড়িয়াছে, তারে সাধিবার তরে ॥ ১৬৪ ॥

tāṅra eka śiṣya tāṅra ṭhākurera sevā kare
sevā chāḍiyāche, tāre sādhibāra tare

SYNONYMS

tāṅra—his; *eka*—one; *śiṣya*—disciple; *tāṅra*—his; *ṭhākurera*—of the Deity; *sevā*—service; *kare*—does; *sevā chāḍiyāche*—he has left that service; *tāre*—him; *sādhibāra tare*—to induce.

TRANSLATION

One of Yadunandana Ācārya's disciples had been worshiping the Deity but had left that service. Yadunandana Ācārya wanted Raghunātha dāsa to induce the disciple to take up that service again.

TEXT 165

রঘুনাথে কহে,—"তারে করহ সাধন।
সেবা যেন করে, আর নাহিক ব্রাহ্মণ ॥" ১৬৫ ॥

raghunāthe kahe, —"tāre karaha sādhana
sevā yena kare, āra nāhika brāhmaṇa"

SYNONYMS

raghunāthe kahe—he said to Raghunātha dāsa; *tāre*—him; *karaha sādhana*—induce to accept the service; *sevā*—service; *yena*—that; *kare*—he does; *āra*—other; *nāhika*—there is no; *brāhmaṇa*—*brāhmaṇa.*

TRANSLATION

Yadunandana Ācārya requested Raghunātha dāsa, "Please induce the brāhmaṇa to resume the service, for there is no other brāhmaṇa to do it."

TEXT 166

এত কহি' রঘুনাথে লঞা চলিলা।
রক্ষক সব শেষরাত্রে নিদ্রায় পড়িলা ॥ ১৬৬ ॥

eta kahi' raghunāthe lañā calilā
rakṣaka saba śeṣa-rātre nidrāya paḍilā

SYNONYMS

eta kahi'—saying this; *raghunāthe lañā*—taking Raghunātha dāsa; *calilā*—he went out; *rakṣaka saba*—all the watchmen; *śeṣa-rātre*—at the end of night; *nidrāya paḍilā*—fell asleep.

TRANSLATION

After saying this, Yadunandana Ācārya took Raghunātha dāsa with him and went out. By that time all the watchmen were deeply asleep because it was the end of the night.

TEXT 167

আচার্যের ঘর ইহার পূর্বদিশাতে।
কহিতে শুনিতে দুঁহে চলে সেই পথে॥ ১৬৭॥

ācāryera ghara ihāra pūrva-diśāte
kahite śunite duṅhe cale sei pathe

SYNONYMS

ācāryera ghara—the house of Yadunandana Ācārya; *ihāra*—of this; *pūrva-diśāte*—to the east; *kahite*—talking; *śunite*—listening; *duṅhe*—both of them; *cale*—go; *sei pathe*—on that path.

TRANSLATION

East of the house of Raghunātha dāsa was the house of Yadunandana Ācārya. Yadunandana Ācārya and Raghunātha dāsa talked together as they went toward that house.

TEXT 168

অর্ধপথে রঘুনাথ কহে গুরুর চরণে।
"আমি সেই বিপ্রে সাধি' পাঠাইমু তোমা স্থানে॥

ardha-pathe raghunātha kahe gurura caraṇe
"āmi sei vipre sādhi' pāṭhāimu tomā sthāne

SYNONYMS

ardha-pathe—halfway along the path; *raghunātha kahe*—Raghunātha dāsa said; *gurura caraṇe*—unto the lotus feet of his spiritual master; *āmi*—I; *sei*—that; *vipre*—*brāhmaṇa; sādhi'*—inducing; *pāṭhāimu*—shall send; *tomā sthāne*—to your place.

TRANSLATION

Halfway along the path, Raghunātha dāsa submitted at the lotus feet of his spiritual master, "I shall go to the home of that brāhmaṇa, induce him to return, and send him to your home.

TEXT 169

তুমি সুখে ঘরে যাহ—মোরে আজ্ঞা হয়" ।
এই ছলে আজ্ঞা মাগি' করিলা নিশ্চয় ॥ ১৬৯ ॥

tumi sukhe ghare yāha——more ājñā haya"
ei chale ājñā māgi' karilā niścaya

SYNONYMS

tumi—you; *sukhe*—in happiness; *ghare yāha*—go to your place; *more*—to me; *ājñā*—order; *haya*—is; *ei chale*—on this plea; *ājñā māgi'*—asking permission; *karilā niścaya*—decided.

TRANSLATION

"You may go home without anxiety. Following your order, I shall persuade the brāhmaṇa." On this plea, after asking permission, he decided to go away.

TEXT 170

"সেবক রক্ষক আর কেহ নাহি সঙ্গে ।
পলাইতে আমার ভাল এইত প্রসঙ্গে ॥" ১৭০ ॥

"sevaka rakṣaka āra keha nāhi saṅge
palāite āmāra bhāla eita prasaṅge

SYNONYMS

sevaka—servant; *rakṣaka*—watchman; *āra*—and; *keha nāhi*—there is no one; *saṅge*—along; *palāite*—to go away; *āmāra*—my; *bhāla*—good; *eita*—this; *prasaṅge*—opportunity.

TRANSLATION

Raghunātha dāsa thought, "This is the greatest opportunity to go away because this time there are no servants or watchmen with me."

TEXT 171

এত চিন্তি' পূর্বমুখে করিলা গমন।
উলটিয়া চাহে পাছে,—নাহি কোন জন ॥ ১৭১ ॥

eta cinti' pūrva-mukhe karilā gamana
ulaṭiyā cāhe pāche, ——nāhi kona jana

SYNONYMS

eta cinti'—thinking this; *pūrva-mukhe*—toward the east; *karilā gamana*—began to proceed; *ulaṭiyā*—turning around; *cāhe*—looks; *pāche*—behind; *nāhi kona jana*—there was no one.

TRANSLATION

Thinking in this way, he quickly proceeded toward the east. Sometimes he turned around and looked back, but no one was following him.

TEXT 172

শ্রীচৈতন্য-নিত্যানন্দ-চরণ চিন্তিয়া।
পথ ছাড়ি' উপপথে যায়েন ধাঞা ॥ ১৭২ ॥

śrī-caitanya-nityānanda-caraṇa cintiyā
patha chāḍi' upapathe yāyena dhāñā

SYNONYMS

śrī-caitanya—of Śrī Caitanya Mahāprabhu; *nityānanda*—of Lord Nityānanda Prabhu; *caraṇa*—the lotus feet; *cintiyā*—thinking of; *patha chāḍi'*—giving up the general pathway; *upapathe*—by the path not generally used; *yāyena dhāñā*—he went very swiftly.

TRANSLATION

Thinking of the lotus feet of Śrī Caitanya Mahāprabhu and Lord Nityānanda Prabhu, he left the general path and proceeded with great haste on the one not generally used.

TEXT 173

গ্রামে-গ্রামের পথ ছাড়ি' যায় বনে বনে।
কায়মনোবাক্যে চিন্তে চৈতন্য-চরণে ॥ ১৭৩ ॥

grāme-grāmera patha chāḍi' yāya vane vane
kāya-mano-vākye cinte caitanya-caraṇe

SYNONYMS

grāme-grāmera—from village to village; *patha*—the general path; *chāḍi'*—giving up; *yāya*—goes; *vane vane*—through the jungles; *kāya-manaḥ-vākye*—with body, mind and words; *cinte*—thinks; *caitanya caraṇe*—of the lotus feet of Śrī Caitanya Mahāprabhu.

TRANSLATION

Giving up the general path from village to village, he passed through the jungles, thinking with heart and soul about the lotus feet of Śrī Caitanya Mahāprabhu.

TEXT 174

পঞ্চদশ-ক্রোশ-পথ চলি' গেলা একদিনে।
সন্ধ্যাকালে রহিলা এক গোপের বাথানে॥ ১৭৪॥

pañca-daśa-krośa-patha cali' gelā eka-dine
sandhyā-kāle rahilā eka gopera bāthāne

SYNONYMS

pañca-daśa-krośa—about thirty miles; *patha cali'*—walking on the path; *gelā*—went; *eka-dine*—in one day; *sandhyā-kāle*—in the evening; *rahilā*—remained; *eka gopera*—of a milkman; *bāthāne*—in the cowshed.

TRANSLATION

He walked about thirty miles in one day, and in the evening he took rest in the cowshed of a milkman.

TEXT 175

উপবাসী দেখি' গোপ দুগ্ধ আনি' দিলা।
সেই দুগ্ধ পান করি' পড়িয়া রহিলা॥ ১৭৫॥

upavāsī dekhi' gopa dugdha āni' dilā
sei dugdha pāna kari' paḍiyā rahilā

SYNONYMS

upavāsī—fasting; *dekhi'*—seeing; *gopa*—the milkman; *dugdha*—milk; *āni'*—bringing; *dilā*—gave; *sei dugdha*—that milk; *pāna kari'*—drinking; *paḍiyā*—lying down; *rahilā*—he remained.

TRANSLATION

When the milkman saw that Raghunātha dāsa was fasting, he gave him some milk. Raghunātha dāsa drank the milk and lay down to rest there for the night.

TEXT 176

এথা তাঁর সেবক রক্ষক তাঁরে না দেখিয়া।
তাঁর গুরুপাশে বার্তা পুছিলেন গিয়া॥ ১৭৬॥

ethā tāṅra sevaka rakṣaka tāṅre nā dekhiyā
tāṅra guru-pāśe vārtā puchilena giyā

SYNONYMS

ethā—here, at his home; *tāṅra*—his; *sevaka*—servant; *rakṣaka*—watchman; *tāṅre*—him; *nā dekhiyā*—not seeing; *tāṅra guru-pāśe*—from his spiritual master; *vārtā*—news; *puchilena*—inquired; *giyā*—going.

TRANSLATION

At the house of Raghunātha dāsa, the servant and watchman, not seeing him there, immediately went to inquire about him from his spiritual master, Yadunandana Ācārya.

TEXT 177

তেঁহ কহে, 'আজ্ঞা মাগি' গেলা নিজ-ঘর।'
'পলাইল রঘুনাথ'—উঠিল কোলাহল॥ ১৭৭॥

teṅha kahe, 'ājñā māgi' gelā nija-ghara'
'palāila raghunātha'——uṭhila kolāhala

SYNONYMS

teṅha kahe—he said; *ājñā māgi'*—asking my permission; *gelā*—went; *nija ghara*—to his home; *palāila raghunātha*—Raghunātha dāsa has gone away; *uṭhila*—arose; *kolāhala*—a tumultuous sound.

TRANSLATION

Yadunandana Ācārya said, "He has already asked my permission and returned home." Thus there arose a tumultuous sound, as everyone cried, "Now Raghunātha has gone away!"

TEXT 178

তাঁর পিতা কহে,—"গৌড়ের সব ভক্তগণ ।
প্রভু-স্থানে নীলাচলে করিলা গমন ॥ ১৭৮ ॥

tāṅra pitā kahe, —"gauḍera saba bhakta-gaṇa
prabhu-sthāne nīlācale karilā gamana

SYNONYMS

tāṅra—his; *pitā*—father; *kahe*—said; *gauḍera*—of Bengal; *saba*—all; *bhakta-gaṇa*—the devotees; *prabhu-sthāne*—to the place of Śrī Caitanya Mahāprabhu; *nīlācale*—at Jagannātha Purī; *karilā gamana*—have gone.

TRANSLATION

Raghunātha dāsa's father said, "Now all the devotees from Bengal have gone to Jagannātha Purī to see Lord Śrī Caitanya Mahāprabhu.

TEXT 179

সেই-সঙ্গে রঘুনাথ গেল পলাঞা ।
দশ জন যাহ, তারে আনহ ধরিয়া ॥" ১৭৯ ॥

sei-saṅge raghunātha gela palāñā
daśa jana yāha, tāre ānaha dhariyā"

SYNONYMS

sei-saṅge—with them; *raghunātha*—Raghunātha dāsa; *gela palāñā*—has fled; *daśa jana*—ten men; *yāha*—go; *tāre*—him; *ānaha*—bring; *dhariyā*—catching.

TRANSLATION

"Raghunātha dāsa has fled with them. Ten men should immediately go catch him and bring him back."

TEXT 180

শিবানন্দে পত্রী দিল বিনয় করিয়া ।
'আমার পুত্রেরে তুমি দিবা বাহুড়িয়া' ॥ ১৮০ ॥

śivānande patrī dila vinaya kariyā
'āmāra putrere tumi dibā bāhuḍiyā'

SYNONYMS

śivānande—unto Śivānanda Sena; *patrī*—a letter; *dila*—sent; *vinaya kariyā*—with great humility; *āmāra putrere*—my son; *tumi*—you; *dibā*—please give; *bāhuḍiyā*—returning.

TRANSLATION

Raghunātha dāsa's father wrote a letter to Śivānanda Sena, asking him with great humility, "Please return my son."

TEXT 181

ঝাঁকরা পর্যন্ত গেল সেই দশ জনে ।
ঝাঁকরাতে পাইল গিয়া বৈষ্ণবের গণে ॥ ১৮১ ॥

jhāṅkarā paryanta gela sei daśa jane
jhāṅkarāte pāila giyā vaiṣṇavera gaṇe

SYNONYMS

jhāṅkarā paryanta—to the place known as Jhāṅkarā; *gela*—went; *sei daśa jane*—those ten men; *jhāṅkarāte*—at Jhāṅkarā; *pāila*—caught up to; *giyā*—going; *vaiṣṇavera gaṇe*—the group of Vaiṣṇavas.

TRANSLATION

In Jhāṅkarā, the ten men caught up with the group of Vaiṣṇavas going to Nīlācala.

TEXT 182

পত্রী দিয়া শিবানন্দে বার্তা পুছিল ।
শিবানন্দ কহে,—'তেঁহ এথা না আইল' ॥ ১৮২ ॥

patrī diyā śivānande vārtā puchila
śivānanda kahe, —'teṅha ethā nā āila'

SYNONYMS

patrī—letter; *diyā*—delivering; *śivānande*—unto Śivānanda Sena; *vārtā*—news; *puchila*—inquired; *śivānanda kahe*—Śivānanda said; *teṅha*—he; *ethā*—here; *nā āila*—did not come.

TRANSLATION

After delivering the letter, the men inquired from Śivānanda Sena about Raghunātha dāsa, but Śivānanda Sena replied, "He did not come here."

TEXT 183

বাহুড়িয়া সেই দশ জন আইল ঘর।
তাঁর মাতা-পিতা হইল চিন্তিত অন্তর ॥ ১৮৩ ॥

bāhuḍiyā sei daśa jana āila ghara
tāṅra mātā-pitā ha-ila cintita antara

SYNONYMS

bāhuḍiyā—returning; *sei*—those; *daśa jana*—ten men; *āila ghara*—came back home; *tāṅra*—his; *mātā-pitā*—mother and father; *ha-ila*—became; *cintita*—full of anxiety; *antara*—within themselves.

TRANSLATION

The ten men returned home, and Raghunātha dāsa's father and mother were filled with anxiety.

TEXT 184

এথা রঘুনাথ-দাস প্রভাতে উঠিয়া।
পূর্বমুখ ছাড়ি' চলে দক্ষিণ-মুখ হঞা ॥ ১৮৪ ॥

ethā raghunātha-dāsa prabhāte uṭhiyā
pūrva-mukha chāḍi' cale dakṣiṇa-mukha hañā

SYNONYMS

ethā—here; *raghunātha-dāsa*—Raghunātha dāsa; *prabhāte*—early in the morning; *uṭhiyā*—rising; *pūrva-mukha*—facing the east; *chāḍi'*—giving up; *cale*—began to proceed; *dakṣiṇa-mukha*—facing south; *hañā*—being.

TRANSLATION

Raghunātha dāsa, who had been resting at the milkman's house, got up early in the morning. Instead of going to the east, he turned his face south and proceeded.

TEXT 185

ছত্রভোগ পার হঞা ছাড়িয়া সরাণ।
কুগ্রাম দিয়া দিয়া করিল প্রয়াণ ॥ ১৮৫ ॥

chatrabhoga pāra hañā chāḍiyā sarāṇa
kugrāma diyā diyā karila prayāṇa

SYNONYMS

chatra-bhoga—the place named Chatrabhoga; *pāra hañā*—crossing; *chāḍiyā*—giving up; *sarāṇa*—the royal road; *kugrāma diyā diyā*—going through village pathways; *karila prayāṇa*—proceeded.

TRANSLATION

He crossed Chatrabhoga, but instead of going on the general path, he proceeded on the path that went from village to village.

PURPORT

Chatrabhoga, known now as Chāḍa-khāḍi, is in the district of twenty-four pargaṇās in West Bengal. It is situated near the celebrated village Jayanagara-majilapura. Formerly the Ganges or some of its branches flowed through this region. Sometimes Chatrabhoga is misunderstood to have been a village on the River Kāṅsāi-nadī in Benāpola.

TEXT 186

ভক্ষণ অপেক্ষা নাহি, সমস্ত দিবস গমন ।
ক্ষুধা নাহি বাধে, চৈতন্যচরণ-প্রাপ্ত্যে মন ॥ ১৮৬ ॥

bhakṣaṇa apekṣā nāhi, samasta divasa gamana
kṣudhā nāhi bādhe, caitanya-caraṇa-prāptye mana

SYNONYMS

bhakṣaṇa apekṣā nāhi—did not care for eating; *samasta divasa*—all day; *gamana*—traveling; *kṣudhā*—hunger; *nāhi bādhe*—did not become an impediment; *caitanya-caraṇa*—the lotus feet of Śrī Caitanya Mahāprabhu; *prāptye*—on obtaining; *mana*—mind.

TRANSLATION

Not caring about eating, he traveled all day. Hunger was not an impediment, for his mind was concentrated upon obtaining shelter at the lotus feet of Śrī Caitanya Mahāprabhu.

TEXT 187

কভু চর্বণ, কভু রন্ধন, কভু দুগ্ধপান ।
যবে যেই মিলে, তাহে রাখে নিজ প্রাণ ॥ ১৮৭ ॥

kabhu carvaṇa, kabhu randhana, kabhu dugdha-pāna
yabe yei mile, tāhe rākhe nija prāṇa

SYNONYMS

kabhu carvaṇa—sometimes chewing; *kabhu randhana*—sometimes cooking; *kabhu dugdha-pāna*—sometimes drinking milk; *yabe*—when; *yei*—whoever; *mile*—meets; *tāhe*—in that way; *rākhe*—keeps; *nija prāṇa*—his life.

TRANSLATION

Sometimes he chewed fried grains, sometimes he cooked, and sometimes he drank milk. In this way he kept his life and soul together with whatever was available wherever he went.

TEXT 188

বার দিনে চলি' গেলা শ্রীপুরুষোত্তম।
পথে তিনদিন মাত্র করিলা ভোজন ॥ ১৮৮ ॥

bāra dine cali' gelā śrī-puruṣottama
pathe tina-dina mātra karilā bhojana

SYNONYMS

bāra dine—for twelve days; *cali'*—traveling; *gelā*—reached; *śrī-puruṣottama*—Jagannātha Purī, or Nīlācala, the place of Puruṣottama; *pathe*—on the path; *tina-dina*—on three days; *mātra*—only; *karilā bhojana*—he ate.

TRANSLATION

He reached Jagannātha Purī in twelve days but could only eat for three days on the way.

TEXT 189

স্বরূপাদি-সহ গোসাঞি আছেন বসিয়া।
হেনকালে রঘুনাথ মিলিল আসিয়া ॥ ১৮৯ ॥

svarūpādi-saha gosāñi āchena vasiyā
hena-kāle raghunātha milila āsiyā

SYNONYMS

svarūpa-ādi-saha—in the company of devotees, headed by Svarūpa Dāmodara; *gosāñi*—Lord Śrī Caitanya Mahāprabhu; *āchena vasiyā*—was sitting; *hena-kāle*—at this time; *raghunātha*—Raghunātha dāsa; *milila*—met; *āsiyā*—coming.

TRANSLATION

When Raghunātha dāsa met Śrī Caitanya Mahāprabhu, the Lord was sitting with His companions, headed by Svarūpa Dāmodara.

TEXT 190

অঙ্গনেতে দূরে রহি' করেন প্রণিপাত ।
মুকুন্দ-দত্ত কহে,—'এই আইল রঘুনাথ' ॥ ১৯০ ॥

aṅganete dūre rahi' karena praṇipāta
mukunda-datta kahe, —'ei āila raghunātha'

SYNONYMS

aṅganete—in the courtyard; *dūre rahi'*—keeping himself at a distant place; *karena praṇipāta*—offered his obeisances; *mukunda-datta kahe*—Mukunda Datta said; *ei*—this; *āila*—has come; *raghunātha*—Raghunātha dāsa.

TRANSLATION

Staying at a distant place in the courtyard, he fell down to offer obeisances. Then Mukunda Datta said, "Here is Raghunātha."

TEXT 191

প্রভু কহেন,—'আইস', তেঁহো ধরিলা চরণ ।
উঠি' প্রভু কৃপায় তাঁরে কৈলা আলিঙ্গন ॥ ১৯১ ॥

prabhu kahena, —'āisa', teṅho dharilā caraṇa
uṭhi' prabhu kṛpāya tāṅre kailā āliṅgana

SYNONYMS

prabhu kahena—the Lord said; *āisa*—come here; *teṅho*—he; *dharilā caraṇa*—caught His lotus feet; *uṭhi'*—standing up; *prabhu*—the Lord; *kṛpāya*—out of mercy; *tāṅre*—him; *kailā āliṅgana*—embraced.

TRANSLATION

As soon as Śrī Caitanya Mahāprabhu heard these words, He immediately welcomed Raghunātha dāsa. "Come here," He said. Raghunātha dāsa then clasped the lotus feet of the Lord, but the Lord stood up and embraced him out of His causeless mercy.

TEXT 192

স্বরূপাদি সব ভক্তের চরণ বন্দিলা ।
প্রভু-কৃপা দেখি' সবে আলিঙ্গন কৈলা ॥ ১৯২ ॥

svarūpādi saba bhaktera caraṇa vandilā
prabhu-kṛpā dekhi' sabe āliṅgana kailā

SYNONYMS

svarūpa-ādi—headed by Svarūpa Dāmodara; *saba bhaktera*—of all the devotees; *caraṇa vandilā*—offered prayers to the lotus feet; *prabhu-kṛpā*—the mercy of Lord Caitanya; *dekhi'*—seeing; *sabe*—all of them; *āliṅgana kailā*—embraced.

TRANSLATION

Raghunātha dāsa offered prayers at the lotus feet of all the devotees, headed by Svarūpa Dāmodara Gosvāmī. Seeing the special mercy Śrī Caitanya Mahāprabhu had bestowed upon Raghunātha dāsa, they embraced him also.

TEXT 193

প্রভু কহে,—"কৃষ্ণকৃপা বলিষ্ঠ সবা হৈতে।
তোমারে কাড়িল বিষয়-বিষ্ঠা-গর্ত হৈতে॥" ১৯৩॥

prabhu kahe, —"kṛṣṇa-kṛpā baliṣṭha sabā haite
tomāre kāḍila viṣaya-viṣṭhā-garta haite"

SYNONYMS

prabhu kahe—Lord Śrī Caitanya Mahāprabhu said; *kṛṣṇa-kṛpā*—the mercy of Lord Kṛṣṇa; *baliṣṭha*—more powerful; *sabā haite*—than anything; *tomāre*—you; *kāḍila*—He has delivered; *viṣaya*—of material enjoyment; *viṣṭhā*—of stool; *garta*—the ditch; *haite*—from.

TRANSLATION

Lord Śrī Caitanya Mahāprabhu said, "The mercy of Lord Kṛṣṇa is stronger than anything else. Therefore the Lord has delivered you from the ditch of materialistic life, which is like a hole into which people pass stool."

PURPORT

According to the law of *karma,* everyone is destined to suffer or enjoy according to a certain material standard, but the mercy of Lord Kṛṣṇa is so powerful that the Lord can change all the reactions of one's past *karma,* or fruitive activities. Lord Śrī Caitanya Mahāprabhu specifically drew attention to the mercy of Lord Kṛṣṇa. That mercy is more powerful than anything else, for it had saved Raghunātha dāsa from the strong bondage of materialistic life, which the Lord compared to a hole where people pass stool. Śrī Caitanya Mahāprabhu gave His verdict that those addicted to the materialistic way of life are like worms that are living in stool but cannot give it up. A *gṛhavrata,* one who has decided to live in a comfortable home although it is actually miserable, is in a condemned position. Only the mercy of Kṛṣṇa can save one from such misery. Without Kṛṣṇa's mercy, one cannot get out of the filthy entanglement of materialistic life. The poor living entity cannot give up his materialistic position on his own; only when granted the special mercy of Kṛṣṇa can he give it up. Lord Caitanya Mahāprabhu knew very well that Raghunātha dāsa was already liberated. Nevertheless He emphasized that Raghunātha dāsa's life of material comfort as a very rich man's son with a very beautiful wife and many servants to attend him was like a ditch of stool. The Lord thus specifically indicated that ordinary men who are very happy with material comforts and family life are in no better position than worms in stool.

TEXT 194

রঘুনাথ মনে কহে,—'কৃষ্ণ নাহি জানি।
তব কৃপা কাড়িল আমা,—এই আমি মানি॥' ১৯৪॥

raghunātha mane kahe, ——'kṛṣṇa nāhi jāni
tava kṛpā kāḍila āmā, ——ei āmi māni'

SYNONYMS

raghunātha—Raghunātha dāsa; *mane kahe*—answered within his mind; *kṛṣṇa*—Lord Kṛṣṇa; *nāhi jāni*—I do not know; *tava*—Your; *kṛpā*—mercy; *kāḍila*—has delivered; *āmā*—me; *ei*—this; *āmi māni*—I accept.

TRANSLATION

Raghunātha dāsa answered within his mind, "I do not know who Kṛṣṇa is. I simply know that Your mercy, O my Lord, has saved me from my family life."

TEXT 195

প্রভু কহেন,—"তোমার পিতা-জ্যেঠা দুই জনে।
চক্রবর্তি-সম্বন্ধে হাম 'আজা' করি' মানে॥ ১৯৫॥

prabhu kahena, ——"tomāra pitā-jyeṭhā dui jane
cakravarti-sambandhe hāma 'ājā' kari' māne

SYNONYMS

prabhu kahena—Lord Caitanya Mahāprabhu said; *tomāra*—your; *pitā-jyeṭhā*—father and his elder brother; *dui jane*—both of them; *cakravarti-sambandhe*—because of a relationship with Nīlāmbara Cakravartī; *hāma*—I; *ājā kari'*—as My grandfathers; *māne*—consider.

TRANSLATION

The Lord continued, "Your father and his elder brother are both related as brothers to My grandfather, Nīlāmbara Cakravartī. Therefore I consider them My grandfathers.

PURPORT

Nīlāmbara Cakravartī, the grandfather of Śrī Caitanya Mahāprabhu, was very intimately related to Raghunātha dāsa's father and uncle. Nīlāmbara Cakravartī used to call them his younger brothers because both of them were very devoted to the *brāhmaṇas* and were very respectable gentlemen. Similarly, they used to call him Dādā Cakravartī, addressing him as an elder brother *brāhmaṇa*. Raghunātha dāsa, however, was almost the same age as Lord Śrī Caitanya Mahāprabhu. Generally a grandchild may joke about his grandfather. Therefore Śrī Caitanya Mahāprabhu took advantage of the relationship between His grandfather and Raghunātha dāsa's father and uncle to speak in a joking way.

TEXT 196

চক্রবর্তীর দুহে হয় ভ্রাতৃরূপ দাস।
অতএব তারে আমি করি পরিহাস ॥ ১৯৬ ॥

cakravartīra duhe haya bhrātṛ-rūpa dāsa
ataeva tāre āmi kari parihāsa

SYNONYMS

cakravartīra—of Nīlāmbara Cakravartī; *duhe*—both; *haya*—are; *bhrātṛ-rūpa dāsa*—servants as younger brothers; *ataeva*—therefore; *tāre*—unto them; *āmi*—I; *kari parihāsa*—say something jokingly.

TRANSLATION

"Since your father and his elder brother are younger brothers of Nīlāmbara Cakravartī, I may joke about them in this way.

TEXT 197

তোমার বাপ-জ্যেঠা —বিষয়বিষ্ঠা-গর্তের কীড়া।
সুখ করি' মানে বিষয়-বিষের মহাপীড়া ॥ ১৯৭ ॥

tomāra bāpa-jyeṭhā——viṣaya-viṣṭhā-gartera kīḍā
sukha kari' māne viṣaya-viṣera mahā-pīḍā

SYNONYMS

tomāra—your; *bāpa*—father; *jyeṭhā*—his elder brother; *viṣaya*—of material enjoyment; *viṣṭhā*—stool; *gartera*—of the ditch; *kīḍā*—worms; *sukha kari'*—as happiness; *māne*—they consider; *viṣaya*—of material enjoyment; *viṣera*—of the poison; *mahā-pīḍā*—the great disease.

TRANSLATION

"My dear Raghunātha dāsa, your father and his elder brother are just like worms in stool in the ditch of material enjoyment, for the great disease of the poison of material enjoyment is what they consider happiness.

PURPORT

When a man is attached to material enjoyment, he is attached to many miserable conditions, but nevertheless he accepts his condemned position as one of happiness. Sense enjoyment is so strong for such a person that he cannot give it up, exactly as a worm in stool cannot give up the stool. From the spiritual point of view, when a person is too absorbed in material enjoyment, he is exactly like a worm in stool. Although such a position is utterly miserable to the eyes of liberated souls, the materialistic enjoyer is greatly attached to it.

TEXT 198

যদ্যপি ব্রহ্মণ্য করে ব্রাহ্মণের সহায়।
'শুদ্ধবৈষ্ণব' নহে, হয়ে 'বৈষ্ণবের প্রায়' ॥ ১৯৮ ॥

yadyadi brahmaṇya kare brāhmaṇera sahāya
'śuddha-vaiṣṇava' nahe, haye 'vaiṣṇavera prāya'

SYNONYMS

yadyapi—although; *brahmaṇya kare*—give charity to the *brāhmaṇas; brāhmaṇera sahāya*—great helpers to the *brāhmaṇas; śuddha-vaiṣṇava*—pure Vaiṣṇavas; *nahe*—not; *haye*—they are; *vaiṣṇavera prāya*—almost like Vaiṣṇavas.

TRANSLATION

"Although your father and uncle are charitable to brāhmaṇas and greatly help them, they are nevertheless not pure Vaiṣṇavas. However, they are almost like Vaiṣṇavas.

PURPORT

As stated by Śrīla Bhaktivinoda Ṭhākura in his *Amṛta-pravāha-bhāṣya,* some people, usually very rich men, dress like Vaiṣṇavas and give charity to *brāhmaṇas.* They are also attached to Deity worship, but because of their attachment to material enjoyment, they cannot be pure Vaiṣṇavas. *Anyābhilāṣitā-śūnyaṁ jñāna-karmādy-anāvṛtam.* The pure Vaiṣṇava has no desire for material enjoyment. That is the basic qualification of a pure Vaiṣṇava. There are men, especially rich men, who regularly worship the Deity, give charity to *brāhmaṇas* and are pious in every respect, but they cannot be pure Vaiṣṇavas. Despite their outward show of Vaiṣṇavism and charity, their inner desire is to enjoy a higher standard of material life. Raghunātha dāsa's father, Hiraṇya dāsa, and uncle, Govardhana, were both very charitable to *brāhmaṇas.* Indeed, the *brāhmaṇas* from the Gauḍīya district were practically dependent upon them. Thus they were accepted as very pious gentlemen. However, they presented themselves as Vaiṣṇavas to the eyes of people in general, although from a purely spiritual point of view they were ordinary human beings, not pure Vaiṣṇavas. Actual Vaiṣṇavas considered them almost Vaiṣṇavas, not pure Vaiṣṇavas. In other words, they were *kaniṣṭha-adhikārīs,* for they were ignorant of higher Vaiṣṇava regulative principles. Nevertheless, they could not be called *viṣayīs,* or blind materialistic enjoyers.

TEXT 199

তথাপি বিষয়ের স্বভাব—করে মহা-অন্ধ ।
সেই কর্ম করায়, যাতে হয় ভব-বন্ধ ॥ ১৯৯ ॥

tathāpi viṣayera svabhāva——kare mahā-andha
sei karma karāya, yāte haya bhava-bandha

SYNONYMS

tathāpi—still; *viṣayera svabhāva*—the potency of material enjoyment; *kare mahā-andha*—makes one completely blind; *sei karma karāya*—causes one to act in that way; *yāte*—by which; *haya*—there is; *bhava-bandha*—the bondage of birth and death.

TRANSLATION

"Those who are attached to materialistic life and are blind to spiritual life must act in such a way that they are bound to repeated birth and death by the actions and reactions of their activities.

PURPORT

As clearly stated in *Bhagavad-gītā* (3.9), *yajñārthāt karmaṇo 'nyatra loko 'yaṁ karma-bandhanaḥ:* If one does not act as a pure devotee, whatever acts he performs will produce reactions of fruitive bondage (*karma-bandhanaḥ*). In *Śrīmad-Bhāgavatam* it is said:

nūnaṁ pramattaḥ kurute vikarma
yad-indriya-prītaya āpṛṇoti
na sādhu manye yata ātmano 'yam
asann api kleśada āsa dehaḥ

"A materialistic person, madly engaged in activities for sense enjoyment, does not know that he is entangling himself in repeated birth and death and that his body, although temporary, is full of miseries." (*Śrīmad-Bhāgavatam* 5.5.4) A *viṣayī*, a person blindly caught in a web of materialistic life, remains in the cycle of birth and death perpetually. Such a person cannot understand how to execute pure devotional service, and therefore he acts as a *karmī, jñānī, yogī* or something else, according to his desire, but he does not know that the activities of *karma, jñāna* and *yoga* simply bind one to the cycle of birth and death.

TEXT 200

হেন 'বিষয়' হৈতে কৃষ্ণ উদ্ধারিলা তোমা' ।
কহন না যায় কৃষ্ণকৃপার মহিমা ॥" ২০০ ॥

hena 'viṣaya' haite kṛṣṇa uddhārilā tomā'
kahana nā yāya kṛṣṇa-kṛpāra mahimā"

SYNONYMS

hena viṣaya—such a fallen condition of material enjoyment; *haite*—from; *kṛṣṇa*—Lord Kṛṣṇa; *uddhārilā tomā'*—has delivered you; *kahana nā yāya*—cannot be described; *kṛṣṇa-kṛpāra*—of the mercy of Lord Kṛṣṇa; *mahimā*—the glories.

TRANSLATION

"By His own free will, Lord Kṛṣṇa has delivered you from such a condemned materialistic life. Therefore the glories of Lord Kṛṣṇa's causeless mercy cannot be expressed."

PURPORT

In the *Brahma-saṁhitā* (5.54) it is said, *karmāṇi nirdahati kintu ca bhakti-bhājām.* Lord Kṛṣṇa is so merciful that He can stop the reaction of *karma* for His devotee. Everyone—from a small insect called *indra-gopa* up to Indra, the King of heaven—is bound by the reactions of fruitive activities.

yas tv indra-gopam athavendram aho sva-karma-
bandhānurūpa-phala-bhājanam ātanoti
karmāṇi nirdahati kintu ca bhakti-bhājāṁ
govindam ādi-puruṣaṁ tam ahaṁ bhajāmi

Everyone, whether like an insect or the King of heaven, is entangled and bound by the actions and reactions of his *karma.* However, when one becomes a pure devotee, free from material desires and from bondage to *karma, jñāna* and *yoga,* one is freed from material actions and reactions by the causeless mercy of Kṛṣṇa. One cannot express sufficient gratitude to Kṛṣṇa for being freed from the materialistic way of life.

TEXT 201

রঘুনাথের ক্ষীণতা-মালিন্য দেখিয়া ।
স্বরূপেরে কহেন প্রভু কৃপার্দ্র-চিত্ত হঞা ॥ ২০১ ॥

raghunāthera kṣīṇatā-mālinya dekhiyā
svarūpere kahena prabhu kṛpārdra-citta hañā

SYNONYMS

raghunāthera—of Raghunātha dāsa; *kṣīṇatā*—thinness; *mālinya*—dirty condition of the body; *dekhiyā*—seeing; *svarūpere kahena*—said to Svarūpa Dāmodara Gosvāmī; *prabhu*—Lord Caitanya Mahāprabhu; *kṛpā*—out of mercy; *ārdra*—melted; *citta*—heart; *hañā*—being.

TRANSLATION

Seeing Raghunātha dāsa skinny and dirty because of having traveled for twelve days and fasted, Lord Śrī Caitanya Mahāprabhu, His heart melting due to causeless mercy, spoke to Svarūpa Dāmodara.

TEXT 202

"এই রঘুনাথে আমি সঁপিনু তোমারে ।
পুত্র-ভৃত্য-রূপে তুমি কর অঙ্গীকারে ॥ ২০২ ॥

"ei raghunāthe āmi saṅpinu tomāre
putra-bhṛtya-rūpe tumi kara aṅgīkāre

SYNONYMS

ei raghunāthe—this Raghunātha dāsa; *āmi*—I; *saṅpinu tomāre*—am entrusting to you; *putra*—son; *bhṛtya*—servant; *rūpe*—as; *tumi*—you (Svarūpa Dāmodara Gosvāmī); *kara aṅgīkāre*—please accept.

TRANSLATION

"My dear Svarūpa," He said, "I entrust this Raghunātha dāsa to you. Please accept him as your son or servant.

TEXT 203

তিন 'রঘুনাথ'-নাম হয় আমার গণে ।
'স্বরূপের রঘু'— আজি হৈতে ইহার নামে ॥"২০৩ ॥

tina 'raghunātha'-nāma haya āmāra gaṇe
'svarūpera raghu'——āji haite ihāra nāme"

SYNONYMS

tina raghunātha—three Raghunāthas; *nāma*—named; *haya*—are; *āmāra gaṇe*—among My associates; *svarūpera raghu*—the Raghunātha of Svarūpa Dāmodara; *āji haite*—from this day; *ihāra*—of this one; *nāme*—the name.

TRANSLATION

"There are now three Raghunāthas among My associates. From this day forward, this Raghunātha should be known as the Raghu of Svarūpa Dāmodara."

PURPORT

Lord Śrī Caitanya Mahāprabhu had three Raghus among His associates—Vaidya Raghunātha (vide *Ādi-līlā* 11.22), Bhaṭṭa Raghunātha and Dāsa Raghunātha. Dāsa Raghunātha became celebrated as the Raghunātha of Svarūpa.

TEXT 204

এত কহি' রঘুনাথের হস্ত ধরিলা ।
স্বরূপের হস্তে তাঁরে সমর্পণ কৈলা ॥ ২০৪ ॥

eta kahi' raghunāthera hasta dharilā
svarūpera haste tāṅre samarpaṇa kailā

SYNONYMS

eta kahi'—saying this; *raghunāthera*—of Raghunātha dāsa; *hasta dharilā*—caught the hand; *svarūpera haste*—in the hands of Svarūpa Dāmodara; *tāṅre*—him; *samarpaṇa kailā*—entrusted.

TRANSLATION

Saying this, Śrī Caitanya Mahāprabhu grasped the hand of Raghunātha dāsa and entrusted him to the hands of Svarūpa Dāmodara Gosvāmī.

TEXT 205

স্বরূপ কহে,—'মহাপ্রভুর যে আজ্ঞা হৈল'।
এত কহি' রঘুনাথে পুনঃ আলিঙ্গিল ॥ ২০৫ ॥

svarūpa kahe, —'mahāprabhura ye ājñā haila'
eta kahi' raghunāthe punaḥ āliṅgila

SYNONYMS

svarūpa kahe—Svarūpa Dāmodara said; *mahāprabhura*—of Śrī Caitanya Mahāprabhu; *ye*—whatever; *ājñā*—order; *haila*—there is; *eta kahi'*—saying this; *raghunāthe*—Raghunātha dāsa; *punaḥ*—again; *āliṅgila*—he embraced.

TRANSLATION

Svarūpa Dāmodara Gosvāmī accepted Raghunātha dāsa, saying, "Śrī Caitanya Mahāprabhu, whatever You order is accepted." He then embraced Raghunātha dāsa again.

TEXT 206

চৈতন্যের ভক্তবাৎসল্য কহিতে না পারি।
গোবিন্দেরে কহে রঘুনাথে দয়া করি' ॥ ২০৬ ॥

caitanyera bhakta-vātsalya kahite nā pāri
govindere kahe raghunāthe dayā kari'

SYNONYMS

caitanyera—of Lord Śrī Caitanya Mahāprabhu; *bhakta-vātsalya*—affection for devotees; *kahite nā pāri*—I cannot express properly; *govindere*—to Govinda; *kahe*—He said; *raghunāthe*—upon Raghunātha; *dayā kari'*—being very merciful.

TRANSLATION

I cannot properly express the affection of Śrī Caitanya Mahāprabhu for His devotees. Being merciful toward Raghunātha dāsa, the Lord spoke as follows to Govinda.

TEXT 207

"পথে ইঁহ করিয়াছে বহুত লঙ্ঘন ।
কতদিন কর ইহার ভাল সন্তর্পণ ॥" ২০৭ ॥

"pathe iṅha kariyāche bahuta laṅghana
kata-dina kara ihāra bhāla santarpaṇa"

SYNONYMS

pathe—on the way; *iṅha*—this Raghunātha dāsa; *kariyāche*—has done; *bahuta*—much; *laṅghana*—fasting and difficult endeavor; *kata-dina*—for some days; *kara*—do; *ihāra*—of him; *bhāla*—good; *santarpaṇa*—attention.

TRANSLATION

"On the way, Raghunātha dāsa has fasted and undergone hardships for many days. Therefore, take good care of him for some days so that he may eat to his satisfaction."

TEXT 208

রঘুনাথে কহে—"যাঞা, কর সিন্ধুস্নান ।
জগন্নাথ দেখি' আসি' করহ ভোজন ॥" ২০৮ ॥

raghunāthe kahe—"yāñā, kara sindhu-snāna
jagannātha dekhi' āsi' karaha bhojana"

SYNONYMS

raghunāthe kahe—He said to Raghunātha dāsa; *yāñā*—going; *kara sindhu-snāna*—bathe in the sea; *jagannātha dekhi'*—after seeing Lord Jagannātha; *āsi'*—after coming; *karaha bhojana*—take your meal.

TRANSLATION

Then Śrī Caitanya Mahāprabhu told Raghunātha dāsa, "Go bathe in the sea. Then see Lord Jagannātha in the temple and return here to take your meal."

TEXT 209

এত বলি' প্রভু মধ্যাহ্ন করিতে উঠিলা ।
রঘুনাথ-দাস সব ভক্তেরে মিলিলা ॥ ২০৯ ॥

eta bali' prabhu madhyāhna karite uṭhilā
raghunātha-dāsa saba bhaktere mililā

SYNONYMS

eta bali'—after saying this; *prabhu*—Śrī Caitanya Mahāprabhu; *madhyāhna karite*—for performing His midday duties; *uṭhilā*—got up; *raghunātha-dāsa*—Raghunātha dāsa; *saba*—all; *bhaktere*—devotees; *mililā*—met.

TRANSLATION

After saying this, Śrī Caitanya Mahāprabhu got up and went to perform His midday duties, and Raghunātha met all the devotees present.

TEXT 210

রঘুনাথে প্রভুর কৃপা দেখি, ভক্তগণ ।
বিস্মিত হঞা করে তাঁর ভাগ্য-প্রশংসন ॥ ২১০ ॥

raghunāthe prabhura kṛpā dekhi, bhakta-gaṇa
vismita hañā kare tāṅra bhāgya-praśaṁsana

SYNONYMS

raghunāthe—unto Raghunātha dāsa; *prabhura*—of Śrī Caitanya Mahāprabhu; *kṛpā*—mercy; *dekhi*—seeing; *bhakta-gaṇa*—all the devotees; *vismita*—struck with wonder; *hañā*—being; *kare*—do; *tāṅra*—his; *bhāgya*—fortune; *praśaṁsana*—praise.

TRANSLATION

Having seen the causeless mercy of Śrī Caitanya Mahāprabhu upon Raghunātha dāsa, all the devotees, struck with wonder, praised his good fortune.

TEXT 211

রঘুনাথ সমুদ্রে যাঞা স্নান করিলা ।
জগন্নাথ দেখি' পুনঃ গোবিন্দ-পাশ আইলা ॥ ২১১ ॥

raghunātha samudre yāñā snāna karilā
jagannātha dekhi' punaḥ govinda-pāśa āilā

SYNONYMS

raghunātha—Raghunātha dāsa; *samudre*—to the sea; *yāñā*—going; *snāna karilā*—took a bath; *jagannātha dekhi'*—after seeing Lord Jagannātha; *punaḥ*—again; *govinda-pāśa āilā*—came to Govinda.

TRANSLATION

Raghunātha dāsa took his bath in the sea and saw Lord Jagannātha. Then he returned to Govinda, the personal servant of Śrī Caitanya Mahāprabhu.

TEXT 212

প্রভুর অবশিষ্ট পাত্র গোবিন্দ তাঁরে দিলা।
আনন্দিত হঞা রঘুনাথ প্রসাদ পাইলা ॥ ২১২ ॥

prabhura avaśiṣṭa pātra govinda tāṅre dilā
ānandita hañā raghunātha prasāda pāilā

SYNONYMS

prabhura—of Śrī Caitanya Mahāprabhu; *avaśiṣṭa pātra*—a plate of remnants of food; *govinda*—the personal servant of the Lord; *tāṅre*—to him; *dilā*—offered; *ānandita hañā*—becoming very happy; *raghunātha*—Raghunātha dāsa; *prasāda pāilā*—accepted the *prasāda.*

TRANSLATION

Govinda offered him a plate with the remnants of food left by Śrī Caitanya Mahāprabhu, and Raghunātha dāsa accepted the prasāda with great happiness.

TEXT 213

এইমত রহে তেঁহ স্বরূপ-চরণে।
গোবিন্দ প্রসাদ তাঁরে দিল পঞ্চ দিনে ॥ ২১৩ ॥

ei-mata rahe teṅha svarūpa-caraṇe
govinda prasāda tāṅre dila pañca dine

SYNONYMS

ei-mata—in this way; *rahe*—remained; *teṅha*—he; *svarūpa-caraṇe*—under the shelter of Svarūpa Dāmodara Gosvāmī; *govinda*—the personal servant of Śrī Caitanya Mahāprabhu; *prasāda*—the remnants of the food of Śrī Caitanya Mahāprabhu; *tāṅre*—unto him; *dila*—gave; *pañca dine*—for five days.

TRANSLATION

Raghunātha dāsa stayed under the care of Svarūpa Dāmodara Gosvāmī, and Govinda supplied him remnants of Śrī Caitanya Mahāprabhu's food for five days.

TEXT 214

আর দিন হৈতে 'পুষ্প-অঞ্জলি' দেখিয়া ।
সিংহদ্বারে খাড়া রহে ভিক্ষার লাগিয়া ॥ ২১৪ ॥

āra dina haite 'puṣpa-añjali' dekhiyā
siṁha-dvāre khāḍā rahe bhikṣāra lāgiyā

SYNONYMS

āra dina—the next day; *haite*—from; *puṣpa-añjali*—the ceremony of offering flowers to the Lord; *dekhiyā*—after seeing; *siṁha-dvāre*—at the main gate; *khāḍā rahe*—remains standing; *bhikṣāra lāgiyā*—for begging some alms.

TRANSLATION

Beginning from the sixth day, Raghunātha dāsa would stand at the gate known as Siṁha-dvāra to beg alms after the puṣpa-añjali ceremony, in which flowers were offered to the Lord.

TEXT 215

জগন্নাথের সেবক যত—'বিষয়ীর গণ' ।
সেবা সারি' রাত্র্যে করে গৃহেতে গমন ॥ ২১৫ ॥

jagannāthera sevaka yata——'viṣayīra gaṇa'
sevā sāri' rātrye kare gṛhete gamana

SYNONYMS

jagannāthera—of Lord Jagannātha; *sevaka*—servants; *yata*—all; *viṣayīra gaṇa*—generally known as *viṣayī; sevā sāri'*—after finishing their service; *rātrye*—at night; *kare*—do; *gṛhete gamana*—returning home.

TRANSLATION

After finishing their prescribed duties, the many servants of Lord Jagannātha, who are known as viṣayīs, return home at night.

TEXT 216

সিংহদ্বারে অন্নার্থী বৈষ্ণবে দেখিয়া ।
পসারির ঠাঞি অন্ন দেন কৃপা ত' করিয়া ॥ ২১৬ ॥

siṁha-dvāre annārthī vaiṣṇave dekhiyā
pasārira ṭhāñi anna dena kṛpā ta' kariyā

SYNONYMS

siṁha-dvāre—at the Siṁha gate; *anna-arthī*—in need of some eatables; *vaiṣṇave*—Vaiṣṇavas; *dekhiyā*—seeing; *pasārira ṭhāñi*—from the shopkeepers; *anna dena*—deliver some eatables; *kṛpā ta' kariyā*—out of mercy.

TRANSLATION

If they see a Vaiṣṇava standing at the Siṁha-dvāra begging alms, out of mercy they arrange with the shopkeepers to give him something to eat.

TEXT 217

এইমত সর্বকাল আছে ব্যবহার।
নিষ্কিঞ্চন ভক্ত খাড়া হয় সিংহদ্বার ॥ ২১৭ ॥

ei-mata sarva-kāla āche vyavahāra
niṣkiñcana bhakta khāḍā haya siṁha-dvāra

SYNONYMS

ei-mata—in this way; *sarva-kāla*—for all time; *āche*—is; *vyavahāra*—the etiquette; *niṣkiñcana bhakta*—a devotee who has no other support; *khāḍā haya*—stands; *siṁha-dvāra*—at the gate known as Siṁha-dvāra.

TRANSLATION

Thus it is a custom for all time that a devotee who has no other means of support stands at the Siṁha-dvāra gate to receive alms from the servants.

TEXT 218

সর্বদিন করেন বৈষ্ণব নাম-সঙ্কীর্তন।
স্বচ্ছন্দে করেন জগন্নাথ দরশন ॥ ২১৮ ॥

sarva-dina karena vaiṣṇava nāma-saṅkīrtana
svacchande karena jagannātha daraśana

SYNONYMS

sarva-dina—the whole day; *karena*—performs; *vaiṣṇava*—a Vaiṣṇava; *nāma-saṅkīrtana*—chanting of the holy name of the Lord; *svacchande*—with full freedom; *karena*—does; *jagannātha daraśana*—seeing Lord Jagannātha.

TRANSLATION

A completely dependent Vaiṣṇava thus chants the holy name of the Lord all day and sees Lord Jagannātha with full freedom.

TEXT 219

কেহ ছত্রে মাগি' খায়, যেবা কিছু পায়।
কেহ রাত্রে ভিক্ষা লাগি' সিংহদ্বারে রয় ॥ ২১৯ ॥

keha chatre māgi' khāya, yebā kichu pāya
keha rātre bhikṣā lāgi' siṁha-dvāre raya

SYNONYMS

keha—some; *chatre*—at the almshouse; *māgi'*—begging; *khāya*—eat; *yebā*—whatever; *kichu*—little; *pāya*—they receive; *keha*—some; *rātre*—at night; *bhikṣā lāgi'*—for begging alms; *siṁha-dvāre raya*—stand at the gate known as Siṁha-dvāra.

TRANSLATION

It is a custom for some Vaiṣṇavas to beg from the charity booths and eat whatever they obtain, whereas others stand at night at the Siṁha-dvāra gate, begging alms from the servants.

TEXT 220

মহাপ্রভুর ভক্তগণের বৈরাগ্য প্রধান।
যাহা দেখি' প্রীত হন গৌর-ভগবান্ ॥ ২২০ ॥

mahāprabhura bhakta-gaṇera vairāgya pradhāna
yāhā dekhi' prīta hana gaura-bhagavān

SYNONYMS

mahāprabhura—of Śrī Caitanya Mahāprabhu; *bhakta-gaṇera*—of the devotees; *vairāgya*—renunciation; *pradhāna*—the basic principle; *yāhā dekhi'*—seeing which; *prīta hana*—becomes satisfied; *gaura-bhagavān*—Śrī Caitanya Mahāprabhu, the Supreme Personality of Godhead.

TRANSLATION

Renunciation is the basic principle sustaining the lives of Śrī Caitanya Mahāprabhu's devotees. Seeing this renunciation, Śrī Caitanya Mahāprabhu, the Supreme Personality of Godhead, is extremely satisfied.

PURPORT

Anyone, whether an ordinary materialistic person or a pure devotee, can understand the behavior of Śrī Caitanya Mahāprabhu's devotees if he studies it minutely. One will thus find that the devotees of Śrī Caitanya Mahāprabhu are not at all attached to any kind of material enjoyment. They have completely given up sense enjoyment to engage fully in the service of Lord Śrī Kṛṣṇa and dedicate their lives and souls to serving Kṛṣṇa without material desires. Because their devotional service is free from material desires, it is unimpeded by material circumstances. Although ordinary men have great difficulty understanding this attitude of the devotees, it is greatly appreciated by the Supreme Personality of Godhead, Lord Śrī Caitanya Mahāprabhu.

TEXT 221

প্রভুরে গোবিন্দ কহে,—"রঘুনাথ 'প্রসাদ' না লয়।
রাত্র্যে সিংহদ্বারে খাড়া হঞা মাগি' খায়॥" ২২১ ॥

prabhure govinda kahe, —"raghunātha 'prasāda' nā laya
rātrye siṁha-dvāre khāḍā hañā māgi' khāya"

SYNONYMS

prabhure—unto Lord Śrī Caitanya Mahāprabhu; *govinda kahe*—Govinda said; *raghunātha*—Raghunātha dāsa; *prasāda nā laya*—does not take *prasāda; rātrye*—at night; *siṁha-dvāre*—at the Siṁha-dvāra gate; *khāḍā hañā*—standing; *māgi'*—begging; *khāya*—he eats.

TRANSLATION

Govinda said to Śrī Caitanya Mahāprabhu, "Raghunātha dāsa no longer takes prasāda here. Now he stands at the Siṁha-dvāra, where he begs some alms to eat."

TEXT 222

শুনি' তুষ্ট হঞা প্রভু কহিতে লাগিল।
"ভাল কৈল, বৈরাগীর ধর্ম আচরিল॥ ২২২ ॥

śuni' tuṣṭa hañā prabhu kahite lāgila
"bhāla kaila, vairāgīra dharma ācarila

SYNONYMS

śuni'—hearing; *tuṣṭa hañā*—being very satisfied; *prabhu*—Lord Śrī Caitanya Mahāprabhu; *kahite lāgila*—began to say; *bhāla kaila*—he has done well;

vairāgīra—of a person in the renounced order; *dharma*—the principles; *ācarila*—he has performed.

TRANSLATION

When Śrī Caitanya Mahāprabhu heard this, He was greatly satisfied. "Raghunātha dāsa has done well," He said. "He has acted suitably for a person in the renounced order.

TEXT 223

বৈরাগী করিবে সদা নাম-সঙ্কীর্তন ।
মাগিয়া খাঞা করে জীবন রক্ষণ ॥ ২২৩ ॥

vairāgī karibe sadā nāma-saṅkīrtana
māgiyā khāñā kare jīvana rakṣaṇa

SYNONYMS

vairāgī—a person in the renounced order; *karibe*—will do; *sadā*—always; *nāma-saṅkīrtana*—chanting of the holy name of the Lord; *māgiyā*—by begging; *khāñā*—eating; *kare jīvana rakṣaṇa*—he sustains his life.

TRANSLATION

"A person in the renounced order should always chant the holy name of the Lord. He should beg some alms to eat, and he should sustain his life in this way.

PURPORT

As stated in the *Hari-bhakti-vilāsa* at the end of the Twentieth *Vilāsa* (366, 379, 382):

kṛtyānyetāni tu prāyo
gṛhiṇāṁ dhaninām satām
likhitāni na tu tyakta-
parigraha-mahātmanām

prabhāte cārdha-rātre ca
madhyāhne divasa-kṣaye
kīrtayanti hariṁ ye vai
te taranti bhavārṇavam

evam ekāntināṁ prāyaḥ
kīrtanaṁ smaraṇaṁ prabhoḥ

kurvatāṁ parama-prītyā
kṛtyam anyan na rocate

A well-to-do householder Vaiṣṇava cannot live like a person in the renounced order who completely takes shelter of the holy name. Such a householder should chant the holy name of Kṛṣṇa in the morning, at midday and in the evening. Then he will be able to cross beyond nescience. Pure devotees in the renounced order, however, who fully surrender to the lotus feet of Kṛṣṇa, should chant the holy name of the Lord with great love and faith, always thinking of Kṛṣṇa's lotus feet. They should have no other occupation than chanting the holy name of the Lord. In the *Bhakti-sandarbha,* Śrīla Jīva Gosvāmī says:

yadyapi śrī-bhāgavata-mate pañca-rātrādivad-arcana-mārgasyāvaśyakatvaṁ nāsti, tad vināpi śaraṇāpattyādīnām ekatareṇāpi puruṣārtha-siddher abhihitatvāt.

TEXT 224

বৈরাগী হঞা যেবা করে পরাপেক্ষা ।
কার্যসিদ্ধি নহে, কৃষ্ণ করেন উপেক্ষা ॥ ২২৪ ॥

vairāgī hañā yebā kare parāpekṣā
kārya-siddhi nahe, kṛṣṇa karena upekṣā

SYNONYMS

vairāgī hañā—being in the renounced order; *yebā*—anyone who; *kare*—does; *parāpekṣā*—dependence on others; *kārya-siddhi nahe*—he does not become successful; *kṛṣṇa*—Lord Kṛṣṇa; *karena upekṣā*—neglects.

TRANSLATION

"A vairāgī [a person in the renounced order] should not depend on others. If he does so, he will be unsuccessful, and he will be neglected by Kṛṣṇa.

TEXT 225

বৈরাগী হঞা করে জিহ্বার লালস ।
পরমার্থ যায়, আর হয় রসের বশ ॥ ২২৫ ॥

vairāgī hañā kare jihvāra lālasa
paramārtha yāya, āra haya rasera vaśa

SYNONYMS

vairāgī hañā—being in the renounced order; *kare*—does; *jihvāra*—of the tongue; *lālasa*—lust; *parama-artha*—the goal of life; *yāya*—goes; *āra*—and; *haya*—becomes; *rasera vaśa*—dependent on taste.

TRANSLATION

"If a renunciant is eager for his tongue to taste different foods, his spiritual life will be lost, and he will be subservient to the tastes of his tongue.

TEXT 226

বৈরাগীর কৃত্য—সদা নাম-সঙ্কীর্তন ।
শাক-পত্র-ফল-মূলে উদর-ভরণ ॥ ২২৬ ॥

vairāgīra kṛtya——sadā nāma-saṅkīrtana
śāka-patra-phala-mūle udara-bharaṇa

SYNONYMS

vairāgīra—of a person in the renounced order; *kṛtya*—duty; *sadā*—always; *nāma-saṅkīrtana*—chanting the holy name of the Lord; *śāka*—vegetables; *patra*—leaves; *phala*—fruit; *mūle*—by roots; *udara-bharaṇa*—filling the belly.

TRANSLATION

"The duty of a person in the renounced order is to chant the Hare Kṛṣṇa mantra always. He should satisfy his belly with whatever vegetables, leaves, fruits and roots are available.

TEXT 227

জিহ্বার লালসে যেই ইতি-উতি ধায় ।
শিশ্নোদরপরায়ণ কৃষ্ণ নাহি পায় ॥" ২২৭ ॥

jihvāra lālase yei iti-uti dhāya
śiśnodara-parāyaṇa kṛṣṇa nāhi pāya"

SYNONYMS

jihvāra—of the tongue; *lālase*—because of greed; *yei*—anyone who; *iti-uti*—here and there; *dhāya*—goes; *śiśna*—genitals; *udara*—belly; *parāyaṇa*—devoted to; *kṛṣṇa*—Lord Kṛṣṇa; *nāhi pāya*—does not get.

TRANSLATION

"One who is subservient to the tongue and who thus goes here and there, devoted to the genitals and the belly, cannot attain Kṛṣṇa."

TEXT 228

আর দিন রঘুনাথ স্বরূপ-চরণে।
আপনার কৃত্য লাগি' কৈলা নিবেদনে ॥ ২২৮ ॥

āra dina raghunātha svarūpa-caraṇe
āpanāra kṛtya lāgi' kailā nivedane

SYNONYMS

āra dina—the next day; *raghunātha*—Raghunātha dāsa; *svarūpa-caraṇe*—unto the lotus feet of Svarūpa Dāmodara Gosvāmī; *āpanāra*—his; *kṛtya*—duty; *lāgi'*—for; *kailā nivedane*—submitted.

TRANSLATION

The next day, Raghunātha dāsa inquired at the lotus feet of Svarūpa Dāmodara about his duty.

TEXT 229

"কি লাগি' ছাড়াইলা ঘর, না জানি উদ্দেশ।
কি মোর কর্তব্য, প্রভু কর উপদেশ ॥" ২২৯ ॥

"ki lāgi' chāḍāilā ghara, nā jāni uddeśa
ki mora kartavya, prabhu kara upadeśa"

SYNONYMS

ki lāgi'—for what reason; *chāḍāilā ghara*—have I been obliged to give up my household life; *nā jāni*—I do not know; *uddeśa*—the purpose; *ki*—what; *mora kartavya*—my duty; *prabhu*—my dear Lord; *kara upadeśa*—please give instruction.

TRANSLATION

"I do not know why I have given up household life," he said. "What is my duty? Kindly give me instructions."

TEXT 230

প্রভুর আগে কথা-মাত্র না কহে রঘুনাথ ।
স্বরূপ-গোবিন্দ-দ্বারা কহায় নিজ-বাত্ ॥ ২৩০ ॥

prabhura āge kathā-mātra nā kahe raghunātha
svarūpa-govinda-dvārā kahāya nija-vāt

SYNONYMS

prabhura āge—in front of Śrī Caitanya Mahāprabhu; *kathā-mātra*—any speaking; *nā kahe*—does not say; *raghunātha*—Raghunātha dāsa; *svarūpa-govinda-dvārā*—through Govinda and Svarūpa Dāmodara Gosvāmī; *kahāya*—he informs; *nija-vāt*—his intention.

TRANSLATION

Raghunātha dāsa never even spoke a word before the Lord. Instead, he informed the Lord of his desires through Svarūpa Dāmodara Gosvāmī and Govinda.

TEXT 231

প্রভুর আগে স্বরূপ নিবেদিলা আর দিনে ।
রঘুনাথ নিবেদয় প্রভুর চরণে ॥ ২৩১ ॥

prabhura āge svarūpa nivedilā āra dine
raghunātha nivedaya prabhura caraṇe

SYNONYMS

prabhura age—in front of Śrī Caitanya Mahāprabhu; *svarūpa*—Svarūpa Dāmodara Gosvāmī; *nivedilā*—submitted; *āra dine*—on the next day; *raghunātha nivedaya*—Raghunātha dāsa inquires; *prabhura caraṇe*—at the lotus feet of Lord Śrī Caitanya Mahāprabhu.

TRANSLATION

The next day, Svarūpa Dāmodara Gosvāmī submitted to Lord Śrī Caitanya Mahāprabhu, "Raghunātha dāsa has this to say at Your lotus feet.

TEXT 232

"কি মোর কর্তব্য, মুঞি না জানি উদ্দেশ ।
আপনি শ্রীমুখে মোরে কর উপদেশ ॥" ২৩২ ॥

"ki mora kartavya, muñi nā jāni uddeśa
āpani śrī-mukhe more kara upadeśa"

SYNONYMS

ki—what; *mora kartavya*—my duty; *muñi*—I; *nā jāni*—do not know; *uddeśa*—the goal of my life; *āpani*—personally; *śrī-mukhe*—through Your transcendental mouth; *more*—unto me; *kara upadeśa*—please give instructions.

TRANSLATION

" 'I do not know my duty or the goal of my life. Therefore, please personally give me instructions from Your transcendental mouth.' "

TEXT 233

হাসি' মহাপ্রভু রঘুনাথেরে কহিল ।
"তোমার উপদেষ্টা করি' স্বরূপেরে দিল ॥ ২৩৩ ॥

hāsi' mahāprabhu raghunāthere kahila
"tomāra upadeṣṭā kari' svarūpere dila

SYNONYMS

hāsi'—smiling; *mahāprabhu*—Śrī Caitanya Mahāprabhu; *raghunāthere*—to Raghunātha dāsa; *kahila*—said; *tomāra*—your; *upadeṣṭā*—instructor; *kari'*—as; *svarūpere dila*—I have appointed Svarūpa Dāmodara Gosvāmī.

TRANSLATION

Smiling, Śrī Caitanya Mahāprabhu told Raghunātha dāsa, "I have already appointed Svarūpa Dāmodara Gosvāmī as your instructor.

TEXT 234

'সাধ্য'-'সাধন'-তত্ত্ব শিখ ইঁহার স্থানে ।
আমি তত নাহি জানি, ইঁহো যত জানে ॥ ২৩৪ ॥

'sādhya'-'sādhana'-tattva śikha iṅhāra sthāne
āmi tata nāhi jāni, iṅho yata jāne

SYNONYMS

sādhya—duty; *sādhana*—how to execute it; *tattva*—truth; *śikha*—learn; *iṅhāra sthāne*—from him; *āmi*—I; *tata*—so much; *nāhi jāni*—do not know; *iṅho*—he; *yata*—as much as; *jāne*—knows.

TRANSLATION

"You may learn from him what your duty is and how to discharge it. I do not know as much as he.

TEXT 235

তথাপি আমার আজ্ঞায় শ্রদ্ধা যদি হয়।
আমার এই বাক্যে তবে করিহ নিশ্চয় ॥ ২৩৫ ॥

tathāpi āmāra ājñāya śraddhā yadi haya
āmāra ei vākye tabe kariha niścaya

SYNONYMS

tathāpi—still; *āmāra ājñāya*—in My instruction; *śraddhā*—faith; *yadi*—if; *haya*—there is; *āmāra*—My; *ei*—these; *vākye*—by words; *tabe*—then; *kariha niścaya*—you can ascertain.

TRANSLATION

"Nevertheless, if you want to take instructions from Me with faith and love, you may ascertain your duties from the following words.

TEXT 236

গ্রাম্যকথা না শুনিবে, গ্রাম্যবার্তা না কহিবে।
ভাল না খাইবে আর ভাল না পরিবে ॥ ২৩৬ ॥

grāmya-kathā nā śunibe, grāmya-vārtā nā kahibe
bhāla nā khāibe āra bhāla nā paribe

SYNONYMS

grāmya-kathā—ordinary talks of common men; *nā śunibe*—never hear; *grāmya-vārtā*—ordinary news; *nā kahibe*—do not speak; *bhāla*—well; *nā khāibe*—do not eat; *āra*—and; *bhāla*—nicely; *nā paribe*—do not dress.

TRANSLATION

"Do not talk like people in general or hear what they say. You should not eat very palatable food, nor should you dress very nicely.

TEXT 237

অমানী মানদ হঞা কৃষ্ণনাম সদা ল'বে।
ব্রজে রাধাকৃষ্ণ-সেবা মানসে করিবে ॥ ২৩৭ ॥

amānī mānada hañā kṛṣṇa-nāma sadā la'be
vraje rādhā-kṛṣṇa-sevā mānase karibe

SYNONYMS

amānī—not expecting any respect; *māna-da*—offering respect to others; *hañā*—becoming; *kṛṣṇa-nāma*—the holy name of the Lord; *sadā*—always; *la'be*—you should chant; *vraje*—in Vṛndāvana; *rādhā-kṛṣṇa-sevā*—service to Rādhā and Kṛṣṇa; *mānase*—within the mind; *karibe*—you should do.

TRANSLATION

"Do not expect honor, but offer all respect to others. Always chant the holy name of Lord Kṛṣṇa, and within your mind render service to Rādhā and Kṛṣṇa in Vṛndāvana.

PURPORT

Śrīla Bhaktivinoda Ṭhākura says in his *Amṛta-pravāha-bhāṣya* that when a man and woman are married, they beget children and are thus entangled in family life. Talk concerning such family life is called *grāmya-kathā*. A person in the renounced order never indulges in either hearing or talking about such subjects. He should not eat palatable dishes, since that is unfit for a person in the renounced order. He should show all respect to others, but should not expect respect for himself. In this way, one should chant the holy name of the Lord and think of how to serve Rādhā and Kṛṣṇa in Vṛndāvana.

TEXT 238

এই ত' সংক্ষেপে আমি কৈলুঁ উপদেশ ।
স্বরূপের ঠাঞি ইহার পাইবে বিশেষ ॥ ২৩৮ ॥

ei ta' saṅkṣepe āmi kailuṅ upadeśa
svarūpera ṭhāñi ihāra pāibe viśeṣa

SYNONYMS

ei—this; *ta'*—certainly; *saṅkṣepe*—in brief; *āmi*—I; *kailuṅ upadeśa*—have given instruction; *svarūpera ṭhāñi*—from Svarūpa Dāmodara; *ihāra*—of this instruction; *pāibe*—you will get; *viśeṣa*—all details.

TRANSLATION

"I have briefly given you My instructions. Now you will get all details about them from Svarūpa Dāmodara.

TEXT 239

তৃণাদপি সুনীচেন তরোরিব সহিষ্ণুনা ।
অমানিনা মানদেন কীর্তনীয়ঃ সদা হরিঃ ॥" ২৩৯ ॥

tṛṇād api sunīcena
taror iva sahiṣṇunā
amāninā mānadena
kīrtanīyaḥ sadā hariḥ"

SYNONYMS

tṛṇāt api—than downtrodden grass; *sunīcena*—being lower; *taroḥ*—than a tree; *iva*—indeed; *sahiṣṇunā*—with more tolerance; *amāninā*—without being puffed up by false pride; *mānadena*—giving respect to all; *kīrtanīyaḥ*—to be chanted; *sadā*—always; *hariḥ*—the holy name of the Lord.

TRANSLATION

"One who thinks himself lower than grass, who is more tolerant than a tree, and who does not expect personal honor but is always prepared to give respect to others, can very easily always chant the holy name of the Lord."

TEXT 240

এত শুনি' রঘুনাথ বন্দিলা চরণ ।
মহাপ্রভু কৈলা তাঁরে কৃপা-আলিঙ্গন ॥ ২৪০ ॥

eta śuni' raghunātha vandilā caraṇa
mahāprabhu kailā tāṅre kṛpā-āliṅgana

SYNONYMS

eta śuni'—hearing this; *raghunātha*—Raghunātha dāsa; *vandilā caraṇa*—offered prayers to the lotus feet; *mahāprabhu*—Śrī Caitanya Mahāprabhu; *kailā*—did; *tāṅre*—him; *kṛpā-āliṅgana*—embracing out of mercy.

TRANSLATION

Having heard this, Raghunātha dāsa offered prayers at the lotus feet of Śrī Caitanya Mahāprabhu, and the Lord, with great mercy, embraced him.

TEXT 241

পুনঃ সমর্পিলা তাঁরে স্বরূপের স্থানে ।
'অন্তরঙ্গ-সেবা' করে স্বরূপের সনে ॥ ২৪১ ॥

punaḥ samarpilā tāṅre svarūpera sthāne
'antaraṅga-sevā' kare svarūpera sane

SYNONYMS

punaḥ—again; *samarpilā*—handed over; *tāṅre*—him; *svarūpera sthāne*—to Svarūpa Dāmodara; *antaraṅga-sevā*—very confidential service; *kare*—he renders; *svarūpera sane*—with Svarūpa Dāmodara.

TRANSLATION

Śrī Caitanya Mahāprabhu again entrusted him to Svarūpa Dāmodara. Thus Raghunātha dāsa rendered very confidential service with Svarūpa Dāmodara Gosvāmī.

PURPORT

Antaraṅga-sevā refers to service performed in one's spiritual body. Svarūpa Dāmodara Gosvāmī was formerly Lalitādevī. Raghunātha dāsa Gosvāmī, who was among his assistants, now also began to serve Rādhā and Kṛṣṇa within his mind.

TEXT 242

হেন-কালে আইলা সব গৌড়ের ভক্তগণ ।
পূর্ব্ববৎ প্রভু সবায় করিলা মিলন ॥ ২৪২ ॥

hena-kāle āilā saba gauḍera bhakta-gaṇa
pūrvavat prabhu sabāya karilā milana

SYNONYMS

hena-kāle—at this time; *āilā*—came; *saba*—all; *gauḍera bhakta-gaṇa*—devotees from Bengal; *pūrva-vat*—as formerly; *prabhu*—Śrī Caitanya Mahāprabhu; *sabāya*—every one of them; *karilā milana*—met.

TRANSLATION

At this time, all the devotees from Bengal arrived, and, as previously, Śrī Caitanya Mahāprabhu met them with great feeling.

TEXT 243

সবা লঞা কৈলা প্রভু গুণ্ডিচা-মার্জন ।
সবা লঞা কৈলা প্রভু বন্য-ভোজন ॥ ২৪৩ ॥

sabā lañā kailā prabhu guṇḍicā-mārjana
sabā lañā kailā prabhu vanya-bhojana

SYNONYMS

sabā lañā—taking all of them; *kailā*—performed; *prabhu*—Śrī Caitanya Mahāprabhu; *guṇḍicā-mārjana*—washing of the Guṇḍicā temple; *sabā lañā*—with all of them; *kailā*—performed; *prabhu*—Śrī Caitanya; *vanya-bhojana*—eating in the garden.

TRANSLATION

As He had previously done, He cleansed the Guṇḍicā temple and held a picnic feast in the garden with the devotees.

TEXT 244

রথযাত্রায় সবা লঞা করিলা নর্তন।
দেখি' রঘুনাথের চমৎকার হৈল মন ॥ ২৪৪ ॥

ratha-yātrāya sabā lañā karilā nartana
dekhi' raghunāthera camatkāra haila mana

SYNONYMS

ratha-yātrāya—during the Ratha-yātrā performance; *sabā lañā*—taking all of them; *karilā nartana*—danced; *dekhi'*—seeing; *raghunāthera*—of Raghunātha dāsa; *camatkāra*—struck with wonder; *haila*—became; *mana*—the mind.

TRANSLATION

The Lord again danced with the devotees during the Ratha-yātrā festival. Seeing this, Raghunātha dāsa was struck with wonder.

TEXT 245

রঘুনাথ-দাস যবে সবারে মিলিলা।
অদ্বৈত-আচার্য তাঁরে বহু কৃপা কৈলা ॥ ২৪৫ ॥

raghunātha-dāsa yabe sabāre mililā
advaita-ācārya tāṅre bahu kṛpā kailā

SYNONYMS

raghunātha-dāsa—Raghunātha dāsa; *yabe*—when; *sabāre mililā*—met all the devotees; *advaita-ācārya*—Advaita Ācārya; *tāṅre*—unto him; *bahu*—much; *kṛpā*—mercy; *kailā*—did.

TRANSLATION

When Raghunātha dāsa met all the devotees, Advaita Ācārya showed him great mercy.

TEXT 246

শিবানন্দ-সেন তাঁরে কহেন বিবরণ ।
তোমা লৈতে তোমার পিতা পাঠাইল দশ জন ॥২৪৬

śivānanda-sena tāṅre kahena vivaraṇa
tomā laite tomāra pitā pāṭhāila daśa jana

SYNONYMS

śivānanda-sena—Śivānanda Sena; *tāṅre*—unto him; *kahena*—says; *vivaraṇa*—description; *tomā laite*—to take you; *tomāra pitā*—your father; *pāṭhāila*—sent; *daśa jana*—ten men.

TRANSLATION

He also met Śivānanda Sena, who informed him, "Your father sent ten men to take you away.

TEXT 247

তোমারে পাঠাইতে পত্রী পাঠাইল মোরে ।
ঝাঁকরা হইতে তোমা না পাঞা গেল ঘরে ॥ ২৪৭ ॥

tomāre pāṭhāite patrī pāṭhāila more
jhāṅkarā ha-ite tomā nā pāñā gela ghare

SYNONYMS

tomāre—you; *pāṭhāite*—to send back; *patrī*—letter; *pāṭhāila more*—sent to me; *jhāṅkarā ha-ite*—from Jhāṅkarā; *tomā*—you; *nā pāñā*—not getting; *gela ghare*—returned home.

TRANSLATION

"He wrote me a letter asking me to send you back, but when those ten men received no information about you, they returned home from Jhāṅkarā."

TEXT 248

চারি মাস রহি' ভক্তগণ গৌড়ে গেলা ।
শুনি' রঘুনাথের পিতা মনুষ্য পাঠাইলা ॥ ২৪৮ ॥

cāri māsa rahi' bhakta-gaṇa gauḍe gelā
śuni' raghunāthera pitā manuṣya pāṭhāilā

SYNONYMS

cāri māsa—for four months; *rahi'*—remaining; *bhakta-gaṇa*—all the devotees; *gauḍe gelā*—returned to Bengal; *śuni'*—hearing; *raghunāthera pitā*—the father of Raghunātha dāsa; *manuṣya*—a man; *pāṭhāilā*—sent.

TRANSLATION

When all the devotees from Bengal returned home after staying at Jagannātha Purī for four months, Raghunātha dāsa's father heard about their arrival and therefore sent a man to Śivānanda Sena.

TEXT 249

সে মনুষ্য শিবানন্দ-সেনেরে পুছিল ।
"মহাপ্রভুর স্থানে এক 'বৈরাগী' দেখিল ॥ ২৪৯ ॥

se manuṣya śivānanda-senere puchila
"mahāprabhura sthāne eka 'vairāgī' dekhila

SYNONYMS

se manuṣya—that messenger; *śivānanda-senere*—from Śivānanda Sena; *puchila*—inquired; *mahāprabhura sthāne*—at the place of Śrī Caitanya Mahāprabhu; *eka vairāgī*—a person in the renounced order; *dekhila*—did you see.

TRANSLATION

That man inquired from Śivānanda Sena, "Did you see anyone in the renounced order at the residence of Śrī Caitanya Mahāprabhu?

TEXT 250

গোবর্ধনের পুত্র তেঁহো, নাম – 'রঘুনাথ' ।
নীলাচলে পরিচয় আছে তোমার সাথ ?" ২৫০ ॥

govardhanera putra teṅho, nāma——'raghunātha'
nīlācale paricaya āche tomāra sātha?"

SYNONYMS

govardhanera—of Govardhana; *putra*—the son; *teṅho*—he; *nāma*—named; *raghunātha*—Raghunātha dāsa; *nīlācale*—in Nīlācala; *paricaya āche*—is there acquaintance; *tomāra sātha*—with you.

TRANSLATION

"That person is Raghunātha dāsa, the son of Govardhana Majumadāra. Did you meet him in Nīlācala?"

TEXT 251

শিবানন্দ কহে,—"তেঁহো হয় প্রভুর স্থানে ।
পরম বিখ্যাত তেঁহো, কেবা নাহি জানে ॥ ২৫১ ॥

śivānanda kahe, —"teṅho haya prabhura sthāne
parama vikhyāta teṅho, kebā nāhi jāne

SYNONYMS

śivānanda kahe—Śivānanda Sena replied; *teṅho*—he; *haya*—is; *prabhura sthāne*—with Lord Śrī Caitanya Mahāprabhu; *parama vikhyāta*—very famous; *teṅho*—he; *kebā*—who; *nāhi jāne*—does not know.

TRANSLATION

Śivānanda Sena replied, "Yes, sir. Raghunātha dāsa is with Śrī Caitanya Mahāprabhu and is a very famous man. Who does not know him?

TEXT 252

স্বরূপের স্থানে তারে করিয়াছেন সমর্পণ ।
প্রভুর ভক্তগণের তেঁহো হয় প্রাণসম ॥ ২৫২ ॥

svarūpera sthāne tāre kariyāchena samarpaṇa
prabhura bhakta-gaṇera teṅho haya prāṇa-sama

SYNONYMS

svarūpera sthāne—to Svarūpa Dāmodara; *tāre*—him; *kariyāchena samarpaṇa*—Lord Caitanya has given charge of; *prabhura*—of Śrī Caitanya Mahāprabhu; *bhakta-gaṇera*—of all the devotees; *teṅho*—he; *haya*—is; *prāṇa*—the life; *sama*—like.

TRANSLATION

"Śrī Caitanya Mahāprabhu has placed him under the charge of Svarūpa Dāmodara. Raghunātha dāsa has become just like the life of all the Lord's devotees.

TEXT 253

রাত্রি-দিন করে তেঁহো নাম-সঙ্কীর্তন।
ক্ষণমাত্র নাহি ছাড়ে প্রভুর চরণ ॥ ২৫৩ ॥

rātri-dina kare teṅho nāma-saṅkīrtana
kṣaṇa-mātra nāhi chāḍe prabhura caraṇa

SYNONYMS

rātri-dina—all day and night; *kare*—performs; *teṅho*—he; *nāma-saṅkīrtana*—chanting of the Hare Kṛṣṇa *mantra; kṣaṇa-mātra*—even for a moment; *nāhi chāḍe*—does not give up; *prabhura caraṇa*—the lotus feet of Śrī Caitanya Mahāprabhu.

TRANSLATION

"He chants the Hare Kṛṣṇa mahā-mantra all day and night. He never gives up the shelter of Śrī Caitanya Mahāprabhu, not even for a moment.

TEXT 254

পরম বৈরাগ্য তার, নাহি ভক্ষ্য-পরিধান।
যৈছে তৈছে আহার করি' রাখয়ে পরাণ ॥ ২৫৪ ॥

parama vairāgya tāra, nāhi bhakṣya-paridhāna
yaiche taiche āhāra kari' rākhaye parāṇa

SYNONYMS

parama—supreme; *vairāgya*—renunciation; *tāra*—his; *nāhi*—not; *bhakṣya*—eating; *paridhāna*—dressing; *yaiche taiche*—somehow or other; *āhāra kari'*—eating; *rākhaye parāṇa*—keeps life.

TRANSLATION

"He is in the supreme order of renounced life. Indeed, he does not care about eating or dressing. Somehow or other he eats and maintains his life.

TEXT 255

দশদণ্ড রাত্রি গেলে 'পুষ্পাঞ্জলি' দেখিয়া ।
সিংহদ্বারে খাড়া হয় আহার লাগিয়া ॥ ২৫৫ ॥

daśa-daṇḍa rātri gele 'puṣpāñjali' dekhiyā
siṁha-dvāre khāḍā haya āhāra lāgiyā

SYNONYMS

daśa-daṇḍa—ten *daṇḍas* (240 minutes); *rātri*—night; *gele*—having gone; *puṣpāñjali*—the *puṣpāñjali* performance; *dekhiyā*—after seeing; *siṁha-dvāre*—at the Siṁha-dvāra gate; *khāḍā haya*—stands; *āhāra lāgiyā*—to get some alms for eating.

TRANSLATION

"After ten daṇḍas [four hours] of the night have passed and Raghunātha dāsa has seen the performance of puṣpāñjali, he stands at the Siṁha-dvāra gate to beg some alms to eat.

TEXT 256

কেহ যদি দেয়, তবে করয়ে ভক্ষণ ।
কভু উপবাস, কভু করয়ে চর্বণ ॥" ২৫৬ ॥

keha yadi deya, tabe karaye bhakṣaṇa
kabhu upavāsa, kabhu karaye carvaṇa"

SYNONYMS

keha—someone; *yadi*—if; *deya*—offers; *tabe*—then; *karaye bhakṣaṇa*—he eats; *kabhu*—sometimes; *upavāsa*—fasting; *kabhu*—sometimes; *karaye carvaṇa*—he chews.

TRANSLATION

"He eats if someone gives him something to eat. Sometimes he fasts, and sometimes he chews fried grains."

TEXT 257

এত শুনি' সেই মনুষ্য গোবর্ধন-স্থানে ।
কহিল গিয়া সব রঘুনাথ-বিবরণে ॥ ২৫৭ ॥

eta śuni' sei manuṣya govardhana-sthāne
kahila giyā saba raghunātha-vivaraṇe

SYNONYMS

eta śuni'—hearing this; *sei manuṣya*—that messenger; *govardhana-sthāne*—to Govardhana Majumadāra; *kahila*—spoke; *giyā*—going; *saba*—everything; *raghunātha-vivaraṇe*—the description of Raghunātha dāsa.

TRANSLATION

After hearing this, the messenger returned to Govardhana Majumadāra and informed him all about Raghunātha dāsa.

TEXT 258

শুনি' তাঁর মাতা পিতা দুঃখিত হইল ।
পুত্র-ঠাঞি দ্রব্য-মনুষ্য পাঠাইতে মন কৈল ॥ ২৫৮ ॥

śuni' tāṅra mātā pitā duḥkhita ha-ila
putra-ṭhāñi dravya-manuṣya pāṭhāite mana kaila

SYNONYMS

śuni'—hearing; *tāṅra*—his; *mātā pitā*—father and mother; *duḥkhita ha-ila*—became very unhappy; *putra-ṭhāñi*—to their son; *dravya-manuṣya*—articles and men; *pāṭhāite*—to send; *mana kaila*—decided.

TRANSLATION

Hearing the description of Raghunātha dāsa's behavior in the renounced order, his father and mother were very unhappy. Therefore they decided to send him some men with goods for his comfort.

TEXT 259

চারিশত মুদ্রা, দুই ভৃত্য, এক ব্রাহ্মণ ।
শিবানন্দের ঠাঞি পাঠাইল ততক্ষণ ॥ ২৫৯ ॥

cāri-śata mudrā, dui bhṛtya, eka brāhmaṇa
śivānandera ṭhāñi pāṭhāila tata-kṣaṇa

SYNONYMS

cāri-śata mudrā—four hundred coins; *dui bhṛtya*—two servants; *eka brāhmaṇa*—one *brāhmaṇa; śivānandera ṭhāñi*—to Śivānanda Sena; *pāṭhāila*—sent; *tata-kṣaṇa*—immediately.

TRANSLATION

Raghunātha dāsa's father immediately sent four hundred coins, two servants and one brāhmaṇa to Śivānanda Sena.

TEXT 260

শিবানন্দ কহে,—"তুমি সব যাইতে নারিবা ।
আমি যাই যবে, আমার সঙ্গে যাইবা ॥ ২৬০ ॥

śivānanda kahe, —"tumi saba yāite nāribā
āmi yāi yabe, āmāra saṅge yāibā

SYNONYMS

śivānanda kahe—Śivānanda Sena said; *tumi*—you; *saba*—all; *yāite nāribā*—cannot go; *āmi yāi*—I go; *yabe*—when; *āmāra saṅge*—with me; *yāibā*—you will go.

TRANSLATION

Śivānanda Sena informed them, "You cannot go to Jagannātha Purī directly. When I go there, you may accompany me.

TEXT 261

এবে ঘর যাহ, যবে আমি সব চলিমু ।
তবে তোমা সবাকারে সঙ্গে লঞা যামু ॥ ২৬১ ॥

ebe ghara yāha, yabe āmi saba calimu
tabe tomā sabākāre saṅge lañā yāmu

SYNONYMS

ebe—now; *ghara yāha*—go home; *yabe*—when; *āmi*—we; *saba*—all; *calimu*—will go; *tabe*—then; *tomā sabākāre*—all of you; *saṅge*—with; *lañā*—taking; *yāmu*—I shall go.

TRANSLATION

"Now go home. When all of us go, I shall take all of you with me."

TEXT 262

এই ত' প্রস্তাবে শ্রীকবিকর্ণপূর।
রঘুনাথ-মহিমা গ্রন্থে লিখিলা প্রচুর ॥ ২৬২ ॥

ei ta' prastāve śrī kavi-karṇapūra
raghunātha-mahimā granthe likhilā pracura

SYNONYMS

ei ta' prastāve—in this connection; *śrī kavi-karṇapūra*—the poet named Kavi-karṇapūra; *raghunātha-mahimā*—the glories of Raghunātha dāsa; *granthe*—in his book; *likhilā*—wrote; *pracura*—much.

TRANSLATION

Describing this incident, the great poet Śrī Kavi-karṇapūra has written extensively about the glorious activities of Raghunātha dāsa in his book.

TEXT 263

আচার্যো যদুনন্দনঃ সুমধুরঃ শ্রীবাসুদেবপ্রিয়-
স্তচ্ছিষ্যো রঘুনাথ ইত্যধিগুণঃ প্রাণাধিকো মাদৃশাম্।
শ্রীচৈতন্যকৃপাতিরেকসততস্নিগ্ধঃ স্বরূপানুগো
বৈরাগ্যৈকনিধির্ন কস্য বিদিতো নীলাচলে তিষ্ঠতাম্ ॥২৬৩॥

ācāryo yadunandanaḥ sumadhuraḥ śrī-vāsudeva-priyas
tac-chiṣyo raghunātha ity adhiguṇaḥ prāṇādhiko mādṛśām
śrī-caitanya-kṛpātireka-satata-snigdhaḥ svarūpānugo
vairāgyaika-nidhir na kasya vidito nīlācale tiṣṭhatām

SYNONYMS

ācāryaḥ yadunandanaḥ—Yadunandana Ācārya; *su-madhuraḥ*—very well behaved; *śrī-vāsudeva-priyaḥ*—very dear to Śrī Vāsudeva Datta Ṭhākura; *tat-śiṣyaḥ*—his disciple; *raghunāthaḥ*—Raghunātha dāsa; *iti*—thus; *adhiguṇaḥ*—so qualified; *prāṇa-adhikaḥ*—more dear than life; *mā-dṛśām*—of all the devotees of Śrī Caitanya Mahāprabhu like me; *śrī-caitanya-kṛpā*—by the mercy of Śrī Caitanya Mahāprabhu; *atireka*—excess; *satata-snigdhaḥ*—always pleasing; *svarūpa-anugaḥ*—following in the footsteps of Svarūpa Dāmodara; *vairāgya*—of renunciation; *eka-nidhiḥ*—the ocean; *na*—not; *kasya*—by whom; *viditaḥ*—known; *nīlācale*—at Jagannātha Purī; *tiṣṭhatām*—of those who were staying.

TRANSLATION

"Raghunātha dāsa is a disciple of Yadunandana Ācārya, who is very gentle and is extremely dear to Vāsudeva Datta, a resident of Kāñcanapallī. Because of Raghunātha dāsa's transcendental qualities, he is always more dear than life for all of us devotees of Śrī Caitanya Mahāprabhu. Since he has been favored by the abundant mercy of Śrī Caitanya Mahāprabhu, he is always pleasing. Vividly providing a superior example for the renounced order, this very dear follower of Svarūpa Dāmodara Gosvāmī is the ocean of renunciation. Who among the residents of Nīlācala [Jagannātha Purī] does not know him very well?

PURPORT

This verse is from *Śrī Caitanya-candrodaya-nāṭaka* (10.3) of Kavi-karṇapūra.

TEXT 264

যঃ সর্বলোকৈকমনোভিরুচ্যা
সৌভাগ্যভূঃ কাচিদকৃষ্টপচ্যা ।
যত্রায়মারোপণতুল্যকালং
তৎপ্রেমশাখী ফলবানতুল্যঃ ॥ ২৬৪ ॥

yaḥ sarva-lokaika-manobhirucyā
saubhāgya-bhūḥ kācid akṛṣṭa-pacyā
yatrāyam āropaṇa-tulya-kālaṁ
tat-prema-śākhī phalavān atulyaḥ

SYNONYMS

yaḥ—who; *sarva-loka*—of all the devotees in Purī; *eka*—foremost; *manaḥ*—of the minds; *abhirucyā*—by the affection; *saubhāgya-bhūḥ*—the ground of good fortune; *kācit*—indescribable; *akṛṣṭa-pacyā*—perfect without tilling or perfect without practice; *yatra*—in which; *ayam*—this; *āropaṇa-tulya-kālam*—at the same time as the sowing of the seed; *tat-prema-śākhī*—a tree of the love of Śrī Caitanya Mahāprabhu; *phalavān*—fruitful; *atulyaḥ*—the matchless.

TRANSLATION

"Because he is very pleasing to all the devotees, Raghunātha dāsa Gosvāmī easily became like the fertile earth of good fortune in which it was suitable for the seed of Lord Caitanya Mahāprabhu to be sown. At the same time that the seed was sown, it grew into a matchless tree of the love of Śrī Caitanya Mahāprabhu and produced fruit."

PURPORT

This is the next verse from *Śrī Caitanya-candrodaya-nāṭaka* (10.4).

TEXT 265

শিবানন্দ যৈছে সেই মনুষ্যে কহিলা ।
কর্ণপূর সেইরূপে শ্লোক বর্ণিলা ॥ ২৬৫ ॥

śivānanda yaiche sei manuṣye kahilā
karṇapūra sei-rūpe śloka varṇilā

SYNONYMS

śivānanda—Śivānanda Sena; *yaiche*—as; *sei*—unto the; *manuṣye*—messenger; *kahilā*—said; *karṇapūra*—the great poet Kavi-karṇapūra; *sei rūpe*—in that way; *śloka varṇilā*—composed verses.

TRANSLATION

In these verses, the great poet Kavi-karṇapūra gives the same information that Śivānanda Sena conveyed to the messenger from Raghunātha dāsa's father.

TEXT 266

বর্ষান্তরে শিবানন্দ চলে নীলাচলে ।
রঘুনাথের সেবক, বিপ্র তাঁর সঙ্গে চলে ॥ ২৬৬ ॥

varṣāntare śivānanda cale nīlācale
raghunāthera sevaka, vipra tāṅra saṅge cale

SYNONYMS

varṣa-antare—the next year; *śivānanda*—Śivānanda Sena; *cale nīlācale*—was going to Jagannātha Purī; *raghunāthera*—of Raghunātha dāsa; *sevaka*—the servants; *vipra*—and the *brāhmaṇa; tāṅra saṅge*—with him; *cale*—go.

TRANSLATION

The next year, when Śivānanda Sena was going to Jagannātha Purī as usual, the servants and the brāhmaṇa, who was a cook, went with him.

TEXT 267

সেই বিপ্র ভৃত্য, চারি-শত মুদ্রা লঞা ।
নীলাচলে রঘুনাথে মিলিলা আসিয়া ॥ ২৬৭ ॥

sei vipra bhṛtya, cāri-śata mudrā lañā
nīlācale raghunāthe mililā āsiyā

SYNONYMS

sei vipra—that *brāhmaṇa; bhṛtya*—the servants; *cāri-śata mudrā*—four hundred coins; *lañā*—bringing; *nīlācale*—at Jagannātha Purī; *raghunāthe*—with Raghunātha dāsa; *mililā*—met; *āsiyā*—coming.

TRANSLATION

The servants and brāhmaṇa brought four hundred coins to Jagannātha Purī, and there they met Raghunātha dāsa.

TEXT 268

রঘুনাথ-দাস অঙ্গীকার না করিল ।
দ্রব্য লঞা দুইজন তাহাঁই রহিল ॥ ২৬৮ ॥

raghunātha-dāsa aṅgīkāra nā karila
dravya lañā dui-jana tāhāṅi rahila

SYNONYMS

raghunātha-dāsa—Raghunātha dāsa; *aṅgīkāra nā karila*—did not accept; *dravya lañā*—taking the wealth; *dui-jana*—two persons; *tāhāṅi rahila*—remained there.

TRANSLATION

Raghunātha dāsa did not accept the money and men sent by his father. Therefore a servant and the brāhmaṇa stayed there with the money.

TEXT 269

তবে রঘুনাথ করি' অনেক যতন ।
মাসে দুইদিন কৈলা প্রভুর নিমন্ত্রণ ॥ ২৬৯ ॥

tabe raghunātha kari' aneka yatana
māse dui-dina kailā prabhura nimantraṇa

SYNONYMS

tabe—at that time; *raghunātha*—Raghunātha dāsa; *kari' aneka yatana*—with great attention; *māse*—every month; *dui-dina*—two days; *kailā*—he made; *prabhura nimantraṇa*—invitation to Lord Śrī Caitanya Mahāprabhu.

TRANSLATION

At that time, Raghunātha dāsa invited Śrī Caitanya Mahāprabhu to his house with great attention for two days every month.

TEXT 270

দুই নিমন্ত্রণে লাগে কৌড়ি অষ্টপণ ।
ব্রাহ্মণ-ভৃত্য-ঠাঞি করেন এতেক গ্রহণ ॥ ২৭০ ॥

dui nimantraṇe lāge kauḍi aṣṭa-paṇa
brāhmaṇa-bhṛtya-ṭhāñi karena eteka grahaṇa

SYNONYMS

dui nimantraṇe—these two invitations; *lāge*—cost; *kauḍi aṣṭa-paṇa*—640 *kauḍis; brāhmaṇa-bhṛtya-ṭhāñi*—from the *brāhmaṇa* and the servant; *karena*—does; *eteka*—so much; *grahaṇa*—accepting.

TRANSLATION

The cost for these two occasions was 640 kauḍis. Therefore he would take that much from the servant and the brāhmaṇa.

TEXT 271

এইমত নিমন্ত্রণ বর্ষ দুই কৈলা ।
পাছে রঘুনাথ নিমন্ত্রণ ছাড়ি' দিলা ॥ ২৭১ ॥

ei-mata nimantraṇa varṣa dui kailā
pāche raghunātha nimantraṇa chāḍi' dilā

SYNONYMS

ei-mata—in this way; *nimantraṇa*—invitation; *varṣa dui*—for two years; *kailā*—continued; *pāche*—at the end; *raghunātha*—Raghunātha dāsa; *nimantraṇa*—invitation; *chāḍi' dilā*—gave up.

TRANSLATION

Raghunātha dāsa continued to invite Śrī Caitanya Mahāprabhu in this way for two years, but at the end of the second year he stopped.

TEXT 272

মাস-দুই যবে রঘুনাথ না করে নিমন্ত্রণ ।
স্বরূপে পুছিলা তবে শচীর নন্দন ॥ ২৭২ ॥

māsa-dui yabe raghunātha nā kare nimantraṇa
svarūpe puchilā tabe śacīra nandana

SYNONYMS

māsa-dui—for two months; *yabe*—when; *raghunātha*—Raghunātha dāsa; *nā kare nimantraṇa*—does not invite; *svarūpe puchilā*—inquired from Svarūpa Dāmodara; *tabe*—at that time; *śacīra nandana*—the son of mother Śacī, Śrī Caitanya Mahāprabhu.

TRANSLATION

When Raghunātha dāsa neglected to invite Lord Śrī Caitanya Mahāprabhu for two consecutive months, the Lord, the son of Śacī, questioned Svarūpa Dāmodara.

TEXT 273

'রঘু কেনে আমায় নিমন্ত্রণ ছাড়ি' দিল ?'
স্বরূপ কহে,—"মনে কিছু বিচার করিল ॥ ২৭৩ ॥

'raghu kene āmāya nimantraṇa chāḍi' dila?'
svarūpa kahe, —"mane kichu vicāra karila

SYNONYMS

raghu—Raghunātha dāsa; *kene*—why; *āmāya*—to Me; *nimantraṇa*—invitation; *chāḍi' dila*—has stopped; *svarūpa kahe*—Svarūpa Dāmodara replied; *mane*—within his mind; *kichu*—something; *vicāra karila*—he has thought.

TRANSLATION

The Lord asked, "Why has Raghunātha dāsa stopped inviting Me?" Svarūpa Dāmodara replied, "He must have reconsidered something in his mind.

TEXT 274

বিষয়ীর দ্রব্য লঞা করি নিমন্ত্রণ ।
প্রসন্ন না হয় ইহায় জানি প্রভুর মন ॥ ২৭৪ ॥

viṣayīra dravya lañā kari nimantraṇa
prasanna nā haya ihāya jāni prabhura mana

SYNONYMS

viṣayīra dravya—things supplied by materialistic men; *lañā*—accepting; *kari nimantraṇa*—I invite; *prasanna*—satisfied; *nā haya*—is not; *ihāya*—in this connection; *jāni*—I can understand; *prabhura mana*—the mind of Lord Śrī Caitanya Mahāprabhu.

TRANSLATION

" 'I invite Śrī Caitanya Mahāprabhu by accepting goods from materialistic people. I know that the Lord's mind is not satisfied by this.

TEXT 275

মোর চিত্ত দ্রব্য লইতে না হয় নির্মল ।
এই নিমন্ত্রণে দেখি,—'প্রতিষ্ঠা'-মাত্র ফল ॥ ২৭৫ ॥

mora citta dravya la-ite nā haya nirmala
ei nimantraṇe dekhi, —'pratiṣṭhā'-mātra phala

SYNONYMS

mora citta—my consciousness; *dravya la-ite*—to accept the goods; *nā haya*—is not; *nirmala*—pure; *ei nimantraṇe*—by this invitation; *dekhi*—I see; *pratiṣṭhā*—reputation; *mātra*—only; *phala*—the result.

TRANSLATION

" 'My consciousness is impure because I accept all these goods from people who are interested only in pounds, shillings and pence. Therefore by this kind of invitation I only get some material reputation.

PURPORT

Śrīla Bhaktisiddhānta Sarasvatī Ṭhākura remarks that people who are under the bodily conception of life are called materialists. If we accept the offerings of such people, place them before the Lord and invite Vaiṣṇavas to partake of the *prasāda,* that attempt will gain us only a material reputation, not the actual benefit of service to a pure Vaiṣṇava. One should therefore try to serve the Supreme Personality of Godhead by fully surrendering at His lotus feet. If one engages for the service of the Lord whatever money one has honestly earned, that is spiritual service to the Supreme Personality of Godhead, the spiritual master and the Vaiṣṇavas.

TEXT 276

উপরোধে প্রভু মোর মানেন নিমন্ত্রণ ।
না মানিলে দুঃখী হইবেক মূর্খ জন ॥ ২৭৬ ॥

uparodhe prabhu mora mānena nimantraṇa
nā mānile duḥkhī ha-ibeka mūrkha jana

SYNONYMS

uparodhe—by my request; *prabhu*—Lord Śrī Caitanya Mahāprabhu; *mora*—my; *mānena*—accepts; *nimantraṇa*—invitation; *nā mānile*—if He does not accept; *duḥkhī*—unhappy; *ha-ibeka*—will become; *mūrkha jana*—foolish person.

TRANSLATION

" 'At my request Śrī Caitanya Mahāprabhu accepts the invitations because He knows that a foolish person like me would be unhappy if He did not accept them.'

PURPORT

Śrīla Bhaktisiddhānta Sarasvatī Ṭhākura says that people who are advanced in learning but attached to material enjoyment, who are puffed up by material possessions, by birth in an elevated aristocratic family or by education, may offer showbottle devotional service to the Deity and also offer *prasāda* to Vaiṣṇavas. Because of their ignorance, however, they cannot understand that since their minds are materially polluted, neither the Supreme Personality of Godhead, Lord Kṛṣṇa, nor the Vaiṣṇavas accept their offerings. If one accepts money from such materialistic persons to offer food to the Deity and Vaiṣṇavas, a pure Vaiṣṇava does not accept it. This causes unhappiness for the materialists because they are fully absorbed in the bodily conception of life. Therefore they sometimes turn against the Vaiṣṇavas.

TEXT 277

এত বিচারিয়া নিমন্ত্রণ ছাড়ি' দিল" ।
শুনি' মহাপ্রভু হাসি' বলিতে লাগিল ॥ ২৭৭ ॥

eta vicāriyā nimantraṇa chāḍi' dila"
śuni' mahāprabhu hāsi' balite lāgila

SYNONYMS

eta vicāriyā—considering this; *nimantraṇa*—invitation; *chāḍi' dila*—he has stopped; *śuni'*—hearing; *mahāprabhu*—Śrī Caitanya Mahāprabhu; *hāsi'*—smiling; *balite lāgila*—began to say.

TRANSLATION

"Considering all these points," Svarūpa Dāmodara concluded, "he has stopped inviting You." Hearing this, Śrī Caitanya Mahāprabhu smiled and spoke as follows.

TEXT 278

"বিষয়ীর অন্ন খাইলে মলিন হয় মন ।
মলিন মন হৈলে নহে কৃষ্ণের স্মরণ ॥ ২৭৮ ॥

"viṣayīra anna khāile malina haya mana
malina mana haile nahe kṛṣṇera smaraṇa

SYNONYMS

viṣayīra—of materialistic persons; *anna*—food; *khāile*—if one eats; *malina*—contaminated; *haya mana*—the mind becomes; *malina*—contaminated; *mana haile*—when the mind becomes; *nahe*—is not; *kṛṣṇera*—of Lord Kṛṣṇa; *smaraṇa*—remembrance.

TRANSLATION

"When one eats food offered by a materialistic man, one's mind becomes contaminated, and when the mind is contaminated, one is unable to think of Kṛṣṇa properly.

PURPORT

Śrīla Bhaktisiddhānta Sarasvatī Ṭhākura suggests that people who are materialistically inclined and *sahajiyās,* or so-called Vaiṣṇavas who take everything very casually, are both *viṣayī,* materialists. Eating food offered by them causes contamination, and as a result of such contamination, even a serious devotee becomes like a materialistic man. There are six kinds of association—giving charity, accepting charity, accepting food, offering food, talking confidentially and inquiring confidentially. One should very carefully avoid associating with both the *sahajiyās,* who are sometimes known as Vaiṣṇavas, and the non-Vaiṣṇavas, or *avaiṣṇavas.* Their association changes the transcendental devotional service of Lord Kṛṣṇa into sense gratification, and when sense gratification enters the mind of a devotee, he is contaminated. The materialistic person who aspires after sense gratification cannot properly think of Kṛṣṇa.

TEXT 279

বিষয়ীর অন্ন হয় 'রাজস' নিমন্ত্রণ ।
দাতা, ভোক্তা—দুঁহার মলিন হয় মন ॥ ২৭৯ ॥

viṣayīra anna haya 'rājasa' nimantraṇa
dātā, bhoktā——duṅhāra malina haya mana

SYNONYMS

viṣayīra—offered by materialistic men; *anna*—food; *haya*—is; *rājasa*—in the mode of passion; *nimantraṇa*—invitation; *dātā*—the person who offers; *bhoktā*—

the person who accepts such an offering; *duṅhāra*—of both of them; *malina*—contaminated; *haya mana*—the mind becomes.

TRANSLATION

"When one accepts an invitation from a person contaminated by the material mode of passion, the person who offers the food and the person who accepts it are both mentally contaminated.

PURPORT

Śrīla Bhaktivinoda Ṭhākura says that there are three varieties of invitations—those in the mode of goodness, those in passion and those in ignorance. An invitation accepted from a pure devotee is in the mode of goodness, an invitation accepted from a person who is pious but materially attached is in the mode of passion, and an invitation accepted from a person who is materially very sinful is in the mode of ignorance.

TEXT 280

ইँहार সঙ্কোচে আমি এত দিন নিল।
ভাল হৈল—জানিয়া আপনি ছাড়িদিল ॥"২৮০ ॥

iṅhāra saṅkoce āmi eta dina nila
bhāla haila——jāniyā āpani chāḍi dila"

SYNONYMS

iṅhāra saṅkoce—because of his eagerness; *āmi*—I; *eta dina*—for so many days; *nila*—I accepted; *bhāla haila*—it is very good; *jāniyā*—knowing; *āpani*—automatically; *chāḍi dila*—he has given up.

TRANSLATION

"Because of Raghunātha dāsa's eagerness, I accepted his invitation for many days. It is very good that Raghunātha dāsa, knowing this, has now automatically given up this practice."

TEXT 281

কত দিনে রঘুনাথ সিংহদ্বার ছাড়িলা।
ছত্রে যাই' মাগিয়া খাইতে আরম্ভ করিলা ॥ ২৮১ ॥

kata dine raghunātha siṁha-dvāra chāḍilā
chatre yāi' māgiyā khāite ārambha karilā

SYNONYMS

kata dine—after some days; *raghunātha*—Raghunātha dāsa; *siṁha-dvāra chāḍilā*—gave up standing at the gate known as Siṁha-dvāra; *chatre yāi'*—going to an alms booth; *māgiyā*—begging; *khāite*—to eat; *ārambha karilā*—he began.

TRANSLATION

After some days, Raghunātha dāsa gave up standing near the Siṁha-dvāra gate and instead began eating by begging alms from a booth for free distribution of food.

TEXT 282

গোবিন্দ-পাশ শুনি' প্রভু পুছেন স্বরূপেরে ।
'রঘু ভিক্ষা লাগি' ঠাড় কেনে নহে সিংহদ্বারে' ?২৮২॥

govinda-pāśa śuni' prabhu puchena svarūpere
'raghu bhikṣā lāgi' ṭhāḍa kene nahe siṁha-dvāre'?

SYNONYMS

govinda-pāśa—from Govinda; *śuni'*—hearing; *prabhu*—Śrī Caitanya Mahāprabhu; *puchena svarūpere*—inquired from Svarūpa Dāmodara Gosvāmī; *raghu*—Raghunātha dāsa; *bhikṣā lāgi'*—for begging; *ṭhāḍa kene nahe*—why does he not stand; *siṁha-dvāre*—at the Siṁha-dvāra gate.

TRANSLATION

When Śrī Caitanya Mahāprabhu heard this news from Govinda, He inquired from Svarūpa Dāmodara, "Why does Raghunātha dāsa no longer stand at the Siṁha-dvāra gate to beg alms?"

TEXT 283

স্বরূপ কহে,—"সিংহদ্বারে দুঃখ অনুভবিয়া ।
ছত্রে মাগি' খায় মধ্যাহ্নকালে গিয়া ॥"২৮৩ ॥

svarūpa kahe, —"siṁha-dvāre duḥkha anubhaviyā
chatre māgi' khāya madhyāhna-kāle giyā"

SYNONYMS

svarūpa kahe—Svarūpa Dāmodara replied; *siṁha-dvāre*—at the Siṁha-dvāra gate; *duḥkha anubhaviyā*—feeling unhappy; *chatre*—at the charity booth; *māgi'*—begging; *khāya*—he eats; *madhyāhna-kāle*—at midday; *giyā*—going.

TRANSLATION

Svarūpa Dāmodara replied, "Raghunātha dāsa felt unhappy standing at the Siṁha-dvāra. Therefore he is now going at midday to beg alms from the charity booth."

TEXT 284

প্রভু কহে,—“ভাল কৈল, ছাড়িল সিংহদ্বার ।
সিংহদ্বারে ভিক্ষা-বৃত্তি—বেশ্যার আচার ॥২৮৪ ॥

prabhu kahe, —"bhāla kaila, chāḍila siṁha-dvāra
siṁha-dvāre bhikṣā-vṛtti—veṣyāra ācāra

SYNONYMS

prabhu kahe—Śrī Caitanya Mahāprabhu said; *bhāla kaila*—he has done well; *chāḍila siṁha-dvāra*—he has given up standing at the Siṁha-dvāra; *siṁha-dvāre bhikṣā-vṛtti*—to beg alms standing at the Siṁha-dvāra; *veśyāra ācāra*—the behavior of a prostitute.

TRANSLATION

Hearing this news, Śrī Caitanya Mahāprabhu said, "He has done very well by no longer standing at the Siṁha-dvāra gate. Such begging of alms resembles the behavior of a prostitute.

TEXT 285

তথাহি—কিমর্থময়মাগচ্ছতি, অয়ং দাস্যতি, অনেন দত্তময়-
মপরঃ । সমেত্যয়ং দাস্যতি,অনেনাপি ন দত্তমন্যঃ সমেষ্যতি,
স দাস্যতি ইত্যাদি ॥ ২৮৫ ॥

kim artham ayam āgacchati, ayaṁ dāsyati, anena dattam ayam
aparaḥ. samety ayaṁ dāsyati, anenāpi na dattam
anyaḥ sameṣyati, sa dāsyati ity ādi.

SYNONYMS

kim artham—why; *ayam*—this person; *āgacchati*—is coming; *ayam*—this person; *dāsyati*—will give; *anena*—by this person; *dattam*—given; *ayam*—this; *aparaḥ*—other; *sameti*—comes near; *ayam*—this person; *dāsyati*—will give; *anena*—by this person; *api*—also; *na*—not; *dattam*—given; *anyaḥ*—another; *sameṣyati*—will come near; *saḥ*—he; *dāsyati*—will give; *iti*—thus; *ādi*—and so on.

TRANSLATION

" 'Here is a person coming near. He will give me something. This person gave me something last night. Now another person is coming near. He may give me something. The person who just passed did not give me anything, but another person will come, and he will give me something.' Thus a person in the renounced order gives up his neutrality and depends on the charity of this person or that. Thinking in this way, he adopts the occupation of a prostitute.

TEXT 286

ছত্রে যাই যথা-লাভ উদর-ভরণ ।
অন্য কথা নাহি, সুখে কৃষ্ণসঙ্কীর্তন ॥"২৮৬ ॥

chatre yāi yathā-lābha udara-bharaṇa
anya kathā nāhi, sukhe kṛṣṇa-saṅkīrtana"

SYNONYMS

chatre yāi—going to the booth for free food distribution; *yathā-lābha*—with whatever is obtained; *udara-bharaṇa*—filling the belly; *anya*—other; *kathā*—talk; *nāhi*—there is not; *sukhe*—happily; *kṛṣṇa-saṅkīrtana*—chanting the Hare Kṛṣṇa *mahā-mantra.*

TRANSLATION

"If one goes to the booth where free food is distributed and fills his belly with whatever he obtains, there is no chance of further unwanted talk, and one can very peacefully chant the Hare Kṛṣṇa mahā-mantra."

TEXT 287

এত বলি' তাঁরে পুনঃ প্রসাদ করিলা ।
'গোবর্ধনের শিলা', 'গুঞ্জা-মালা' তাঁরে দিলা ॥২৮৭॥

eta bali' tāṅre punaḥ prasāda karilā
'govardhanera śilā', 'guñjā-mālā' tāṅre dilā

SYNONYMS

eta bali'—saying this; *tāṅre*—unto him; *punaḥ*—again; *prasāda karilā*—gave something in mercy; *govardhanera śilā*—a stone from Govardhana Hill; *guñjā-mālā*—a garland of small conchshells; *tāṅre dilā*—delivered to him.

TRANSLATION

After saying this, Śrī Caitanya Mahāprabhu again bestowed His mercy upon Raghunātha dāsa by giving him a piece of stone from Govardhana Hill and a garland of small conchshells.

TEXT 288

শঙ্করানন্দ-সরস্বতী বৃন্দাবন হৈতে আইলা ।
তেঁহ সেই শিলা-গুঞ্জামালা লঞা গেলা ॥ ২৮৮ ॥

śaṅkarānanda-sarasvatī vṛndāvana haite āilā
teṅha sei śilā-guñjā-mālā lañā gelā

SYNONYMS

śaṅkarānanda-sarasvatī—one of the devotees of Śrī Caitanya Mahāprabhu; *vṛndāvana haite*—from Vṛndāvana; *āilā*—came; *teṅha*—he; *sei*—that; *śilā-guñjā-mālā*—stone and the garland of small conchshells; *lañā*—taking; *gelā*—went.

TRANSLATION

Previously, when Śaṅkarānanda Sarasvatī had returned from Vṛndāvana, he had brought the piece of stone from Govardhana Hill and also the garland of conchshells.

TEXT 289

পার্শ্বে গাঁথা গুঞ্জামালা, গোবর্ধনশিলা ।
দুই বস্তু মহাপ্রভুর আগে আনি' দিলা ॥ ২৮৯ ॥

pārśve gāṅthā guñjā-mālā, govardhana-śilā
dui vastu mahāprabhura āge āni' dilā

SYNONYMS

pārśve—on one side; *gāṅthā*—strung together; *guñjā-mālā*—the garland of small conchshells; *govardhana-śilā*—the stone from Govardhana; *dui vastu*—two things; *mahāprabhura āge*—in front of Śrī Caitanya Mahāprabhu; *āni' dilā*—presented.

TRANSLATION

He presented Śrī Caitanya Mahāprabhu these two items—the garland of conchshells and the stone from Govardhana Hill.

TEXT 290

দুই অপূর্ব-বস্তু পাঞা প্রভু তুষ্ট হৈলা ।
স্মরণের কালে গলে পরে গুঞ্জামালা ॥ ২৯০ ॥

dui apūrva-vastu pāñā prabhu tuṣṭa hailā
smaraṇera kāle gale pare guñjā-mālā

SYNONYMS

dui—two; *apūrva-vastu*—uncommon things; *pāñā*—getting; *prabhu*—Lord Śrī Caitanya Mahāprabhu; *tuṣṭa hailā*—became very happy; *smaraṇera kāle*—at the time of remembering (when He was chanting Hare Kṛṣṇa); *gale*—on the neck; *pare*—wears; *guñjā-mālā*—the garland of small conchshells.

TRANSLATION

Upon receiving these two uncommon items, Śrī Caitanya Mahāprabhu was extremely happy. While chanting, He would put the garland around His neck.

TEXT 291

গোবর্ধন-শিলা প্রভু হৃদয়ে-নেত্রে ধরে ।
কভু নাসায় ঘ্রাণ লয়, কভু শিরে করে ॥ ২৯১ ॥

govardhana-śilā prabhu hṛdaye-netre dhare
kabhu nāsāya ghrāṇa laya, kabhu śire kare

SYNONYMS

govardhana-śilā—the stone from Govardhana Hill; *prabhu*—Śrī Caitanya Mahāprabhu; *hṛdaye*—on the heart; *netre*—on the eyes; *dhare*—puts; *kabhu*—sometimes; *nāsāya*—with the nose; *ghrāṇa laya*—smells; *kabhu*—sometimes; *śire kare*—He puts on His head.

TRANSLATION

The Lord would put the stone to His heart or sometimes to His eyes. Sometimes He would smell it with His nose and sometimes place it on His head.

TEXT 292

নেত্রজলে সেই শিলা ভিজে নিরন্তর ।
শিলারে কহেন প্রভু—'কৃষ্ণ-কলেবর' ॥ ২৯২ ॥

netra-jale sei śilā bhije nirantara
śilāre kahena prabhu——'kṛṣṇa-kalevara'

SYNONYMS

netra-jale—by the tears of His eyes; *sei*—that; *śilā*—stone; *bhije*—remains wet; *nirantara*—always; *śilāre*—the stone; *kahena*—says; *prabhu*—Śrī Caitanya Mahāprabhu; *kṛṣṇa-kalevara*—the body of Lord Kṛṣṇa.

TRANSLATION

The stone from Govardhana was always moist with tears from His eyes. Śrī Caitanya Mahāprabhu would say, "This stone is directly the body of Lord Kṛṣṇa."

TEXT 293

এইমত তিনবৎসর শিলা-মালা ধরিলা।
তুষ্ট হঞা শিলা-মালা রঘুনাথে দিলা ॥ ২৯৩ ॥

ei-mata tina-vatsara śilā-mālā dharilā
tuṣṭa hañā śilā-mālā raghunāthe dilā

SYNONYMS

ei-mata—in this way; *tina-vatsara*—for three years; *śilā-mālā*—the stone and the garland of conchshells; *dharilā*—He kept; *tuṣṭa hañā*—when He became very happy; *śilā-mālā*—the stone and the garland; *raghunāthe*—to Raghunātha dāsa; *dilā*—He delivered.

TRANSLATION

For three years He kept the stone and garland. Then, greatly satisfied by the behavior of Raghunātha dāsa, the Lord delivered both of them to him.

TEXT 294

প্রভু কহে,—"এই শিলা কৃষ্ণের বিগ্রহ।
ইঁহার সেবা কর তুমি করিয়া আগ্রহ ॥ ২৯৪ ॥

prabhu kahe, ——"ei śilā kṛṣṇera vigraha
iṅhāra sevā kara tumi kariyā āgraha

SYNONYMS

prabhu kahe—Śrī Caitanya Mahāprabhu said; *ei śilā*—this stone; *kṛṣṇera vigraha*—the form of Lord Kṛṣṇa; *iṅhāra*—of this; *sevā*—worship; *kara*—do; *tumi*—you; *kariyā āgraha*—with great eagerness.

TRANSLATION

Śrī Caitanya Mahāprabhu instructed Raghunātha dāsa, "This stone is the transcendental form of Lord Kṛṣṇa. Worship the stone with great eagerness."

PURPORT

Śrīla Bhaktisiddhānta Sarasvatī Ṭhākura writes in his *Anubhāṣya* that in the opinion of Śrī Caitanya Mahāprabhu, the *govardhana-śilā,* the stone from Govardhana Hill, was directly the form of Kṛṣṇa, the son of Mahārāja Nanda. The Lord used the stone for three years, and then in the heart of Raghunātha dāsa the Lord awakened devotional service to the stone. The Lord then gave the stone to Raghunātha dāsa, accepting him as one of His most confidential servants. However, some envious people conclude that because Raghunātha dāsa had not taken birth in the family of a *brāhmaṇa,* Śrī Caitanya Mahāprabhu did not give him the right to worship the Deity directly, but instead gave him a stone from Govardhana. This kind of thought is *nārakī,* or hellish. As stated in the *Padma Purāṇa, arcye viṣṇau śilādhīr guruṣu nara-matir vaiṣṇave jāti-buddhiḥ...yasya vā nārakī saḥ:* "One who considers the *arcā-mūrti* (the worshipable Deity of Lord Viṣṇu) to be stone, the spiritual master to be an ordinary human being, or a Vaiṣṇava to belong to a particular creed is possessed of hellish intelligence." If one thinks that the worshipable *śālagrāma-śilā* is a mere stone, that the spiritual master is an ordinary human being or that a pure Vaiṣṇava preaching the *bhakti* cult all over the world is a member of a particular caste or material division of society, he is considered a *nārakī,* a candidate for hellish life. When Śrī Caitanya Mahāprabhu instructed that the *govardhana-śilā,* the stone taken from Govardhana, is nondifferent from the body of Śrī Kṛṣṇa, the Supreme Personality of Godhead, He indirectly advised such foolish persons that one should not be envious of a Vaiṣṇava who belongs to a different caste or sect. One should accept a Vaiṣṇava as transcendental. In this way one can be saved; otherwise, one is surely awaiting a hellish life.

TEXT 295

এই শিলার কর তুমি সাত্ত্বিক পূজন ।
অচিরাৎ পাবে তুমি কৃষ্ণপ্রেমধন ॥ ২৯৫ ॥

ei śilāra kara tumi sāttvika pūjana
acirāt pābe tumi kṛṣṇa-prema-dhana

SYNONYMS

ei śilāra—of this stone; *kara*—do; *tumi*—you; *sāttvika pūjana*—worshiping like a perfect *brāhmaṇa,* or in the mode of goodness; *acirāt*—very soon; *pābe tumi*—you will get; *kṛṣṇa-prema*—ecstatic love of Kṛṣṇa; *dhana*—wealth.

TRANSLATION

Śrī Caitanya Mahāprabhu continued, "Worship this stone in the mode of goodness like a perfect brāhmaṇa, for by such worship you will surely attain ecstatic love of Kṛṣṇa without delay.

TEXT 296

এক কুঁজা জল আর তুলসী-মঞ্জরী ।
সাত্ত্বিক-সেবা এই—শুদ্ধভাবে করি ॥ ২৯৬ ॥

eka kuṅjā jala āra tulasī-mañjarī
sāttvika-sevā ei——śuddha-bhāve kari

SYNONYMS

eka—one; *kuṅjā*—jug; *jala*—water; *āra*—and; *tulasī-mañjarī*—flowers of the *tulasī* tree; *sāttvika-sevā*—worship in goodness; *ei*—this; *śuddha-bhāve*—in complete purity; *kari*—performing.

TRANSLATION

"For such worship, one needs a jug of water and a few flowers from a tulasī tree. This is worship in complete goodness when performed in complete purity.

TEXT 297

দুইদিকে দুইপত্র মধ্যে কোমল মঞ্জরী ।
এইমত অষ্টমঞ্জরী দিবে শ্রদ্ধা করি' ॥" ২৯৭ ॥

dui-dike dui-patra madhye komala mañjarī
ei-mata aṣṭa-mañjarī dibe śraddhā kari' "

SYNONYMS

dui-dike—on two sides; *dui-patra*—two *tulasī* leaves; *madhye*—within; *komala mañjarī*—very soft *tulasī* flower; *ei-mata*—in this way; *aṣṭa-mañjarī*—eight *tulasī* flowers; *dibe*—you should offer; *śraddhā kari'*—with faith and love.

TRANSLATION

"With faith and love, you should offer eight soft tulasī flowers, each with two tulasī leaves, one on each side of each flower."

TEXT 298

শ্রীহস্তে শিলা দিয়া এই আজ্ঞা দিলা ।
আনন্দে রঘুনাথ সেবা করিতে লাগিলা ॥ ২৯৮ ॥

śrī-haste śilā diyā ei ājñā dilā
ānande raghunātha sevā karite lāgilā

SYNONYMS

śrī-haste—by His own transcendental hand; *śilā*—the stone from Govardhana Hill; *diyā*—delivering; *ei ājñā*—this order; *dilā*—He gave; *ānande*—in great happiness; *raghunātha*—Raghunātha dāsa; *sevā karite lāgilā*—began to worship.

TRANSLATION

After thus advising him how to worship, Lord Śrī Caitanya Mahāprabhu personally offered Raghunātha dāsa the govardhana-śilā with His transcendental hand. As advised by the Lord, Raghunātha dāsa worshiped the śilā in great transcendental jubilation.

TEXT 299

এক-বিতস্তি দুইবস্ত্র, পিঁড়া একখানি ।
স্বরূপ দিলেন কুঁজা আনিবারে পানি ॥ ২৯৯ ॥

eka-vitasti dui-vastra, piṅḍā eka-khāni
svarūpa dilena kuṅjā ānibāre pāni

SYNONYMS

eka-vitasti—about six inches long; *dui-vastra*—two cloths; *piṅḍā eka-khāni*—one wooden platform; *svarūpa dilena*—Svarūpa Dāmodara Gosvāmī delivered; *kuṅjā*—a jug; *ānibāre pāni*—for bringing water.

TRANSLATION

Svarūpa Dāmodara gave Raghunātha dāsa two cloths, each about six inches long, a wooden platform and a jug in which to keep water.

TEXT 300

এইমত রঘুনাথ করেন পূজন ।
পূজা-কালে দেখে শিলায় 'ব্রজেন্দ্রনন্দন' ॥ ৩০০ ॥

ei-mata raghunātha karena pūjana
pūjā-kāle dekhe śilāya 'vrajendra-nandana'

SYNONYMS

ei-mata—in this way; *raghunātha*—Raghunātha dāsa Gosvāmī; *karena pūjana*—worships; *pūjā-kāle*—while worshiping; *dekhe*—he sees; *śilāya*—in the stone from Govardhana; *vrajendra-nandana*—the son of Nanda Mahārāja.

TRANSLATION

Thus Raghunātha dāsa began worshiping the stone from Govardhana, and as he worshiped he saw the Supreme Personality of Godhead, Kṛṣṇa, the son of Nanda Mahārāja, directly in the stone.

TEXT 301

'প্রভুর স্বহস্ত-দত্ত গোবর্ধন-শিলা।
এই চিন্তি' রঘুনাথ প্রেমে ভাসি' গেলা ॥ ৩০১ ॥

'prabhura svahasta-datta govardhana-śilā
ei cinti' raghunātha preme bhāsi' gelā

SYNONYMS

prabhura—of Śrī Caitanya Mahāprabhu; *sva-hasta*—own hand; *datta*—handed over by; *govardhana-śilā*—the stone from Govardhana Hill; *ei cinti'*—thinking this; *raghunātha*—Raghunātha dāsa; *preme*—in ecstatic love; *bhāsi' gelā*—became overflooded.

TRANSLATION

Thinking of how he had received the govardhana-śilā directly from the hands of Śrī Caitanya Mahāprabhu, Raghunātha dāsa was always overflooded with ecstatic love.

TEXT 302

জল-তুলসীর সেবায় তাঁর যত সুখোদয়।
ষোড়শোপচার-পূজায় তত সুখ নয় ॥ ৩০২ ॥

jala-tulasīra sevāya tāṅra yata sukhodaya
ṣoḍaśopacāra-pūjāya tata sukha naya

SYNONYMS

jala-tulasīra sevāya—by worshiping with water and *tulasī; tāṅra*—his; *yata*—as much as; *sukha-udaya*—rise of transcendental happiness; *ṣoḍaśa-upacāra-pū-jāya*—by worshiping with sixteen kinds of paraphernalia; *tata*—so much; *sukha*—happiness; *naya*—is not.

TRANSLATION

The amount of transcendental bliss that Raghunātha dāsa enjoyed simply by offering water and tulasī is impossible to achieve even if one worships the Deity with sixteen kinds of paraphernalia.

TEXT 303

এইমত কত দিন করেন পূজন ।
তবে স্বরূপ-গোসাঞি তাঁরে কহিলা বচন ॥ ৩০৩ ॥

ei-mata kata dina karena pūjana
tabe svarūpa-gosāñi tāṅre kahilā vacana

SYNONYMS

ei-mata—in this way; *kata dina*—for some days; *karena pūjana*—he worshiped; *tabe*—at that time; *svarūpa-gosāñi*—Svarūpa Dāmodara Gosvāmī; *tāṅre*—to him; *kahilā vacana*—said some words.

TRANSLATION

After Raghunātha dāsa had thus worshiped the govardhana-śilā for some time, Svarūpa Dāmodara one day spoke to him as follows.

TEXT 304

"অষ্ট-কৌড়ির খাজা-সন্দেশ কর সমর্পণ ।
শ্রদ্ধা করি' দিলে, সেই অমৃতের সম ॥" ৩০৪ ॥

"aṣṭa-kauḍira khājā-sandeśa kara samarpaṇa
śraddhā kari' dile, sei amṛtera sama

SYNONYMS

aṣṭa-kauḍira—costing eight *kauḍis; khājā-sandeśa*—*khājā* and *sandeśa* sweetmeats; *kara samarpaṇa*—offer; *śraddhā kari'*—with love and faith; *dile*—if you offer; *sei*—that; *amṛtera sama*—just like nectar.

TRANSLATION

"Offer the Govardhana stone eight kauḍis worth of the first-class sweetmeats known as khājā and sandeśa. If you offer them with faith and love, they will be just like nectar."

TEXT 305

তবে অষ্ট-কৌড়ির খাজা করে সমর্পণ ।
স্বরূপ-আজ্ঞায় গোবিন্দ তাহা করে সমাধান ॥ ৩০৫ ॥

tabe aṣṭa-kauḍira khājā kare samarpaṇa
svarūpa-ājñāya govinda tāhā kare samādhāna

SYNONYMS

tabe—then; *aṣṭa-kauḍira*—costing eight *kauḍis; khājā*—the sweetmeat named *khājā; kare samarpaṇa*—offers; *svarūpa-ājñāya*—by the order of Svarūpa Dāmodara; *govinda*—the personal servant of Śrī Caitanya Mahāprabhu; *tāhā*—that; *kare samādhāna*—arranges.

TRANSLATION

Raghunātha dāsa then began offering the costly sweetmeats known as khājā, which Govinda, following the order of Svarūpa Dāmodara, would supply.

TEXT 306

রঘুনাথ সেই শিলা-মালা যবে পাইলা ।
গোসাঞির অভিপ্রায় এই ভাবনা করিলা ॥ ৩০৬ ॥

raghunātha sei śilā-mālā yabe pāilā
gosāñira abhiprāya ei bhāvanā karilā

SYNONYMS

raghunātha—Raghunātha dāsa Gosvāmī; *sei śilā*—that stone; *mālā*—garland; *yabe*—when; *pāilā*—he got; *gosāñira*—of Śrī Caitanya Mahāprabhu; *abhiprāya*—intention; *ei*—this; *bhāvanā karilā*—he thought.

TRANSLATION

When Raghunātha dāsa received from Śrī Caitanya Mahāprabhu the stone and the garland of conchshells, he could understand the Lord's intention. Thus he thought as follows.

TEXT 307

"শিলা দিয়া গোসাঞি সমর্পিলা 'গোবর্ধনে'।
গুঞ্জামালা দিয়া দিলা 'রাধিকা-চরণে' ॥" ৩০৭ ॥

"śilā diyā gosāñi samarpilā 'govardhane'
guñjā-mālā diyā dilā 'rādhikā-caraṇe'

SYNONYMS

śilā diyā—by offering this stone; *gosāñi*—Śrī Caitanya Mahāprabhu; *samarpilā*—offered; *govardhane*—a place near Govardhana Hill; *guñjā-mālā diyā*—by offering the garland of small conchshells; *dilā*—offered; *rādhikā-caraṇe*—shelter at the lotus feet of Śrīmatī Rādhārāṇī.

TRANSLATION

"By offering me the govardhana-śilā, Śrī Caitanya Mahāprabhu has offered me a place near Govardhana Hill, and by offering me the garland of conch shells, He has offered me shelter at the lotus feet of Śrīmatī Rādhārāṇī."

TEXT 308

আনন্দে রঘুনাথের বাহ্য বিস্মরণ।
কায়মনে সেবিলেন গৌরাঙ্গ-চরণ ॥ ৩০৮ ॥

ānande raghunāthera bāhya vismaraṇa
kāya-mane sevilena gaurāṅga-caraṇa

SYNONYMS

ānande—in transcendental bliss; *raghunāthera*—of Raghunātha dāsa; *bāhya vismaraṇa*—forgetting everything external; *kāya-mane*—by mind and body; *sevilena*—served; *gaurāṅga-caraṇa*—the lotus feet of Śrī Caitanya Mahāprabhu.

TRANSLATION

Raghunātha dāsa's transcendental bliss was boundless. Forgetting everything external, he served the lotus feet of Śrī Caitanya Mahāprabhu with his body and mind.

TEXT 309

অনন্ত গুণ রঘুনাথের কে করিবে লেখা ?
রঘুনাথের নিয়ম,—যেন পাষাণের রেখা ॥ ৩০৯ ॥

ananta guṇa raghunāthera ke karibe lekhā?
raghunāthera niyama, ——yena pāṣāṇera rekhā

SYNONYMS

ananta guṇa—unlimited transcendental attributes; *raghunāthera*—of Raghunātha dāsa; *ke*—who; *karibe lekhā*—can write; *raghunāthera*—of Raghunātha dāsa; *niyama*—the strict regulative principles; *yena*—like; *pāṣāṇera rekhā*—lines on a stone.

TRANSLATION

Who could list the unlimited transcendental attributes of Raghunātha dāsa? His strict regulative principles were exactly like lines on a stone.

PURPORT

The words *pāṣāṇera rekhā* are very significant. Raghunātha dāsa Gosvāmī followed the regulative principles so strictly and rigidly that they were compared to the lines on a stone. As such lines cannot be erased at any time, so the regulative principles observed by Śrī Raghunātha dāsa Gosvāmī could not be changed under any circumstances.

TEXT 310

সাড়ে সাত প্রহর যায় কীর্তন-স্মরণে ।
আহার-নিদ্রা চারি দণ্ড সেহ নহে কোন দিনে ॥৩১০

sāḍe sāta prahara yāya kīrtana-smaraṇe
āhāra-nidrā cāri daṇḍa seha nahe kona dine

SYNONYMS

sāḍe sāta prahara—7.5 *praharas* (one *prahara* equals three hours); *yāya*—is spent; *kīrtana-smaraṇe*—in chanting the Hare Kṛṣṇa *mahā-mantra* and remembering the lotus feet of Kṛṣṇa; *āhāra-nidrā*—eating and sleeping; *cāri daṇḍa*—four *daṇḍas* (one *daṇḍa* equals twenty-four minutes); *seha*—that; *nahe*—is not; *kona dine*—some days.

TRANSLATION

Raghunātha dāsa spent more than twenty-two hours out of every twenty-four chanting the Hare Kṛṣṇa mahā-mantra and remembering the lotus feet of the Lord. He ate and slept for less than an hour and a half, and on some days that also was impossible.

TEXT 311

বৈরাগ্যের কথা তাঁর অদ্ভুত-কথন।
আজন্ম না দিল জিহ্বায় রসের স্পর্শন॥ ৩১১॥

vairāgyera kathā tāṅra adbhuta-kathana
ājanma nā dila jihvāya rasera sparśana

SYNONYMS

vairāgyera—of the renunciation; *kathā*—talks; *tāṅra*—of him; *adbhuta-kathana*—wonderful topics; *ā-janma*—from birth; *nā dila*—did not allow; *jihvāya*—to the tongue; *rasera sparśana*—tasting.

TRANSLATION

Topics concerning his renunciation are wonderful. Throughout his life he never allowed his tongue sense gratification.

TEXT 312

ছিণ্ডা কানি কাঁথা বিনা না পরে বসন।
সাবধানে প্রভুর কৈলা আজ্ঞার পালন॥ ৩১২॥

chiṇḍā kāni kāṅthā vinā nā pare vasana
sāvadhāne prabhura kailā ājñāra pālana

SYNONYMS

chiṇḍā kāni—a small torn cloth; *kāṅthā*—a patchwork cotton wrapper; *vinā*—except; *nā pare*—does not wear; *vasana*—clothing; *sāvadhāne*—with great care; *prabhura*—of Śrī Caitanya Mahāprabhu; *kaila*—performed; *ājñāra pālana*—execution of the order.

TRANSLATION

He never touched anything to wear except a small torn cloth and a patchwork wrapper. Thus he very rigidly executed the order of Śrī Caitanya Mahāprabhu.

PURPORT

The principle of very rigidly carrying out the order of the spiritual master must be observed. The spiritual master gives different orders to different people. For example, Śrī Caitanya Mahāprabhu ordered Jīva Gosvāmī, Rūpa Gosvāmī and

Sanātana Gosvāmī to preach, and He ordered Raghunātha dāsa Gosvāmī to strictly follow the rules and regulations of the renounced order. All six Gosvāmīs strictly followed the instructions of Śrī Caitanya Mahāprabhu. This is the principle for progress in devotional service. After receiving an order from the spiritual master, one must strictly try to execute the order. That is the way of success.

TEXT 313

প্রাণ-রক্ষা লাগি' যেবা করেন ভক্ষণ।
তাহা খাঞা আপনাকে কহে নির্বেদ-বচন ॥ ৩১৩ ॥

prāṇa-rakṣā lāgi' yebā karena bhakṣaṇa
tāhā khāñā āpanāke kahe nirveda-vacana

SYNONYMS

prāṇa-rakṣā lāgi'—to maintain life; *yebā*—whatever; *karena bhakṣaṇa*—he ate; *tāhā khāñā*—eating that; *āpanāke*—to himself; *kahe*—said; *nirveda-vacana*—words of reproach.

TRANSLATION

Whatever he ate was only to keep his body and soul together, and when he ate he would reproach himself thus.

TEXT 314

আত্মানং চেদ্বিজানীয়াৎ পরং জ্ঞানধূতাশয়ঃ।
কিমিচ্ছন্ কস্য বা হেতোর্দেহং পুষ্ণাতি লম্পটঃ ॥ ৩১৪ ॥

ātmānaṁ ced vijānīyāt
paraṁ jñāna-dhūtāśayaḥ
kim icchan kasya vā hetor
dehaṁ puṣṇāti lampaṭaḥ

SYNONYMS

ātmānam—the soul; *cet*—if; *vijānīyāt*—one understands; *param*—supreme; *jñāna*—by knowledge; *dhūta*—thrown off; *āśayaḥ*—material desires; *kim*—what; *icchan*—desiring; *kasya*—what; *vā*—or; *hetoḥ*—for reason; *deham*—the material body; *puṣṇāti*—maintains; *lampaṭaḥ*—debauchee.

TRANSLATION

"If one's heart has been cleansed by perfect knowledge and one has understood Kṛṣṇa, the Supreme Brahman, he then gains everything. Why should

such a person act like a debauchee by trying very carefully to maintain his material body?"

PURPORT

This verse (*Bhāg.* 7.15.40) was spoken by Nārada to Yudhiṣṭhira Mahārāja regarding a householder's liberation from material bondage. On the spiritual platform, one does not unnecessarily care for the body. Śrīla Narottama dāsa Ṭhākura has said, *deha-smṛti nāhi yāra, saṁsāra bandhana kāhāṅ tāra.* One who is spiritually situated does not think that he is the body. Therefore he can transcendentally execute severe penances in the renounced order of life. The best example of such renunciation is Raghunātha dāsa Gosvāmī.

TEXT 315

প্রসাদান্ন পসারির যত না বিকায়।
দুই-তিন দিন হৈলে ভাত সড়ি' যায় ॥ ৩১৫ ॥

prasādānna pasārira yata nā vikāya
dui-tina dina haile bhāta saḍi' yāya

SYNONYMS

prasāda-anna—food of Jagannātha; *pasārira*—of the shopkeepers; *yata*—as much as; *nā vikāya*—is not sold; *dui-tina dina*—two and three days; *haile*—after; *bhāta*—the rice; *saḍi' yāya*—becomes decomposed.

TRANSLATION

Lord Jagannātha's prasāda is sold by shopkeepers, and that which is not sold decomposes after two or three days.

TEXT 316

সিংহদ্বারে গাভী-আগে সেই ভাত ডারে।
সড়া-গন্ধে তৈলঙ্গী-গাই খাইতে না পারে ॥ ৩১৬ ॥

siṁha-dvāre gābhī-āge sei bhāta ḍāre
saḍā-gandhe tailaṅgī-gāi khāite nā pāre

SYNONYMS

siṁha-dvāre—at the gate known as Siṁha-dvāra; *gābhī-āge*—in front of the cows; *sei bhāta*—that food; *ḍāre*—they throw; *saḍā-gandhe*—because of a rotten smell; *tailaṅgī-gāi*—the cows from Tailaṅga; *khāite nā pāre*—cannot eat.

TRANSLATION

All the decomposed food is thrown before the cows from Tailaṅga at the Siṁha-dvāra gate. Because of its rotten odor, even the cows cannot eat it.

TEXT 317

সেই ভাত রঘুনাথ রাত্রে ঘরে আনি'।
ভাত পাখালিয়া ফেলে ঘরে দিয়া বহু পানি ॥৩১৭॥

sei bhāta raghunātha rātre ghare āni'
bhāta pākhāliyā phele ghare diyā bahu pāni

SYNONYMS

sei bhāta—that rejected rice; *raghunātha*—Raghunātha dāsa; *rātre*—at night; *ghare āni'*—bringing home; *bhāta*—the rice; *pākhāliyā*—washing; *phele*—throws; *ghare*—at home; *diyā*—putting; *bahu pāni*—much water.

TRANSLATION

At night Raghunātha dāsa would collect that decomposed rice, bring it home and wash it with ample water.

TEXT 318

ভিতরের দৃঢ় যেই মাজি ভাত পায়।
লবণ দিয়া রঘুনাথ সেই অন্ন খায় ॥ ৩১৮ ॥

bhitarera dṛḍha yei māji bhāta pāya
lavaṇa diyā raghunātha sei anna khāya

SYNONYMS

bhitarera—within; *dṛḍha*—the harder portion; *yei*—which; *māji*—the core; *bhāta*—rice; *pāya*—he gets; *lavaṇa diyā*—with a little salt; *raghunātha*—Raghunātha dāsa Gosvāmī; *sei anna*—that rice; *khāya*—eats.

TRANSLATION

Then he ate the hard inner portion of the rice with salt.

TEXT 319

একদিন স্বরূপ তাহা করিতে দেখিলা।
হাসিয়া তাহার কিছু মাগিয়া খাইলা ॥ ৩১৯ ॥

eka-dina svarūpa tāhā karite dekhilā
hāsiyā tāhāra kichu māgiyā khāilā

SYNONYMS

eka-dina—one day; *svarūpa*—Svarūpa Dāmodara Gosvāmī; *tāhā*—that; *karite*—doing; *dekhilā*—saw; *hāsiyā*—smiling; *tāhāra*—of that; *kichu*—some; *māgiyā khāilā*—he begged and ate.

TRANSLATION

One day Svarūpa Dāmodara saw the activities of Raghunātha dāsa. Thus he smiled and asked for a small portion of that food and ate it.

TEXT 320

স্বরূপ কহে,—"ঐছে অমৃত খাও নিতি-নিতি ।
আমা-সবায় নাহি দেহ',—কি তোমার প্রকৃতি ?"৩২০॥

svarūpa kahe, —"aiche amṛta khāo niti-niti
āmā-sabāya nāhi deha', —ki tomāra prakṛti?"

SYNONYMS

svarūpa kahe—Svarūpa Dāmodara said; *aiche*—such; *amṛta*—nectar; *khāo*—you eat; *niti-niti*—daily; *āmā-sabāya*—to us; *nāhi deha'*—you do not offer; *ki*—what; *tomāra*—your; *prakṛti*—nature.

TRANSLATION

Svarūpa Dāmodara said, "You eat such nectar every day, but you never offer it to us. Where is your character?"

TEXT 321

গোবিন্দের মুখে প্রভু সে বার্তা শুনিলা ।
আর দিন আসি' প্রভু কহিতে লাগিলা ॥ ৩২১ ॥

govindera mukhe prabhu se vārtā śunilā
āra dina āsi' prabhu kahite lāgilā

SYNONYMS

govindera mukhe—from the mouth of Govinda; *prabhu*—Śrī Caitanya Mahāprabhu; *se vārtā*—that news; *śunilā*—heard; *āra dina*—the next day; *āsi'*—coming; *prabhu*—Śrī Caitanya Mahāprabhu; *kahite lāgilā*—began to say.

TRANSLATION

When Śrī Caitanya Mahāprabhu heard news of this from the mouth of Govinda, He went there the next day and spoke as follows.

TEXT 322

কাঁহা বস্তু খাও সবে, মোরে না দেহ' কেনে ?'
এত বলি' এক গ্রাস করিলা ভক্ষণে ॥ ৩২২ ॥

kāṅhā vastu khāo sabe, more nā deha' kene?'
eta bali' eka grāsa karilā bhakṣaṇe

SYNONYMS

kāṅhā—what; *vastu*—things; *khāo*—you eat; *sabe*—all; *more*—to Me; *nā deha' kene*—why do you not give; *eta bali'*—saying this; *eka grāsa*—one morsel; *karilā bhakṣaṇe*—ate.

TRANSLATION

"What nice things are you eating? Why don't you give anything to Me?" Saying this, He forcibly took a morsel and began to eat.

TEXT 323

আর গ্রাস লৈতে স্বরূপ হাতেতে ধরিলা ।
'তব যোগ্য নহে' বলি' বলে কাড়ি' নিলা ॥ ৩২৩ ॥

āra grāsa laite svarūpa hātete dharilā
'tava yogya nahe' bali' bale kāḍi' nilā

SYNONYMS

āra—another; *grāsa*—morsel; *laite*—taking; *svarūpa*—Svarūpa Dāmodara; *hātete*—the hand; *dharilā*—caught; *tava*—for You; *yogya*—fit; *nahe*—is not; *bali'*—saying; *bale*—by force; *kāḍi'*—snatching; *nilā*—he took.

TRANSLATION

When Śrī Caitanya Mahāprabhu was taking another morsel of food, Svarūpa Dāmodara caught Him by the hand and said, "It is not fit for You." Thus he forcibly took the food away.

TEXT 324

প্রভু বলে,—"নিতি-নিতি নানা প্রসাদ খাই ।
ঐছে স্বাদ আর কোন প্রসাদে না পাই ॥ ৩২৪ ॥"

prabhu bale, —"niti-niti nānā prasāda khāi
aiche svāda āra kona prasāde nā pāi"

SYNONYMS

prabhu bale—Lord Śrī Caitanya Mahāprabhu said; *niti-niti*—day after day; *nānā prasāda*—varieties of *prasāda; khāi*—I eat; *aiche svāda*—such a nice taste; *āra*—other; *kona*—any; *prasāde*—in the remnants of Lord Jagannātha's food; *nā pāi*—I do not get.

TRANSLATION

Śrī Caitanya Mahāprabhu said, "Of course, every day I eat varieties of prasāda, but I have never tasted such nice prasāda as that which Raghunātha is eating."

TEXT 325

এইমত মহাপ্রভু নানা লীলা করে ।
রঘুনাথের বৈরাগ্য দেখি' সন্তোষ অন্তরে ॥ ৩২৫ ॥

ei-mata mahāprabhu nānā līlā kare
raghunāthera vairāgya dekhi' santoṣa antare

SYNONYMS

ei-mata—in this way; *mahāprabhu*—Śrī Caitanya Mahāprabhu; *nānā līlā*—many pastimes; *kare*—performs; *raghunāthera*—of Raghunātha dāsa; *vairāgya*—renunciation; *dekhi'*—by seeing; *santoṣa antare*—satisfied within.

TRANSLATION

Thus Śrī Caitanya Mahāprabhu performed many pastimes at Jagannātha Purī. Seeing the severe penances performed by Raghunātha dāsa in the renounced order, the Lord was greatly satisfied.

TEXT 326

আপন-উদ্ধার এই রঘুনাথদাস ।
'গৌরাঙ্গস্তবকল্পবৃক্ষে' করিয়াছেন প্রকাশ ॥ ৩২৬ ॥

āpana-uddhāra ei raghunātha-dāsa
'gaurāṅga-stava-kalpa-vṛkṣe' kariyāchena prakāśa

SYNONYMS

āpana-uddhāra—his personal deliverance; *ei raghunātha-dāsa*—this Raghunātha dāsa Gosvāmī; *gaurāṅga-stava-kalpa-vṛkṣe*—in his poem known as *Gaurāṅga-stava-kalpavṛkṣa; kariyāchena prakāśa*—has manifested.

TRANSLATION

In his own poem known as the Gaurāṅga-stava-kalpavṛkṣa, Raghunātha dāsa has described his personal deliverance.

TEXT 327

মহাসম্পদ্দাবাদপি পতিতমুদ্ধৃত্য কৃপয়া
স্বরূপে যঃ স্বীয়ে কুজনমপি মাং ন্যস্য মুদিতঃ ।
উরোগুঞ্জাহারং প্রিয়মপি চ গোবর্ধনশিলাং
দদৌ মে গৌরাঙ্গো হৃদয় উদয়ন্মাং মদয়তি ॥ ৩২৭ ॥

mahā-sampad-dāvād api patitam uddhṛtya kṛpayā
svarūpe yaḥ svīye kujanam api māṁ nyasya muditaḥ
uro-guñjā-hāraṁ priyam api ca govardhana-śilāṁ
dadau me gaurāṅgo hṛdaya udayan māṁ madayati

SYNONYMS

mahā-sampat—of profuse material opulence; *dāvāt*—from a forest fire; *api*—although; *patitam*—fallen; *uddhṛtya*—delivering; *kṛpayā*—by mercy; *svarūpe*—unto Svarūpa Dāmodara Gosvāmī; *yaḥ*—He who (Lord Śrī Caitanya Mahāprabhu); *svīye*—His personal associate; *ku-janam*—low person; *api*—although; *mām*—me; *nyasya*—having delivered; *muditaḥ*—pleased; *uraḥ*—of the chest; *guñjā-hāram*—the garland of conchshells; *priyam*—dear; *api*—although; *ca*—and; *govardhana-śilām*—a stone from Govardhana Hill; *dadau*—delivered; *me*—to me; *gaurāṅgaḥ*—Lord Gaurāṅga; *hṛdaye*—in my heart; *udayan*—by manifesting; *mām*—me; *madayati*—maddens.

TRANSLATION

"Although I am a fallen soul, the lowest of men, Śrī Caitanya Mahāprabhu delivered me from the blazing forest fire of great material opulence by His mercy. He handed me over in great pleasure to Svarūpa Dāmodara, His per-

sonal associate. The Lord also gave me the garland of small conchshells that He wore on His chest and a stone from Govardhana Hill, although they were very dear to Him. That same Lord Śrī Caitanya Mahāprabhu awakens within my heart and makes me mad after Him."

PURPORT

This verse is from *Śrī Gaurāṅga-stava-kalpavṛkṣa* (11), written by Raghunātha dāsa Gosvāmī.

TEXT 328

এই ত' কহিলুঁ রঘুনাথের মিলন ।
ইহা যেই শুনে পায় চৈতন্যচরণ ॥ ৩২৮ ॥

ei ta' kahiluṅ raghunāthera milana
ihā yei śune pāya caitanya-caraṇa

SYNONYMS

ei—this; *ta'*—certainly; *kahiluṅ*—I have described; *raghunāthera milana*—the meeting of Raghunātha dāsa; *ihā*—this; *yei*—anyone who; *śune*—hears; *pāya*—gets; *caitanya-caraṇa*—the lotus feet of Śrī Caitanya Mahāprabhu.

TRANSLATION

Thus I have described the meeting of Raghunātha dāsa with Śrī Caitanya Mahāprabhu. Anyone who hears about this incident attains the lotus feet of Śrī Caitanya Mahāprabhu.

TEXT 329

শ্রীরূপ-রঘুনাথ-পদে যার আশ ।
চৈতন্যচরিতামৃত কহে কৃষ্ণদাস ॥ ৩২৯ ॥

śrī-rūpa-raghunātha-pade yāra āśa,
caitanya-caritāmṛta kahe kṛṣṇadāsa

SYNONYMS

śrī-rūpa—Śrīla Rūpa Gosvāmī; *raghunātha*—Śrīla Raghunātha dāsa Gosvāmī; *pade*—at the lotus feet; *yāra*—whose; *āśa*—expectation; *caitanya-caritāmṛta*—the book named *Caitanya-caritāmṛta; kahe*—describes; *kṛṣṇadāsa*—Śrīla Kṛṣṇadāsa Kavirāja Gosvāmī.

TRANSLATION

Praying at the lotus feet of Śrī Rūpa and Śrī Raghunātha, always desiring their mercy, I, Kṛṣṇadāsa, narrate Śrī Caitanya-caritāmṛta, following in their footsteps.

Thus end the Bhaktivedanta purports to the Śrī Caitanya-caritāmṛta, Antya-līlā, *Sixth Chapter, describing Lord Caitanya's meeting with Raghunātha dāsa Gosvāmī.*

References

The statements of *Śrī Caitanya-caritāmṛta* are all confirmed by standard Vedic authorities. The following authentic scriptures are quoted in this book on the pages listed. Numerals in bold type refer the reader to *Śrī Caitanya-caritāmṛta's* translations. Numerals in regular type are references to its purports.

Amṛta-pravāha-bhāṣya (Bhaktivinoda Ṭhākura), 1-2, 117, 126, 158, 203-204, 215, 291, 310

Anubhāṣya (Bhaktisiddhānta Sarasvatī), **232,** 337

Bhagavad-gītā, **85,** 86, 173, 176, 194, 291

Bhakti-rasāmṛta-sindhu (Rūpa Gosvāmī), **108,** 164-165

Bhakti-ratnākara (Narahari Cakravartī), 108, 110

Bhakti-sandarbha (Jīva Gosvāmī), 35-36, 304

Bhāvārtha-dīpikā (Śrīdhara Svāmī), 183

Brahma-saṁhitā, 292-293

Bṛhad-bhāgavatāmṛta (Sanātana Gosvāmī), 36, **106**

Garuḍa Purāṇa, 96

Gaurāṅga-stava-kalpavṛkṣa (Raghunātha dāsa Gosvāmī), 352-353

Hari-bhakti-vilāsa (Sanātana Gosvāmī), **107,** 108, 303-304

Kalyāṇa-kalpataru (Bhaktivinoda Ṭhākura), 82

Kūrma Purāṇa, 181

Nāmāṣṭaka (Rūpa Gosvāmī), 36

Padma Purāṇa, 92, 175, 337

Śikṣāṣṭaka (Caitanya Mahāprabhu), 37

Glossary

A

Ācārya—one who teaches by example.

Acintya-bhedābheda-tattva—Lord Caitanya's "simultaneously one and different" doctrine, which establishes the inconceivable simultaneous existence of the Absolute Truth as both personal and impersonal.

Ahaṅgrahopāsaka-māyāvādī—a person engaged in fruitive activities or a person interested only in sense gratification.

Ajña—a description of Kṛṣṇa indicating that nothing is unknown to Him.

Anamra—one who offers obeisances to no one.

Antaraṅga-sevā—service performed in one's spiritual body.

Anurasa—imitation transcendental mellows.

Aparasa—opposing transcendental mellows.

Arcā-mūrti—worshipable Deity of Lord Viṣṇu.

Āśramas—the four spiritual orders of life—*brahmācārya, gṛhastha, vanaprāstha* and *sannyāsa.*

Aṣṭāṅga-yoga—the mystic *yoga* system to control the senses.

A-tattva-jña—one who has no knowledge of the Absolute Truth or who worships his own body as the Supreme Personality of Godhead.

B

Baddha-jña—a conditioned soul who distinguishes between the Lord's body and soul.

Bhagavān—one who possesses all opulences in full.

Bāliśa—innocent, as a young boy.

Bandhu-ham—the killer of *māyā.*

Brahmaloka—topmost planet in this universe.

Brahman—the all-pervading impersonal aspect of Kṛṣṇa.

Brahma-bhūta—stage of realization at which one becomes joyful knowing he is not the body.

Brāhmaṇas—the intelligent class of men.

C

Caṇḍāla—dog-eaters.

Catuḥsama—mixture of sandalwood pulp, camphor, aguru, and musk.

D

Dakṣiṇa—an offering made by the disciple to the spiritual master at the time of initiation.

Deva-dāsīs—māhārīs, professional dancing and singing girls trained to dramatize Vaiṣṇava ideology.
Dola-yātrā ceremony—swing festival for the Deities.
Durgā-maṇḍapa—the place in a house where mother Durgā is worshiped.

G

Gosvāmī—one who controls his sense gratification and serves Caitanya.
Govardhana-śilā—a stone from Govardhana hill in Vṛndāvana which is worshipable as Kṛṣṇa Himself.
Grāmya-kathā—talk concerning family life.
Grāmya-kavi—one who writes only about the relationship between man and woman.
Gṛham andhakūpam—family affection.
Gṛhastha—a householder who follows the rules of saintly life.
Gṛhavrata—one who is attached to living in a confortable home although it is actually miserable.
Gṛhavratas—those determined to continue following the materialistic way of life.
Guru—spiritual master.

I

Impersonal monism—philosophy that everything is one, and that the Absolute Truth is not a person.
Indra—the King of heaven.

J

Jagad-guru—the spiritual master of the entire world.
Jñāna—knowledge.
Jñānī—a transcendentalist interested in speculative philosophy.

K

Kaniṣṭha-adhikārī—lowest class of devotee.
Karma—fruitive work, for which one must accept good or bad reactions.
Karma-bandanaḥ—bondage to the reactions of fruitive activities.
Karmī—a fruitive worker.
Khājā—a kind of light sweetmeat.
Kṛṣṇa-kathā—topics of Kṛṣṇa.

M

Mahā-mantra—the great chanting of deliverance: Hare Kṛṣṇa, Hare Kṛṣṇa, Kṛṣṇa Kṛṣṇa, Hare Hare/ Hare Rāma, Hare Rāma, Rāma Rāma, Hare Hare.
Martya—a description of Kṛṣṇa indicating that because of His affection for His devotees, He appears like an ordinary human being.
Māyā—illusion; Kṛṣṇa's external energy.

N

Nārakī—candidate for hellish life.

P

Paṇḍita—one greatly learned in the *Vedānta-sūtras.*
Paṇḍita-mānī—word indicating that Kṛṣṇa is honored even by learned scholars.
Paramahaṁsa—topmost swanlike devotee.
Paramātmā—Supersoul; Kṛṣṇa as He is present within every heart and every atom.
Prabhu-datta deśa—place of residence given by the spiritual master or Lord Kṛṣṇa.
Prahara—three hours.
Prākṛta-sahajiyā—materialistic so-called devotees who take everything very lightly.
Prasāda—the mercy of the Lord; or foodstuffs offered to Him.
Purāṇas—the eighteen very old books which are histories of this and other planets.
Puruṣa-adhama—the Personality of Godhead, under whom all other persons remain.
Puṣpa-añjali—the ceremony of offering flowers to the Lord.

R

Rasa—mellow.
Rāsa-līlā—Kṛṣṇa's pastime of dancing with the *gopīs.*
Ratha-yātrā festival—Lord Jagannātha's car festival.

S

Sac-cid-ānanda-vigraha—the form of eternality, bliss and knowledge—characteristic of Kṛṣṇa.
Sahajiyās—*See: Prākṛta-sahajiyās.*
Sajātīyāśaya-snigdha—pleasing to the same class of people.
Śālagrāma-śilā—a special stone worshipable as Lord Viṣṇu.
Sandeśa—a delicate sweetmeat made with curd and sugar.

Sannyāsī—one in the renounced order of life.
Sarasvatī—goddess of learning.
Śarīrī—the owner of the body.
Śāstra—revealed scripture.
Siṁha-dvāra—the main gate of the Jagannātha temple.
Śūdra—the working or servant class of men.
Śvapaca—lowborn person.
Svarāt—independent quality of the Supreme Lord.

T

Tulasī—a great devotee in the form of a plant. This plant is very dear to the Lord, and its leaves are always offered to His lotus feet.

U

Upala-bhoga—morning refreshments offered to the Deity.
Uparasa—submellows.
Uttama-śloka—name of Kṛṣṇa which means "one who is praised by sublime prayers."

V

Vācāla—a person who can speak according to Vedic authority.
Vairāgī—a person in the renounced order of life.
Vaiṣṇava-aparādha—an offense to the devotee of Kṛṣṇa.
Varṇas—the social orders—*brāhmaṇa, kṣatriya, vaiśya* and *śūdra.*
Viṣayīs—blind materialistic enjoyers.
Vṛndāvana—the site of Kṛṣṇa's transcendental village pastimes, exhibited when He was present on earth about 5,000 years ago.

Y

Yadvā-tadvā kavi—one who writes poetry without proper knowledge.
Yoga—process of linking with the Supreme Lord.
Yogī—one who practices faithfully a system of *yoga.*

Bengali Pronunciation Guide

BENGALI DIACRITICAL EQUIVALENTS AND PRONUNCIATION

Vowels

অ a   আ ā   ই i   ঈ ī   উ u   ঊ ū   ঋ ṛ

ৠ ṝ   এ e   ঐ ai   ও o   ঔ au

ং ṁ *(anusvāra)*   ঁ ṅ *(candra-bindu)*   ঃ ḥ *(visarga)*

Consonants

Gutterals:	ক ka	খ kha	গ ga	ঘ gha	ঙ ṅa
Palatals:	চ ca	ছ cha	জ ja	ঝ jha	ঞ ña
Cerebrals:	ট ṭa	ঠ ṭha	ড ḍa	ঢ ḍha	ণ ṇa
Dentals:	ত ta	থ tha	দ da	ধ dha	ন na
Labials:	প pa	ফ pha	ব ba	ভ bha	ম ma
Semivowels:	য ya	র ra	ল la	ব va	
Sibilants:	শ śa	ষ ṣa	স sa	হ ha	

Vowel Symbols

The vowels are written as follows after a consonant:

া ā   ি i   ী ī   ু u   ূ ū   ৃ ṛ   ৄ ṝ   ে e   ৈ ai   ো o   ৌ au

For example: কা kā   কি ki   কী kī   কু ku   কূ kū   কৃ kṛ

কৄ kṝ   কে ke   কৈ kai   কো ko   কৌ kau

The letter *a* is implied after a consonant with no vowel symbol.

The symbol *virāma* (্) indicates that there is no final vowel. ক্ k

The letters above should be pronounced as follows:

a –like the *o* in h*o*t; sometimes like the *o* in go; final *a* is usually silent.
ā –like the *a* in f*a*r.
i, ī –like the *ee* in m*ee*t.
u, ū –like the *u* in r*u*le.
ṛ –like the *ri* in *ri*m.
ṝ –like the *ree* in *ree*d.
e –like the *ai* in p*ai*n; rarely like *e* in b*e*t.
ai –like the *oi* in b*oi*l.
o –like the *o* in g*o*.
au –like the *ow* in *ow*l.
ṁ –*(anusvāra)* like the *ng* in so*ng*.
ḥ –*(visarga)* a final *h* sound like in Ah.
ṅ –*(candra-bindu)* a nasal *n* sound like in the French word *bon*.
k –like the *k* in *k*ite.
kh –like the *kh* in Ec*kh*art.
g –like the *g* in *g*ot.
gh –like the *gh* in bi*g-h*ouse.
ṅ –like the *n* in ba*n*k.
c –like the *ch* in *ch*alk.
ch –like the *chh* in mu*ch-h*aste.
j –like the *j* in *j*oy.
jh –like the *geh* in colle*ge-h*all.
ñ –like the *n* in bu*n*ch.
ṭ –like the *t* in *t*alk.
ṭh –like the *th* in ho*t-h*ouse.
ḍ –like the *d* in *d*awn.
ḍh –like the *dh* in goo*d-h*ouse.
ṇ –like the *n* in g*n*aw.
t–as in *t*alk but with the tongue against the the teeth.
th–as in ho*t-h*ouse but with the tongue against the teeth.
d–as in *d*awn but with the tongue against the teeth.
dh–as in goo*d-h*ouse but with the tongue against the teeth.
n–as in *n*or but with the tongue against the teeth.
p –like the *p* in *p*ine.
ph –like the *ph* in *ph*ilosopher.
b –like the *b* in *b*ird.
bh –like the *bh* in ru*b-h*ard.
m –like the *m* in *m*other.
y –like the *j* in *j*aw. য
y –like the *y* in *y*ear. য়
r –like the *r* in *r*un.
l –like the *l* in *l*aw.
v –like the *b* in *b*ird or like the *w* in d*w*arf.
ś, ṣ –like the *sh* in *sh*op.
s –like the *s* in *s*un.
h–like the *h* in *h*ome.

This is a general guide to Bengali pronunciation. The Bengali transliterations in this book accurately show the original Bengali spelling of the text. One should note, however, that in Bengali, as in English, spelling is not always a true indication of how a word is pronounced. Tape recordings of His Divine Grace A.C. Bhaktivedanta Swami Prabhupāda chanting the original Bengali verses are available from the International Society for Krishna Consciousness, 3959 Landmark St., Culver City, California 90230.

Index of Bengali and Sanskrit Verses

This index constitutes a complete alphabetical listing of the first and third line of each four-line verse and both lines of each two-line verse in *Śrī Caitanya-caritāmṛta.* In the first column the transliteration is given, and in the second and third columns respectively the chapter-verse references and page number for each verse are to be found.

A

B

C

D

E

G

H

I

J

K

L

M

N

R

S

U

V

General Index

Numerals in bold type indicate references to *Śrī Caitanya-caritāmṛta's* verses. Numerals in regular type are references to its purports.

A

Absolute Truth
as master of material energy, **182**
Bengali poet has no knowledge of, 177
understood from three angles of vision, 180
See also: Kṛṣṇa, Supreme Lord

Activities
of devotee are spiritual, **141**

Ādi-līlā
cited on India, 49

Advaita Ācārya
as ocean of mercy, **119**
false followers of, 273
Yadunandana Ācārya initiated by, **274**

Affection
for devotees causes Kṛṣṇa's appearance as ordinary human being, **192**

Ami ta' vaiṣṇava, e-buddhi ha-ile
verses quoted, 82

Amṛta-pravāha-bhāṣya
cited on caste *brāhmaṇas,* 158
cited on entanglement in family life, 310
cited on those who are almost Vaiṣṇavas, 291
Fourth Chapter summarized in, 1-2
quoted on *kāyastha* community, 215
quoted on Rāmānanda Rāya's dancing girls, 126
summary of Chapter Six in, 203-204
summary of Fifth Chapter in, 117

Anubhāṣya
cited on *govardhana śilā,* 337
devotees of Nityānanda described in, **232**

Anupama
as good devotee of Raghunātha (Rāmacandra), **14**
as younger brother of Sanātana and Rūpa Gosvāmīs, **14-16**

Anupama
determination of fixed on serving Raghunātha dāsa, **18-20**
heard *Bhāgavatam* from Rūpa and Sanātana, **16**
requests initiation into Kṛṣṇa *mantra,* **18**
Vallabha a name of, **17**

Anyābhilāṣitā-śūnyaṁ jñāna
quoted, 291

Arcye viṣṇau śilādhīr guruṣu
quoted, 92, 175, 337

Āśrama
duties performed according to, **122**

Association
six kinds of, 329
with devotees required to understand devotional service, **187**

Austerity
devotional service satisfies Kṛṣṇa more than, **28**

B

Balabhadra Bhaṭṭācārya
gave Sanātana Gosvāmī Caitanya's route, **101**

Balarāma
ate with Kṛṣṇa on banks of Yamunā, **242**

Bandhu-han
Kṛṣṇa as, **193-**194

Bengal
brāhmaṇa from wrote drama about Caitanya, **161**
Caitanya met devotees from, **312**
devotees of went to Jagannātha Purī, **272**
kāyastha community highly honored in, 215
offense committed by poet of, 177, **184, 188-**189

L

S